"The secret of hi... ⟨⟩ **SO-AXU-694** ... ...
unequaled capacity for suffering."

—Ludwig Lewisohn

AUGUST STRINDBERG

was born in Sweden on January 22, 1849. His life was a
tangle of misfortune—unhappy school years, followed by
a bewildering sequence of occupations, three tormented
marriages, innumerable spiritual revolutions, and periods
of genuine insanity. Yet he continued to pour out plays,
novels and stories of undisputed genius and technical
mastery. His fame as a dramatist spread gradually
throughout Europe, but he received the public acclaim
he deserved only in the last five years before his death
in 1912.

ON THIS TRANSLATION

"This translation is of a very high quality, both from a
linguistic and a literary point of view. It has caught
Strindberg's style, primary quality, originality, and keen-
ness of repartee."

—The Swedish American Tribune

SEVEN PLAYS
BY AUGUST STRINDBERG

•

The definitive modern translation by
Arvid Paulson

•

With a general introduction
and prefaces to the plays by
John Gassner

SEVEN PLAYS BY AUGUST STRINDBERG
Published as a Bantam Classic November 1960
2nd printing ..... January 1964   3rd printing ... December 1964
4th printing ..... February 1966
Bantam World Drama edition published March 1968
6th printing

Bantam Books are published by Bantam Books, Inc., a subsidiary
of Grosset & Dunlap, Inc. Its trade-mark, consisting of the words
"Bantam Books" and the portrayal of a bantam, is registered in the
United States Patent Office and in other countries. Marca Registrada.
Bantam Books, Inc., 271 Madison Avenue, New York, N.Y. 10016.

CONTENTS

NOTE ON THE TRANSLATOR

Born and educated in Sweden, Arvid Paulson came to America as a young man. He quickly distinguished himself in the theater as actor and producer. Mr. Paulson's mastery of both Swedish and English, his close association with the theater, and his lifelong devotion to Scandinavian literature, qualify him perhaps better than anyone in the world for the job of translating Strindberg.

Among his other Strindberg translations are *Letters to Harriet Bosse, Eight Expressionist Plays,* and the novels *The Natives of Hemsö* and *The Scapegoat.*

Mr. Paulson has been knighted by the King of Sweden for strengthening the cultural and literary ties between the United States and Sweden. He was recently awarded the Gold Medal of the Royal Swedish Academy of Letters—the first time the award has been given for translations of Swedish literature.

INTRODUCTION

BY JOHN GASSNER

Strindberg and the Modern Drama

Without a doubt the most fascinating modern playwright
and one of the greatest, August Strindberg continues to
attract attention wherever dramatic art is respected. Although
Ibsen's junior by twenty-one years, Strindberg made such
singular advances in playwriting before the end of the
nineteenth century that he came to be bracketed with the
older writer as the modern theatre's founding-father. Ibsen
himself considered Strindberg potentially the superior
dramatist. Strindberg, who usually knew his own worth and
at times tended to overestimate it, gave every indication of
entertaining the same opinion, and posterity has tended to
endorse it. The twentieth century theatre is, in fact, doubly
indebted to him since he not only deepened realism but
transcended it with pioneering experiments in non-realistic
drama. Strindberg is doubly celebrated as the first modern
master of both psychological realism and expressionism.

The close collaboration between this dramatist's life and
talent has been a subject for proper interest to both his
admirers and detractors. It accounts for both the compulsive
passionateness and uniquely personal feeling of his writing.
His manner is rarely ordinary. And the sequence of trau-
matic experiences that constituted his life from early childhood to the end of his days supplied him with much of his
source material as well as animus. Personal experience ac-
counted for the obsessiveness with which he pursued his
favorite topic of ineluctable conflict between man and

vii

woman and led him to add the war of the classes to the war of the sexes, the grievance of the underdog to the protest of the male. The close relationship between his private tensions and literary career was indeed so vividly present to Strindberg's own consciousness as to inspire book after book of confession and self-analysis. *The Son of a Servant, The Confession of a Fool, Inferno* and other personal testaments written by him over a period of years are among the most remarkable autobiographies ever published.

It has been said that the first and greatest of Strindberg's misfortunes was his birth. His mother, successively a servant, a waitress and a barmaid, and a housekeeper, had borne her steamship agent lover Carl Oscar Strindberg two illegitimate children before they were legally married. The future author, baptized Johan August, was born on January 22, 1849 in Stockholm. Growing up in a frugal household full of children, he received slight consideration from either parent, and then acquired an uncongenial stepmother at the age of thirteen—only a few months after his mother's death in 1862. He became a moody and cantankerous child who felt himself badgered, humiliated, and both emotionally and intellectually isolated. "Family!" he exclaimed in *The Son of a Servant,* "thou art the home of all social evil, a charitable refuge for indolent women, an anchorage for fathers, and a hell for children." He was also painfully conscious of his mother's inferior position, referring to himself as the servant's or bondwoman's son who "shall not be heir with the free woman's son" and resenting "the blood of the slave" in his veins. In later life, he was torn not only between adoration and contempt for women, but between Nietzschean scorn for the common people and democratic identification with them. At one period of his life, he actually became a champion of the working class and shortly before he died he was honored by trade union sympathizers and other admirers with a torchlight procession.

Strindberg's schooling was irregular, discipline made him rebellious, and the level of education at the schools he attended was too low for his precocious mind. Nor were his encounters with higher education materially more successful. He entered the University of Uppsala in the fall of 1867, with no more financial assistance from his father than a box of cigars, and left after the first semester when his meager savings gave out. Idealistically he turned to teaching, but quickly abandoned his position; it was at the school in which he had been himself an uneasy pupil ten years before! He found a congenial environment only when he became a tutor in the fall of 1868 in the household of a cultivated Jewish physician, Dr. Axel Lamm, who aroused his interest in literature and science. Encouraged by Dr. Lamm to study medicine, Strindberg returned to the University, but only to drop the project in 1869 after failing to pass the qualifying examination in chemistry.

Acting attracted him next, and he made an inconspicuous début at the Royal Theatre in the fall of 1869, following which he was relegated to the Theatre's School of Acting. His prospects in the profession dwindled rapidly and he was demoted to the job of prompter at the school. It was soon after this humiliating experience that he discovered his talent for writing and wrote his first play, *A Name-Day Gift*. In the spring of 1870 he returned to the University, this time with a small legacy from his mother (now that he had reached his majority), and with a resolve to prepare himself for authorship by pursuing political and philological studies. Languages and history ultimately formed a large part of his encyclopaedic (if not invariably reliable) knowledge; but poor grades and dwindling resources ended his academic career forever. By then, however, he was determined to pursue his writing, having already turned out several plays. One of these, a romantic one-act piece in poetic prose called *The Outlaw,* produced at the Royal Theatre in 1871, had even brought him a small stipend from King Carl XV, who had seen and liked the play. In 1872 he wrote his first important work, a five-act historical play in prose, *Master Olof*. He revised this drama of the Protestant Reformation in Sweden frequently, but without getting it accepted for production until considerably later in his career. His situation improved materially only when he received an appointment in 1874 at the age of twenty-five to the Royal Library as assistant librarian, a position entailing little labor and bearing the honorable title of Royal Secretary which he held for some eight years.

Within a year, however, Strindberg succeeded in unsettling his life again by falling in love with a young married woman of the nobility, Siri von Essen. She became the great love and bane of his life. Her marriage to a Baron Wrangel dissolved in 1876, she married Strindberg in December 1877, shortly before the birth of their first child. The marriage of an ambitious and vivacious woman and a morbidly jealous husband, both egregiously self-centered individuals, was doomed from the start. He was becoming known as a writer, and in 1879, at the age of thirty, he enjoyed popular success with a realistic novel about Stockholm's literary and artistic circles, *The Red Room*. But his private life became increasingly unbearable and his irritability and suspicions (he suspected his wife of having lovers of both sexes) aggravated his relations with Siri. Strindberg tried at first to subordinate himself to her determined pursuit of professional success as an actress and her intemperate bohemianism, but the rift between them grew with the years. Their tempestuous marriage was dissolved in 1891 after nearly fourteen years; their last years together were embittered by recriminations that assumed the proportions of a public scandal. Although it was Strindberg who petitioned for the divorce, Siri acquired custody of their three children, and the court's decision was a severe blow to him.

The only way Strindberg could discharge his tensions was to write about them, and some of his most devastating plays, including *The Father* and *Miss Julie*, as well as rather indiscreet autobiographical works, came out of the period of his "love-hatred" for Siri. This was also the period in which he developed his so-called misogyny, which made him regard woman as man's natural enemy; he derided the species of emancipated woman now arising, and he loathed Ibsen, "the Norwegian bluestocking," as a fatuous supporter of the cult of feminine emancipation. Strindberg also became afflicted with abnormal sensitivity about personal relations and with suspiciousness that verged on persecution mania. And the end of his marriage, along with disappointments in the theatre, left him too dispirited for creative writing. He found compensation in extravagant scientific experiments, cultivated an interest in the supernatural, took to alchemy and astrology, as well as astronomy, fancied himself the possessor of magical powers, and plunged into dissipation in a Berlin artists' dive.

But his marital misadventures were by no means over. Misogyny, which he himself described as only "the reverse side of my fearful attraction towards the other sex," did not long stand in the way of his contracting a second marriage in 1893. At the age of 44, he married a precocious Austrian journalist, Frida Uhl, who was not yet of age to marry without her father's consent. Apparently he turned to her more out of need for a wife than out of love and soon felt managed and weakened by this vigorous young person who earned her own living as a newspaper correspondent and had maintained her own apartment in Berlin. Only pride kept them from ending their marriage, which had been a newspaper sensation. But even the birth of a daughter could not keep them together long. Frida separated from him in 1894, while he stayed in Paris and went through his severest mental crisis; and in 1897 she concluded the divorce proceedings she had started in Vienna. A third marriage the 52-year-old Strindberg contracted with a talented 22-year-old actress, Harriet Bosse, in 1901, also began to deteriorate almost immediately after the wedding. It came to an end three and a half years later, in 1904.

*   *   *

In each of his unfortunate marriages Strindberg appears to have experienced a fateful attraction to a spirited modern woman bent upon maintaining her independence and realizing her individuality. Yet his deepest longings were for a woman he could totally possess and subordinate to his need for inner security. He appears to have been constantly in search of a mother (a wife who would perhaps substitute for the mother he lost at an early age) only to discover that he had married a rival. He was, no doubt, often as unreasonable in his demands as he was suspicious and tempestuous by temperament. Nervous tensions had plagued him before, and he had attempted suicide twice in his youth. During his stormy marriages with Siri and her successors he was on the brink of madness as his anxieties and delusions of persecution multiplied. He submitted to psychiatric treatment twice during the acute mental crisis that followed the collapse of his marriage to Frida Uhl. But Strindberg is remarkable for his genius rather than his misfortunes. Neither his marital disasters (his romantic persistence brought him to the threshold of a fourth affair, toward the close of his life, with a 19-year-old actress and art student, Fanny Falkner) nor his clinical symptoms diminish his right to be considered a major figure in the modern theatre.

That Strindberg's mind was unmistakably clouded during a period of acute stress is less important than the fact that he recovered sufficiently to be able to write work after work with distinction; and less important, of course, than the lucidity he evinced in his delineation of character, his analysis of motivations, and his conscious exercise of craftsmanship. It is undoubtedly true that Strindberg was apt to be extravagant in treating sexual conflict (no more so, however, than D. H. Lawrence) and that his *obiter dicta* on the state of marriage in the modern world tended to be extreme. But his earned and unearned sufferings fed his insights. His embarrassing confessional candor drew attention to realities the Victorianism of his age normally concealed. He jolted equally the philistine complacencies of middle-class society and the blithe optimism of its would-be reformers who put their trust in such palliatives as careers and ballots for women. His very vehemence was tonic amid the torpor of received opinion, whether conservative or liberal; and I believe his honesty has continued to be tonic to this day. He noted guile in the face of innocence, rivalry and rage in the human heart, conversion of love into hatred, and guilt in the jungle of the human comedy. He felt the imminence of disaster and hungered for salvation. Strindberg's fateful marriages were, so to speak, marriages of heaven and hell from which the sufferer distilled a knowledge of good and evil found only in the work of the great writers of fiction from Dostoevski in the nineteenth century to Proust and Mann in the twentieth.

It is difficult to select one special quality out of the many that made Strindberg an outstanding writer rather than a psychopathic Don Quixote of the bedroom. He was, it must be immediately apparent to his readers, an acute observer of environments, customs, and manners, and a master of the concrete whether he dealt with city or provincial life, the upper or the lower classes, historical or contemporary situations. He wrote with spontaneity and verve. He wrote with noteworthy simplicity, too. Yet his plays never lacked eloquence whenever eloquence was dramatically justifiable, or intensity whenever his characters were joined in conflict. A neutral style was foreign to his nature; his works usually convey an impression of violent involvement with characters and issues. Nevertheless, this intensely "engaged" writer, who was more often than not openly partisan, proved himself perfectly capable of giving the other side its due and even allowing it to have its say. In the conflicts between husband and wife in *The Father*, and between mistress and valet in *Miss Julie*, for example, the antagonists reveal themselves and expose each other as complex and contradictory. The wife's ruthless behavior to her husband in *The Father* is deplorable, but the latter's irascibility, susciousness, and claims to authority in his household are less than ingratiating. For all his proclaimed anti-feminism, Strindberg weighs men and women in the scales of a strict judgment once he proceeds to produce drama out of the clash of personalities. Strindberg even undercuts his own verdict, whether or not he knows it, by exposing a total human being rather than a mere culprit. His characterizing power is patently too great to be kept in check by any thesis. This power appears to be an instinctive insight, disturbing and perhaps repellent now and then, but frequently sound and even compassionate, bearing out the familiar leitmotiv of his *A Dream Play* that mankind is to be pitied.

Paradox, indeed, seems to be the key to Strindberg as man and artist. Paradox, along with plain speaking and "plain-showing" (such as the Captain's hurling a lighted lamp at his wife and being later coaxed into a strait jacket by his loving old Nurse in *The Father*), is an essential element in his many-faceted plays. He perceived this himself in his famous *Preface* to *Miss Julie*, when he prided himself on supplying his character with a "multiplicity of motives" and decried old-fashioned methods of characterization that yielded only stereotypes on the stage. Paradox is inseparable in his case from depth of understanding, and it is plainly his comprehension of ambivalence and inner conflict that made him the prime creator of modern psychological drama. His mastery of his *métiér* has not yet found its match in the work of his twentieth-century successors in the theatre despite the exertions of Wedekind, O'Neill, Williams, and others, and despite the vogue of Freudian depth-psychology.

It is also a paradox, no doubt, that after having made himself a master of realistic techniques, Strindberg should have come under the spell of Maeterlinck, turned to symbolist drama, and then gone on to create a virtually new style of non-realistic playwriting in his latter-day (post-1897) expressionist works such as *To Damascus, A Dream Play, The Ghost Sonata,* and *The Great Highway*. But the revolutionary effort he made in these plays to express the ineffable was only a part of the greater aptitude that ultimately qualified him as a true artist rather than as a neurotic who accidentally produced art. Strindberg had the true artist's drive and capacity to make the unknown known, the hidden revealed, the unconscious conscious. If only ultra-realistic dramaturgy would enable him to accomplish this at one stage of his career, he would endeavor to make the most of "naturalism,"

or modify it to suit his purpose. And if non-realistic
dramaturgy would enable him to make subjective experience
and vision objective, he would just as confidently evolve a
new style of theatre. It would simply be another effort to
make order out of disorder and let Ego prevail where Id
was. Strindberg's instinct for health and instinct for art were
nearly identical. And if Strindberg was fortunate in this respect, so was the formative modern theatre.

*   *   *

Indebtedness to Strindberg has been frequently acknowledged in our century. The debt was unequivocally acknowledged by Eugene O'Neill. He declared that "it was the reading of his plays that above all gave the vision of what
modern drama could be and first inspired me with the urge
to write for the theatre myself." Although less eloquent on
the subject and primarily Ibsen's disciple, Shaw was also
distinctly appreciative. He once called Strindberg perhaps
the "noblest Roman of us all." Shaw urged Ibsen's nineteenth-
century translator William Archer to turn to Strindberg's
plays and perform the same service of translation for the
Swedish master that he had performed for the Norwegian.
Many years later Shaw used his Nobel Prize to establish the
Anglo-Swedish Foundation for the purpose of facilitating
translations from the Swedish. New translations of plays by
Strindberg were the first volumes to be published. O'Casey
and Thornton Wilder also expressed a high opinion of Strindberg, and Tennessee Williams may well trace his descent
from him.

It must be noted, however, that Strindberg achieved his
reputation by persistent and logical craftsmanship rather
than by erratic inspiration. He was a thoroughly professional writer, and his ample productiveness alone could lead
to no other conclusion. At his death in 1912 in his sixty-third
year, he left plays, novels, collections of stories, autobiographies, histories, works on science and philology, political
treatises, and speculative writings that might have occupied
several reasonably busy lifetimes. His dramatic output alone
consisted of 58 full-length and one-act pieces, and among
these were not only domestic dramas but folk-plays such as
The Bridal Crown (or *The Crown Bride*), fairy plays such as
Swanwhite, "pilgrimage plays" such as *Lucky Per's Journey,
The Keys of Heaven,* and *The Great Highway,* and historical
dramas (*Queen Christina, Charles XII, Gustav Vasa*)

unexcelled in the modern theatre. The amplitude of his writing for the stage was matched, moreover, by concentration on technical accomplishment as well as attention to the problems of stage production.

He made himself a master of the one-act form and condensed full-length playwriting to such a degree that he could dispense with intermissions in dramatizing emotional crises. (*Miss Julie* is the outstanding example of a one-act "full-length" play.) He ignited the dramatic action of plays at once, reducing the role of exposition and pedestrian preparation to the vanishing point. He accomplished condensation also in his non-realistic experiments, employing many scenes but telescoping time and place until past and present fuse and scene blends into scene as if space, too, were annihilated by psychological reality. His last experiments were undertaken with a view to developing "chamber plays" suitable for presentation in the *Intimate Theatre*, seating only 161 spectators, which he had founded in Stockholm in 1907 with a young actor-manager, August Falck. For this theatre, patterned after Max Reinhardt's *Kleines Theater* (Little Theatre) in Berlin, as well as the Paris *Théâtre Libre* and other avant-garde groups, Strindberg wrote five plays (including the expressionist masterpiece *The Ghost Sonata*) which were intended to stand in relation to ordinary drama as chamber music stands in relation to large orchestral compositions. "Professionalism" led Strindberg to consider not only dramatic details but acting style, décor, and problems of lighting the stage. Thus he decided to abolish footlights at the *Intimate Theatre,* and provided sound reasons for his decision. It is one more paradox that the most subjective of important modern playwrights should have been capable of so much professional meticulousness.

Strindberg gave proof of his attentiveness to dramaturgy and theatre art throughout his career. The masterly *Preface* to *Miss Julie*, his "naturalist" manifesto of the year 1888 (see page 62), was followed in 1889 by the significant essay *On Modern Drama and Theatre*. Twenty years later he was still publishing comments on dramatic art, including the provocative *Open Letters to the Intimate Theatre* (1907–1909). In 1902, in his prefatory note to *A Dream Play,* he outlined the major features of expressionism in describing how he had attempted "to reproduce the detached and disunited—although apparently logical—form of dreams." Most important, in the 1889 essay, he virtually redefined naturalism, distinguishing between "the misunderstood naturalism" and "the great naturalism." He deplored the slice-of-life photography that "includes everything, even the grain of dust on the lens of the camera." He identified the "great" style with a "deep probing of the human soul," making the naturalistic delineation of characters identical with psychological drama. He rejected impersonal naturalistic writing, moreover, by maintaining that art should be "a piece of nature seen through a temperament." And he got to the heart of the matter by insisting that "the great naturalism" presents the unusual rather than the usual, "seeks out the points where the great battles are fought," and takes delight in "the clash of natural forces."

The decisive fact about his own work is of course that his best theatrical writing is just that: It is reality filtered through a strong temperament. It also seeks out points of maximum conflict and presents in the conflicts of his characters the powerful clash of natural forces. By 1889 Strindberg entertained a dream of a theatre in which everything hitherto concealed behind moralistic and esthetic veils could be seen, a "free theatre" (this pronouncement came within two years of the founding of Antoine's "free theatre," the *Théâtre Libre* in Paris) where one had freedom for everything but talentlessness, hypocrisy, and fatuity. Strindberg went far toward realizing his dream with the seven plays contained in the present volume—and about a dozen others one could mention.

* * *

No attempt is made in the present collection to represent Strindberg's most exotic ventures into imaginative theatre art. His extreme expressionist experiments (the *To Damascus* trilogy, *A Dream Play*, *The Ghost Sonata*, and *The Great Highway*) would be presented to best advantage if collected and introduced separately. His historical dramas (he left 21 of these) also qualify for separate presentation. For all their effectiveness in dramatic characterization and action, most of these historical works require a knowledge of Swedish national history.

The plays in this Bantam collection, all newly translated by Strindberg's indefatigable American champion Arvid Paulson, who has been acclaimed as a sensitive and expert translator by both American critics and Swedish specialists, cover much ground. They span the playwright's most fruitful years, from 1886 when he wrote *Comrades* to 1900 when he completed *Easter*. They represent the Strindberg who won success both at home and abroad and who exerted the most fecund influence in the modern theatre, from his native Sweden to distant Japan. They also convey a wider range of dramatic interest than we usually associate with Strindberg. We encounter here not only a desperately earnest author of tragedies and quasi-tragedies of sex, in *The Father, Miss Julie,* and *The Bond,* but a humorist or rather ironist, in *Comrades* and *Crimes and Crimes,* who may remind us of Shaw's statement (published in 1921 in *The London Mercury*) that "Ibsen, Strindberg, and Tolstoy wrote tragi-comedies, supplying a much grimmer entertainment than tragedy." We meet not only the formidable naturalist of *The Father* and *Miss Julie* who made Ibsen seem by comparison a tame playwright, but an unusually subdued writer in the poetic and wistful mood of *Easter,* Strindberg's drama of forgiveness and reconciliation. In *Easter* Strindberg, having found comfort in religion after his breakdown, will be seen leaning toward the symbolist style and mysticism that came into vogue at the turn of the century. And in *Crimes and Crimes* we see him approaching expressionism by giving reality a fantastic turn that has the attributes of a nightmare.

In the frequently performed little comedy *The Stronger* —a minuscule masterpiece which is simple only on the surface—we observe the ultimate result of Strindberg's ideal of dramatic compression. All the action of a domestic drama is reduced to a scene of discovery in the telescopic form of a dramatic monologue. But *The Bond,* too, is stripped playwriting. It starts with a crisis, ends in a catastrophe for the principals, and is perhaps the most shattering divorce drama in all dramatic literature. And with *Miss Julie,* the acknowledged masterpiece of compressed dramaturgy in the modern theatre, and *The Father,* a naturalistic variant on the classic Clytemnestra-Agamemnon theme in domestic tragedy, Strindberg opened avenues of escape from placid middle-class drama that have as yet been only intermittently explored.

He accomplished this necessary feat by digging deeper into human nature than any other nineteenth-century playwright (though not deeper than Stendhal or Dostoevski in the nineteenth-century novel) and by virtue of almost uncanny introspection.

While Strindberg's autobiographical books exhibit the raw power of self-examination, *The Father* and *Miss Julie* translate the introspection into viable dramatic art. The two plays show the will of one person clashing with the will of another closely-linked person. Other writers have also viewed drama as a conflict of will. But Strindberg took the next necessary step by plunging into the irrational to find the will no simple and transparent thing at all.

This is the case even though Strindberg supplies a considerable amount of intellectual fencing and self-analysis by exceptionally articulate characters. It is indeed another Strindbergian paradox that self-awareness, intellectuality, and irrationality should be congruent in the case of such driven or driving characters as the neurotic Captain, the man-eating Laura, and the sex-starved Julie. Personal anguish brought Strindberg into the underground that was subsequently to be so investigated by Sigmund Freud and his associates. It is from obscure levels of their selves, rarely illuminated by reason, illogical or crazily logical, that the characters dredge up their anxieties and resentments; passions erupt out of the depths; dangerous emotions well up from suppression; unreason escapes from the restraints ordained by reasonable middle-class society.

All things considered, Strindberg has his say in the seven plays contained in the present volume. In the realistic genre, the only major omission is *The Dance of Death,* a two-part "sex-duel" tragedy of formidable proportions. The seven examples of his craft included in this volume reveal Strindberg's dramatic talent in much of its significance as well as variety. They also introduce readers to much that is distinctly "modern" about the modern and contemporary theatre.

THE FATHER

A TRAGEDY IN THREE ACTS

The Father (*Fadren*) was written in 1887 and first performed on November 14 of the same year in Copenhagen; it was presented in Sweden early the following year on January 12, 1888. It is one of the clearest as well as most forceful and widely known of Strindberg's plays, and the most famous of his dramas of the sex-duel.

While a hasty reading or an inept stage production (or a flat translation) can leave us unconvinced, closer inspection of the text will reveal a work of great dramatic power. No doubt the author goes to extremes and verges on melodrama, but he probes the conduct of the conflicting couple brilliantly and provides complex characterizations. The play, which dramatizes a conflict of wills in terms of mental struggle (the conflict is between the mind of Laura and the mind of her husband—nothing else in the play really matters), proves to be too multifaceted to be dismissed or denigrated as mere melodrama. It also contains much modern discussion, as well as modern psychology, and the play is definitely addressed to the intelligence as well as to the readily available emotions of the adult reader and playgoer.

The Father is plainly animated by Strindberg's miseries and resentments accumulated during his turbulent first marriage. Laura is patterned after the author's first wife, Siri von Essen. And Strindberg obviously sees himself in Laura's husband, the impressionable and greatly wronged Captain. The conflict between them is probably the most compelling redaction of classical dramatic material (the conflict of Agamemnon and Clytemnestra) by a modern playwright. Only O'Neill in the first two parts of his *Mourning Becomes Electra* trilogy approaches the effectiveness of Strindberg's transformation of the classic story into modern terms. That the transformation

3

is so successful is probably partly due to its intensely felt personal quality: "Strindberg's own fear and doubts had been woven into the texture, doubts as to the paternity of his children, fears as to his own madness, as well as his reading of works on suggestion and hypnotism." (*Strindberg,* by Brita E. Mortensen and Brian W. Downs, 1949.) But the objective artistry of this work on the technical side remains inviolate; the classic unities are observed: the cast of characters is small, and the action is single, transpiring in one room and within twenty-four hours.

The Father, regarded as "too morbid" by its first audience, was quickly acclaimed as a masterpiece of naturalism. It was published in French with a preface written by Emile Zola, the head of the naturalist literary movement, and was accepted for production at the *Théâtre Libre* by Antoine. The play was first produced in France, however, by a rival little theatre, Lugné-Poë's new *Théâtre de l'Oeuvre,* on December 13, 1894. It was first presented in New York at the Lyceum Theatre in April 1912 with Warner Oland and Rosalind Ivan in the principal roles.

The *Freie Bühne* première in Berlin, on October 12, 1890, with Emmanuel Reicher in the role of the Captain, gave Strindberg his first claim to a European reputation. His own production at the *Intimate Theatre* in Stockholm in 1908 had a run of 77 performances, and the play has had numerous presentations in Europe and South America. In the English-speaking world, *The Father* found such redoubtable champions as George Jean Nathan and St. John Ervine. London first saw the play in 1911, and in 1927 it was revived with considerable success by the distinguished actor-manager Robert Loraine, who played the Captain while Haidée Wright performed as Laura. The British critic Ernest Short recalled that "the monstrous and the horrible assumed a strange loveliness" in this production and observed that "the plays of Strindberg offer telling examples of the extension of the meaning attached to the word 'beauty' in modern aesthetics." Loraine "persuaded British playgoers of the greatness of Strindberg." (Ernest Short, *Theatrical Cavalcade,* London, 1942, pp. 140–143.)

Two productions of *The Father* were given in New York in 1949, the centenary year of Strindberg's birth. The Broadway production in which Mady Christians played Laura and Raymond Massey the Captain proved only half-successful and familiar charges of extremism were made against the author at that time. One critic, Richard Watts, Jr., complained of "the inequality of the combatants." Another question that occurred at that time, as also on previous occasions, was whether *The Father* was a tragedy at all rather than a melodrama. At the mid-century point it was evident that the play would need an exceptionally sensitive and controlled production before it could be expected to prevail on the New York stage. But it could also be remarked that Broadway criteria should not be construed as decisive opinion in judging a work that has impressed critics and playgoers in other parts of the world for about three-quarters of a century.

PERSONS IN THE PLAY

The Captain
Laura, his wife
Bertha, their daughter
Doctor Östermark
The Pastor
Margret, a nurse-maid
Nöjd
The Orderly

(The action takes place in the Captain's quarters at a regimental [cavalry] establishment in a Swedish country town.)

ACT I

(THE SETTING.—A living-room in THE CAPTAIN's home. There is a door in the rear, on the left. In the center of the room, a large round table with a lighted lamp on it; also a number of newspapers and periodicals. On the left is a leather-covered sofa and a small table, and in the corner, left, a door covered by wallpaper. On the right, a high-backed chiffonier-writing desk. On top of it stands a pendulum clock. On the same side of the room there is also a door leading to the rest of the rooms on the first floor. On the walls are hung firearms, including shotguns, and game bags. Army service coats hang on a rack with pegs by the door.)

THE CAPTAIN. *(He is seated on the sofa with THE PASTOR. He is dressed in the fatigue uniform of a cavalry officer and wears riding boots with spurs. THE PASTOR is dressed in black, with white tie instead of the usual clergyman's bands. He is smoking a pipe. THE CAPTAIN gets up, and jerks the bell-pull.)*

THE ORDERLY *(enters)*. You rang, Captain?

THE CAPTAIN. Is Nöjd outside?

THE ORDERLY. Nöjd is in the kitchen, sir. Waiting for orders, sir.

THE CAPTAIN. So he is in the kitchen again? Send him in to me at once!

THE ORDERLY. I'll tell him, sir.   *(He goes out.)*

THE PASTOR. Has anything gone wrong?

THE CAPTAIN. Oh, the rascal has got the kitchen maid into trouble again. He just doesn't know how to control himself!

7

THE PASTOR. Is it that fellow Nöjd again? He was in the same difficulty last spring, wasn't he?

THE CAPTAIN. Yes, you remember—don't you? I wish you would help me—give him some fatherly advice, it might have some effect. I have sworn at him, and I have horse-whipped him, but it hasn't done the slightest bit of good.

THE PASTOR. And now you want me to read a sermon to him? What impression could the word of God possibly have on a cavalryman, do you think?

THE CAPTAIN. Well, you know, my dear brother-in-law, how much of an impression it makes on me, don't you . . .

THE PASTOR. Alas, I know it all too well!

THE CAPTAIN. But it may do him some good. At any rate, try! (*Nöjd enters.*) What have you been up to this time, Nöjd?

NÖJD. May God save you, Captain—but I couldn't go into that, sir, not with the Pastor here.

THE PASTOR. Oh, don't let that embarrass you, young man!

THE CAPTAIN. Tell the truth now—the whole truth—or you know what will happen to you.

NÖJD. Well, you see, sir, it was like this. We was at a dance at Gabriel's—and then—well, and then Ludvig said—he said . . .

THE CAPTAIN. What has Ludvig to do with this? Stick to the truth!

NÖJD. Well . . . and then Emma said we was to go into the barn . . .

THE CAPTAIN. Is that so? I suppose it was Emma who led you astray?

NÖJD. Well—that's not far from the truth. And all I have to say is, that if the girl isn't willing—then nothing will happen . . .

THE CAPTAIN. Give me a straight answer now: *are* you the child's father, or are you *not*?

NÖJD. How am I to know?

THE CAPTAIN. What's that you say? Don't you know?

NÖJD. Why, no, sir—a fellow can't really be sure.

THE CAPTAIN. Were there others?

NÖJD. Not *that* time—but just the same—how can I be sure I was the only one.

THE CAPTAIN. Are you trying to put the blame on Ludvig now? Are you?

NÖJD. It isn't so easy to say just who to put the blame on . . .

THE CAPTAIN. Yes, but you told Emma you would marry her, didn't you?

NÖJD. Well—but you see you always have to tell them that . . .

THE CAPTAIN (*to* THE PASTOR). This is really dreadful—dreadful!

THE PASTOR. It's the same old story! But listen to me now, Nöjd! Surely you are man enough to know whether you *are* or are *not* the father . . .

NÖJD. Well, I don't deny I had something to do with her —but the pastor sure must know himself that nothing need to happen for all that!

THE PASTOR. Look here, young man, we are talking about you now! You are not going to leave the girl in the lurch with her child, are you? I don't suppose you can be compelled to marry her, but you must provide for the child! That you must do!

NÖJD. Well—then Ludvig must too.

THE CAPTAIN. The case must go to the court, that's all! I can't make head or tail of all this—and, after all, it's not the kind of thing I care to have anything to do with. Be off with you now!

THE PASTOR. Just a moment, Nöjd. H'm. Don't you think it is nothing short of dishonesty to leave a girl with a child to take care of without any support whatever? Don't you? Eh? Don't you think that such conduct . . . h'm . . . h'm

NÖJD. Well, yes, if I—if I was sure I was the father of the child, yes,—but you know, Pastor, that's something you can never be sure of. And to be slaving all your life for someone who's not your own, that's not much fun. You must see that for yourself, Pastor,—and the Captain sure can understand that, too!

THE CAPTAIN. Be on your way, Nöjd!

NÖJD. God save you, Captain! (*He goes out.*)

THE CAPTAIN (*calls after him*). And stay out of the kitchen after this, you rascal! (*To* THE PASTOR.) Why didn't you give it to him good and hard?

THE PASTOR. What? Didn't I give him enough of a drubbing?

THE CAPTAIN. Bah! You only sat there muttering to yourself!

THE PASTOR. To tell the truth, I really don't know what to say about it. I feel sorry for the girl, of course; but I feel sorry for the boy, too. Suppose that he is not the father! The girl can suckle the child for four months at the maternity home, and after that the child will be taken care of for the rest of its days. But the young man—he can't suckle, you know. . . . The girl will then be given a decent place in a better family; but the boy's future might be ruined if he were to be given a dishonorable discharge from the regiment.

THE CAPTAIN. Upon my soul, I wouldn't like to be the judge and have to pass sentence in this case. I don't think the boy is entirely innocent—but how can one be sure? But there is one thing that is certain: if anyone is to be blamed, it is the girl.

THE PASTOR. Well . . . well, I am not going to sit in judgment! But what was it we were discussing when this blessed interlude came up?—Oh, yes, we were speaking about Bertha and her confirmation, weren't we?

THE CAPTAIN. It wasn't exactly about her confirmation but about her upbringing as a whole that we were talking. This house is full of women—and they all want to bring up my child in their own particular way. My mother-in-law would like to see her a spiritualist; Laura wants her to be an artist; the governess would have her a Methodist; old Margret would like to see her become a Baptist; and the servant-girls, a salvationist. You can't patch a soul together that way, least of all when I—who primarily am responsible for the molding of her character—am constantly being opposed in all that I do. That is why I must take her out of this house.

THE PASTOR. There are too many women trying to run your house.

THE CAPTAIN. Yes—you agree with me, I see! It's like going into a cage of tigers! And if I didn't hold a red-hot poker under their noses, they would soon pounce on me and tear me to pieces! Yes, you may laugh, you rogue. . . . It wasn't enough that I took your sister for my wife—you made me take in your old stepmother also.

THE PASTOR. Yes, by God, one should never have stepmothers in one's house.

THE CAPTAIN. No—but you think it fitting to have mothers-in-law—as long as they stay in somebody else's house.

THE PASTOR. Well . . . well, we have all been given our own burden to bear in life.

THE CAPTAIN. Yes, but I think *I* have been given more than my share. And to cap it all, I have my old wet-nurse, too, and she treats me as if I still wore a bib. To be sure, she is a very good-hearted woman, but she ought not be staying here!

THE PASTOR. When you deal with women, my dear brother-in-law, you must take hold of the reins. You allow them to rule you.

THE CAPTAIN. I would like to know how one manages women.

THE PASTOR. Speaking seriously . . . Laura—and I say this although she is my own sister—Laura has always been a little hard to handle.

THE CAPTAIN. Laura may have her little faults, but they are not serious.

THE PASTOR. Oh, come! You can sing out—I know her!

THE CAPTAIN. She was brought up with romantic notions, that is why she finds it a little difficult to face reality. Nonetheless—she is my wife, and . . .

THE PASTOR. And that is why you think no one could be better! No, my dear brother-in-law, I think it is she who galls you most.

THE CAPTAIN. Be that as it may, the whole house is upside down. Laura refuses absolutely to let Bertha leave, but I cannot possibly let her remain in this madhouse!

THE PASTOR. So-o? Laura refuses absolutely! Well, in that case, I fear for the worst. As a child she would lie prostrate, as if she were dead, until she got what she wanted. And when she succeeded in getting it, she gave it back—whatever it was that she had feigned being dead for —with the explanation that it was not the thing itself that she wanted, but simply to have her own way.

THE CAPTAIN. You don't say? She acted like that even as a child, did she? H'm. To tell the truth, there are times when she acts so hysterical that I think she must be ill, and can't help being concerned for her.

THE PASTOR. But exactly what is it you have in mind for Bertha that causes so much friction and seems so difficult for you to agree upon? Isn't it possible to work out a compromise?

THE CAPTAIN. I don't want you to think that I have any

desire to make her into a prodigy, or into some sort of image of myself. And I don't care to act as procurer for my daughter and educate her for marriage only. For if she should not marry, she might have a difficult life. On the other hand, I do not wish to see her enter a man's profession which would require long preparation and training—and which would be all wasted if she married.

THE PASTOR. What would you like her to do, then?

THE CAPTAIN. I want her to be a teacher. Then, in case she does not marry, she will be able to support herself. And she will be no worse off than the poor teachers who have to spend what they earn on their families. Again, if she does marry, her knowledge would be useful in bringing up her children. Does that sound logical to you?

THE PASTOR. Logical, yes! But what about her talent for painting? Doesn't she have a talent for that? And would you like her to suppress a natural talent such as that?

THE CAPTAIN. Not at all! But I showed a sampling of her work to a distinguished painter. His verdict was that it was merely the kind of painting one learns at school. But last summer a young would-be critic was here—and he understood such things much better! He said she possessed exceptional talent. And with that, the matter was decided in Laura's favor.

THE PASTOR. Was he in love with the girl?

THE CAPTAIN. I take it for granted he was.

THE PASTOR. Then may God be with you, my boy; for I see no way out for you! But this is getting tedious, and Laura is entertaining her supporters inside.

THE CAPTAIN. Yes, of that you may be sure! The whole house is already lighted up, and—between ourselves—it's not exactly a fair and noble battle that is being waged from that quarter.

THE PASTOR (rises). Don't you think I know?

THE CAPTAIN. You mean you also have been through the same thing?

THE PASTOR. Did you say also?

THE CAPTAIN. But the worst of it is that I can't help feeling that Bertha's future is being decided in there by hateful motives. They keep talking about showing the men that women are capable of doing both this and that. Continuously—the whole day long—you hear nothing but chatter about the male and the female as being opposed to each other.

(THE PASTOR *gets up.*) Oh, must you be going? Why don't you stay for the evening? I don't know what we have to offer you, but I wish you would stay. You know I am expecting the new doctor, don't you? Have you met him yet?

THE PASTOR. I caught a passing glimpse of him just now. He gave the impression of being a decent and substantial person.

THE CAPTAIN. So–o? I am glad to hear that. Do you think he might be of some support to me?

THE PASTOR. Who can tell? It depends upon how well he knows women.

THE CAPTAIN. Oh, but why don't you stay?

THE PASTOR. No, thank you, my dear Adolf. . . . I promised my wife to be back in time for supper; and if I don't get there, she starts to worry.

THE CAPTAIN. Starts to worry? You mean she starts to fume, don't you? Well, you do just as you like. . . . Let me help you on with your overcoat.

THE PASTOR. It must be very cold out this evening. (THE CAPTAIN *helps him with his overcoat.*) Thank you. You must take good care of yourself, Adolf. You seem a little unstrung . . .

THE CAPTAIN. You say I look a little unstrung?

THE PASTOR. Y–e–s, you don't look quite well.

THE CAPTAIN. Has Laura put that idea into your head? She treats me as if I were marked for death and ready to die.

THE PASTOR. Laura? Why, of course not—but I am worried about you. Take care of yourself, that's my advice to you. Goodbye, old friend!—But, come to think of it, wasn't it about the confirmation you wanted to talk to me?

THE CAPTAIN. No, no! I assure you that is a matter that will have to take its own course. It will have to be charged to the official conscience—for I am neither a witness to the truth nor some sort of martyr. We have put such things behind us. Goodbye, my friend! Remember me to your wife . . .

THE PASTOR. Goodbye, Adolf! Give my love to Laura!

THE CAPTAIN (*opens the chiffonier-writing desk and seats himself at it, going through his accounts*). Thirty-four—nine—forty-three—seven—eight—fifty-six . . .

LAURA (*enters from the door leading to the rest of the rooms*). Will you be good enough to . . .

THE CAPTAIN. In just a minute! Sixty-six—seventy-one—eighty-four—eighty-nine—ninety-two—one hundred. What was it you said?

LAURA. Perhaps I am disturbing you . . .

THE CAPTAIN. Not at all! The money for the household, I suppose?

LAURA. Yes—the money for the household.

THE CAPTAIN. If you leave the bills here, I'll go through them.

LAURA. The bills?

THE CAPTAIN. Yes.

LAURA. Must we start keeping the bills now?

THE CAPTAIN. Naturally, we must keep the accounts straight. Our position is precarious. If we should have to go into liquidation and have to make a settlement, we must have the bills to show, or we might be held liable for negligence as debtors and be punished.

LAURA. If we are in debt, I am not the one to blame.

THE CAPTAIN. That is exactly what the bills will show.

LAURA. If the tenant farmer fails to pay his rent, it is not my fault.

THE CAPTAIN. Who was it who recommended him so ardently? You! What made you recommend such a . . . well, let us call him a—a careless fellow?

LAURA. Why did you take on such a careless fellow?

THE CAPTAIN. Because I never had any peace—neither when I was eating, nor when I slept, nor at my work—until you had your way. You wanted him here because your brother was anxious to get rid of him—my mother-in-law wanted him because *I* did *not* want him—the governess wanted him because he was a pietist, and old Margret because she had known his grandmother as a child. And that is why he was taken on! And if I had not taken him, I would now be in an insane asylum, or be lying in my grave. However, here is the money for the household and your pin money. You can let me have the bills later.

LAURA (*with a sarcastic smile and a curtsy*). Thank you ever so much! Do *you* also, by the way, keep account of what *you* give out for other than household expenses?

THE CAPTAIN. That does not concern you!

LAURA. No—that's true. It concerns me no more than my child's education and upbringing does. Did you gentlemen come to any conclusion after your plenary session this evening?

THE CAPTAIN. I had already made my decision. Therefore I had only to impart it to the only friend I and the rest of the family have in common. Bertha will be going to town to live. She will be leaving in two weeks.

LAURA. With whom, may I ask, is she going to stay?

THE CAPTAIN. At the home of accountant Sävberg.

LAURA. That freethinker!

THE CAPTAIN. Children are to be brought up in the faith of their father—that is what the law says.

LAURA. And the mother has nothing to say in the matter?

THE CAPTAIN. Nothing whatsoever! When she sells her birthright by legal purchase contract, she surrenders all her rights; and in exchange the husband agrees to support her and her children.

LAURA. Consequently she has no rights over her own child?

THE CAPTAIN. Not the slightest! Once you have sold something, it is not customary to take it back and still keep the money for it.

LAURA. But assume that the father and mother should jointly decide to . . .

THE CAPTAIN. What would happen then? I want her to live in town; you want her to remain at home. The arithmetical solution would be for her to stop halfway between her home and the town: at the railroad station. So you see— it's a question that has no solution.

LAURA. Then it must be solved by force! What was Nöjd doing here?

THE CAPTAIN. That is a professional secret!

LAURA. Which everybody in the kitchen knows!

THE CAPTAIN. Well—then *you* ought to know it, too.

LAURA. I do.

THE CAPTAIN. And have the verdict all ready?

LAURA. It is written in the law!

THE CAPTAIN. The law does not say who is the father of the child.

LAURA. No—but that is not very hard to know.

THE CAPTAIN. People who should know maintain that that is something one can never be sure of.

LAURA. That's strange! You mean to say one can't tell who is the father of a child!

THE CAPTAIN. Yes—that's what they say!

LAURA. That's curious! If that is so, then why should the father have such power over the child?

THE CAPTAIN. He has such rights only if he assumes the

responsibilities, or if they are imposed upon him. And in a marriage, of course, there are no doubts about the paternity.

LAURA. No doubts about the paternity?

THE CAPTAIN. No—I hope not!

LAURA. Well, but what about a wife who has been unfaithful?

THE CAPTAIN. There could be no such question in this case! Is there anything else you would like to ask?

LAURA. Not a thing.

THE CAPTAIN. Then I shall go up to my room. And will you please let me know when the doctor has come. (*He closes the chiffonier-writing desk and gets up.*)

LAURA. I will.

THE CAPTAIN (*leaving by the door in the left wall*). As soon as he is here! For I don't wish to show myself discourteous to him. You understand?   (*He goes out.*)

LAURA. I understand.

(LAURA *is alone. She regards the paper money she holds in her hand.*)

THE VOICE OF THE MOTHER-IN-LAW (*from inside*). Laura!

LAURA. Yes!

THE VOICE OF THE MOTHER-IN-LAW. Is my tea ready?

LAURA (*in the doorway to the inner rooms*). It will be in a moment.

THE ORDERLY (*opens the door leading from the hall and announces*): Dr. Östermark.

(LAURA *goes toward* THE DOCTOR *and stretches out her hand to him.*)

THE DOCTOR. Madam!

LAURA. Welcome, my dear Doctor! A most cordial welcome to our home! The Captain has gone out, but he will be back in a moment.

THE DOCTOR. I hope you will forgive me for being a little late, but I have already started my sickbed visits.

LAURA. Won't you sit down? Please sit down!

THE DOCTOR (*seats himself*). Thank you.

LAURA. Yes, we have quite a few cases of sickness out here at the present time. But nevertheless I hope you will like it here; and for us who live out here in the loneliness of the country, it is of special importance to have a physician who takes an interest in his patients. I have heard so many nice things said about you, Dr. Östermark, that I can only trust our relations will always be the very happiest.

THE DOCTOR. You are much too gracious, Madam,—but

on the other hand I hope that my visits in my capacity as physician will not have to be too frequent. Your family, I understand, are generally in good health, and . . .

LAURA. Well—yes, we have been fortunate enough not to have had any acute illnesses of any kind, but at the same time, things are not precisely as they should be.

THE DOCTOR. No—o?

LAURA. Things are not quite as we could wish them to be.

THE DOCTOR. Why—you startle me!

LAURA. There are certain conditions and situations in a family that one is bound by honor and conscience to conceal from the world . . .

THE DOCTOR. But not from one's physician!

LAURA. It is exactly for that reason I feel it my painful duty to tell you the whole truth from the very first.

THE DOCTOR. Could we not postpone this conversation until I have had the honor of making the Captain's acquaintance?

LAURA. No—I must tell you before you meet him.

THE DOCTOR. It is about him you wish to speak, then?

LAURA (*with a sad expression on her face*). It's about him, my poor, dear husband.

THE DOCTOR. You disturb me, my dear Madam. Believe me, I sympathize with you in your difficulty . . .

LAURA (*takes out her handkerchief*). My husband's mind—is affected. (*She sobs.*) Now you know the whole story—and soon you will be able to judge for yourself.

THE DOCTOR. I can't believe it! I have read and admired the Captain's excellent treatises on mineralogy—and they are clearly written with logic by a powerful intellect.

LAURA. You really think so? It would make me most happy if we—all his relatives, I mean—should be mistaken.

THE DOCTOR. Of course his mind could be disturbed in other ways. . . . Tell me some more.

LAURA. That is just what we have been afraid of! You see, he has at times the most fantastic ideas. This, of course— he being a scholar and a scientist—need not necessarily be disturbing *if* they did not encroach upon the peace and well-being of his family. For instance, he has a compulsion to buy all sorts of things.

THE DOCTOR. That sounds serious. Just exactly what does he buy?

LAURA. Books—whole cases of them—and he never reads them.

THE DOCTOR. Oh well—that a scholar acquires books— that isn't anything so alarming.

LAURA. You do not believe what I am telling you?

THE DOCTOR. Why, yes, my dear Madam, I haven't the slightest doubt you believe what you tell me.

LAURA. And is it reasonable that a person can see what takes place on another planet through a microscope?

THE DOCTOR. Does he say he can do that?

LAURA. That's what he says.

THE DOCTOR. Through a microscope?

LAURA. Yes—through a microscope!

THE DOCTOR. If that is so, then it is a grave sign.

LAURA. If that is so, you say! You can't have much trust in me, Doctor. And here I have been confiding a family secret to you. . . .

THE DOCTOR. Well, I am grateful and honored for that, of course, but as a physician I must first observe and investigate before I can give an opinion. Has the Captain ever shown any symptoms of fickleness, capriciousness—or instability—lack of willpower?

LAURA (sarcastically). Has he? We have been married twenty years, and I have never known him to make a decision without changing his mind about it afterwards.

THE DOCTOR. Is he stubborn?

LAURA. He wants to have his way in everything; but as soon as he gets what he wants, he drops the whole matter and asks me to decide.

THE DOCTOR. All this is serious and requires constant and thorough observation. You know, Madam, the will is the backbone of the mind. When the will is impaired, the mind and the soul disintegrate.

LAURA. And God knows I have had to learn to anticipate and carry out his every wish and fancy during these many long, trying years. Oh, if you only knew what kind of life I have had to endure as his wife! If you only knew! (She sobs in her handkerchief.)

THE DOCTOR. Your misfortune touches me deeply, Madam, and I promise you I shall see what can be done. I sympathize with you from the bottom of my heart, and I assure you you can rely upon me absolutely. But after what I have heard, I must ask this one thing of you: you must avoid giving your sick husband any ideas that will make an intense impression on him. Such ideas do not take long to develop in anyone with a tendency to softening of the brain; and they can easily turn into fixed ideas or monomania. Do you understand me?

LAURA. Yes—you mean—to avoid making him suspicious!

THE DOCTOR. Just that! You see, a sick person will believe anything he is told. He is receptive to anything.

LAURA. I see! Now I understand! Yes!—Yes! (*A bell is heard ringing from inside.*) Excuse me, my mother has something to say to me. I'll be back in a moment. . . . Ah, there is Adolf now.

(LAURA *goes out.* THE CAPTAIN *enters from the door in the left wall.*)

THE CAPTAIN. Ah, you are already here, Doctor! My most cordial welcome to you!

THE DOCTOR. It is a very great pleasure for me to make the acquaintance of such a distinguished scientist as yourself, Captain.

THE CAPTAIN. Oh, don't speak of it! My army duties, unfortunately, do not permit me much time for more profound investigations—but despite that, I believe I am on the verge of making a new discovery.

THE DOCTOR. So—o?

THE CAPTAIN. You see, I have been subjecting meteorites to spectrum analysis, and I have found coal—which confirms the presence of organic life. What do you say to that?

THE DOCTOR. Can you see that with a microscope?

THE CAPTAIN. Hell, no—with the spectroscope!

THE DOCTOR. The spectroscope! Forgive me! Well, then you will soon be able to tell us what is happening on Jupiter!

THE CAPTAIN. Not what *is* happening but what *has* happened there! If only that damned bookseller in Paris would send me those books! But it looks as if all the bookshops in the world were conspiring against me. Think of it, for two months not one of them has honored my requisitions or answered my letters or my insulting telegrams! I am going mad! And I haven't the faintest idea what can be wrong!

THE DOCTOR. Oh, I imagine it's only their usual carelessness. You must not take the matter so to heart.

THE CAPTAIN. No, but damn it, I won't get my treatise finished in time; and I know that some scientists in Berlin are working along the same line. But that's not what we should be talking about now—we should talk about you. If you should care to live *here,* we have a few rooms in the wing for you, unless you prefer to live in the house the former doctor occupied. . . .

THE DOCTOR. Whatever you say, Captain.

THE CAPTAIN. No, it's for you to decide! Make your choice!

THE DOCTOR. It's for you, Captain, to decide!

THE CAPTAIN. No, it is not for me to make the decision. You have to express your preference; I have no preference in the matter—none whatever!

THE DOCTOR. Well, but it is not for me to——

THE CAPTAIN. In heaven's name, man, make up your mind! What do you want? I have no wish in this matter, no opinion, no choice! Are you so lacking in backbone that you don't know what you want? Say what you want? Say what you want, or I shall lose my temper!

THE DOCTOR. Since you leave it to me—I would like to live here.

THE CAPTAIN. Good! Thank you! (*He goes over and jerks the bell-pull.*) Oh, you will forgive me, Doctor, but there is nothing that infuriates me so much as when people say they are indifferent to one thing or another.

(MARGRET *enters.*)

THE CAPTAIN. So—it's you, Margret. Tell me, Margret, do you know whether the rooms in the wing have been made ready for the Doctor?

MARGRET. Yes, sir, they are in order.

THE CAPTAIN. Very well! Then I shan't detain you, Doctor. I imagine you are tired. Goodnight—and again: welcome! We shall see you tomorrow, I hope.

THE DOCTOR. Goodnight, Captain!

THE CAPTAIN. And I imagine my wife gave you an inkling of conditions here, so that you have some idea of how the land lies?

THE DOCTOR. Your excellent wife pointed out a few things that could be of value to anyone who is a stranger here.— Goodnight, Captain.   (THE DOCTOR *leaves.*)

THE CAPTAIN. What is it, my dear? Anything special?

MARGRET. Listen to me, dear Mr. Adolf . . .

THE CAPTAIN. Speak up, Margret! You are the only one I can listen to who does not irritate me.

MARGRET. Now, listen, Mr. Adolf, don't you think you could meet your wife halfway and come to some sort of understanding with her in all this fuss over the child? One has to think of the mother . . .

THE CAPTAIN. And about the father, too, Margret.

MARGRET. Now, now, now! A father has other things than his child to occupy himself with, but a mother has only her child.

THE CAPTAIN. You are quite right there! She has only one burden to carry while I have to carry three. And I have to bear her burden, too. Has it never occurred to you that I would have had a different position in life from that of an old army man, if it had not been for her and the child?

MARGRET. Well, but it was not about that I wanted to talk.

THE CAPTAIN. I am quite aware of that, for what you are trying to do is to make me admit I am in the wrong, isn't it?

MARGRET. Don't you believe I have your welfare at heart?

THE CAPTAIN. Yes, my dear Margret, that I believe—but you don't really know what is best for me. Don't you see, it is not enough for me to have given life to my child; I want her to have the essence of myself, my intellect, my ideals, as well.

MARGRET. Well—all that is something I know nothing about. But, just the same, I don't understand why people should not be able to agree.

THE CAPTAIN. You are not my friend, Margret!

MARGRET. I? Why—what in heaven's name are you saying, Mr. Adolf? Do you think I could forget that I suckled and nursed you when you were a baby?—Do you?

THE CAPTAIN. No, Margret, my darling . . . and I have never forgotten it. Have I? You have been like a mother to me. You have stood by me in the past. But now, when I need you most—now you turn away from me and desert me for the enemy!

MARGRET. The enemy?

THE CAPTAIN. Yes, the enemy! You know very well what is going on in this house. You have seen it all—from beginning to end.

MARGRET. Yes—I have seen it, yes. But, God in heaven, must two people keep tormenting the life out of each other—two people who otherwise are so kind—and so good to everyone else? Your wife never acts like that to me or to anybody else.

THE CAPTAIN. No, I know—only to me. And I must tell you, Margret, that if you desert me now, you will be doing a sinful thing. For they are spinning a net round me—and that new doctor is not my friend!

MARGRET. Poor Mr. Adolf, you think the worst of everybody! But that's because you have not the true faith . . . yes, that's what's the matter . . .

THE CAPTAIN. But you and the Baptists have found it! You are indeed lucky!

MARGRET (*in a stern voice*). Well—at least I am luckier, and more happy, than you are, Mr. Adolf! If you would only be humble in your heart, and learn to love your neighbor, you would soon see that God will send you happiness.

THE CAPTAIN. It is strange that as soon as you begin to talk about God and love, your voice becomes hard and your eyes full of hate. No, Margret, you cannot possibly have found the true faith.

MARGRET. That's right, be proud! Be proud, and gloat over your learning! It won't help you when you are stuck in the mud . . .

THE CAPTAIN. How can you speak so arrogantly, you with your humble heart? But knowledge means nothing to creatures like you—I am certain of that!

MARGRET. You ought to be ashamed of yourself! But just the same, old Margret still loves her great, big boy best of all, and when the weather is stormy he'll be back again to his Margret—like a good child.

THE CAPTAIN. Margret, forgive me . . . but believe me, there is no one here but you who wishes me well. Help me, for I have a feeling that something is going to happen here. What, I do not know . . . but what is going on here now has nothing of good in it. (*A scream is heard from within.*) What is that? Who is that screaming?

BERTHA (*enters from the rooms within*). Father—father —help me! Save me!

THE CAPTAIN. What is it, my dearest child? Tell me!

BERTHA. Help me! I'm afraid she is going to hurt me!

THE CAPTAIN. Who wants to hurt you? Tell me! Tell me!

BERTHA. Grandmother! But I am to blame. I deceived her.

THE CAPTAIN. Tell me what has happened!

BERTHA. Yes, but you must not give me away! You must promise to tell no one!

THE CAPTAIN. Yes—but tell me what the trouble is!

(MARGRET *leaves*.)

BERTHA. You know, she has a habit of turning the lamp low and then she makes me sit at the table—then she puts a pen in my hand and gives me a sheet of paper, and then she says the spirits will move me to write . . .

THE CAPTAIN. What's that you are saying? And you never told me this before?

BERTHA. I didn't dare to—forgive me!—for grandmother says the spirits will take revenge if one talks about them. And then the pen writes—but if it's I or the spirits I don't know. Sometimes it goes without the slightest difficulty, but then again there are times when the pen won't move. When I am tired, it won't work at all, but she keeps insisting. And this evening I thought I was doing very well, but then grandmother said I was quoting from Stagnelius—and that I was making jest of her and trying to deceive her—and she flew into a terrible rage.

THE CAPTAIN. And do you believe there are spirits?

BERTHA. I don't know . . .

THE CAPTAIN. But *I* know—I know they do not exist!

BERTHA. But grandmother says you do not understand such things and that you, father, have something that is far worse—something you can see other planets with—far away——

THE CAPTAIN. So that's what grandmother says, eh? What else does grandmother say?

BERTHA. She says you can't work magic.

THE CAPTAIN. I never said I could. You know what a meteorite is, don't you? Yes—stones that fall from other heavenly bodies. Those I can examine and analyze and determine whether they contain the same elements as our earth. That is all I can do.

BERTHA. Grandmother says there are things *she* can see and *you* can't.

THE CAPTAIN. Then, my child, she is lying.

BERTHA. Grandmother does not tell lies!

THE CAPTAIN. What makes you say that?

BERTHA. Then mother must lie, too!

THE CAPTAIN. H'm.

BERTHA. If you say that mother tells lies, I'll never believe another word you say!

THE CAPTAIN. I have never said that, and so you will believe me when I say that for your own good and for the sake of your future you must leave this house! Wouldn't you like to do that? Wouldn't you like to go to the city and live—wouldn't you like to learn something useful? Eh?

BERTHA. Oh, would I! If I could only get to the city—away from here—no matter where! That is, if you will only let me see you occasionally—often! This house is always as gloomy and depressing as a dark winter night! But the moment *you* come into the house, father, it's like—like a morning in early spring when the storm windows are being taken out!

THE CAPTAIN. Oh, my dear child! My darling!

BERTHA. But, father dear, you must be good to mother, do you hear? She cries so often . . .

THE CAPTAIN. H'm.—Then you *would* like to go to town?

BERTHA. Oh yes, yes!

THE CAPTAIN. But if your mother should say no?

BERTHA. She won't, she must not!

THE CAPTAIN. But if she should?

BERTHA. Well—then I don't know what will happen. But she *must* let me go—she *must*!

THE CAPTAIN. Will you ask her?

BERTHA. No—you ask her, ask her in a nice way! If I asked her, she would pay no attention.

THE CAPTAIN. H'm. Well, if *you* want it, and *I* want it, and she still says no—then what are we going to do?

BERTHA. Oh—then our troubles will start all over again! Why can't you two——

LAURA (*enters*). Ah, so Bertha is here. Then perhaps we can hear what *she* has to say, now that the question of her future is to be decided.

THE CAPTAIN. You can scarcely expect the child to have any real opinion about a young girl's life and future, can you? On the other hand, you and I have seen a great many young girls grow up and develop, and therefore we have some knowledge of the problems of their formative years.

LAURA. But as you and I are of different opinions, we may as well let Bertha decide.

THE CAPTAIN. No! I will not let anyone, neither woman nor child, encroach upon my rights! Bertha, you go inside!

(BERTHA *leaves*.)

LAURA. You did not want her to speak because you were afraid she would side with me!

THE CAPTAIN. I know she would like to get away from this house, but I also know that your power over her is great enough to change her mind at will.

LAURA (*sarcastically*). Oh, have I that much power?

THE CAPTAIN. Yes, you have a fiendish, infernal way of getting what you want. Like all unscrupulous people you have no compunction about the means you use. How, for example, did you get rid of Doctor Norling—and what did you have to do with getting the new doctor here?

LAURA. Well, what did I do?

THE CAPTAIN. You kept insulting Dr. Norling until he finally left, and then you used your brother to procure votes for your Doctor Östermark.

LAURA. Well, that was quite simple, and perfectly legal. So—you plan to have Bertha leave home, do you?

THE CAPTAIN. Yes. She leaves in two weeks.

LAURA. You have made up your mind?

THE CAPTAIN. Yes.

LAURA. Have you spoken to Bertha about it?

THE CAPTAIN. Yes.

LAURA. Then I imagine I shall have to try to prevent it!

THE CAPTAIN. You can't.

LAURA. Can't I? Do you think I would let my daughter be among unprincipled people—people who would teach her that everything she has learned from her mother is nothing but worthless drivel? Do you?—Why, she would despise me for the rest of my life!

THE CAPTAIN. Would you have me allow ignorant and self-opinionated women to teach her that her father is a charlatan, would you?

LAURA (scornfully). I would not let that upset me!

THE CAPTAIN. And why not?

LAURA. Because a mother is closer to her child—more so since it has been discovered that no one can be absolutely certain who is the father of a child.

THE CAPTAIN. What bearing has that on this case?

LAURA. You don't know whether you are Bertha's father!

THE CAPTAIN. Don't I?

LAURA. How can you know what no one else knows?

THE CAPTAIN. Are you joking?

LAURA. No—I am simply employing your teachings. Besides, how do you know that I have not been unfaithful to you?

THE CAPTAIN. I can believe many things of you, but not that. And if you had been unfaithful, you would not be talking about it now!

LAURA. Suppose I was prepared to tolerate anything: to be an outcast, to be despised—all for the sake of possessing and keeping my influence over my child—and that I told the truth just now when I said: Bertha is my child, but not yours! Suppose——

THE CAPTAIN. That's enough!

LAURA. Just suppose! Then your power would be over!

THE CAPTAIN. If you could prove that I was not the father, yes!

LAURA. That should not be difficult! Would you like me to?

THE CAPTAIN. Stop it!

LAURA. All I would have to do would be to give the name of the real father, the details—such as time and place—and, by the way, when was Bertha born? In the third year of our marriage . . .

THE CAPTAIN. You had better stop now, or I'll . . .

LAURA. Or what? Yes, let's stop now! But think carefully on what you do and what you decide! And, above all, don't make yourself look ridiculous!

THE CAPTAIN. How about you?

LAURA. Oh, no—I have arranged the whole thing much too well!

THE CAPTAIN. That's what makes it so difficult to fight you.

LAURA. Why do you enter into combat with a superior enemy?

THE CAPTAIN. Superior?

LAURA. Yes! It's curious . . . but I have never been able to look at a man without feeling myself his superior.

THE CAPTAIN. Well—you shall at last meet your superior —and you will never forget it.

LAURA. That will be interesting.

MARGRET (*enters*). Supper is served. Will you please step into the dining-room?

LAURA. Yes, indeed. (THE CAPTAIN *tarries; he seats himself in an armchair by the smaller table.*) Aren't you coming in to supper?

THE CAPTAIN. No, thank you. I want nothing.

LAURA. Why not? Are you not in a good humor?

THE CAPTAIN. Yes—but I am not hungry.

LAURA. You had better come—or there will be questions asked that are unnecessary! Be pleasant now!—Oh, so you won't? Well, then, stay there!   (*She goes out.*)

MARGRET. Mr. Adolf, what is the trouble now?

THE CAPTAIN. I don't know, I don't know. But can you tell me why you women must treat a grown man as if he were a child?

MARGRET. Well, I can't tell you exactly why, but I suppose

it is because you are all children of women—all of you men, big and small.

THE CAPTAIN. But no woman is of man born. Yet I am Bertha's father. Tell me, Margret, you believe I am her father, don't you? Don't you?

MARGRET. May God have mercy, if he isn't childish. Of course, you are your own child's father.—Come and eat now, and don't sit there and sulk. There, now! (*She pats him on the head.*) Come along now!

THE CAPTAIN (*rises*). Out with you, woman! To hell with you, you hags! (*He goes to the door leading to the hall.*) Svärd! Svärd!

THE ORDERLY (*enters*). Yes, Captain!

THE CAPTAIN. Get ready the sleigh at once!

MARGRET. Now, Captain! Listen to me, Captain!

THE CAPTAIN. Out, woman,—out—this minute!

MARGRET (*with an anxious look*). God help us—what is going to happen now?

THE CAPTAIN (*puts on his cap and readies himself to leave*). Don't expect me home before midnight!

(*He goes out.*)

MARGRET. May God help us! What's to be the end of this?

ACT II

(THE SETTING.—*The same as in Act I. The lamp on the table is lighted. It is night.*)

THE DOCTOR. After talking with the Captain I have come to the conclusion that his mental condition can by no means be said to be proved. To begin with, you erred when you said that he had obtained these remarkable results about other celestial bodies by the use of a microscope. Now that I have learned it was through a spectroscope, he is not only freed of the suspicion of being mentally unbalanced but, on the contrary, it shows his services to science to be highly meritorious.

LAURA. Oh, but I never said that!

THE DOCTOR. My dear Madam, I made a note of our conversation; and I recall that I questioned you on that very point because I was afraid I had heard wrong. One must be exceedingly conscientious and scrupulous about one's facts when one makes accusations which might lead to a man's being declared incompetent.

LAURA. Declared incompetent?

THE DOCTOR. You certainly must know that a mentally incompetent person loses his civil and family rights.

LAURA. No—I didn't know that!

THE DOCTOR. There is still another point which can't help but cause suspicion. He mentioned that his letters to book dealers have brought no replies. May I ask whether you have had a hand in this because of some benevolent, although perhaps misguided, motive?

LAURA. Yes, I have. I felt it my duty—for the sake of our home. I could not allow him to ruin and disgrace us all without doing something about it.

28

THE DOCTOR. You will forgive me for saying so—but I am afraid you fail to realize what consequences such intercepting of his mail might have. Should he discover your underhand interference in his affairs, then you would have awakened his suspicions—and after that, they would grow like an avalanche. Furthermore, by doing this you have set yourself against his will and provoked him into even greater irritability. Haven't you yourself felt how maddening it is when your most ardent desires are thwarted—when your will is opposed? Haven't you?

LAURA. If I have? . . .

THE DOCTOR. Well—then imagine how he must feel!

LAURA (rises). It's midnight, and he is not yet back. . . . Now we can expect the worst.

THE DOCTOR. But tell me, Madam, what happened after I left earlier this evening? You must tell me everything.

LAURA. He talked in the most fantastic manner about all sorts of weird ideas he had. Can you imagine—he even came up with the notion that he is not the father of his own child!

THE DOCTOR. How very peculiar! Whatever could have put that idea in his head?

LAURA. I haven't the faintest idea—unless it could have been something in connection with the questioning of one of his men in a paternity case. When I took the girl's part he lost control of himself and said one could never tell who was father of a child. God knows I did all I could to calm him, but I'm afraid he is beyond help now. (She sobs.)

THE DOCTOR. This can't go on, of course. Something must be done about it, but without rousing his suspicions.—Tell me, has the Captain had any such delusions before?

LAURA. Six years ago a similar episode occurred; and at that time he himself admitted—yes, and in a letter to his doctor—that he feared for his sanity.

THE DOCTOR. H'm. H'm. Well, this is a disturbance with deep roots. . . . But the sanctity of family life, and all that, prevents me from—from probing into every phase of it; and so I will only take into consideration the obvious manifestations. What is done can not be undone, unfortunately, and in any case: it is to visible symptoms and manifestations that the remedy should be applied. Where do you think he is now?

LAURA. I haven't the faintest idea. He has so many ridiculous notions these days.

THE DOCTOR. Perhaps you would like me to stay till he comes. Would you? And so that he will not be suspicious, I can say I came to see your mother, since she has not been well.

LAURA. Yes, that is a good idea! Yes, you must not leave us, Doctor. You can't imagine how worried I am. And wouldn't it be better to tell him at once what you think of his condition? Don't you think so?

THE DOCTOR. That's something we don't do when we deal with mental cases—unless the patient himself brings up the subject. And then we do it only under rare circumstances. It depends entirely upon what turn his condition takes. But I think we had best not stay in here. Couldn't I withdraw to the adjoining room so that it would not look quite so designing?

LAURA. Yes, that might be better—and then Margret can sit in here. . . . She always waits up for him when he is out late, and she is the only one who can do anything with him. (*She goes over to the door, right.*) Margret! Margret!

MARGRET. Anything I can do for you, Madam? Is the Captain back?

LAURA. No, I want you to sit up and wait for him in here. And when he comes, tell him that my mother is not well and that the doctor is here on her account.

MARGRET. Yes, indeed, Madam. I'll do just as you say.

LAURA (*opens the door leading to the rest of the rooms on the floor*). Won't you step in here, Doctor?

THE DOCTOR. Thank you, Madam.

MARGRET (*seats herself at the large table and takes out her hymn book and spectacles*). Yes, yes! Yes, yes! (*She starts to read in half audible voice.*)

A vale of tears, and pain, and doubt,
This dreary life soon passes by.
For Death keeps hovering about;
He sends to all the earth his cry:
'Tis Vanity! 'Tis Vanity!

Yes, yes. . . . Yes, yes. . . .

All earthly things with breath and mind
Are struck down by his mighty sword;
But Death leaves only Grief behind—
To write upon the grave this word:
'Tis Vanity. 'Tis Vanity!

(*While she is reading, Bertha has entered with a coffeepot*

*and a piece of needlework. She speaks in a subdued
voice.)*

BERTHA. Do you mind, Margret, if I sit here with you? It
is so dreary up there!

MARGRET. Good heavens, Bertha! Are you still up?

BERTHA. I have to finish my Christmas present for father,
you know. And I brought something good for you . . .

MARGRET. Yes—but, my dear child, this won't do. You
have to be up early in the morning, and it is now past midnight.

BERTHA. Well, what does that matter? I am afraid to stay
up there all alone. . . . I believe the place is haunted.

MARGRET. There now, didn't I tell you? Yes, you may take
my word for it, this house has no good gnome looking after
it. Just what *did* you hear, Bertha?

BERTHA. Why, I heard someone singing up in the attic.

MARGRET. In the attic? At this time of night?

BERTHA. Yes—and it was such a sad, mournful song! I have
never *heard* a more mournful song. And it seemed to come
from the part of the attic where the cradle stands—you
know, to the left.

MARGRET. Oh, dear me, dear me! And with such a frightful storm going on, too! You would think the chimneys
would blow down. (*She reads:*)

O, what is this earthly life
If not pain and grief and strife?
At its best life is not free
From despair, adversity . . .

Well, my dear child, may God grant us a happy Christmas!

BERTHA. Margret, is it true that father is sick?

MARGRET. Yes, I am afraid it is.

BERTHA. Then we can't celebrate Christmas Eve, can we?
But if he is sick, how can he be up?

MARGRET. Because, my child, his sickness is not the kind
that keeps him in bed.—Sh! I hear someone out in the hall.
Go upstairs and go to bed now—and take the coffeepot with
you, or the Captain will be angry. (*Bertha goes out, taking
the coffeepot with her*).

BERTHA (*in the doorway*). Goodnight, Margret!

MARGRET. Goodnight, my child, and may God bless
you. . . .

THE CAPTAIN (*enters; he takes off his overcoat*). Are you
still up? Go to bed!

MARGRET. I was just waiting up . . .

(THE CAPTAIN *lights a candle, then opens the writing desk and seats himself at it. He takes some letters from his pocket, also some newspapers.*)

MARGRET. Mr. Adolf!

THE CAPTAIN. What is it you want?

MARGRET. Your wife's mother is sick. The doctor is here . . .

THE CAPTAIN. Anything serious?

MARGRET. No, I don't think so. It's a cold, that's all.

THE CAPTAIN (*gets up*). Margret, who was the father of your child?

MARGRET. Why, I have told you ever so many times that it was that good-for-nothing fellow Johansson.

THE CAPTAIN. Are you sure it was he who was the father?

MARGRET. Why, how can you talk so childish? Of course, I am sure! Of course he was the only one!

THE CAPTAIN. Yes—but did he know he was the only one? No, he could not be certain of that—only *you* could know absolutely. You see the difference, don't you?

MARGRET. No, I don't.

THE CAPTAIN. No—you wouldn't; but the difference is there nevertheless. (*He opens the photograph album on the large table and starts turning the pages.*) Do you think Bertha looks like me? (*He regards intently a photograph in the album.*)

MARGRET. Why, of course. Two berries couldn't be more alike.

THE CAPTAIN. Did Johansson admit that he was the father? Did he?

MARGRET. Ah, I guess he had to.

THE CAPTAIN. How dreadful!—Here is the doctor . . . (*He goes to greet* THE DOCTOR *who has entered.*) Good evening, Doctor. How is my wife's mother?

THE DOCTOR. Oh, it's nothing serious. Merely a sprained ligament in the left foot—just a slight sprain.

THE CAPTAIN. I thought Margret said it was a cold. There seems to be a difference in diagnosis.—You can go to bed now, Margret. (MARGRET *leaves. There is a silence.* THE CAPTAIN *beckons to* THE DOCTOR *to be seated.*) Please sit down, Doctor Östermark.

THE DOCTOR (*seating himself*). Thank you.

THE CAPTAIN. Is it a fact that when you cross a zebra with a mare, you get striped foals?

THE DOCTOR (*startled*). That is a definite fact.

THE CAPTAIN. Is it a fact that if you continue the breeding with a stud-horse the foals will also be striped?

THE DOCTOR. That, too, is a fact.

THE CAPTAIN. Consequently, a stallion can, in certain circumstances, be the sire to striped foals, and vice versa.

THE DOCTOR. Yes . . . that seems to be the case.

THE CAPTAIN. And that would seem to indicate that the resemblance between the male and his offspring proves nothing.

THE DOCTOR. Oh . . .

THE CAPTAIN. In short: It is impossible to prove who is the father?

THE DOCTOR. Oh—ho!

THE CAPTAIN. You are a widower and you have brought children into the world, haven't you?

THE DOCTOR. Y–e–s . . .

THE CAPTAIN. Haven't there been times when you have felt yourself ridiculous as a father, eh? I can't imagine anything sillier than seeing a man holding on to his child—or hearing a man talking about his children. "My *wife's* children" is what he should say. Did you never realize how false your position was? Were you never assailed by doubts—I shan't say suspicions for, being a gentleman, I assume that your wife was above suspicion?

THE DOCTOR. No—I had no such doubts—none whatsoever. And you see, Captain, we have to accept our children in good faith. I think that's what Goethe says.

THE CAPTAIN. In good faith—when you deal with women? That is taking a risk.

THE DOCTOR. Ah, but there are so many sorts of women.

THE CAPTAIN. The latest investigations show that there is only one kind! When I was young, I was virile and, if I may say so, handsome. There are two impressions—each one momentary—which come back to me; and they are what have made me somewhat apprehensive. My first experience was on board a steamer. I and some friends were seated in the fore-saloon, when the young stewardess suddenly came and sat down beside me, crying hysterically. She told us that her beloved had perished at sea, and we expressed our sorrow. Then I ordered some champagne. After our second glass, I touched her foot, after our fourth, her knee—and before daybreak I had consoled her.

THE DOCTOR. That was merely one of those rare winter flies!

THE CAPTAIN. Now I come to my second experience—

and that was a *summer* fly. I was staying at a seaside resort, and there I met a young married woman who was there with her children. Her husband was occupied in the city. She was religious and extremely severe in her principles, kept preaching morality to me, and I believe, was genuinely honest. I lent her a book—two books; and, remarkably enough, when she left, she returned them both. Three months later I came across her visiting card in one of the books, and on it was quite a candid declaration of love. It was innocent enough—that is to say, as innocent as a declaration of love coming from a married woman to an unknown stranger who had never made any advances to her, is likely to be. And now comes the moral: Never put too much faith in anybody!

THE DOCTOR. Nor too little!

THE CAPTAIN. No, just enough! But don't you see, Doctor, this woman was so absolutely unconscious of her unprincipled behavior that she promptly, brazenly, told her husband of her infatuation for me. And that is just where the danger lies—that they are unaware of their instinctive wickedness. I grant you that these are extenuating circumstances, but they do not reverse the judgment. They only help to mitigate it.

THE DOCTOR. My dear Captain, you let your thoughts take a morbid direction. You ought to guard against that.

THE CAPTAIN. You ought to guard against using the word *morbid*. You must know that a steam boiler explodes when the pressure gauge registers 100° Centigrade. But the boiling point varies and is not the same for all boilers. You understand what I am driving at? However, you are here to keep an eye on me. And if I were not a man, I would be justified in making accusations—or, as it so craftily is called, express regrets. And I might be able to provide you with the full diagnosis—and, what is more, the case history. But I am unfortunately a man; and therefore I can do nothing but fold my arms across my breast and, like the Roman of old, hold my breath until I die. . . . Goodnight!

THE DOCTOR. Captain, if you are ill, it would be no reflection on your honor as a man if you told me everything. I must, of course, hear both sides.

THE CAPTAIN. I imagine you have heard enough from the other side.

THE DOCTOR. No, Captain. And I must confide to you that when I heard Mrs. Alving talk about her dead husband, I thought to myself: "What a damned shame the fellow is unable to talk back from the grave!"

THE CAPTAIN. And do you think he would have spoken, had he lived? And do you think any man risen from the dead would be believed?—Goodnight, Dr. Östermark! You can hear I am quite calm, can't you? So you can confidently go to bed.

THE DOCTOR. Well, then, goodnight, Captain. I can have nothing further to do with this matter.

THE CAPTAIN. Are we enemies?

THE DOCTOR. Far from it. I am only sorry we can't be friends! Goodnight! (*He leaves.* THE CAPTAIN *escorts* THE DOCTOR *to the door, rear; then he goes to the door, right, and opens it slightly.*)

THE CAPTAIN. Come in—and let us have a talk . . . I could hear you while you were busy listening to us . . . (LAURA *enters. She is embarrassed.* THE CAPTAIN *seats himself at the writing desk.*) It is after midnight—but we must get this over with. Sit down! (*There is a silence.*) I have been at the post office this evening and picked up certain letters. They confirm that you have intercepted letters I have written as well as others addressed to me. As a consequence of this I have lost time, and the results I hoped to achieve from my efforts have come to nothing.

LAURA. I did it for your own good. You were pursuing your investigations at the expense of your duties as an army officer.

THE CAPTAIN. It could not have been out of interest for me! You knew only too well that I was bound to achieve greater distinction some day through this work of mine than I ever would through my military career. But you were opposed to my doing anything that might bring me recognition! It would have exposed your own inferiority. And, therefore—in return—I have intercepted letters addressed to you.

LAURA. How very noble of you!

THE CAPTAIN. I am glad you hold me in such high esteem as you say. From these letters it appears that for some time you have been mobilizing all my old friends against me by keeping alive certain rumors about my mental condition. And you have succeeded in your efforts—for now there is no more than one person, from the colonel to the cook, who believes that I am in my right mind. The truth about my condition is that my mind is unimpaired, as you well know: therefore I am capable of taking care of both my duties in the army and my duties as a parent. As long as my will-power remains unbroken, I have my emotions under control. But you have been nagging, and wearing it down, until it is about to fly off its cogs—and suddenly the whole mechanism might snap and whir backwards. I am not appealing to your feelings, for you haven't any—and there is where your strength lies. But I do appeal to your self-interest.

LAURA. I'd like to hear.

THE CAPTAIN. By behaving as you have done, you have roused my suspicions. As a result, my sense of judgment has been befogged and my mind is beginning to drift. You have been waiting for me to fall prey to insanity—little by little —and it may set in at any moment. The question you now have to decide is this: is it of greater advantage to you to have me remain of sound mind, or to be mentally ill . . . Give that a thought! If I should lose my mind, I'll lose my army post—and then you'll be without support. If I should die, you'll have my life insurance. But—if I should take my own life, you'll get nothing. Therefore, you see, it is to your own interest that I live out my life.

LAURA. Is this meant to be a trap of some kind?

THE CAPTAIN. Naturally! You can go around it, or stick your head in it.

LAURA. You talk about killing yourself! (*Scornfully.*) You'll never do that!

THE CAPTAIN. Don't be too sure! Do you think a man can go on living when he has no one to live for—nothing whatever to live for?

LAURA. In other words, you are capitulating.

THE CAPTAIN. No—I propose we have peace.

LAURA. On what conditions?

THE CAPTAIN. That you allow me to keep my reason. Relieve my mind of suspicions and I shall give up the fight.

LAURA. What suspicions?

THE CAPTAIN. About Bertha's parentage.

LAURA. Is there any doubt about that?

THE CAPTAIN. Yes, there is—for me there is—and it is you who have given impulse to it.

LAURA. I?

THE CAPTAIN. Yes, you have been trickling poisonous doubts—like henbane—in my ear, and circumstances made them sprout and grow. Relieve me of the uncertainty—tell me frankly—tell me the truth—and I promise you I shall forgive you.

LAURA. You can't expect me to confess to something I am not guilty of!

THE CAPTAIN. Why should it matter to you? You know only too well I would never reveal it! Do you think a man would spread his shame abroad to the whole world?

LAURA. If I were to tell you it is not true, you would still question my truthfulness. But if I say it *is* true, then you will believe me. You seem to wish it were true.

THE CAPTAIN. Strange to say—yes. But I presume it is only because of the fact that if the first supposition is true, it cannot be proved. Only the second one can.

LAURA. Have you any grounds for your suspicions?

THE CAPTAIN. Yes and no.

LAURA. I believe your aim is to prove me guilty in order to get rid of me so that you alone will have authority over Bertha. But you will not catch me in that trap!

THE CAPTAIN. Do you really think I would assume responsibility for another man's child if I were convinced of your guilt? Do you?

LAURA. No—I quite believe you wouldn't. And now it has become quite evident to me that you lied just now when you said you would be able to forgive me.

THE CAPTAIN (*gets up*). Laura—save me! Don't let me lose my reason! I can't believe you understand what I am trying to say. . . . If the child is not mine, then I have no authority over her, and I don't want any. And that is exactly what you are aiming at! Isn't it? But perhaps you are reaching for still more—for something else, perhaps? You want the child in your power, and at the same time have me support you.

LAURA. In my power, yes. . . . What has all this struggle of life and death been for, if not for power?

THE CAPTAIN. For me—who don't believe in a life hereafter—the child was my life after this. She was the embodiment of my idea of eternal life—perhaps the only conception that has any correspondence to life. If you destroy this thought, this sentiment, then you sentence me to death.

LAURA. Why didn't we part long ago?

THE CAPTAIN. Because the child bound us together. But the bond became a chain. And—how did this come about? How? I never gave this a thought before, but now the memories rise up, accusing . . . yes, and perhaps judging, punishing. We had been married two years, and we had had no child. The reason for that you know best. I was taken ill and lay at death's door. One day, when my fever had momentarily subsided, I heard voices coming from outside, in the drawing-room. It was you and the attorney discussing what resources I still possessed at that time. He explained that you would inherit nothing because you were childless. And then he asked whether you by any chance were pregnant. I did not hear what you answered him. I recovered—and we had a child.—Who is the father?

LAURA. You are.

THE CAPTAIN. No—I am not her father. . . . There is a crime buried here that's beginning to reek! And what a hellish, infernal crime! You women showed yourselves tenderhearted enough when it came to freeing black men from slavery—but white men are still being kept enslaved! I have worked for you, slaved for you, for your child, your mother, your servants! I have sacrificed promotion and my career. I have endured torture; I have been your whipping boy; have gone without sleep, been plagued by anxiety for you and yours until my hair has turned gray—all because I wanted you to live a life without worry, and so that, when you grew old, you might live life over again in your child. I have borne it all without complaining because I believed myself to be the father of the child. . . . This is the vilest form of stealing, the most brutal, most cruel form of slavery. I have been through seventeen years of penal servitude . . . yet have been without guilt. How can you ever make amends for all this?

LAURA. Now you have gone completely mad!

THE CAPTAIN (seating himself). So you hope! I have watched you in your efforts to conceal your crime. I have felt compassion for you because I did not understand what made you downcast; many a time I have caressed your bad conscience until it found peace, thinking I was merely chasing away some morbid thought. I have heard you cry out and speak aloud in your sleep, yet closing my ears to what you uttered. I suddenly remember—the night before last—Bertha's birthday. It was between two and three in the morning, I was sitting up reading, when I heard a scream as if someone were trying to strangle you: "Don't come near me, don't come near me!" I rapped on the wall, for I didn't want to hear any more. I have long had my suspicions, but I didn't have the courage to hear them confirmed. All this I have suffered for you. . . . What will *you* now do for me?

LAURA. What is there I can do? I will swear by God and all that is holy that you are Bertha's father.

THE CAPTAIN. All that is of no help, for you have already said that a mother can and should commit any crime for her child. I implore you—for the sake of our past happy years—I plead with you, as a wounded man pleads for his final death blow, to tell me everything. Can't you see that I am helpless—helpless as a child—can't you hear I am whimpering as to a mother—won't you try to forget that I am a man, that I am a soldier, who by a mere word can tame both men and beasts? All I ask of you is that you show compassion, as to one who is sick. I lay down all authority and I ask for mercy—ask that you let me live!

LAURA (*has come up to him. She lays her hand on his brow*). What do I see! The man is crying!

THE CAPTAIN. Yes—I am crying, even though I am a man. But has a man not eyes? Has a man not hands, limbs, likes, dislikes, passions? Is he not kept alive by the same nourishment, is he not wounded by the same weapons, is he not warmed by the same summer, cooled by the same winter as a woman? If you prick us, do we not bleed—if you tickle us, do we not burst into laughter? If you poison us, do we not die? Then why should not a man complain, a soldier cry? Because it is not manly? Why is it not manly?

LAURA. Weep then, my child, and you will have your mother with you again. Do you remember that it was as your second mother I first came into your life? Do you? You were big of body and strong, but you were lacking in stamina. You were a giant of a child and had either come into the world ahead of time—or perhaps you were unwanted.

THE CAPTAIN. Yes—I am afraid you are right. My father and mother did not want a child; and so I was born without a will of my own. Then, when you and I became one, I felt myself strengthened by your will, and so I allowed you to be the master in the house. I—who was used to giving the commands to my troopers—I now became the one to take orders; and I grew to be part of you—looked up to you as to a superior intelligence—listened to you as if I were your foolish little boy.

LAURA. Yes, that's the way it was, and that is why I loved you as if you were my child. But I don't think you could have helped noticing that each time you approached me as lover, with feelings of another nature, I felt ashamed. . . .

And the joy of being in your embrace turned into a sense of guilt—as if the shame had crept into my very blood. The mother turned mistress! Ugh!

THE CAPTAIN. Yes—I noticed that, but I did not understand. And somehow I—I got the impression that you despised my lack of manhood—and then I made up my mind to win you as woman by being the man.

LAURA. There is where you made your mistake. The mother was your friend, you see, but the woman was your enemy; and love between the sexes produces strife, dissension, conflict. And do not think that I gave myself to you! I took—whatever I wanted. But you had the upper hand in one thing —and I felt it, and wanted you to realize it.

THE CAPTAIN. You always had the upper hand; you could hypnotize me when I was awake so that I would neither see nor hear, but simply obey. You could give me a raw potato and make me think it was a peach; you could make me admire your silly ideas as outbursts of genius. You could have persuaded me to do anything—any crime, anything evil. But you lacked in intelligence and common sense; and instead of carrying out my instructions and admonitions, you acted according to your own whims and ideas. And when I finally woke up and began to realize what was happening and saw that my honor was at stake, I tried to forget these indignities by an achievement of some sort, by some great and noble act, a discovery, or—suicide. I tried to go to war but was not given permission. It was then I began to devote myself to science. And just as I am about to stretch out my hand to receive the fruits of my work, you cut off my arm. I am now dishonored, discredited . . . I don't care to live any longer. For a man cannot live without honor.

LAURA. But a woman can!

THE CAPTAIN. Yes—for she has her children but he hasn't. We two—as so many others in the world—have lived our lives unconsciously, like children, full of fanciful conceits and notions, ideals and illusions, until at last we woke up. That was all very well, but we woke up with our feet on the bed pillow, and we were awakened by someone who was himself a sleepwalker. When women grow old and cease to be women, they get hair on their chins. I wonder what happens to men when they are old and no longer are men? The fowls that crowed were not roosters, they were capons—and the fat pullets answered their call. And so— when the sun should have risen for us, we found ourselves among ruins in the full of moon, exactly as in the good old days. It had only been a little morning slumber with wild dreams. There had been no real awakening.

LAURA. You know, you should have taken up writing—been an author, a poet.

THE CAPTAIN. Who knows!

LAURA. And now I am sleepy! If you have any more fantasies, save them till tomorrow.

THE CAPTAIN. Just one word more—about realities: Do you hate me?

LAURA. I do—sometimes! When you are a man.

THE CAPTAIN. This is like race hatred. If it is true that we are descended from the ape, then it must have been from two separate species. We two are not alike, are we?

LAURA. Just what is it you mean?

THE CAPTAIN. I can see now that one of us must go under in this struggle.

LAURA. Which one of us?

THE CAPTAIN. The weaker one, of course.

LAURA. And the stronger one is in the right, eh?

THE CAPTAIN. The stronger are always in the right because they have the power!

LAURA. Then I am in the right!

THE CAPTAIN. You mean you have the power, then?

LAURA. Yes—and lawful power—when I place you under a guardian tomorrow!

THE CAPTAIN. A guardian?

LAURA. Yes! And that done, I shall bring up my child myself without having to listen to your fantastic nonsense!

THE CAPTAIN. And who will pay for her education when I am gone?

LAURA. Your pension!

THE CAPTAIN (*approaches her threateningly*). How can you have me put under a guardian, tell me?

LAURA (*produces a letter*). By means of this letter, an attested copy of which has been made, and which is now in the hands of the proper authorities!

THE CAPTAIN. What letter is that?

LAURA (*her eyes fixed on* THE CAPTAIN, *she moves backwards toward the door on the right*). Yours! Your own! Your confession to the doctor that you are insane!

(THE CAPTAIN *regards her silently.*)

LAURA. Now you have fulfilled your destiny as a father and family supporter—a function that unfortunately is a necessary one. You are no longer needed . . . and so you must go! Since you don't want to stay and acknowledge what you at last have come to realize: that my intellect is as strong as my will, you must be gotten rid of.

(THE CAPTAIN *goes over to the table and picks up the burning lamp which he throws at* LAURA *who has just passed through the door.*)

ACT III

(THE SETTING.—*The same as in Acts I and II. The door in the left side corner is barricaded with a chair.* LAURA *and* MARGRET *are alone on the stage. From above can be heard* THE CAPTAIN'S *footsteps as he is nervously pacing the floor.*)

LAURA (*to Margret*). Did he give you the keys?

MARGRET. *Give* them to me? No, so help me God, I just took them from his pocket when Nöjd had his clothes out for an airing.

LAURA. Then it's Nöjd who is on duty today?

MARGRET. Yes, it's Nöjd.

LAURA. Let me have the keys.

MARGRET. Yes, but this is like downright stealing! Just listen to him pacing back and forth up there! Back and forth— back and forth—

LAURA. Is the door safely bolted?

MARGRET. Yes, it is. It is safe enough, don't worry!

LAURA (*opens the writing desk and seats herself at it.* MARGRET *starts to sob*). Control yourself, Margret. Now it is a question of keeping calm if we are going to be able to hold our own. (*There is a knock at the door, rear, left.*) Who is there?

MARGRET (*opens the door to the hall*). It's Nöjd.

LAURA. Tell him to come in.

NÖJD (*enters*). A message from the Colonel . . .

LAURA. Give it to me. (*She reads the letter.*) Ah, I see! Nöjd, did you remove all the cartridges from the Captain's guns—and from the game pouches, did you?

NÖJD. I did just as you said, Madam.

LAURA. Then wait outside till I have answered the Colonel's letter.

43

(Nöjd *goes out.* Laura *starts to write. Suddenly the sound of sawing is heard from above.*)

Margret. Listen to that! What in the world can he be doing up there now?

Laura. Don't talk when I am writing!

Margret (*muttering to herself*). May God help us and have mercy on us all! How will this end?

Laura (*her letter finished, she places it in an envelope, addresses it and hands it to* Margret). Here, Margret. Give this to Nöjd. And not a word to my mother about this, do you hear!

(Margret *takes the letter and goes out toward the door leading to the entrance hall.* Laura *pulls out several drawers in the writing desk, examines papers, letters etc. . . .* The Pastor *enters. He pulls up a chair and seats himself close by* Laura.)

The Pastor. Good evening, sister. I have been away all the day as you know and only just returned. You have had a distressing time, I hear.

Laura. Yes, brother! Never in my life have I been through any twenty-four hours like these!

The Pastor. I see, however, that you are none the worse for it.

Laura. No, thank heaven—but you can imagine what *might* have happened.

The Pastor. But tell me about it. How did it all start? I have only heard rumors—all kinds of rumors.

Laura. It began with this crazy notion of his that he was not Bertha's father, and it ended by his throwing the burning lamp in my face.

The Pastor. Why, this is horrible! This is nothing short of complete insanity!—What are we going to do now?

Laura. We must try to prevent any further such violence, and the Doctor has sent to the insane asylum for a strait jacket. In the meantime I have written and explained to the Colonel, and I am now trying to wade through these bills and accounts here. He has managed our affairs in a most reprehensible manner.

The Pastor. What a sorry business this is! But it's what I always expected would happen. When fire and water come together, the result is explosion. (Laura *pulls out another drawer.*) What's that I see there in the drawer?

Laura. Look—he saves everything!

The Pastor (*rummaging through the drawer*). Good

heavens! It's your old doll! And here is your christening cap
—and Bertha's rattle—and your letters—and the locket . . .
(*He wipes a tear from his eyes.*) He must have loved you
deeply, Laura . . . he must have . . . I never kept anything
like that. . .

LAURA. I believe he did love me once, but time—time
changes so many things.

THE PASTOR. What is the large document you have there?
Oh, the contract for your burial plot! Yes—rather the grave
than the asylum. Laura, tell me! Are you in any way to
blame for all this, are you?

LAURA. I? How could I be to blame if a person loses his
mind?

THE PASTOR. Well . . . well . . . I am not saying anything!
After all, blood is thicker than water.

LAURA. Just exactly what have you the audacity to imply?

THE PASTOR (*with a fixed gaze at her*). Oh, you can tell
me! . . .

LAURA. What?

THE PASTOR. Tell me. . . . You can not deny that what you
really want is the right to bring up and have complete
control over your daughter.

LAURA. I don't understand what you mean——

THE PASTOR (*marveling at her boldness*). I can't help ad-
miring you!

LAURA. Me? H'm.

THE PASTOR. And to think that I am to be his guardian—
that freethinker! Frankly, I have always regarded him as a
weed in our family pasture.

LAURA (*emitting an abrupt laugh, which she quickly sup-
presses. Then she suddenly becomes serious*). And you dare to
say this to me, his wife?

THE PASTOR. You are a strong woman, Laura! Unbe-
lievably strong! Like the fox in the trap, you would rather
gnaw off your leg than allow yourself to be caught! Like a
master thief, you have no accomplice—not even your own
conscience! Look at yourself in the mirror! You don't dare!

LAURA. I never use a mirror!

THE PASTOR. No—because you don't dare! Let me look at
your hand! Not a sign of blood to betray you—not a trace
of insidious poison! An innocent murder that cannot be
reached by the law—an unconscious crime—unconscious,
mind you! A clever scheme, a master stroke! Do you hear

how he is working away up there!—Take care, Laura! If that man should ever get loose, he'll saw you in two.

LAURA. You talk as volubly as if you had a bad conscience! Why don't you accuse me, if you can?

THE PASTOR. I can't.

LAURA. You see—you can't! Consequently, I am innocent! Now you just look after your ward—and I'll look after mine! Here is the doctor! (LAURA *rises and greets him.*) Welcome, Dr. Östermark. You, at least, will help me, won't you? You will, won't you? But I am sorry to say there is not much you can do. You hear how he is going on up there, don't you? Will that convince you?

THE DOCTOR. I am convinced that an act of violence has been committed, but the question is whether this should be considered to have been done in a fit of anger or of insanity.

THE PASTOR. But aside from the outburst itself, you must acknowledge that he had fixed ideas.

THE DOCTOR. I think *your* ideas, Pastor, are if anything more so.

THE PASTOR. My views on spiritual matters are deep-rooted and consistent.

THE DOCTOR. Let us not talk about what we think! (*To* LAURA.) It rests with you, Madam, to decide just what your husband's guilt is and whether he should be fined and sent to prison, or put away in an asylum. What is your opinion in this matter?

LAURA. I can't answer that now.

THE DOCTOR. Then you have no definite opinion as to what is best for you and your family?—What do you say, Pastor?

THE PASTOR. Well—no matter which way, there is bound to be scandal. . . . It is not an easy matter to decide.

LAURA. But suppose he should escape with a fine for attempted assault! He might use violence again!

THE DOCTOR. And if he should be sent to prison, it would not be for long.. Considering what is best for all concerned, we must conclude he should at once be adjudged insane.— Where is the nurse?

LAURA. The nurse? Why?

THE DOCTOR. She will have to put the strait jacket on your sick husband—after I have had a talk with him. But not before I tell her. I have the jacket outside. (*He goes out into the hall and returns with a large bundle.*) Will you please ask the nurse to come in here?

(LAURA *jerks the bell-pull.*)

THE PASTOR. This is frightful! Frightful!

(MARGRET *enters.*)

THE DOCTOR (*unwraps the bundle and takes out the strait jacket*). Please listen closely to what I say! In case I find it necessary to prevent further outbreaks of violence by the Captain, I want you to slip this jacket on him from behind —but so that he doesn't realize what you are doing. As you see, the sleeves are unusually long. That is because they are intended to hinder his movements. Then you tie the sleeves in a knot on the back. And here are two straps—you put them through these small buckles and fasten them to the arm of the chair or the sofa, whichever you think is easiest. Now— do you think you can do this?

MARGRET. No, sir! I can't do it! I never could!

LAURA. Why don't *you* do it, Doctor?

THE DOCTOR. Because the Captain does not trust me. You yourself would really be the proper person to do it; but I am afraid he has not much confidence in you, either.

(LAURA *makes a grimace.*)

THE DOCTOR. Perhaps you, Pastor . . .

THE PASTOR. No, no—I must ask to be excused!

(*There is a knock at the door, rear, and* NÖJD *enters.*)

LAURA. Did you deliver my note?

NÖJD. Yes, Madam.

THE DOCTOR. Ah, it's you, Nöjd! You know what's going on here and that the Captain is suffering from a mental disorder. I expect you to help us to take care of your sick Captain.

NÖJD. If there is anything I can do for the Captain, you may be sure I will do it, Doctor.

THE DOCTOR. I want you to put this jacket on him.

MARGRET. No—I don't want Nöjd to lay hands on him! He mustn't do him any harm! Then I'd rather do it myself—I can do it gently, gently! But let Nöjd stand outside—he can give me a hand if I need any help . . . yes, he can do that.

(*There is a sudden pounding on the door in the left wall.*)

THE DOCTOR. There he is! Put away the jacket—put it on the chair there—cover it with your shawl! Now all of you go out, and the Pastor and I will look after him! But hurry! That door won't hold many more minutes!—Go, go!

MARGRET (*goes out, right*). Help us, Jesus! Help us!

(LAURA *quickly locks the writing desk and then leaves,*

right. NÖJD *goes out, rear. Suddenly the wallpaper-covered door is flung open with such force that the chair, barricading it, catapults into the room and the lock falls to the floor.* THE CAPTAIN *emerges with a bundle of books under his arm.*)

THE CAPTAIN (*piles the books on the large table*). Here you can read it—the whole thing—and in every one of these books. So you see I wasn't so mad after all! Here you see it in the first canto of the *Odyssey*, verse 215, page 6, in the Uppsala translation. Telemachus, speaking to Athene, says: "Though my mother avers that he, Odysseus, is my father, I myself cannot be certain; for no one has yet known his origin." And the same suspicion Telemachus held of Penelope, the most virtuous of women. A fine state of affairs, isn't it? And here . . . (*He picks up another book from the pile.*) . . . here we have the prophet Ezekiel: "The fool saith: Lo, here is my father; but who can tell whose loins have engendered him." That's plain enough, isn't it?—But let us see what this book says . . . (*He picks up still another volume from the pile on the table.*) *A History of Russian Literature* by Merzlyakov. (*He reads.*) "Alexander Pushkin, Russia's greatest poet, died in torture. This could be attributed in a lesser degree to the bullet that was lodged in his chest during a duel than to rumors spread abroad that his wife had been unfaithful. On his deathbed he swore that she was innocent." Ass! What an ass! How could he swear to that! At any rate, you can see I read my books, can't you?—Why, Jonas! Are you here? And the Doctor, of course. Did I ever tell you how I answered an English lady when she complained of a habit a certain Irishman had of throwing a lighted lamp in his wife's face?—"God, what women," I answered her. "Women?" she stammered. "Why, certainly," I told her. "When things go so far that a man who has loved and adored a woman picks up a lighted lamp and flings it in her face, then you may be sure . . ."

THE PASTOR. Be sure of what?

THE CAPTAIN. Of nothing! We can never be sure of anything; we can only believe. Isn't that so, Jonas? If we believe, we shall be saved! Yes, we shall, indeed!—Oh no, my experience has been that a man can be accursed by believing. I have learned that.

THE DOCTOR. Captain!

THE CAPTAIN. Keep quiet! I have nothing to say to you! I don't care to hear you relay all the gossip from in there.

(*He makes a gesture in the direction of the other rooms.*)
You know what I mean—in there! Tell me, Jonas, are you
sure you are the father of your children? I seem to remember you once had a good-looking tutor in your house,
whom people used to talk about.

THE PASTOR. Take care what you say, Adolf.

THE CAPTAIN. If you raise your wig a little, I wouldn't be
surprised if you found two bumps shooting out. Upon my
soul, I believe he is turning pale! Well, well—all that was
only gossip, of course; but there certainly was enough of it!
Still—we married men make both sorry and comical rep-
robates. Don't you agree with me, Doctor? How about *your*
marriage couch? Didn't you have a lieutenant staying with
you? Didn't you? Wait, I am trying to think. . . . His name
was . . . (*He whispers in* THE DOCTOR's *ear.*) What do I see?
He, too, is turning pale! But don't let that distress you.
She is dead and buried; and what is done cannot be undone.
I knew him, by the way—and he is now. . . . Look at me,
Doctor! No, look me straight in the eye! He is now a major
of Dragoons! By God, if I don't believe *he* has horns too!

THE DOCTOR. Will you please change the subject, Captain!

THE CAPTAIN (*to* THE PASTOR *and* THE DOCTOR). You see!
He immediately wants to speak about something else the moment I begin to talk about horns.

THE PASTOR. Has it ever occurred to you, Adolf, that you
are not of sound mind?

THE CAPTAIN. Yes, I know that only too well. But if I had
the chance to go to work on your master brains for a
while, I would soon have you put away too. Yes—I am
mad. But how did it come about? That is something you are
not interested in—nor is anyone else. (*He picks up the photograph album on the large table.*) God in heaven, there is
my child! Mine? But how can we be sure? Let me tell you
what to do in order to be sure. . . . First you marry so that
you will be accepted by the community; and as soon as that
is over with, you get a divorce and live together as lover and
mistress. Then you adopt the children; and in that way one
can at least be certain that they are one's adopted children.
Don't you think that's the right idea? But all that is of no
help to me now! How can anything be of help to me now—
now that you have robbed me of my conception of a life
after death? What good is science and philosophy to me when
I no longer have anything to live for? What use is life, with

no honor left? I grafted my right arm and half of my brain and half of my spinal cord onto another family tree and I thought they would grow together and become as one in a still more perfect tree. And then someone put a knife to it and made a cut below the graft; and now I am only half a tree. But the other half, with my arm and the rest of my brain, keeps growing, while I—I am withering and dying . . . for what I gave away was the better part of myself. And now I don't care to live any longer! You may do what you like with me—my life is at an end!

(THE DOCTOR *whispers to* THE PASTOR. *They go into the room, right. Soon after,* BERTHA *enters.* THE CAPTAIN *seats himself at the large table. He is now bent and shrunken.*)

BERTHA (*comes up to him*). Are you sick, papa?

THE CAPTAIN (*looks up, offended*). I—sick?

BERTHA. Do you know what you have done? Do you realize you threw the lamp at Mamma?

THE CAPTAIN. Did I?

BERTHA. Yes, that's what you did. Suppose she had been hurt!

THE CAPTAIN. What if she had been!

BERTHA. You can't be my father if you say a thing like that!

THE CAPTAIN. What's that you say? Am I not your father? How can you know? Who has been telling you that? Who is your father, then? Who is he?

BERTHA. I know it can't be you!

THE CAPTAIN. You keep saying I am not your father! Who is your father, then? Who is? You seem to know so much! Who has told you that? And I should live to hear this—to have my own child tell me to my face that I am not her father! And don't you understand that when you say such a thing, you defame your mother as well? Don't you realize that if it were true it would bring shame upon her?

BERTHA. I don't want you to say anything bad about Mamma, do you hear?

THE CAPTAIN. Yes, you all stick together against me! That's what you have been doing right along . . .

BERTHA. Papa!

THE CAPTAIN. Never call me that again!

BERTHA (*breaks down and sobs*). Papa! Papa!

THE CAPTAIN (*draws her to him*). Bertha, my beloved child . . . you *are* my child, aren't you? Yes, yes—you

couldn't be anyone else's. You are mine! All that I said was
nothing but sickly thoughts that came with the wind, just like
fever and pestilence. . . . Look at me and let me find my
soul in your eyes! But I find *her* soul there, too! You have
two souls—and with one of them you love me, with the
other one you hate me.— But I want you to love *me*
only! You must have only one soul, or you will never have
peace—nor will I! You must have only one mind—you
child of my mind; only one will—and that, mine!

BERTHA. I don't want that! I want to be myself!

THE CAPTAIN. I won't let you! I am a cannibal, you see,
and I shall devour you. Your mother wanted to devour me,
but I wouldn't let her. I am Saturn who devoured his children because it had been foretold that they would otherwise
devour him. To eat or to be eaten, that is the question! If I
do not eat you, you will eat me; and you have already bared
your teeth to me! But be not afraid, my darling child. I
will never hurt you! (*He goes over to the wall where the
weapons are hanging and takes down a revolver.*)

BERTHA (*frightened, she tries to escape*). Help! Mamma!
Help, he is going to murder me!

MARGRET (*comes rushing in*). Mr. Adolf! What is it?

THE CAPTAIN (*examining the revolver, he turns to
MARGRET*). Did *you* remove the cartridges?

MARGRET. Yes, I put them away when I was cleaning; but if
you will calm yourself and sit down here, I'll give them to
you.

(*She takes THE CAPTAIN by the arm and places him
in the chair. He remains seated there; he appears dull
and feeble. Then she reaches for the strait jacket, while
standing behind the chair. BERTHA steals out, right.*)

MARGRET. Mr. Adolf, do you remember when you were my
darling little child and I used to tuck you in at night and
read "God who loves the children dearly" to you? Do you?
And do you remember how I used to get up during the night
and bring you a drink of water? Do you remember how I
would light a candle and tell you lovely fairy tales when you
had had a bad dream and couldn't go back to sleep? Do you
remember that?

THE CAPTAIN. Keep talking to me, Margret—it soothes
me—it calms me to hear you. Talk to me some more!

MARGRET. Why, yes—but then you must listen to me! Do
you remember the time you got hold of the large kitchen
knife and wanted to carve some boats, and how I caught

sight of you and had to coax the knife away from you because you didn't think any of us knew what was good for you. "Give me that snake," I said, "before he bites you!" Then you let go the knife! (*She takes the revolver from his hand.*) . . . And the many times I told you to get dressed and you refused to. I had to coax you and promise you I would get you a coat of gold so that you would be dressed like a prince. And then I took the tiny garment which was only made of green wool and held it in front of you, and said: "Now put your arms in the sleeves—both of them"; and then I said: "Sit still now, very still, while I button you up in the back!" (*During the preceding scene she has managed to put the strait jacket on him.*) And then I said: "Now stand up—and then walk across the floor and let me see how it fits . . ." (*She leads him to the sofa.*) And then I said: "Now you are going to bed."

THE CAPTAIN. What's that you say? Should I be going to bed with my clothes on?—Hell and damnation, woman! What have you done to me? (*He tries to free himself from the jacket.*) Oh, you foxy she-devil! Who would have thought you were that cunning? (*He lies down on the sofa.*) Trapped —outwitted—deprived of everything . . . and they will not let me die!

MARGRET. Forgive me, Mr. Adolf! Please forgive me! . . . But I couldn't let you kill the poor child!

THE CAPTAIN. Why didn't you let me do it? Life is a hell, and death is the kingdom of heaven . . . and the children belong to heaven!

MARGRET. What do *you* know about the hereafter and life after death?

THE CAPTAIN. It is the only thing we do know—we know nothing of life! Oh, if we could only have known from the beginning!

MARGRET. Humble your hardened heart, Mr. Adolf, and pray to God that He have mercy on you while there still is time! It was not too late for the thief on the Cross when the Saviour said to him: "Today thou shalt be with me in Paradise!"

THE CAPTAIN. You are already croaking for a corpse, you old crow! (MARGRET *takes her hymnbook from her pocket.*)

THE CAPTAIN (*calls out*). Nöjd? Are you there, Nöjd? (NÖJD *enters.*)

THE CAPTAIN. Throw this woman out! She wants to read

the life out of me with her hymns! Throw her out the window, or down the chimney! I don't care what you do with her as long as you get rid of her!

Nöjd (with a glance at Margret). God save you, Captain—and I mean that sincerely—but I can't do that. I just can't! If it had been six men, why. . . . But a woman—no!

The Captain. You mean to say you can't handle one woman?

Nöjd. Sure, I can handle her—but when it comes to laying hands on a woman—well, that's different . . .

The Captain. Why is it so different? Haven't *they* laid hands on me?

Nöjd. Yes—but I just can't do it, Captain. It's exactly as if you was to ask me to strike the Pastor. It's something what's in your bones, in your blood—like religion! I just couldn't do it!

(Laura enters. She beckons to Nöjd to leave. He does so.)

The Captain. Omphale! Omphale! Now you have the club in your hand while Hercules is spinning your wool.

Laura (goes over to the sofa). Adolf! Look at me! Do you really think I am your enemy?

The Captain. Yes—I do. I believe you all are my enemies! My mother—who didn't want to bring me into the world because childbirth would give her pain—was my enemy when she sapped the nourishment from the first seed of life in me and made a misfit of me. My sister was my enemy when she forced me to be subservient to her. The first woman I embraced was my enemy, for she gave me ten years of a sickness in return for the love I gave her. My daughter became my enemy when she had to choose between you and me. And you, my wife,—you *are* and *have been* my deadly enemy—for you never let go your hold on me until no life was left in me . . .

Laura. I don't know that I ever gave a thought to doing what you imagine I did. I wouldn't say I may not have had some vague urge within me to get you out of the way— and if you see anything resembling a plan in what I have done, it might have been there although I was not conscious of it. I have never really reflected over what has been taking place: it has all developed along the lines you yourself laid down. Even if I should not be innocent, before God, and in my conscience, I feel I am. You weighed on my heart like a stone that pressed and pressed until at last I tried to shake off the oppressive burden. That is no doubt what happened; and if I have struck you down without meaning to, I ask you to forgive me.

THE CAPTAIN. All that sounds credible enough! But how does that help me? And where does the fault lie? Perhaps in our spiritual, Platonic marital relations. One used to marry a woman for love; but nowadays one enters into partnership with a business or professional woman—or one shares one's bed and board with a mistress! And then one has illegal intercourse with the partner—or one casts a stigma upon the mistress! But what becomes of love—healthy, sensuous love? It dies as a result! And what happens to the offspring of this sort of love in shares, payable to the bearer, without any mutual responsibility? And who is the bearer when the crash comes? Who is the physical father of the spiritual child?

LAURA. Let me say that your suspicions about the child are entirely groundless.

THE CAPTAIN. That is exactly what makes it so terrible! If my suspicions at least had some foundation, then one would have something tangible, something to go by. . . . Now there is nothing but shadows that bury themselves in the thickets and stick out their heads and laugh derisively; now it's like battling with air, like fighting a sham battle with blank cartridges. A dangerous reality would have inspired one to resistance, strained every nerve in one's body and soul to action . . . but now—my thoughts keep evaporating and my brain grinding at empty thoughts until it burns out. . . . Let me have a pillow to put under my head! And something to cover me with—I am freezing! I am so frightfully cold!

(LAURA *takes off her shawl and covers him with it.* MARGRET *goes to fetch a pillow.*)

LAURA. Give me your hand, my dear!

THE CAPTAIN. My hand—which you have tied. . . .Omphale! Omphale! . . . But I can feel your shawl touching my lips. It is as warm and soft as your hand and has the fragrance of vanilla, like your hair when you were young. . . . Laura, when you were young and we went for walks in the birchwoods, where primrose grew and the thrush was singing—it was glorious! Think upon the past—how beautiful it was—and what it has come to. . . . You did not wish it to become like this, nor did I—and yet it has. . . . Who is it who rules our lives?

LAURA. God alone . . .

THE CAPTAIN. The God of War and Strife, then! Or I should say, nowadays, the Goddess of Strife! Take away the cat that's lying on me—take it away! (MARGRET *enters with a pillow. She places it under his head and then removes the shawl.*) Give me my tunic! Throw it over me! (MARGRET *goes over to the clothes rack and brings* THE CAPTAIN *his tunic, which she lays over him.*) Alas, my stout lion skin that you tried to take away from me! Omphale! Omphale! You treacherous woman! You pretended you were for peace and started disarmament! Wake up, Hercules, before they take your club away from you! You will try to take our armor away from us, too, by stealth, under the pretext that it is mere tinsel. No, I say . . . it was iron—iron before it was made of tinsel. In olden days it was the smith who forged the armored suit—now it is the needlewoman! Omphale! Omphale! Rude strength has given way before weakness fortified by treachery. A curse on you, woman of Satan, and may all your sex be damned! (*He raises himself to spit on her but sinks back on the sofa.*) What kind of pillow is this you have given me, Margret? It is so hard and so cold—so cold! Come and sit down here on the chair beside me. . . . There! Let me put my head in your lap! There! It's so nice and warm! Lean over me so that I feel your breast!—Oh, how wonderful to fall asleep at a woman's breast—whether mother or mistress . . . but most wonderful at a mother's!

LAURA. Would you like to see your child, Adolf? Would you?

THE CAPTAIN. My child? A man has no children—it is only women who bear children—and that is why the future may be theirs when we die without offspring!—Oh God who loves the children dearly . . .

MARGRET. Listen—he is praying to God!

THE CAPTAIN. No—to you . . . you must lull me to sleep, for I am tired—so tired! Goodnight, Margret, and blessed be you among women! (*He sits up for a brief moment—then his head falls down into* MARGRET'S *lap while he emits a cry of anguish.* LAURA *walks over to the right and summons* THE DOCTOR *who promptly enters with* THE PASTOR.)

LAURA. Help us, Doctor, if it is not too late! See, he is no longer breathing!

THE DOCTOR (*feeling* THE CAPTAIN'S *pulse*). He has had a stroke!

THE PASTOR. Is he dead?

THE DOCTOR. No, he may still come back to life . . . but to what kind of awakening—that we cannot tell.

THE PASTOR. Once dead, then comes the judgment . . .

THE DOCTOR. Let us have no judgment—and no accusations. You who believe there is a God who rules human destiny—you will have to take this matter up with Him.

MARGRET. Just think, Pastor, his last words were a prayer to God!

THE PASTOR (*to* LAURA). Is this true?

LAURA. That is true!

THE DOCTOR. If it is—and I know as little about that as I do about his illness—then my skill is of no use. Now you see what you can do, Pastor.

LAURA. Is this all you have to say at this moment of death, Dr. Östermark?

THE DOCTOR. That is all! I have said all I know. Let Him who is better able to judge, speak.

BERTHA (*comes running from the right, crying*). Mamma! Mamma!

LAURA. My child! My own child!

THE PASTOR. Amen!

MISS JULIE
A NATURALISTIC TRAGEDY IN ONE ACT

In writing *Miss Julie* (*Fröken Julie*) in 1888, Strindberg was greatly influenced by the example of French naturalistic playwrights associated with the *Théâtre Libre* in Paris. He advocated the abolition of act divisions and intermissions; during which the playgoer might escape the suggestive influence of the playwright, or "author-mesmerist." But it is doubtful that this explanation or apology is necessary. The action of *Miss Julie* is *naturally* continuous; it deals with a single explosion of repressed nature and its immediate consequences.

Miss Julie has commanded attention for more than technical reasons. It has, in the first place, a powerful dramatic action in which the sex duel is augmented and intensified by social contrasts; the struggle is not merely between woman and man but between mistress and servant. And the action, consisting of an eruption of sexual drives hitherto suppressed, is *psychological action* which could not be more modern if it were written today. Underlying the dramatic art of *Miss Julie,* moreover, is a view of characterization and of realistic theatre that is highly important. Strindberg's explanation (in the famous *Preface,* which follows) requires no additional editorial comment; he takes pride in having used multiple motivation, or a complex of motives, as the source of Miss Julie's behavior.

Published in 1888 with its author's *Preface, Miss Julie* was originally presented at the Students Association of the University of Copenhagen on March 14, 1889 and, having been banned in Denmark, was first produced for the general public by the avant-garde little theatre of Berlin, *Die Freie Bühne,* on April 3, 1892, with the distinguished actress Rosa Bertens in the principal role. Antoine's *Théâtre Libre,* the first of the experimental theatres of the naturalistic movement, presented the play successfully in Paris on January 16, 1893. It appears indeed that Strindberg wrote *Miss Julie* with the *Théâtre Libre* in mind. The first American performance of the play was in New York in 1905, with the great actress Nazimova playing the part of Julie in Russian. Strindberg's first wife, Siri von Essen, was the first Julie, and many outstanding actresses have played this exacting role. A recent American production was given by the Phoenix Theatre in New York in February 1956 with Viveca Lindfors and James Daly in the main roles. More noteworthy was the success of the play, in Arvid Paulson's translation, when presented as a "Play of the Week" television drama in 1960; Lois Smith excelled in the role of Julie.

Some comment on Strindberg's *Preface* may also be in order. It should be noted, first of all, that the preface is a defense of his previously presented naturalistic tragedy *The Father* (which had outraged some Swedish playgoers), as well as an introduction to the text of *Miss Julie*. In the second place, we observe Strindberg reaching for a naturalistic theory of tragedy. His defense of naturalistic practice is based on "social Darwinism" and the "will-to-power" philosophy of Friedrich Nietzsche, with whom he corresponded for a time. The law of life is struggle ("the hawk eats the dove and the flea eats the hawk . . ."); it is a joyous thing to see weakness swept away ("the national forests cleared of rotting and superannuated trees"); and the "joy of life" is to be found "in its violent and cruel struggles." Life, in brief, is tragic; it is full of suffering but also exciting, bracing, and elevating. If life is irrational, our readiness to face it "scientifically," objectively and truthfully, constitutes heroism. To accept life on these hard terms is tragic exaltation.

It is possible to conclude, nevertheless, that Strindberg does not quite distinguish between pathological and heroic drama. It is questionable whether the heroic mood is at all sustained in *Miss Julie*. As Herbert J. Muller (*The Spirit of Tragedy*) puts it, "the neurotic Miss Julie is much too mean to be a tragic figure; at most she stirs some pity—more than Strindberg intended, if we take him at his own word—in her utter bafflement." And we can boggle at Strindberg's implication, in the *Preface*, that the conflict between the neurotic Julie and the gross valet Jean is one of "the great conflicts," or "the battle of elemental powers," to which he refers so confidently. The play possesses abundant interest for us on *other* grounds than its viability as high tragedy.

The above qualifications do not, of course, reduce the historical and critical significance of the *Preface*. Its importance was immediately apparent to the leaders of the progressive stage, and the critic Paul Schlenther, one of the founders and directors of the *Freie Bühne,* read the essay aloud to the audience at the Berlin première. Antoine, at the *Théâtre Libre,* considered the *Preface* so important that he distributed a translation to the audience at his production of the play.

THE AUTHOR'S PREFACE

In common with art generally, the theatre has long seemed to me to be a *biblia pauperum,* i.e. a bible in pictures for those who cannot read the written or printed word. Similarly, the playwright has the semblance of being a lay preacher presenting the views and sentiments of his time in popular form—and in a form sufficiently popular so that the middle classes, from which theatre audiences are chiefly drawn, can understand what it is all about without racking their brains.

Thus the theatre has long been a public school for the young, for people not too well educated, and for women who still possess that primitive faculty of deceiving themselves and letting themselves be deceived, or, in brief, who are impressionable to illusion and susceptible to the suggestions of the author. For the self-same reason it has seemed to me as if, in our time—when the rudimentary, immature way of thinking (which is a process of the imagination) appears to be developing into reflection, inquiry and analysis—the theatre, like religion, is in the throes of being abandoned as a moribund form of art for which we lack the conditions requisite to enjoyment. The profound crisis now sweeping through the whole of Europe gives credence to this assumption, and not least the fact that in those countries of culture which have given us the greatest thinkers of the age, namely England and Germany, the drama, in common with most of the other fine arts, is dead.

In other countries, however, efforts have been made to create a new form of drama by employing elements reflecting the ideas of modern times within the framework of the old forms. But on the one hand, there has not been sufficient time for these new ideas to have been so generally accepted that the audiences can fathom their purport and implication; on the other hand, some of the audiences have been so impassioned by partisan polemics and propaganda that it has been impossible to enjoy the play in a purely objective manner while one's innermost feelings and convictions are being assailed, and when an applauding or hissing majority displays a tyranny so openly as only a theatre affords an opportunity for. And, furthermore, the new content has as yet been given no fresh form; as a result, the new wine has burst the old bottles.

In the present drama I have not attempted to create anything new (for that is an impossibility) but merely to modernize the form to meet the demands which, it occurs to me, people of our time are likely to make upon this art. To this end I have chosen (or rather, been captured by) a theme which may be said to lie outside the partisan and controversial issues of the day. The problem of social rise or downfall, of who is higher or lower, or who is better or worse, whether man or woman, is, has been and shall be of enduring interest. When I chose this theme from real life—as I heard it related a number of years ago, at which time I was greatly moved by the story—I saw in it the ingredients of a tragic drama. To see an individual on whom fortune has heaped an abundance of gifts go to her ruin and destruction, leaves us with a tragic feeling; to see a whole line die out is still more tragic. But perhaps there will come a time when we will be so enlightened that we will view with indifference the brutal, cynical and heartless spectacle that life has to offer—perhaps when we have done with our imperfect, unreliable thought mechanisms which we call feelings, and which may be superfluous when our reflective organs have developed.

The fact that the heroine in this play arouses our pity and compassion is due solely to our weakness and inability to resist such a feeling for fear that we ourselves may meet with the self-same fate. And the over-sensitive spectator may still not be content with feeling pity and compassion; the man with faith in the future may demand some sort of positive action or suggestion for doing away with the evil—in short, some stroke of policy. But, first of all, there is nothing absolutely evil; for the extinction of one family is nothing short of luck for another family that gets a chance to rise in the world. And the succession of rise and fall is one of life's greatest fascinations as luck is only relative.

And to the man with a program who desires to rectify the unfortunate fact that the bird of prey devours the dove and that the lice eat the bird of prey, I wish to put this question: "Why should it be rectified?" Life is not so mathematically idiotic that it allows only the big to eat the small, for it happens just as often that the bee kills the lion or at least drives it mad.

That my tragedy has a depressing effect upon the many is the fault of these many. When we have grown as hardened as the first French revolutionaries were, then it will without question produce only a happy and wholesome impression to see the crown parks weeded out and ridded of rotting, super-annuated trees that too long have stood in the way of others, equally entitled to their day of vegetation—the kind of impression one experiences when one sees somebody with an incurable disease taken by death.

Not long ago I was upbraided by someone who thought my tragedy *The Father* was too sad. As if a tragedy were meant to be amusing! People are constantly clamoring pretentiously for *the joy of life,* and play producers keep demanding farces—as if the joy of life consisted in being ludicrous and in depicting all human beings as if they were suffering from St. Vitus' dance, or idiocy. For my part, I find the joy of life in the hard and cruel battles of life; and to be able to add to my store of knowledge, to learn something, is enjoyment to me. It is for that reason I have chosen an unusual situation—yet one that teaches a moral; an exception, in brief,—but a rare exception that proves the rule and that no doubt will make all those who love the commonplace, feel offended. The next thing that will offend the simple-minded is the fact that my motivation for the action is not a simple one and that the *raison d'être* is not a single one. A happening in life—and this is a fairly recent discovery!—is generally brought about by a whole series of more or less deeplying motives; but as a rule the spectator selects the one which in his opinion seems the easiest to understand or that is most flattering to his own best judgment. A suicide takes place. "Bad business!" says the burgher. "Unrequited love!" say the women. "Physical illness!" says the invalid. "Crushed hopes!" says the human derelict. But now it is possible that the motive may be all or none of these things, and that the deceased may have concealed the actual motive by letting another be known that would cast a more favorable light over his memory!

The sad fate of Miss Julie I have motivated by a host of circumstances: the mother's fundamental instincts, the father's wrong upbringing of the girl, her own strange nature, and the suggestive influence of her fiancé upon an insipid, vapid and degenerated mind. In addition, and more directly, the festal mood of Midsummer Eve, the absence of her father, her monthly period, her preoccupancy with animals, the excitement of the dance, the long twilight of the night, the strongly aphrodisiac influence of the flowers, and lastly, the chance bringing together of the two alone in a secluded room—not to mention the aroused passion of a bold and aggressive man. Consequently my mode of procedure has been neither one-sidedly physiological nor psychological: I have neither placed the blame exclusively on traits inherited from the mother nor have I cast the blame on the girl's physical indisposition. By the same token, I have not put the blame solely on "immorality," and I have not merely preached a moral. For want of a priest, I have left this task to the cook.

I commend myself for the introduction of this multiplicity of motives; they are in keeping with the times. And if others have done the same thing before me, I will acknowledge with pride that I was not alone in my paradoxes—as all discoveries are called.

With regard to the delineation of the characters, I have made them somewhat lacking in character for the following reasons:

In the course of time the word *character* has been given many meanings. Originally it no doubt denoted the dominant trait in the soul-complex and was confused with temperament. With time it became the middle-class term for an automaton, an individual who had become so fixed in his nature—or who had adapted himself to a particular role in life and who, in a word, had ceased to grow—that people called him *a character*. On the other hand, a man who continued to develop, an able navigator on the river of life, who sailed not with sheets set fast but who veered down the wind to steer closer to the wind again—this man was called lacking in character. And this, of course, in a derogatory sense —because he was so hard to capture, to categorize, to keep an eye on.

This bourgeois notion of the fixed state of the soul was transmitted to the stage, where the middle-class element has always been in dominance. There a character became synonymous with a man permanently settled and finished, one who at all times appeared as a drunkard, a jolly jester, or as a deplorable, miserable figure. And for the purpose of characterization nothing more was needed than some physical defect such as a clubfoot, a wooden leg, a red nose—or that the actor in the role be given some repetitious phrase such as: "That's splendid!" or "Barkis will be glad to do it!", and so forth.

This one-sided manner of looking at human beings still survives in the great Molière. Harpagon is a miser and nothing else, although he could have been both a miser and an excellent financier, a fine father, a good man in his community. And what is worse, his infirmity is precisely of utmost advantage to his son-in-law and daughter who are his heirs. For that reason they ought not to take him to task, even if they have to wait a little before they take to their nuptial bed. I do not believe, therefore, in simplified characters for the stage. An author's summary judgment upon men (this man is a fool; that one brutal; this one is jealous; that one stingy, etc.) ought to be challenged and rejected by the Naturalists who are aware of the richness of the human soul and who know that vice has another side to it that is very like virtue.

I have depicted my characters as modern characters, living in an age of transition at least more breathlessly hysterical than the period immediately preceding it. Thus I have made them more vacillating, disjointed: a blending of the old and the new. And it seems not improbable to me that modern ideas, absorbed through conversations and newspapers, could have filtered down to the domain of the domestics.

My souls (characters) are conglomerates of a past stage of civilization and our present one, scraps from books and newspapers, pieces of humanity, torn-off tatters of holiday clothes that have disintegrated and become rags—exactly as the soul is patched together. I have, besides, contributed a small fragment of evolutionary history by having the weaker character parrot words purloined from the stronger one, and by having the souls (the characters) borrow "ideas" (or suggestions, as they are called) from one another.

Miss Julie is a modern character. Not that the half-woman, the man-hater, has not existed since time immemorial but because she has now been discovered, has trod into the open and begun to create a stir. The half-woman of today is a type who pushes herself forward; today she is selling herself for power, decorations, aggrandizement, diplomas, as she did formerly for money; and the type is indicative of degeneration. It is not a wholesome type and it is not enduring, but unfortunately it can reproduce and transplant its misery in another generation. And degenerate men seem instinctively to choose their mates from among such women; and so they multiply and bring into the world progeny of indeterminate sex, to whom life becomes a torture. Fortunately, however, they come to an end, either from being unable to face and withstand life, or from the irresistible rebellion of their suppressed desires, or because their hope of coming up to men has been thwarted. It is a tragic type, revealing the spectacle of a desperate struggle against nature; tragic also as a Romantic inheritance now being put to flight by Naturalism, whose aim is only for happiness; for in order to achieve happiness, strong, virile and wholesome types are required.

But Miss Julie is also a remnant of the old war nobility, which is now giving way to the new aristocracy of the mind with its nervous driving force. She is a victim of the discord which a mother's "crime" produces in a family; a victim also of the delusions and deceptions of her time, of circumstances, of her own defective constitution—all of which adds up to the "fate" or "universal law" of days now past. The Naturalist has done away with the idea of guilt, as well as God; but the consequences of the act: punishment, imprisonment (or the fear of it)—*that* he cannot do away with for the simple reason that they are bound to remain. They will remain whether he (the Naturalist) lets the protagonists go free or not; for the injured parties are never so good-natured as outsiders (who have not been wronged) can be—at a price.

Even if the father for compelling reasons should take no vengeance, the daughter would avenge herself—as she does here—from that innate or acquired sense of honor which the upper classes have as their inheritance. From where? From the barbarian ages, from the original homeland of the Aryans, or from the chivalry of the Middle Ages? It is a beautiful thing, but these days it has become somewhat of a disadvantage to the preservation of the race. It is the nobleman's hara-kiri—which is the law of the Japanese, of his innermost conscience, that bids him cut open his own abdomen after receiving an insult from another man. The custom survives, in modified form, in the duel, also a privilege of the upper classes. And that is why Jean, the valet, re-

mains alive; but Miss Julie cannot go on living once she has
lost her honor. This is the advantage the serf has over the
earl: that he is without this deadly superstition about honor.
In all of us Aryans there is something of the nobleman, or
Don Quixote, which makes us sympathize with the man who
takes his own life after he has committed a dishonorable
deed and so lost his honor. And we are noblemen enough to
suffer when we see a person once considered great, suddenly
topple and then be looked upon as dead and a nuisance. Yes
—even if he should raise himself up again and make up for
the past by performing an act of nobility. Jean, the valet, is
a procreator, and he has acquired a distinct and separate
character. He was born the son of a farmhand and has gradually taken on the characteristics of a gentleman. He finds it
easy to learn, his senses are well developed (smell, taste, vision), and he has a feeling for beauty. He has already come
up in the world; and he is hard and unscrupulous enough
not to allow sensitiveness to interfere when it comes to using
others for his purposes. He is already a stranger to those
around him (the servants and farmhands) whom he looks
down upon, as he does upon the life he has turned his back
on. He avoids the menials and fears them because they know
his secrets, pry into his schemings, watch with envy as he
betters himself, and anticipate his downfall with glee. This
accounts for the duality of his indeterminate character,
which vacillates between love of power and glory and hatred against those who have it. He thinks of himself as an
aristocrat. He has learned the secrets of good society. He is
polished on the surface, but the inside is uncouth and vulgar. He has learned to wear formal clothes with taste, but
one cannot be so certain that his body is clean.

He has respect for Miss Julie but is timid and apprehensive about Kristin (the cook), for she knows his precarious
secrets. He is also sufficiently callous not to let the night's
happenings interfere with his plans for the future. With the
brutality of the serf and the lack of squeamishness of the
ruler he can see blood without losing consciousness, and he
can throw off any hardship or adversity. Consequently he
emerges from the battlefield unscarred, and no doubt he will
end up as a hotelkeeper; and if he fails to become a Rou-
manian count, his son will probably attend a university and
may end up as a petty official.

For the rest, Jean gives a rather enlightening insight into
the lower classes' conception of life—of life as they see it

—when he speaks the truth, which he infrequently does; for rather than adhere to the truth he asks what will do him most good. When Miss Julie suggests that the lower classes must feel oppressed by those above them, Jean naturally agrees with her because his aim is to gain sympathy. But when he realizes that it is to his advantage to place himself apart from the common herd, he quickly takes back his words.

Aside from the fact that Jean is well on his way up in the world, he possesses an advantage over Miss Julie because of being a man. Sexually he is the aristocrat because of his male strength, his more acutely developed senses, and his capacity for taking the initiative.

His feeling of inferiority can principally be ascribed to the temporary social environment in which he lives, and he can probably rid himself of it when he sheds his servant's livery.

The mental attitude of the slave manifests itself in his inordinate respect for the count (as exemplified in the scene with the boots), and in his religious superstition. But his respectfulness is chiefly inspired by the fact that the count occupies a position of rank which he himself would like to attain. And this deference remains with him after he has won the affections of the count's daughter and seen the emptiness within the shell.

I find it hard to believe that a relationship of love in a higher sense could exist between two souls so different in nature. For this reason I have made Miss Julie imagine that she is in love—to justify her behavior, to blot out her transgression; and I let Jean think that if social conditions were different, he might be able to love her. I imagine love is much like the hyacinth: it has to strike roots in darkness *before* it can produce a healthy, hardy flower. In this instance, it shoots up instantaneously—and therefore the plant withers and dies so soon.

Finally there is Kristin. She is a female slave, obsequious and dull (from standing at the hot stove) and laden with morality and religion that serve as a cloak for her own immorality, and as a scapegoat. Her church-going is a means of lightheartedly and glibly unloading on Jesus her household thieveries and taking on a new lease of guiltlessness. Otherwise she is a subordinate figure, and therefore intentionally sketched much in the manner of the Pastor and the Doctor in *The Father*—the reason for this being that I wanted to have precisely this type of ordinary human being (such as country clergymen and country doctors usually are).

If these subordinate figures of mine have appeared as abstractions to some, it is because everyday people go about their work in a somewhat detached manner. By that I mean that they are impersonal and that they show only *one* side of their personality. And as long as the spectator feels no need of seeing the other sides of their personality, my abstract characterization of them is quite correct.

As far as the dialogue is concerned, I have, to a certain degree, broken with tradition by not making catechists out of my characters; that is, they do not keep asking silly questions merely for the sake of bringing forth a clever or jocular retort. I have avoided the symmetrical, mathematical construction commonly used by the French in their dialogue. Instead I have had my characters use their brains only intermittently as people do in real life where, during a conversation, one cog in a person's brain may find itself, more or less by chance, geared into another cog; and where no topic is completely exhausted. That is the very reason that the dialogue rambles. In the early scenes it piles up material which is later worked up, gone over, repeated, expanded, rearranged and developed much like the theme in a musical composition.

The plot is tolerable enough, and as it is really concerned with only two persons, I have concentrated my attention on them. I have added only one other character, a minor one: Kristin (the cook), and have kept the spirit of the unfortunate father hovering over and in the background of the entire action. I have done this because I seem to have observed that the psychological course of events is what interests the people of our time most. I have also noticed that our souls, so hungry for knowledge, find no satisfaction in merely seeing something done; we want to know *how* and *why* it is done! What we want to see are the wires—the machinery! We want to examine the box with the false bottom, take hold of and feel the magic ring in an attempt to find where it is joined together; we want to scrutinize the cards and try to discover how they are marked.

In this attempt of mine I have had in mind the brothers de Goncourt's monographic novels which, among all literature of modern times, have appealed to me most.

As far as the technical side is concerned, I have, as an experiment, done away with the division into acts. This I have done because I seem to have found that our decreasing capacity for illusion might be disturbed by intermissions, dur-

ing which the theatregoer would have time to engage in reflection and thereby escape the author-mesmerizer's suggestive influence. The performance of Miss Julie will probably
last one hour and a half. As people can listen to a lecture, a
sermon, or a parliamentary proceeding lasting that length of
time or longer, it has struck me that a theatrical piece ought
not to fatigue an audience in a similar space of time. Already in 1872, in one of my earlier playwriting experiments,
The Outlaw, I tried using this concentrated form, although
without much success. The play was originally written in
five acts, and when it was completed, I was cognizant of the
chaotic and alarming effect it had upon me. I burned the
manuscript and from out of the ashes rose a single, well-
constructed act, fifty printed pages in length, that took one
hour to perform. While the form of *Miss Julie* is not absolutely original, it nevertheless seems to be my own innovation; and as public taste appears to be changing, there may
be prospects for its being accepted in our time.

My hope is that we may some day have audiences so educated that they will sit through a whole evening's performance
of a play consisting only in one act. But to attain this, tests
would have to be made.

In order, however, to provide momentary interludes (or
rest stops) for the audience and the actors without allowing
the spectators to lose the illusion that the play has created,
I have included three art forms, all integral parts of the
drama, namely: the monologue, the pantomime, and the
ballet. Originally they were part of the tragedies of antiquity,
the monologue having been derived from the monody and
the ballet from the chorus.

The monologue has now been condemned by our realists
as not being true to life; but if its motivation is sound, it
can be made believable, and consequently it can be used to
good advantage. It is, for instance, quite natural that an
orator should walk up and down in his home practising aloud
his speech by himself; not at all improbable that an actor
should rehearse the lines of his role in a stage voice; that a
servant girl should babble to her cat; that a mother should
prattle to her little child; that an old spinster should chatter
with her parrot; that anyone might talk in his sleep. And in
order that the actor, for once, may have an opportunity to
do some independent work, free from any interference,
suggestions or directions from the author, it may be pref-
erable that the monologue scenes not be written out (in

so many words) but merely indicated. For it is of small importance what is being said by a person in his sleep, or to a parrot, or a cat—it has no influence on the action in the play. A gifted actor may, however, improvise such a scene better than the author can, because the actor has become part and parcel of the situation and is imbued with the mood of it. In short, the author has no way of determining in advance how much small talk may be used and how long it should last without having the audience awakened from the spell it is under.

It is general knowledge that certain theatres in Italy have gone back to the art of improvising—and as a result have produced some creative artists. They follow, however, the author's general outline and suggestions; and this may well prove to be a step forward, not to say a new art form which may truly be said to be *creative*.

Wherever the monologue, on the other hand, has made for improbability, I have resorted to the pantomime; and there I have given the actors still wider scope for creating imagery—and to win individual acclaim. To prevent the audience from being strained to the utmost, I have designated that the music—for which there is ample justification owing to the fact that it is Midsummer Eve, with its traditional dancing—exert its seductive influence while the pantomime is going on. And I address a plea to the musical director that he consider carefully his choice of music selections, lest he conjure forth an atmosphere foreign to the play and lest he induce remembrances of strains from current operettas, or reminders of popular dance music, or of primitive folk airs which are too pronouncedly ethnographic.

The ballet which I have introduced could not have been replaced by a so called mob (or ensemble) scene. Such scenes are generally badly acted and afford a lot of grinning fools, bent on attracting attention to themselves, an opportunity to shatter the illusion. As rustics usually do not improvise into ditties their derision and jeers, but make use of already existing material (which frequently carries a double meaning) I have not composed their scurrilous innuendo but have chosen a little-known dance game, which I came across in the vicinity of Stockholm and wrote down. The words fit the actual happenings only to a degree and not entirely; but that is exactly my intention—for the wiliness and insidiousness in the slave makes him shrink from attacking in the open. Thus there must be no cackling buffoons in a serious drama such as this, no exhibition of coarse grinning in a situation which forever places the lid on the coffin of a family lineage.

With regard to the scenery, I have borrowed from impressionistic painting its asymmetry, its terse and pregnant concision, and in this way I think I have increased the possibilities for creating illusion. The very fact that the room is not seen in its entirety (nor all of its furnishings), gives us the incentive to conjecture. In brief, our imagination is set to work and fills in what is lacking before our eyes. I have also gained something by getting rid of the tiresome exits through doors, primarily because the doors in a stage set are made of canvas and move at the slightest touch. They can not even give expression to an angry father's temper when he, after an execrable dinner, gets up and leaves, slamming the door after him "so that the whole house shakes." On the stage "the whole house" (of canvas!) moves unsteadily from one side to the other. Similarly, I have used only one single setting, and this for two purposes: to blend the figures into the environment, and to break with the habit of using extravagant scenery. And with only one setting, one can expect it to be realistic in appearance. Yet there is nothing so hard to find on the stage as an interior set that comes close to looking as a room *should* look, no matter how convincingly the scenic artist otherwise can produce a volcano in eruption, or a waterfall. We may have to tolerate walls made of canvas, but it is about time that we stopped having shelves and kitchen utensils painted on it. There are so many other conventions on the stage that strain our imagination; certainly we might be freed from overexerting ourselves in an effort to believe that pots and pans painted on the scenery are real.

I have placed the rear wall and the table obliquely across the stage for the purpose of showing the actors full face and in half-profile while they face each other across the table. I once saw a setting in the opera *Aïda* that had a slanting backdrop, and it opened up to the eye unknown perspectives; and this arrangement did not have the look of having been made in a spirit of rebellion against the trying straight line.

Another innovation that is much needed is the removal of the footlights. The lighting is designed to make the actors appear plumper of face. But now let me ask: Why must all actors have plump faces? Does not the light from below tend to erase many of the sensitive, subtle character traits of the lower part of the face, and especially round the mouth? And does it not change the shape of the nose and cast a shadow effect above the eyes? Even if this were not so, there is one thing that is certain: that the eyes of the actors are suffering under a strain, making it difficult for them fully and effectively to project the varying expressions of the eyes across the footlights. For the light strikes the retina in places that under ordinary circumstances are protected (except in the case of sailors: they get the glare of the sun from the water), and consequently one seldom witnesses anything but a glare, a stare, or a crude rolling of the eyes—in the direction of the wings or upward toward the balconies—so that the whites of the eyes show. Very likely this also accounts for the tiresome habit of blinking with the eyelashes, especially by actresses. And whenever anyone on the stage has to speak with his eyes, there is only one way in which he can do it (and that a bad one): to gaze straight out into the audience, and so come in close contact with it from the stage apron outside the curtain line. Rightly or wrongly, this nuisance has been referred to as: "Greeting one's acquaintances!"

Would not sufficiently powerful lighting from the sides (with parabolas or similar devices, for instance) be of help to the actor and enable him to project more completely the sensibility of expression and mobility of the eyes, which are the most important means of facial expression?

I have no illusions about being able to persuade the actors to play *for* the audience and not *to* it, although this would be highly desirable. Nor do I look forward with much hope to the day when I shall see an actor turn his back completely to the audience throughout an important scene; but I do wish that crucial scenes would not be given close to the prompter's box (in the center of the stage) as though the actors were performing a duet and expected it to be received by applause. I would like to have each scene played at the very place where the situation demands it to be played.

And so there must be no revolutionary changes, only minor modifications. To transform the stage into a room with the fourth wall removed, and to carry out the effect of realism by placing some pieces of furniture with their backs to the audience would, for the present, provoke an outcry.

And I would also like to say a word about the make-up, although I dare not hope that the actresses will pay much attention to me. They much prefer to look beautiful rather than look their part in the play. But it might be well to give a thought to whether it is expedient and becoming for the actor to smear his face with make-up until it becomes an abstraction and its character is obliterated by a mask. Let us imagine an actor who—in order to achieve an irascible, choleric look—applies a couple of bold, black lines between the eyes and that he, still looking wrathful with his in-eradicable expression, has to smile in response to somebody's remark! What a horrible grimace it will result in! And again, how can the old man possibly wrinkle the false forehead of his wig (which is smooth as a billiard ball!) when he flies into a rage?

Presented on a small stage, a modern psychological drama, in which the most subtle reactions of the soul must be reflected by facial expression rather than by gesture, shouting and meaningless sound, would be the most practic-able testing ground for the use of powerful lighting from the sides, with the participating actors using no make-up, or at least very little.

If, in addition, the visible orchestra with the disturbing glare from the lamps (on the music stands), and with the faces of orchestra members turned toward the audience, could be made invisible; and if the parquet ("orchestra") could be elevated so that the eyes of the spectators focused on a level higher than the actors' knees; if the stage boxes, with their giggling, snickering late dinner and supper party arrivals, could be got rid of; and if, in addition, we could have absolute darkness in the auditorium while the play is in progress; and if we, first and foremost, could have an intimate stage and an intimate theatre—then we may see the inception of a new drama, and the theatre could again become an institution for the entertainment of the cultured.

While waiting for this kind of theatre to come into being, we may as well continue our writing and file it away in preparation for the repertory that is to come.

I have made an attempt! If I have not succeeded, there is time enough to make another!

PERSONS IN THE PLAY

Miss Julie, 25 years old
Jean, butler and valet, 30 years old
Kristin, cook, 35 years old

(The action takes place in the count's kitchen on Midsummer-Night's Eve.)

(THE SETTING.—*A large kitchen the ceiling and side walls of which are masked by borders and draperies. The rear wall runs diagonally across the stage, from the right of the stage to the left, at a slight angle. On the wall, to the right, are two shelves with utensils of copper, iron, tin and other metals. The shelves are trimmed with fancy paper. Further over, on the left, can be seen three-quarters of a great arched doorway, which has two glass doors; through these doors are seen a fountain with a figure of Cupid, lilac shrubs in bloom and the tops of some Lombardy poplars. On the right, the corner of a large stove, faced with glazed bricks; a part of its hood is also seen. On the left, one end of the servants' dining table of white pine; around it are a few chairs. The stove is decorated with branches of birch, and twigs of juniper are strewn on the floor. On the table stands a large Japanese spice jar, filled with lilac blossoms. An ice-box, a kitchen table, and a sink. Above the door, a big, old-fashioned bell; to the right of the door, a speaking tube. Down stage, left, there is a triangular opening in the wall, inside which are doors upstage and downstage leading to JEAN'S and KRISTIN'S rooms. Only the door leading to JEAN'S room (upstage) is visible. KRISTIN is standing at the stove. She is busy frying something. She wears a light-colored cotton dress and a kitchen apron. JEAN enters. He is wearing livery and carries a pair of large riding-boots with spurs which he puts down on the floor so that they are in full view of the audience.*)

JEAN. Now Miss Julie's mad again—absolutely mad!
KRISTIN. So—you are back again, are you?
JEAN. I took the count to the station, and when I came

back and went by the barn. I stepped inside and had a
dance. And there I saw Miss Julie leading the dance with
the gamekeeper. But the instant she set eyes on me, she
dashed straight over to me and asked me to dance the next
waltz with her; and from that moment on she has been
waltzing with me—and never in my life have I known anything like it! She is stark mad!

KRISTIN. She's always been crazy—but after the engagement was broken off two weeks ago, she is worse than ever.

JEAN. Just what was the trouble, I wonder? I thought he
was a fine young man, even if he didn't have any money to
speak of. . . . Oh, but they all have so many queer notions!
(*He seats himself at one end of the table.*) Anyhow, don't
you think it's strange that a lady like her—h'm—should
want to stay at home with the help instead of going away
with her father to visit some of their relatives?

KRISTIN. I suppose she is sort of embarrassed after the
break-up with her fiancé—

JEAN. I shouldn't be surprised! But I must say, he was the
sort who could stand up for himself. Did you hear, Kristin,
how the whole thing happened? I watched it from beginning
to end—although I never let on that I did.

KRISTIN. You don't mean it? You saw it—did you?

JEAN. I certainly did! They were together out in the stableyard one evening—and Miss Julie was trying to "train" him,
as she called it. What do you think she did? She had him
jump over her riding-crop—the way you train a dog to
jump! And each time she gave him a whack with her riding
crop. But the third time he snatched the whip from her
hand and broke it to bits! And then he left.

KRISTIN. So that's what happened! Well, I never—

JEAN. Yes, that's the way it happened. . . . But now—what
have you that's good to eat, Kristin?

KRISTIN (*dishes out from the pan and places a plate before
Jean*). Oh, it's only a piece of kidney that I cut from the
veal steak.

JEAN (*smells the food*). Splendid! That's my special *délice.*
. . . (*He feels the plate.*) But you didn't heat the plate!

KRISTIN. I must say—you are more of a fuss-box than the
count himself when he wants to be particular. (*She runs
her hand through his hair caressingly.*)

JEAN (*crossly*). Stop that—stop pulling my hair! You know
how sensitive I am about that!

KRISTIN. Why, why—you know I only do it because I love you—don't you know that!

JEAN (*eats.* KRISTIN *uncorks a bottle of ale*). Beer on Midsummer Eve! No, thanks! I have something better than that. (*He pulls out a table drawer and produces a bottle of red wine with yellow seal.*) You see the yellow seal, don't you? Now bring me a glass! A glass with stem—*always*—when you drink it undiluted.

KRISTIN (*goes over to the stove and puts a small pan on the fire. Then she brings him a wine glass.*) God help the woman who gets you for a husband! I never knew anyone to fuss like you!

JEAN. Don't talk nonsense! You ought to be glad to get a fellow as fine as I! And I don't think it's hurt you any to have them call me your sweetheart! (*He tastes the wine.*) Good! Very good! Could be just a trifle warmer. (*He warms the glass with his hands.*) We bought this in Dijon. Four francs a liter from the cask—not counting the duty. What are you cooking over there that smells so horrible?

KRISTIN. Oh, it's some devilish mess that Miss Julie has me cook for Diana.

JEAN. You might be a little more careful with your expressions, Kristin!—But I don't see why you should stand and cook for that damned cur on Midsummer Eve! Is anything the matter with the bitch?

KRISTIN. Yes, she is sick. She has been sneaking out with the gatekeeper's pugdog, and now she's in trouble—and that's just what Miss Julie doesn't want, don't you see?

JEAN. The young lady is too haughty in some respects, and in others she has no pride at all—exactly like her mother, the countess, when she was alive. She was especially at home in the kitchen and in the stables, but she would never drive behind one horse only—she had to have at least two. She went around with dirty cuffs, but she had to have a crest on each button. And speaking of Miss Julie, she shows a lack of self-respect. She has no regard for her position. I could almost say she lacks refinement. Why, just now when she was dancing out there in the barn, she pulled the gamekeeper away from Anna and started to dance with him, without any ado. Would we do anything like that? We would not!—But that's what happens when aristocrats try to act like the common people—they become—common! But she is splendid to look at! Gorgeous! Ah, what shoulders! And what—etcetera—

KRISTIN. Oh, stop your ranting! Haven't I heard what Clara says about her?—and she dresses her.

JEAN. Oh! Clara! You women are always jealous of each other! But don't *I* go out riding with her? . . . And can she dance!

KRISTIN. Listen, Jean—how about a dance with me when I get through with my work here?

JEAN. Why, certainly—why not?

KRISTIN. Is that a promise?

JEAN. Do I have to take an oath? When I say I'll do a thing, I do it!—Well, thanks for the snack, anyhow . . . it tasted good! (*He corks the wine bottle with gusto.*)

MISS JULIE (*appears suddenly in the doorway. She speaks to someone outside.*) I'll be back immediately—you just wait there . . .

JEAN (*He quickly slips the bottle into the table drawer; then he rises respectfully. MISS JULIE enters and goes over to Kristin by the mirror.*) Well, Kristin, is it ready?

(KRISTIN *indicates* JEAN's *presence.*)

JEAN (*with gallantry*). Do you ladies have secrets between you?

MISS JULIE (*with a flip of her handkerchief in his face*). No inquisitiveness!

JEAN. Ah—what lovely fragrance—the smell of violets—

MISS JULIE (*coquettishly*). So—you are impertinent, are you? Are you a connoisseur of scents, too? You are an expert at dancing. Now, now—no peeking! Go away!

JEAN (*impudently, yet with a semblance of politeness*). Is it some sort of witches' brew for Midsummer Night that you two ladies are concocting? Something to help you look into the future and see what your lucky star has in store for you —and get a glimpse of your intended?

MISS JULIE (*tartly*). You have to have good eyes for that! (*To* KRISTIN.) Pour it into a small bottle and put the cork in tight.—Now come and dance a schottische with me, Jean.

JEAN (*hesitantly*). I don't mean to be disrespectful, but I promised Kristin this dance . . .

MISS JULIE. Oh, she can dance the next one with you instead. How about it, Kristin? You'll loan me Jean, won't you?

KRISTIN. That's not for me to say. (*To* JEAN.) If Miss Julie condescends, it's not for you to say no. Go on, Jean, and be thankful to Miss Julie for the honor!

JEAN. If you will permit me to speak frankly, Miss Julie—

and I hope you won't be offended—I wonder whether it's wise of you to dance more than one dance with the same partner . . . especially as people here are only too prone to misinterpret, to imagine things . . .

MISS JULIE (*flares up*). What do you mean? What kind of interpretations? Just what is it you mean?

JEAN (*servilely*). Since you refuse to understand, Miss Julie, I'll have to speak more plainly. It doesn't look good to single out one of your domestics in preference to some of the others, who would like to have the same honor paid to them . . .

MISS JULIE. Single out? Preference? What an idea! I am astonished! I—the mistress of the house—honor the people by attending their dance . . . and when I feel like dancing, I want to dance with someone who knows how to lead! I don't want to dance with someone who makes me look ridiculous!

JEAN. Just as you say, Miss Julie! I am at your service!

MISS JULIE (*in an appeasing tone of voice*). Don't take it as an order now! Tonight we are celebrating! We all want to enjoy the holiday! We are all happy—and all just plain human beings . . . and rank doesn't count! Come now, give me your arm! You don't have to worry, Kristin—I am not going to take your sweetheart away from you!

(JEAN *offers her his arm; she takes it, and they go out.*)

(*The following scene is entirely in pantomime. It is to be played as if the actress were alone on the stage. Whenever necessary, she should turn her back to the audience and she should not look in the direction of the audience. She must be in no hurry, as though afraid that the audience might become impatient.* KRISTIN *is alone. The faint sound of violin music in the distance, played in schottische tempo, is heard. She hums the tune while clearing* JEAN'S *place at the table, washes the dishes and utensils in the sink, dries them and puts them away in the cupboard. Then she removes her apron, takes out a small mirror from a drawer and places it on the table, supporting the mirror against the jar of lilacs. She lights a candle and heats a hairpin, with which she curls her forelock. This done, she goes to the door and stands there listening. Then she goes back to the table and discovers* MISS JULIE'S *forgotten handkerchief. She sniffs of it; then she distractedly smoothes it out and folds it carefully.*)

JEAN (*enters alone*). She is mad, really! Dancing the way

she does! The people are standing behind the doors, grinning at her. . . . What do you think has got into her, Kristin?

KRISTIN. Oh, she's having her period—and then she is always so peculiar.—Well, do you want to dance with me now?

JEAN. I hope you are not cross with me because I let you down a moment ago, are you?

KRISTIN. Certainly not! Not for a little thing like that— you ought to know that! And I know my place . . .

JEAN (*puts his arm round her waist*). You show good sense, Kristin. You'll make a good wife. . . .

MISS JULIE (*enters. She is unpleasantly surprised. She speaks with forced good humor*). Well—you are a fine young swain—running away from your partner!

JEAN. On the contrary, Miss Julie, I just hastened back to the one I deserted . . .

MISS JULIE (*changing tactics*). Do you know—you dance as nobody else! But why do you wear your livery on a holiday like this? Take it off—this minute!

JEAN. Well—then I must ask you, Miss Julie, to step outside for a moment. . . . My black coat is hanging . over there— (*He points toward it and goes over to the left.*)

MISS JULIE. You are not embarrassed because of me, are you? Just to change your coat?—Go into your room, then, and come back when you have changed. . . . Or you can stay here, and I'll turn my back.

JEAN. If you'll excuse me, then, Miss Julie. (*He goes to his room, on the left. One sees the movement of his arm while he is changing coats.*)

MISS JULIE (*to* KRISTIN). Tell me, Kristin, is Jean your fiancé, is he? You seem to be so intimate.

KRISTIN. Fiancé? Well—yes, if you like! We call it being engaged.

MISS JULIE. Oh, you do?

KRISTIN. Well, you have been engaged yourself, Miss Julie, and . . .

MISS JULIE. Yes, but *we* were *properly* engaged.

KRISTIN. Just the same, nothing came of it.

(JEAN *re-enters, now dressed in a black cutaway and carrying a black bowler.*)

MISS JULIE (*regards him admiringly*). *Très gentil, Monsieur Jean. Très gentil.*

JEAN. *Vous voulez plaisanter, madame!*

MISS JULIE. *Et vous voulez parler français?* Where have you learned that?

JEAN. In Switzerland—when I was steward in one of the largest hotels in Lucerne.

MISS JULIE. Why, you look a real gentleman in that cutaway! *Charmant!* (*She seats herself at the table.*)

JEAN. Oh, you flatter me!

MISS JULIE (*offended*). Flatter you?

JEAN. My natural modesty forbids me to believe that you could honestly pay compliments to anyone like me—and that is why I had the audacity to assume that you were merely exaggerating—or, as it is called, engaging in flattery.

MISS JULIE. Where did you learn to phrase your words so nimbly? You must have visited the theatres a good deal?

JEAN. I've done that, too! Yes, I have been to many places.

MISS JULIE. But you were born here in the neighborhood, weren't you?

JEAN. My father was a farmhand on the county prosecutor's estate nearby. I remember seeing you when you were a child. But you never took any notice of me.

MISS JULIE. Oh, you do, really?

JEAN. Yes, and I especially remember one time . . . oh, but I can't tell you about that.

MISS JULIE. Oh yes, do—go on—Why not? This is just the time . . .

JEAN. No, really—I can't . . . not now! Some other time, perhaps . . .

MISS JULIE. Another time may be never. Is it anything so shocking?

JEAN. No, it isn't anything shocking at all—just the same I feel a little squeamish about it. Look at her there. (*He points to* KRISTIN *who has gone to sleep in a chair by the stove.*)

MISS JULIE. She'll make a delightful wife, won't she? Perhaps she snores, too?

JEAN. No—but she talks in her sleep.

MISS JULIE (*with sarcasm*). How do you know?

JEAN (*with bravado*). I have heard her. (*There is a silence. They eye each other.*)

MISS JULIE. Why don't you sit down?

JEAN. I couldn't—not in your presence!

MISS JULIE. And if I order you to?

JEAN. I would obey.

MISS JULIE. Sit down, then!—Oh, wait! Would you get me something to drink first . . .

JEAN. I don't know what there is in the ice-box here. I think there is only some beer.

MISS JULIE. That's not to be despised—and my tastes are so simple that I prefer it to wine.

JEAN (*takes out a bottle of ale from the ice-box, and opens it. Then he goes to the cupboard and brings out a glass and a plate, and serves her.*) If you please!

MISS JULIE. Thank you! Wouldn't you like some yourself?

JEAN. I am not particularly fond of beer—but since you insist . . .

MISS JULIE. Insist? I should think ordinary good manners would prompt you to keep me company . . .

JEAN. You are quite right, Miss Julie! (*He uncorks a bottle of ale and brings out another glass from the cupboard; then pours himself a glass of ale.*)

MISS JULIE. Now drink a toast to me! (JEAN *hesitates.*) Old as you are, I believe you are bashful.

JEAN (*kneeling, he raises his glass and jestingly parodies:*) To my sovereign and mistress!

MISS JULIE. Bravo! Now you must kiss my foot—as a crowning touch!

(JEAN *hesitates, and then he boldly takes her foot and gives it a light kiss.*)

MISS JULIE. Superb! You should have been an actor!

JEAN (*rises*). We must not go on like this, Miss Julie . . . someone might come in and catch us—

MISS JULIE. Why should that matter?

JEAN. Because people would start to gossip, that's the reason! You should have heard their tongues wagging out there just now . . .

MISS JULIE. What did they say? Go on, tell me! Sit down . . .

JEAN (*sits down*). I don't wish to hurt your feelings, Miss Julie—but they used expressions . . . that . . . well, they blurted out suspicions of a kind that . . . well, you can well imagine what kind— You are not a child, Miss Julie, and if you see a lady drinking alone with a man—and especially a servant—and at night—why—

MISS JULIE. What then? And besides, we are not alone. . . . Kristin is here, isn't she?

JEAN. Yes—asleep!

MISS JULIE. I'll wake her up! (*She rises.*) Kristin, are you asleep?

KRISTIN (*in her sleep*). Bla-bla-bla-bla . . .

MISS JULIE. Kristin!—She is sound asleep!

KRISTIN (*still in her sleep*). The count's boots are polished —put on the coffee—I'll do it this minute—this very minute —phew—pish—ho— (*She snores.*)

MISS JULIE (*twists her nose*). Wake up, will you?

JEAN (*sternly*). One should never disturb people when they are asleep!

MISS JULIE (*in a sharp tone of voice*). What's that?

JEAN. Anyone who stands at the stove all day long has a right to be tired at the end of the day. And sleep should be respected.

MISS JULIE (*in a different tone*). It's considerate of you to think like that—it does you credit! Thank you! (*She extends her hand to him.*) Come outside with me and pick a few lilacs . . .

(KRISTIN *wakes, rises and goes sleepily to her bedroom, on the left.*)

JEAN. With you, Miss Julie?

MISS JULIE. Yes, with me!

JEAN. It would never do! Absolutely not!

MISS JULIE. I don't understand what you mean. . . . You couldn't possibly be imagining things, could you?

JEAN. No—not I . . . but the people.

MISS JULIE. What? That I am in love with a domestic?

JEAN. I am not conceited—but such things *have* happened. . . . And nothing is sacred to anybody.

MISS JULIE (*tartly*). You talk like an aristocrat!

JEAN. Yes—and I *am*!

MISS JULIE. And *I*—am I lowering myself?

JEAN. Take my advice, Miss Julie, do not lower yourself! No one will believe you did it innocently. People will always say that you fell!

MISS JULIE. I have a higher opinion of people than you have. Come and let us see if I am right!—Come on! (*She gives him a challenging glance.*)

JEAN. You know, Miss Julie, you are a very strange young lady!

MISS JULIE. Perhaps I am—but so are you strange! For that matter, everything is strange! Life, human beings— everything is scum and slime that floats and drifts on the surface until it sinks—sinks to the bottom! It makes me think of a dream that comes back to me ever so often: I am perched on top of a tall column and can see no way of getting down. When I gaze below, I feel dizzy. Yet I must get down; but I haven't the courage to jump. There is nothing to hold on to, and I hope that I may fall—but I don't. . . . Nevertheless I feel I cannot be at peace until I am down, down on the ground. . . . And if I should once reach the ground, I would want to be buried in the earth. Have you ever had such a feeling?

JEAN. No! *I* usually dream that I am lying underneath a tall tree in a dark forest. I have a desire to get up high, to the very top of the tree and look out over the bright landscape where the sun is shining—and to rob the bird's nest up there of its golden eggs. And I climb and climb; but the tree's trunk is so thick and so slippery, and the lowest branches are so high up. But I know that if I can only reach the first branch, I'll get to the top as easily as on a ladder. So far I have never reached it, but I am going to—even if it's only in my dreams.

MISS JULIE. Here I stand talking about dreams with you. . . . Come now! Only into the garden! (*She offers him her arm and they go out.*)

JEAN. We must sleep on nine midsummer blossoms tonight, Miss Julie; then our dreams will come true.

(MISS JULIE *and* JEAN *turn at the door.* JEAN *suddenly covers one eye with his hand.*)

MISS JULIE. Let me see what you have in your eye.

JEAN. Oh, it's nothing . . . just a speck of dust. It'll disappear in a minute.

MISS JULIE. It was from my sleeve—it brushed against your eye. Sit down and let me help you! (*She takes him by the arm and leads him to a chair, takes hold of his head and bends it backward, then tries to remove the speck from his eye with the tip of her handkerchief.*) Sit still now, very still! (*She slaps him on the hand.*) Will you do as I tell you! —I believe the great, big, strong fellow is trembling! (*She feels his biceps.*) With arms like yours!

JEAN (*tries to dissuade her*). Miss Julie!

MISS JULIE. Yes, Monsieur Jean!

JEAN. *Attention! Je ne suis qu'un homme!*

MISS JULIE. Will you sit still!—There now! I got it out! Kiss my hand now and say "thank you"!

JEAN (*gets up from the chair*). Miss Julie, will you please listen to me!—Kristin has gone to bed now.—Will you listen to me!

MISS JULIE. Kiss my hand first!

JEAN. Very well—but the blame will be yours!

MISS JULIE. Blame for what?

JEAN. For what? You are twenty-five years old, aren't you, and not a child? Don't you know it's dangerous to play with fire?

MISS JULIE. Not for me. I'm insured.

JEAN (boldly). No, you are not! And if you are, you are not far from danger—you may trigger a combustion!

MISS JULIE. I presume you mean yourself!

JEAN. Yes. Not because it is I, but because I am a man, and young!

MISS JULIE. Of prepossessing appearance. . . . What incredible conceit! Another Don Juan, perhaps! Or a Joseph! Upon my soul, I believe you are another Joseph!

JEAN. You do, do you?

MISS JULIE. Yes, I almost think so . . .

(JEAN boldly goes up to her and tries to embrace and kiss her.)

MISS JULIE (boxes his ears). That'll teach you manners!

JEAN. Were you serious or were you jesting?

MISS JULIE. Serious.

JEAN. In that case, you were serious a moment ago also? You play much too seriously—and there is where the danger lies! Now I am tired of playing and beg to be excused so that I can go back to my work. The count has to have his boots ready when he returns, and it's long past midnight. (He picks up a pair of boots.)

MISS JULIE. Put down those boots!

JEAN. No. This is my work which I am hired to do—but I was never hired to be your playmate, and that's something I can never be. . . . I consider myself above that!

MISS JULIE. You are proud.

JEAN. In certain ways, yes—not in others.

MISS JULIE. Have you ever been in love?

JEAN. We don't use that word; but I have been fond of many girls—and once I felt sick because I couldn't have the one I wanted: sick, you know, like the princes in A Thousand and One Nights—who could neither eat nor drink merely for love!

MISS JULIE. Who was the girl? (JEAN does not answer.) Who was she?

JEAN. That's something you couldn't force out of me.

MISS JULIE. If I ask you as an equal, ask you as a—friend. . . . Who was she?

JEAN. It was you!

MISS JULIE (*seats herself*). How priceless!

JEAN. Yes, you may call it that! It was preposterous!—You see—it was that incident I was loath to tell you about, a moment ago—but now I shall. . . . Do you know how your world looks from below? No, you don't. Like hawks and falcons—whose backs we rarely see because they are always soaring high up in the sky. . . . I lived in my father's little shack with seven brothers and sisters and one pig out in the gray, barren fields where not even a tree grew. But from the windows I could see the wall enclosing the count's park, with the apple trees rising above it. That was to me the Garden of Eden; and it was protected by a multitude of fierce angels with flaming swords. In spite of their presence, I and some other boys found our way to the tree of life. . . . Now you despise me, don't you?

MISS JULIE. Heavens, no—all boys steal apples!

JEAN. You say so now, but you have contempt for me just the same. . . . Well—one time I went into the Garden of Paradise with my mother, to weed the onion beds. Near the vegetable garden there was a Turkish pavilion standing in the shade of jasmine, and overgrown with honeysuckle. I had no idea what it could be used for; but I had never seen such a beautiful building. . . . People went inside, then came out again; and one day the door was left open. I sneaked in and saw the walls were covered with pictures of emperors and kings; and, hanging at the windows were red curtains with tassels. Now you understand where I was . . . I . . . (*He breaks off a spray of lilac and holds it close to her nostrils.*) I had never been inside the castle, and had never seen any place as grand as the church, but this was if anything more beautiful. . . . And no matter which way my thoughts went, they always returned to—to that place. . . . And gradually it developed into a yearning to experience some day all of its splendor and charm.—*Enfin*, I stole inside, gazed and admired, but just then I heard someone coming! There was only one exit for cultivated people—but for me there was another; and I had no choice but to take it . . .

(MISS JULIE *who meanwhile has accepted the lilac spray from* JEAN, *lets it drop on the table.*)

JEAN . . . and then I took to my heels, plunged through a raspberry hedge, dashed across the strawberry patches and found myself on the rose terrace. There I gazed at a figure in pink dress and white stockings—it was you. I hid underneath a heap of weeds and lay there—lay there, imagine, with thistles pricking me and under dank, stinking earth. And as I watched you among the roses, I thought to myself: If it is true that a thief can get to heaven and be with the angels, why should it be impossible for a poor peasant child here on God's earth, to get into the castle park and play with the count's daughter . . .

MISS JULIE (*with an expression of pain*). Do you think all poor children have the same thoughts that you had?

JEAN (*at first hesitantly, then with conviction*). That all poor children . . . Yes—of course—of course . . .

MISS JULIE. It must be terrible to be poor!

JEAN. Oh, Miss Julie—oh! A dog may lie on the countess's sofa—a horse have his nose stroked by a young lady—but a lackey . . . (*In a changed tone.*) Oh, of course, there are some who have the right stuff in them and who swing themselves up in the world—but that doesn't happen every day. Anyhow, do you know what I did? I ran down to the mill-pond and jumped in, with my clothes on. I was dragged out and given a thrashing. But the following Sunday when my father and the rest of the family had gone to visit my grandmother, I schemed to stay at home. I then washed myself with soap and warm water, put on my best clothes and went to church—where I knew I would see you! I saw you and went back home, determined to die. . . . But I wanted to die beautifully and comfortably, without pain. I suddenly remembered that it was dangerous to sleep beneath an alder bush. We had a large one that was just blooming. I stripped it of its flowers; then made a bed of them in the oats-bin. Did you ever notice how smooth and silken oats are? Soft to the touch as the human skin. Well, I closed the lid, shut my eyes, and fell asleep. And when I woke up, I was very, very sick! . . . But as you see, I didn't die. What was in my mind, I really don't know! . . . I had no hope of ever winning you, of course—but you represented to me the hopelessness of ever rising above the social level to which I was born.

MISS JULIE. You know, you express yourself charmingly! Did you ever go to school?

JEAN. Briefly. But I have read a great many novels. And I have gone to the theatre. Also I have listened to cultured people talking, and I've learned most from that.

MISS JULIE. You stand and listen to what we say?

JEAN. Certainly! And I have heard much—much—when I've been sitting on the carriage-box and when I've been at the oars in the rowboat. I once heard you, Miss Julie, and a girl friend of yours . . .

MISS JULIE. Oh!—What did you hear?

JEAN. Well, I don't know that I can tell you. . . . But I must say I was rather surprised; and I couldn't imagine where you had learned words like that. After all, perhaps there isn't such a great difference between people as one thinks—

MISS JULIE. Shame on you! We don't behave like you do when we are engaged!

JEAN (with a penetrating look). Are you so sure? There is no use making yourself out so innocent, Miss Julie . . .

MISS JULIE. The man I gave my love to turned out to be a blackguard!

JEAN. That's what you always say—when it's over.

MISS JULIE. Always?

JEAN. Yes, always—at least that's what I think, having heard the same expression before—under such circumstances.

MISS JULIE. What sort of circumstances?

JEAN. Such as this one! The last time—

MISS JULIE. Stop! I don't want to hear any more!

JEAN. Strange to say, that's exactly what *she* said!—Well, now I must ask you to let me go to bed . . .

MISS JULIE (softly). Go to bed at this hour—on Midsummer Eve?

JEAN. Yes—I don't care the least bit about dancing with that riff-raff out there . . .

MISS JULIE. Go and get the key to the boathouse and take me for a row on the lake! I want to see the sunrise!

JEAN. Would that be a wise thing to do?

MISS JULIE. It sounds as if you were afraid of your reputation!

JEAN. And why shouldn't I be? I don't want to be made to look ridiculous and I have no desire to be discharged without a reference just when I am hoping to start on my own. And besides, I feel I am under some obligation to Kristin . . .

MISS JULIE. Oh, so it's Kristin again?

JEAN. Yes—but it's you, too. Take my advice: go to bed!

MISS JULIE. Should I take orders from you?

JEAN. Yes, for once—I beg of you—for your own sake! It's long past midnight. Lack of sleep brings on feverish excitement; it intoxicates and makes one reckless. Go to bed! And besides, if I am not mistaken, I hear the people coming this way, and they will be looking for me. . . . If they find us here, you'll be under a cloud!

(*The crowd, approaching, is heard to sing:*)

There came two wedded maids from the wood—
Tridiridi-ralla tridiridi-ra.
The one had wet her little foot
Tridiridi-ralla-la.

They kept talking of nothing but money—
Tridiridi-ralla tridiridi-ra.
Yet they scarcely owned a farthing
Tridiridi-ralla-la.

Your ring I now give back to you
Tridiridi-ralla tridiridi-ra.
For I've another man in view
Tridiridi-ralla-la!

MISS JULIE. I know the people here, and I love them as they love me. Let them come and you'll see!

JEAN. No, Miss Julie, they don't love you. They accept your food, but spit at you behind your back! Believe me! Listen to them! Just listen to what they are singing. . . . No—don't listen!

MISS JULIE (*stands listening*). What is it they are singing?

JEAN. It's an indecent parody! About you and me!

MISS JULIE. It's disgraceful! Shameless! What deceit!

JEAN. People like them are always cowardly! All you can do when you fight with rabble is to flee!

MISS JULIE. Flee? But where? We can't get out, and we can't go into Kristin's room . . .

JEAN. Well—into mine, then? We have to—there is no other way—and you can trust me. I am your friend, truly and respectfully . . .

MISS JULIE. But suppose—suppose they should look for you in your room?

JEAN. I'll bolt the door—and if they try to break in, I'll

shoot! Come! (*He pleads with her, on his knees.*) Come, please!

MISS JULIE (*significantly*). Will you promise me . . .

JEAN. I swear!

(MISS JULIE *goes quickly into his room, left.* JEAN *follows her excitedly.*)

(*Dressed in their holiday best and with flowers in their hats and caps, the farm people enter. Leading them is a fiddler. They place a keg of small beer and a firkin of corn brandy, both decorated with garlands of fresh green leaves, on the table; then they bring out glasses and start drinking, form a ring and begin to dance, singing to the tune of "There came two wedded maids from the wood." When they have finished the dance, they leave, singing.*

MISS JULIE *comes from* JEAN's *room, alone. She sees the kitchen in a deplorable mess, and claps her hands together in dejection. Then she takes out her powder-puff and powders her face.*)

JEAN (*enters with bravado*). Don't you see! Did you hear them? Do you think you can stay here after this?

MISS JULIE. No! I don't think I can! But what are we going to do?

JEAN. Get away from here—travel—go far away from here . . .

MISS JULIE. Go away—travel. Yes, but where?

JEAN. To Switzerland—to the Italian lakes. . . . You have never been there, have you?

MISS JULIE. No—is it beautiful there?

JEAN. Ah! Eternal summer—orange groves—laurel trees. . . . Ah!

MISS JULIE. And when we are there—what shall we do?

JEAN. I'll start a hotel business—everything first class, and for exclusive guests . . .

MISS JULIE. A hotel?

JEAN. That's a lively business, believe me! All the time new faces, new languages, you never have time to worry or to be bored. . . . You nerve yourself against anything—you never have to look for something to do, for there is never any let-up. Bells ring day and night—you hear the train whistles—buses and carriages come and go—and all the time the money keeps rolling in. That's the life, I tell you!

MISS JULIE. Yes—that's living. . . . And what about me?

JEAN. You'll be the mistress of the house—its chief attraction and ornament! With your looks, and your style and manner, why, our success is assured from the start! It'll be colossal! You'll be sitting like a queen in the office and you'll keep the slaves moving by pressing an electric button —the guests file past your throne and place their tribute timidly before you—you have no idea how nervous it makes people to have their bills presented to them. I'll salt the bills, and you'll sugar them with your sweetest smile. . . . Ah, please—let us get away from here! (*He takes out a time-table from his pocket.*) Without delay—by the next train! We'll be in Malmö at six-thirty—in Hamburg at eight-forty in the morning—in Frankfort and Basel within a day—and we'll get to Como, by way of St. Gothard, in—let me see— in three days. Three days!

MISS JULIE. That's all very well—but, Jean—you must give me courage. Tell me that you love me! Come and take me in your arms!

JEAN (*hesitates*). I want to—but I lack the courage . . . ever to do it in this house again. I love you—you know that —you can't doubt that, can you, Miss Julie?

MISS JULIE (*shyly, with true womanly feeling*). Miss Julie? Call me Julie! Between us there can no longer be any barriers! Call me Julie!

JEAN (*pathetically*). I can't! As long as we are in this house, there are barriers between us. There is tradition—and there is the count. Never in my life have I met *anyone* who strikes such awe into me! I have only to see his gloves lying on a chair, and I feel servile. . . . I have only to hear him ring upstairs, and I cringe like a shying horse—and even now when I look at his boots standing there so stiff and cocky, I feel a chill down my spine. (*He kicks at the boots.*) Superstition, prejudice, convention—knocked into us from childhood—but that can easily be got rid of. . . . All you have to do is to go to another country, to a republic, and there you will see how they prostrate themselves before my porter's uniform. . . . Yes, they'll bow and scrape—but here is one who won't! I wasn't born to crawl before others—I have the right stuff in me—I have character . . . and if I only get to the first branch, you watch me climb to the top! Today I am a lackey—next year I'll be in business for myself—ten years from now I'll be rich and retire—and then I'll move to Roumania and get myself a decoration—and I may, mark my words, I may end up a count!

MISS JULIE. Very nice, very nice!

JEAN. Yes—for in Roumania you can buy yourself a title —and so you may, after all, be a countess, Miss Julie. . . . *My* countess!

MISS JULIE. All that doesn't interest me at all—I'm leaving all that behind me! Tell me only that you love me . . . for if you don't . . . well—then what would I be?

JEAN. I'll tell you—I'll tell you a thousand times—later on! But not now—not here! And above all, let's not be sentimental, or everything will go wrong! We must look at this matter calmly, soberly, like sensible people. (*Takes out a cigar, bites off the butt end and lights it.*) Now you sit down there, and I'll sit here; then we'll talk it over as if nothing had happened.

MISS JULIE (*desperately*). My God—haven't you any feelings?

JEAN. *If* I have feelings! There isn't a man with more feeling than I! But I know how to control myself!

MISS JULIE. A moment ago you kissed my slipper—and now . . .

JEAN (*brutally*). That was then—now we have other things to think of!

MISS JULIE. Don't speak to me so cruelly!

JEAN. I am speaking sensibly, that's all! One folly has been committed—don't commit any more! The count may be here any moment now; and before he comes, we must settle our future. Now—what do you think of my plans, Miss Julie? Do you approve of them?

MISS JULIE. They seem likely enough—but let me ask one question: Have you sufficient capital to start such a large undertaking?

JEAN (*chewing his cigar*). Have I? Of course I have! I have my training in the business, my vast experience, my linguistic ability! That's a capital to be reckoned with, don't you think?

MISS JULIE. But you couldn't buy a railroad ticket with it, could you?

JEAN (*keeps chewing the cigar*). That's quite true—and that is why I am looking for a partner who can advance the necessary funds.

MISS JULIE. Where do you expect to find such a person in a hurry?

JEAN. That is where *you* come in—if you want to be my partner—

MISS JULIE. I couldn't . . . and I haven't any money of my own. (*There is a silence.*)

JEAN. Then we'll have to drop the whole thing . . .

MISS JULIE. And so . . .

JEAN. And so . . . things remain as they are . . .

MISS JULIE. Do you think I'll remain under this roof as your mistress? Do you think I will allow the people here to point a finger at me? Do you think I could face my father after this? Never! Take me away from here—from this humiliation and disgrace! Oh, my God, what have I done? My God! . . . (*She breaks into tears.*)

JEAN. So, that's the tune you are singing *now*? What you have done?—What many others have done before you . . .

MISS JULIE (*screaming hysterically*). And now you despise me! I'm falling—falling—

JEAN. Fall low enough—fall down to my level—then I'll raise you up again!

MISS JULIE. What dreadful power could have drawn me to you? The attraction of the weak to the strong, the ones on the decline to the ones rising? Or could it have been love? Is this what you call love? Do you know what love is?

JEAN. Do I? You may be sure I do! Do you think I never had an affair before?

MISS JULIE. What a way to speak? And such thoughts!

JEAN. That's the way I was brought up, and that's the way I am! Now don't get excited, and stop acting so prim and prudish! For now you are not a bit better than I am. . . . Come here, my little girl, let me treat you to a glass of something very special! (*He opens the table drawer and brings out the wine bottle; then he fills the two glasses which were used previously.*)

MISS JULIE. Where did you get this wine?

JEAN. From the wine cellar.

MISS JULIE. My father's burgundy!

JEAN. Isn't it good enough for his son-in-law?

MISS JULIE. And I drink beer!

JEAN. That only shows your taste is not as good as mine!

MISS JULIE. Thief!

JEAN. You are not going to give me away, are you?

MISS JULIE. Oh, God! To be the accomplice of a thief—and in my own home! Have I been under the influence of some intoxication? Have I been dreaming this Midsummer Night?—This festival of frolic and innocent merriment?

JEAN (*sarcastically*). Innocent, h'm!

MISS JULIE (*paces back and forth*). Could there be anyone in this world more miserable than I am?

JEAN. Why be miserable—after a conquest like yours? Think of Kristin in there—don't you think that she, too, has feelings . . .

MISS JULIE. I used to think so, but I no longer do! No—once a servant, always a servant!

JEAN. And once a whore—always a whore!

MISS JULIE (*on her knees, her hands clasped*). Oh, God in heaven—put an end to my miserable life! Take me away from this filth—I am sinking down in it! Help me! Save me!

JEAN. I can't help feeling sorry for you. . . . When I lay in the onion bed and watched you in the rose garden, I—yes, I can tell you now—I had the same nasty thoughts that all boys have.

MISS JULIE. And you—you wanted to die for me!

JEAN. You mean in the oats-bin? I just made that up!

MISS JULIE. Just a lie, then!

JEAN (*he is beginning to be sleepy*). Not exactly! I think I once read somewhere in a newspaper about a chimney-sweep who went to sleep in a chest used for firewood. He had filled it with lilacs—because he was sued for non-support of his child . . .

MISS JULIE. So that's the kind of person you are . . .

JEAN. I had to make up something. Glitter and tinsel is what dazzle the women—and catch them.

MISS JULIE. Cad!

JEAN. Garbage!

MISS JULIE. And now you have seen the hawk's back!

JEAN. Not exactly its *back* . . .

MISS JULIE. And I was to be the first branch . . .

JEAN. But the branch was rotten . . .

MISS JULIE. I was to be the hotel sign . . .

JEAN. And I the hotel . . .

MISS JULIE. . . . Sitting behind the desk to attract and lure customers, falsify the bills and overcharge them . . .

JEAN. That would have been *my* business . . .

MISS JULIE. To think that the human soul can be so low, so rotten—

JEAN. Wash it clean, why don't you?

MISS JULIE. You lackey! You menial! Stand up when I speak to you!

JEAN. You—a menial's strumpet—whore to a lackey—keep your mouth shut and get out of here! Is it for you to rake me over the coals for being coarse and uncouth? Never have I seen any of our kind behave so vulgarly as you behaved tonight! Do you think a servant girl would accost a man the way you did? Did you ever see a girl of my class throw herself at a man as you did? That's something I have only seen done by animals and prostitutes!

MISS JULIE (*crushed*). That's right! Stone me—trample on me—I deserve it—all of it! I am a wretched woman! But help me—help me out of this—if there *is* a way out of it!

JEAN (*now in a milder tone of voice*). I would belittle myself if I denied having a share in the honor of my class seducing you; but do you really think that anyone of my class would have dared to cast a glance at you, if you yourself had not sent out the invitation? I still can't get over it—

MISS JULIE. And you take pride in it!

JEAN. Why not?—Although I must confess the victory was much too easy to give me any real intoxication!

MISS JULIE. Keep on being brutal!

JEAN (*rises*). No—on the contrary, I ask you to forgive me for the things I just said! I never strike a defenseless person—least of all a woman. I won't deny that it gives me a certain satisfaction to discover that what dazzled us down below was nothing but cheap tinsel; that the hawk's back was only gray, like the rest of his fine feathers; that the delicate complexion was mere powder; that the polished nails had dirty edges; that the handkerchief could be soiled, despite its perfumed scent. . . . But on the other hand, it hurts me to realize that what I was striving to reach was so unsubstantial and artificial . . . it pains me to see that you have sunk so low that you are far beneath your own cook . . . it saddens me as when I see the autumn leaves torn into tatters by the rain and turned into mud.

MISS JULIE. You talk as if you already feel yourself above me?

JEAN. Of course I am! You see, I might be able to make you a countess—but you could never make me a count.

MISS JULIE. But you are a thief, and I am not!

JEAN. There are worse things than being a thief! Much worse! Besides, when I am employed in a household, I consider myself, in a way, a member of the family, related to it, so to speak; and to pick a berry or two when the bushes are full, is not stealing. . . . (*His passion comes to life again.*) Miss Julie—you are a glorious woman—far too good for one like me! You were under the spell of some sort of intoxication, and now you want to cover up your mistake by deluding yourself that you love me! But you don't! You may be attracted to me physically—and in that case your love is no better than mine! But I am not content with being just an animal, to you; and I can never kindle any love in you for me—

MISS JULIE. Are you so sure of that?

JEAN. Do you mean to say that I could?—I could love you, yes—no doubt of that! You are beautiful, you are refined—(*He comes close to her and takes hold of her hand.*) . . . cultivated, and charming—when you feel like it; and I don't think that any man who has once fallen for you, will ever stop loving you. (*He puts his arm round her waist.*) You are like mulled wine, strongly spiced—and a kiss from you— (*He tries to lead her out of the kitchen. She gently frees herself from him.*)

MISS JULIE. Let me go! You will never win me that way . . .

JEAN. Then *how*? Not *that* way, you say. Not by caresses and pretty words—not by thoughtfulness about the future— trying to save you from disgrace! How then?

MISS JULIE. How? You ask how? I don't know . . . haven't a thought! I loathe you as I loathe a rat—but I can't escape you!

JEAN. Escape *with* me, then!

MISS JULIE (*straightens up*). Escape? Yes, we must get away from here! But I am so tired!—Pour me a glass of wine!

(JEAN *serves her a glass.*)

MISS JULIE (*looking at her watch*). But first we must have a talk—we still have a little time left. (*She empties her glass and holds it out for another drink.*)

JEAN. You must drink moderately, or it'll go to your head.

MISS JULIE. What does it matter?

JEAN. What does it matter? To be intoxicated is a sign of vulgarity. . . . What was it you wanted to tell me?

MISS JULIE. We have to get away from here! But first we must have a talk—that is, I must do the talking—for so far it is you who have done it all. You have told me about your life; now I shall tell you about mine—then we shall really know each other, before we begin our journey together.

JEAN. Wait a second! If you'll pardon my suggestion— don't you think you may regret it afterwards, if you bare your life's secrets?

MISS JULIE. Are you not my friend?

JEAN. Yes—in a way. . . . But don't put too much confidence in me.

MISS JULIE. You don't mean what you say—and besides: everybody knows my secrets. You see, my mother was not an aristocrat by birth. She came of quite simple stock. She was brought up in conformity with the ideas of her generation: equality of the sexes—the emancipation of women— and all that sort of thing. She looked upon marriage with downright aversion. Therefore, when my father proposed marriage to her, she replied that she would never be his wife —but—she married him just the same. I came into the world —against my mother's wishes, as I have learned; and now I was to be reared by my mother as a child of nature and in addition was to be taught all the things a boy has to learn, all in order to prove that a woman is quite as good as any man. I had to wear boy's clothes, had to learn how to handle horses, but I was never allowed in the cattle barn. I had to groom, harness and saddle my horse and had to go hunting —yes, I even had to try my hand at farming! And the farmhands were given women's chores to do, and the women did the men's work—and the upshot of it was that the estate almost went to rack and ruin, and we became the laughingstock of the whole countryside. . . . At last my father seems to have come out of his inertia, for he rebelled; and after that all went according to his will. My mother took sick— what the sickness was I never learned—but she frequently had spasms, shut herself up in the attic, or secluded herself in the garden—and sometimes she stayed out all night. Then came the great fire which you have heard about. The house, the stables, and the cattle barns burned down, and under suspicious circumstances that pointed to arson. The disaster happened, namely, the day after the quarterly insurance period had expired; and the insurance premium, that my father had forwarded by a messenger, had arrived too late because of the messenger's negligence or indifference. (*She fills up her glass, and drinks.*)

JEAN. You mustn't drink any more!

MISS JULIE. Ah, what do I care!—We were left with nothing, and we had no place to sleep, except in the carriages.

My father was desperate; he didn't know where to get money to build again. Then my mother suggested to him that he borrow from an old friend of hers—someone she had known in her youth, a brick manufacturer not far from here. Father got the loan, and without having to pay any interest—and this was a surprise to him. And the estate was rebuilt! (*She drinks again.*) Do you know who set the place on fire?

JEAN. The Countess, your mother . . .

MISS JULIE. Do you know who the brick manufacturer was?

JEAN. Your mother's lover?

MISS JULIE. Do you know whose money it was?

JEAN. Wait a second!—No—I don't—

MISS JULIE. It was my mother's.

JEAN. In other words, your father's—the Count's—unless they had made a marriage settlement.

MISS JULIE. No, there was none. My mother had a little money of her own. She didn't want my father to have charge of it, so she—entrusted it to her friend!

JEAN. And he helped himself to it!

MISS JULIE. Precisely! He appropriated the money. All this my father came to know. He couldn't bring action against him, couldn't repay his wife's lover, couldn't prove that the money was his wife's!—That was the revenge my mother took on him because he had made himself the master in his own house. He was on the verge of committing suicide when all this happened; as a matter of fact, there was a rumor that he tried to and didn't succeed. . . . However, he took a new lease of life, and my mother had to pay the penalty for her behavior! You can imagine what the next five years did to me! I felt sorry for my father, yet I took my mother's part because I didn't know the true circumstances. She had taught me to mistrust and hate men, for she herself hated men, as I told you before—and she made me swear never to become the slave of any man . . .

JEAN. And then you became engaged to the county prosecutor!

MISS JULIE. Yes—in order to make him my slave.

JEAN. And he refused?

MISS JULIE. He would have liked it, don't worry; but I didn't give him the chance. I became bored with him . . .

JEAN. I saw that you did—out in the stableyard.

MISS JULIE. What did you see?

JEAN. Exactly what happened—how he broke off the engagement.

MISS JULIE. That's a lie! It was I who broke the engagement!—Did he tell you he did? The scoundrel!

JEAN. I wouldn't call him a scoundrel. . . . You just hate men, Miss Julie.

MISS JULIE. Yes, I do! Most men! But occasionally—when my weakness comes over me—oh, the shame of it!

JEAN. You hate me, too, don't you?

MISS JULIE. I hate you no end! I should like to have you slaughtered like an animal!

JEAN. As one shoots a mad dog, eh?

MISS JULIE. Precisely!

JEAN. But as there is nothing here to shoot with, and no dog—what are we to do?

MISS JULIE. Get away from here!

JEAN. And then torture each other to death?

MISS JULIE. No—live life for a few brief days, for a week—for as long as we can—and then—die . . .

JEAN. Die? What nonsense! No—I think it would be far better to go into the hotel business.

MISS JULIE (*who, absorbed with her thoughts, has not heard what he said*). . . . by Lake Como, where the sun is always shining—where the laurel tree is still greening at Christmas—and the oranges are golden red—

JEAN. Lake Como is a hole where it rains all the time, and I never saw any oranges there except in the grocery shops. But it's a good place for foreigners—and there are plenty of villas to be rented to lovers—and that is a business that pays! And do you know why? I'll tell you why—because they have to sign a six months' lease, and they never stay longer than three weeks!

MISS JULIE (*naïvely*). Why only three weeks?

JEAN. Because they quarrel, of course. But the rent has to be paid in full just the same. And then the house is rented out again; and that's the way it goes—on and on—for people will always be in love, although their love doesn't last very long . . .

MISS JULIE. Then you don't care to die with me, do you?

JEAN. I don't care to die at all! Not only because I like to live, but because I consider suicide a sin against God, who gave us life.

MISS JULIE. You believe in God—*you*?

JEAN. Of course I do! I go to church every other Sunday. But now—quite frankly—now I am getting tired of all this talk, and I am going to bed.

MISS JULIE. Oh, you are, are you? And you think that will be a satisfactory ending? Do you know what a man owes to a woman he has taken advantage of?

JEAN (*takes out his purse and throws a coin on the table*). There you are! Now I owe you nothing!

MISS JULIE (*pretends to ignore the insult*). Are you aware of the legal consequences?

JEAN. It's too bad that the law provides no punishment for the woman who seduces a man!

MISS JULIE. Can you think of any way out of this—other than going abroad, getting married, and being divorced?

JEAN. Suppose I refuse to enter into such a degrading marriage?

MISS JULIE. Degrading?

JEAN. Yes—for me! For, mind you, my lineage is cleaner and more respectable than yours—I have no pyromaniac in my family—

MISS JULIE. How can you be so sure of that?

JEAN. And how can you prove the opposite? We have no register of our ancestors—except in the police records! But I have seen your genealogical chart in the book on your drawing-room table. Do you know who your first ancestor was? A miller who let his wife sleep with the king one night during the Danish War!—I haven't any ancestors like that! I have no ancestry of any kind—but I can start a family tree of my own!

MISS JULIE. This is what I get for opening my heart to one like you, to an inferior . . . for betraying the honor of my family . . .

JEAN. You mean *dishonor*! . . . Well, I warned you—and now you see— People shouldn't drink, for then they start talking—and people should never be garrulous.

MISS JULIE. Oh, how I regret what I have done! How I regret it! Oh, if—at least—you had loved me!

JEAN. For the last time—what is it you want me to do? Do you want me to burst into tears? Do you want me to jump over your riding whip? Do you want me to kiss you?— to elope with you to Lake Como for three weeks?—and then. . . . What do you want me to do? What is it you want? This is getting to be intolerable! But that's what one gets for sticking one's nose into a female's business! Miss Julie—I

know you must be suffering—but I can't understand you. . . .
We have no such strange notions as you have—we don't
hate as you do! To us love is nothing but playfulness—we
play when our work is done. We haven't the whole day and
the whole night for it like you! I think you must be sick. . . .
Yes, I am sure you are!

MISS JULIE. You must treat me with kindness—you must
speak to me like a human being . . .

JEAN. Yes, if you'll behave like one! You spit on me—
but when I spit back, you object!

MISS JULIE. Oh, help me—help me! Tell me what to do—
and where to go!

JEAN. In the name of Christ, I wish I knew myself!

MISS JULIE. I have behaved like a madwoman . . . but is
there no way out of this?

JEAN. Stay here—and stop worrying! Nobody knows a
thing.

MISS JULIE. I can't! They all know—and Kristin knows—

JEAN. They know nothing—and they wouldn't believe
such a thing!

MISS JULIE (*after a moment's hesitation*). But—it might
happen again!

JEAN. Yes—it might.

MISS JULIE. And have consequences? . . .

JEAN. Consequences? . . . What have I been thinking about?
That never occurred to me!—Then there is only one thing
to do. You must leave—and immediately! If I come with
you, it would look suspicious—therefore you must go alone—
go away—it doesn't matter where.

MISS JULIE. I—alone—but where? I couldn't do it!

JEAN. You must—and before the Count gets back! If you
remain here, we both know what will happen. Having committed one mistake, it's easy to make another because the
damage has already been done. . . . With time one gets more
and more reckless—until, finally one is caught! That's why I
urge you to leave! Later on you can write to the Count and
tell him everything—except that it was I!—He would never
suspect, of course,—and I don't think he would be anxious
to know!

MISS JULIE. I'll go, if you'll come with me . . .

JEAN. Are you stark staring mad, woman? Miss Julie elop-
ing with her lackey! It would be in the newspapers before
another day had passed. The Count would never get over it!

MISS JULIE. I can't go—and I can't stay here! Can't you

help me! I am so tired, so dreadfully tired!—Order me to go! Make me move! I am no longer able to think—I can't bring myself to do anything!

JEAN. Now you see what sort of miserable creature you are, don't you? Why is your sort always so overbearing? Why do you strut with your noses in the air as if you were the lords of Creation?—Very well, then—I shall order you about! Go upstairs and get dressed, take enough money with you for traveling and then come down!

MISS JULIE (*almost in a whisper*). Come upstairs with me—

JEAN. To your room?—Now you are mad again! (*He hesitates a moment.*) No! Go immediately! (*He takes her by the hand and escorts her to the door.*)

MISS JULIE (*walking toward the door*). Why don't you speak gently to me, Jean?

JEAN. An order always sounds harsh.—Now you are beginning to find out how it feels . . .

(JULIE *leaves.* JEAN *is now alone. He gives a sigh of relief, seats himself at the table, takes out a pencil and a notebook, writes down some figures; now and then he counts aloud, all in pantomime, until* KRISTIN *enters. She is dressed for church-going; carries a white tie and a false shirt front with collar, for* JEAN.)

KRISTIN. In heaven's name—look at my kitchen! What's been going on here?

JEAN. Oh—it's Miss Julie—she brought them all inside. . . . Don't tell me you've been sleeping so soundly you didn't hear them?

KRISTIN. Yes, I slept like a log!

JEAN. And you are already dressed for church?

KRISTIN. Sure! You promised to come to communion with me today, didn't you?

JEAN. Why, of course—so I did, didn't I?—And I see you have my outfit there—let's get ready, then!

(JEAN *seats himself, and* KRISTIN *starts to put on him the dickey, collar and tie. There is a silence.*)

JEAN (*sleepily*). What is the text for today?

KRISTIN. Oh—I think it's about the beheading of John the Baptist.

JEAN. Then I imagine it's going to be a terribly long sermon!—Ouch, you are choking me!—Oh, I am so sleepy, so sleepy!

KRISTIN. Well, what have you been doing the whole night —you are all green in the face.

JEAN. I've been sitting here talking to Miss Julie. . . .

KRISTIN. She just has no decency, that one!

(*Silence.*)

JEAN. Tell me, Kristin, don't you think—

KRISTIN. What?

JEAN. Isn't it strange, after all, when you think about it— that she—

KRISTIN. What is it that's so strange?

JEAN. Everything!

(*There is a pause.*)

KRISTIN (*with a glance at the wine glasses that stand on the table, half-filled*). You haven't been drinking together, have you?

JEAN. Yes!

KRISTIN. You ought to be ashamed of yourself! Look me straight in the eye! (JEAN *affirms her suspicions.*) Can it be possible? Can it really be possible?

JEAN (*deliberates for a moment, then answers her*). Yes— that's what happened.

KRISTIN. Why! I would never have believed it! Never! Shame on you! Shame on you!

JEAN. You are not jealous of her, are you?

KRISTIN. No, not of her! If it had been Clara or Sophie— I would have scratched your eyes out! Yes—yes, that's the way I feel—and I can't tell you just why I feel that way! Oh, but this is disgusting—disgusting!

JEAN. Do you hate her for it?

KRISTIN. No—I am furious with you! It was a shameless thing to do—shameless! I pity the girl!—To tell the truth, I don't care to stay in this house any longer—I want to feel some respect for the people I work for . . .

JEAN. Why do we have to have respect for them?

KRISTIN. Well, you tell me—you who know everything! You don't want to work for people who don't behave decently, do you? Do you? . . . I think it's degrading, that's what I think . . .

JEAN. Yes—but it makes you feel good to know that they are not a bit better than we are!

KRISTIN. No—I don't look at it that way at all. If they are no better than we are—what's the use of trying to be like them—of becoming any better than we are? And think of the Count—think of him—who has had so much grief in his day! No—I won't stay here in this house any longer! . . . And with such as you!—Now—if it had been the county prosecutor—or someone who was a little bit better than you—

JEAN. What's that?

KRISTIN. That's just what I said! You may be good enough in your own way, but just the same there is a difference between high and low. . . . No—I'll never be able to get over this!—Miss Julie who was so proud—who acted so superior toward men. . . . You would never have thought that she would have let any man become intimate with her—and, least of all, with a fellow like you! She—who was about to have her poor little Diana shot just because she was running after the gatekeeper's pugdog. . . . Can you imagine it! But I won't stay here any longer—the twenty-fourth of October I quit!

JEAN. And then?

KRISTIN. Well—since you bring the matter up—it's about time you looked around for something to do, for we are going to get married just the same.

JEAN. Yes—but what kind of place am I to look for? If I marry, I couldn't get a place like this.

KRISTIN. No, I know that. But you can get a job as a janitor or porter—or try to get a position in some government bureau. The government doesn't pay much, but it's security—and, besides, the wife and children get a pension.

JEAN (*with a grimace*). That's all very good, but it doesn't exactly fit in with my plans just now to be thinking about dying for the benefit of wife and children. I must confess that my aspirations are aimed at something a little bit higher.

KRISTIN. You and your ideas, yes! But you have responsibilities, too! Try to think of them!

JEAN. Don't make me lose my temper by talking about responsibilities! I know what I have to do! (*He suddenly listens to some sound from outside.*) Anyhow, we have plenty of time to decide just what to do. Go and get ready now so we can go to church.

KRISTIN. Who can that be I hear walking upstairs?

JEAN. I've no idea—unless it's Clara.

KRISTIN (*as she is leaving*). I don't suppose it could be the Count, could it? Could he have come home without anybody hearing him?

JEAN (*panic-stricken*). The Count? Why, no—I would never think so. . . . If he had, he would have rung . . .

KRISTIN. Well, God help us. . . . I've never heard of anything like this! (*She goes out.*)

(*The sun has now risen and casts its rays on the treetops
in the park. The light beams keep moving until they fall
obliquely through the windows.* JEAN *goes over to the
door and gives a sign to* JULIE *outside.*)

MISS JULIE (*comes inside. She is dressed for travel and
carries a small birdcage, covered with a towel. She places
the cage on a chair.*) I am ready now.

JEAN. Ssh! Kristin is awake!

MISS JULIE (*from this moment on, she shows signs of extreme nervousness*). Does she suspect anything?

JEAN. Not a thing! She knows nothing!—Lord in heaven—
how you look!

MISS JULIE. Look? Why—what's the matter?

JEAN. Your face is livid! You look like a corpse . . . and
if you'll pardon me, your face is not clean!

MISS JULIE. Then I must wash my face! (*She goes over to
the sink and washes her face and hands.*) Would you give
me a towel?— Oh . . . I see the sun is rising . . .

JEAN. . . . and now the spell will be broken!

MISS JULIE. Yes, the trolls have been out this night!—But
now, Jean,—you can come with me, do you hear, for I have
all the money we need.

JEAN (*with disbelief and hesitation*). You have enough?

MISS JULIE. Enough to start with. . . . Please come with
me! I can't travel alone now. . . . Imagine my sitting alone
on a stuffy train, squeezed in among crowds of passengers
gaping at me . . . and with long stops at the stations, when I
would like to fly away on wings. . . . No—I can't do it—I
just can't do it! And then I'll be thinking of the past—memories of the midsummer days of my childhood—the church,
covered with wreaths and garlands, with leaves of birch
and with lilac—the festive dinner table—relatives and
friends—and the afternoon in the park, with music and
dancing, games and flowers. . . . Oh—no matter how one
tries to get away from the past, the memories are there,
packed into one's baggage. . . . They pursue one, hitched
onto the tail of the train . . . and then comes remorse—
and the pangs of conscience—

JEAN. I'll come with you, but let's hurry—before it's too
late! We haven't a second to lose!

MISS JULIE. Hurry up and dress! (*She picks up the birdcage.*)

JEAN. But no baggage! Then we would be found out immediately!

MISS JULIE. No, nothing . . . only what we can take with us in our compartment.

JEAN (*who has just reached for his hat, stares at the birdcage*). What's that you have there? What is it?

MISS JULIA. It's only my green siskin . . . I couldn't go without her!

JEAN. Well, of all the— Are we going to take a birdcage with us now? You must be completely out of your mind! (*He tries to take the cage from her.*) Let go of the cage!

MISS JULIE. It's the one thing I am taking with me from my home—the only living thing that loves me since Diana was faithless to me. . . . Don't be cruel! Please let me take her with me!

JEAN. Put that cage down, I tell you—and don't talk so loud! Kristin can hear us!

MISS JULIE. No—I won't part with her to anyone else! I'd rather you killed her . . .

JEAN. Give me the little beast then—I'll chop its head off!

MISS JULIE. Oh—but—don't hurt her, please!—No—I can't let you . . .

JEAN. But I can—and I know how. . . . Give it to me!

MISS JULIE (*takes the bird out of the cage. She kisses it.*) Oh, my poor little Sérine, must your mother lose you—must you die?

JEAN. Let's have no scenes—it's now a question of life and death—of your own future. . . . Quick, now! (*He snatches the bird from her, goes over to the chopping block, and picks up the axe lying on it. MISS JULIE turns away her face.*) You should have learned how to kill chickens instead of how to shoot . . . (*He lets the hatchet fall on the bird's neck.*) . . . then the sight of a little blood wouldn't make you faint!

MISS JULIE (*screams*). Let me die too! Kill me! You—who can take the life of an innocent little creature without even a tremble of the hand! Oh—how I hate you—how I loathe you! Now there is blood between us! I curse the day I was born, the day I was conceived!

JEAN. Stop cursing—it does you no good! Let's be off!

MISS JULIE (*approaches the chopping block, as if drawn to it against her will*). No—I am not ready to go yet—I can't go—I must first see . . . (*She suddenly stops. She stands listening; all the while her eyes are riveted on the chop-*

ping block and the axe.) You think I can't stand the sight of blood! You think I am such a weakling, do you?—Oh, I should like to see your blood—your brain—on the chopping block. . . . I should like to see your whole sex bathing in its own blood, like my little bird! . . . I even think I could drink out of your skull—I would revel in bathing my feet in your caved-in chest—and I could devour your heart roasted! You think I am a weakling—you think that I am in love with you because my womb felt a craving for your seed—you think that I yearn to carry your offspring under my heart, to nourish it with my blood—to bear your child and your name? Come to think of it, what is your name? I have never heard your last name—I guess you haven't any. . . . I was to be Mrs. Gatekeeper—or Mme. Refuseheap— You dog who wear my collar—you lackey with my family crest on your buttons! I was to share you with my cook—a rival of my own servant! Oh, oh, oh!—You think I am a coward and that I am anxious to flee! No—this time I am not leaving —come what may! When father returns he will find his chiffonier ransacked and the money gone! Immediately he will ring that bell—his usual two rings for you, Jean,—and he will send for the sheriff . . . and then—then I shall tell the whole story! The whole story! Oh, what a relief it will be to get it over with. . . . If only that moment were here! And father will have a stroke and die! . . . And that will be the end of our family. And then, at last, we shall be at rest—find peace—eternal peace! . . . And the family coat of arms will be broken against the coffin—the noble line will be extinct—but the lackey's line will go on in an orphanage— reaping laurels in the gutter, and ending in prison . . .

JEAN. There's your royal blood talking! Bravo, Miss Julie! And don't forget to stuff the miller's skeleton in your family closet!

(KRISTIN *enters. She is dressed for church and carries a prayer book.*)

MISS JULIE (*rushes toward her and flings herself into her arms, as if to plead for protection*). Help me, Kristin! Save me from this man!

KRISTIN (*stands cold and unmoved*). What kind of spectacle is this on the sabbath morning? (*She notices the dead bird and the blood on the chopping block.*) And what's this piggish mess you have made here?—What's the meaning of all this? And why are you screaming and making so much noise?

MISS JULIE. Kristin—you are a woman—and you are my friend! Look out for this man—he is a villain!

JEAN (*somewhat abashed and timid*). While you ladies are conversing, I am going in to shave.

(*He goes into his room, left.*)

MISS JULIE. I want you to understand me—I want you to listen to me—

KRISTIN. No—I must say I can't understand all these goings-on! Where are you planning to go—you are dressed for traveling—and Jean had his hat on. . . . Why?—What's going on?

MISS JULIE. Listen to me, Kristin! You must listen to me—and then I'll tell you everything . . .

KRISTIN. I don't care to— I don't want to know . . .

MISS JULIE. You must—you must hear . . .

KRISTIN. Just what is it—what's it all about? Is it about this foolishness with Jean, is it?—Well, I don't let that bother me a bit—it's none of my business. . . . But if you are thinking of tricking him into running away with you— then I'll soon put a stop to that!

MISS JULIE (*with extreme nervousness*). Try to be calm, Kristin, and please listen to me! I can't stay here—and Jean can't stay here—and that is why we must leave . . .

KRISTIN. H'm, h'm!

MISS JULIE (*brightening*). Oh, I know—I have an idea! Suppose the three of us—if we should go abroad—we three together—to Switzerland—and start a hotel business— I have the money, you see. . . . (*She dangles the handbag before Kristin.*) . . . and Jean and I would run the business—and I thought you could take charge of the kitchen. Don't you think that would be perfect?—Say that you will? Do come with us—then everything will be settled! Will you? Say yes! (*She puts her arms round* KRISTIN *and gives her a pat on the back.*)

KRISTIN (*coldly reflective*). H'm, h'm!

MISS JULIE (*presto tempo*). You have never been out in the world, Kristin,—you must travel and see things. You have no idea what fun it is to travel by train! Always new people, new countries! And in Hamburg we stop over and look at the Zoological Garden—you will like that . . . and when we arrive in Munich, we have the museums there—and there you'll see Rubens and Raphael and other great masters, you know. . . . You have heard of Munich, haven't you?—There is where King Ludwig lived—the king, you

know, who lost his mind. . . . And then we'll visit his
castles—his castles still are there; and they are beautiful like
the castles in the fairy tales—and from there, you see, it is
only a short distance to Switzerland—and the Alps! Think
of it, they are covered with snow in the middle of the summer
—and oranges grow there—and laurels that stay green the
year round!

(JEAN *appears from the left. While he is sharpening his
razor on a strop that he holds between his teeth and his
left hand, he is listening with evident satisfaction to
their conversation. Now and then he nods approvingly.*)

MISS JULIE (*tempo prestissimo*). And in Switzerland we'll
buy a hotel—and I'll take care of the accounts while Jean
looks after the guests—does the marketing—attends to the
correspondence. . . . It'll be a hustle and bustle, believe me.
. . . You hear the whistle of the train—the omnibus arrives
—the bells ring, from the hotel rooms and the dining-room.
—I make out the bills—and I know how to salt them, too.
. . . You can't imagine how diffident tourists are when
their bills are presented to them!—And you—you will
preside in the kitchen! You won't have to stand at the stove
yourself, of course,—and you will have to be dressed neatly
and nicely so that you can show yourself among people . . .
and with your looks—yes, I am not trying to flatter you—
with your looks, you might very well get yourself a husband
one fine day!—Some rich Englishman, why not? They
are so easy to . . . (*in a slackened pace*) . . . to capture . . .
and then we'll build ourselves a villa at the edge of Lake
Como. . . . Of course, it rains there a little occasionally,
but . . . (*Her voice fades a little.*) . . . the sun must be
shining there some time—even though the gloom seems to
persist—and—so—well, we can always return home—and
then go back again . . . (*There is a pause.*) . . . here—
or somewhere else . . .

KRISTIN. Miss Julie, do you really believe all this yourself?

MISS JULIE (*crushed*). . . . If I believe it—myself?

KRISTIN. Just that!

MISS JULIE. I don't know . . . I don't believe in anything
any more! (*She sinks down on the bench, puts her head between her hands and drops her head on the table.*) Not in
anything! Not in anything!

KRISTIN (*turning toward the left where* JEAN *is standing*).
So—o, you were going to run away, were you?

JEAN (*crestfallen and looking foolish, he lays the razor*

on the table). Run away? Well—that's a strong word to use! Miss Julie told you about her project, didn't she? Well—she is tired now after being up all night . . . but her plan can very well be carried to success!

KRISTIN. Now you listen to me! Was it your intention that I was to be cook for that one—

JEAN (*sharply*). You will be good enough to speak of your mistress in a proper manner! You understand me, don't you?

KRISTIN. Mistress, yes!

JEAN. Yes, mistress!

KRISTIN. Ha, listen—listen to him!

JEAN. Yes, that's just what *you* should do—listen—and talk a little less! Miss Julie *is* your mistress—and the very same thing that you now look down upon her for, should make you feel contempt for yourself!

KRISTIN. I always had so much respect for myself that . . .

JEAN. . . . that you felt you could show disrespect for others!

KRISTIN. . . . that I could never let myself sink beneath my level! Nobody can say that the Count's cook has had any goings-on with the stablehand, or the fellow who looks after the pigs! No—nobody can say that!

JEAN. Yes—you are lucky to have been able to catch a fine fellow like me, that's all I can say!

KRISTIN. A fine fellow, indeed,—selling the oats from the Count's stable . . .

JEAN. You should talk about that—you, who take a rake-off from the grocer and let the butcher bribe you!

KRISTIN. I don't know what you mean . . .

JEAN. And you—you can't have any respect for the family you are working for! You—you—you!

KRISTIN. Are you coming with me to church now? You could stand a good sermon after your great triumph!

JEAN. No, I am not going to church today. . . . You have to go alone and confess your *own* exploits!

KRISTIN. Yes—that's what I intend to do, and I'll come back with enough forgiveness for us both! The Saviour suffered and died on the Cross for all our sins; and if we come to Him with faith and repentence in our hearts, He will take all our trespasses upon Himself.

JEAN. Including petty grocery frauds?

JULIE (*who suddenly lifts her head*). Do you believe that, Kristin?

KRISTIN. That is my living faith, as sure as I stand here.

It is the faith that was born in me as a child and that I have kept ever since, Miss Julie. . . . And where sin abounds, grace abounds much more . . .

MISS JULIE. Oh—if I only had your trusting faith! Oh, if I . . .

KRISTIN. Yes, but you see you can't have faith without God's special grace—and it is not given to all to receive that.

MISS JULIE. To whom is it given then?

KRISTIN. That, Miss Julie, is the great secret of the gift of grace . . . and God is no respecter of persons: in His Kingdom the last shall be first . . .

MISS JULIE. Well—but in that case He shows preference for the last, doesn't He?

KRISTIN (continues). . . . and it is easier for a camel to go through the eye of a needle than for a rich man to enter the Kingdom of Heaven. You see, Miss Julie, that is the way it is!—But now I am going—alone—and on my way I'll stop and tell the stableman not to let out any of the horses to anybody . . . just in case anybody'd like to get away before the Count returns!—Goodbye! (She goes out.)

JEAN. What a bitch!—And all this just because of a green siskin!

MISS JULIE (apathetically). Never mind the siskin!—Can you see any way out of this? Any way to end it?

JEAN (thinking hard). No—I can't.

MISS JULIE. If you were in my place—what would you do?

JEAN. In your place? Let me think!—As a woman—of noble birth—who has fallen . . . I don't know. . . . Yes—now I think I know—

MISS JULIE (picks up the razor and makes a telling gesture). This, you mean?

JEAN. Yes . . . but I would never do it! Not I—for there is a difference between us two!

MISS JULIE. You mean—because you are a man and I a woman? What, then, is the difference?

JEAN. The same difference—as—between man and woman—

MISS JULIE (with the razor in her hand). I want to do it . . . but I can't!—My father couldn't either—that time when he ought to have done it . . .

JEAN. No—he ought not to have done it! He had to take his revenge first!

Miss Julie. And now my mother gets her revenge once more—through me!

Jean. Did you ever love your father, Miss Julie? Did you?

Miss Julie. Yes, I did—immensely—but, at the same time, I think I must have hated him. . . . I must have done so without being conscious of it! It was he who brought me up to look with contempt upon my own sex—to be part woman and part man! Who is to be blamed for the consequences? My father, my mother, or myself? Myself? Am I then really myself? There is nothing I can call my own; I haven't a thought that wasn't instilled in me by my father—not a passion that I didn't inherit from my mother . . . and that last notion of mine—the idea that all people are equal— that came from him, my fiancé . . . and that is why I call him a mischief-maker, a scoundrel! How can I possibly be to blame? To put the burden of blame on Jesus Christ as Kristin did just now—for that I have too much pride and too much sense, thanks to what my father taught me. . . . And as for the idea that a rich man may not enter Heaven —that's a lie; and Kristin, who has put her savings in the bank, won't get there either, for that matter! Now—who is to blame?—What does it matter who is to blame? After all, it is I who have to bear the burden of guilt and suffer the consequences. . . .

Jean. Yes—but . . . (Two abrupt rings interrupt him. Miss Julie jumps to her feet; Jean quickly changes his coat.) The Count is back! What if Kristin . . . (He goes over to the speaking tube and listens.)

Miss Julie. Could he have been to the chiffonier already?

Jean. Yes, sir—this is Jean. (He listens. The Count's voice is not heard by the audience.) Yes, sir.—Yes, sir. Immediately!—At once, sir!—Yes, sir. In half an hour!

Miss Julie (in extreme agitation). What did he say? For God's sake—what did he say?

Jean. He asked for his boots and his coffee in half an hour.

Miss Julie. Half an hour, then! . . . Oh, I am so tired—I have no strength to do anything—not even to feel repentant—or to get away from here—or to stay here—to live—or to die! . . . Help me, please! Order me to do something—and I'll obey like a dog. . . . Do me this last service! Save my honor—save his good name! You know what I would like to have the will to do—yet don't like to do. . . . Use your willpower on me—and make me do it!

JEAN. I don't know why—but now *I* haven't any willpower either. I can't understand it. . . . It's just as if wearing this coat made it impossible for me to—to give orders to you; and now, after the Count spoke to me, I—well, I—I just can't explain it—but—well, it's the damned menial in me . . . and if the Count should come in here this very minute, and he should order me to cut my throat, I believe I'd do it without the slightest hesitation!

MISS JULIE. Can't you make believe that you are he, and that I am you! You did a good piece of acting just now when you were on your knees—then you acted the nobleman—or, perhaps, you have seen a hypnotist when you've been to the theatre? (JEAN *gives an affirmative nod.*) He tells his subject: "Pick up that broom!"—and he picks it up; he tells him to sweep—and he starts to sweep . . .

JEAN. But he must put his subject to sleep first . . .

MISS JULIE (*ecstatically*). I am already asleep—the whole room is like a cloud of dust and smoke before me—and you look like a tall stove—and the stove looks like a man in black with a top hat—your eyes glow like embers in a fire-place—and your face is merely a patch of white ash . . . (*The sun's rays are now falling across the room and shine on* JEAN.) . . . It's so pleasantly warm . . . (*She rubs her hands together as if she were warming them by the fire.*) And how bright it is—and so peaceful!

JEAN (*takes the razor and places it in her hand*). Here is the broom! Walk outside now while it's still light—out into the barn—and . . . (*He whispers in her ear.*)

MISS JULIE (*awake*). Thank you! I'm going—to find rest. . . . But before I go, tell me—that even those who are among the first, can receive the gift of grace. Please tell me that— even if you do not believe it!

JEAN. Among the first? No—that's something I cannot do. . . . But wait, Miss Julie. . . . Now I know the answer! Since you no longer are one of the first—you must be—among the last!

MISS JULIE. You are right!—I am among the—very last —I am the last! Oh!—But something holds me back again. . . . Tell me once again to go!

JEAN. No—I can't tell you again—I can't—

MISS JULIE. And the first shall be the last . . .

JEAN. Stop thinking—stop thinking! You are robbing me of all my strength—you are making me a coward. . . . What's that? I thought I heard the bell! No—but let's stuff it with paper. . . . Imagine, to be so afraid of a bell! Yes—but it isn't merely a bell—there is someone behind it—a hand that sets it in motion—and something else sets the hand in motion —but you can stop your ears—stop your ears—and then— yes, then it keeps ringing louder than ever—keeps ringing until you answer—and then—it's too late! And then the sheriff appears on the scene—and then . . .

(*Two peremptory rings from the bell.*)

JEAN (*quails; then he straightens himself*). It's horrible! But it's the only way to end it!—Go!

(MISS JULIE, *with the razor in her hand, walks firmly out through the door.*)

COMRADES
A COMEDY IN FOUR ACTS

Comrades (*Kamraterna*), Strindberg's satire on the emancipation of women, was started in 1886 as a five-act work under the title of *Marauders* (*Marodörer*). His domestic tensions intruding into this comedy, Strindberg darkened its humor. Revised about a year later in collaboration with the young Swedish author Axel Lundegård, the work acquired a happy ending with a reconciliation between husband and wife. But in the final form written by Strindberg alone under the ironic title of *Comrades,* the play (published in Helsingborg by Hans Österling, in 1888) became a virtual reproof of the modern ideal of the equality of the sexes or of equal opportunities for men and women. Marriages founded artificially on this principle, according to Strindberg, are doomed to failure, for the wife becomes the husband's rival while at the same time arrogating to herself the time-honored prerogatives of woman. Greedy for success and power and lacking the man's chivalrous principles and sense of fair play, the woman becomes ruthless and overbearing. She uses her new-found opportunity to humiliate and subjugate the man. A marriage founded upon the impossible base of "comradeship" cannot last.

The motives for writing the play were rooted in his own marital conflicts with Siri von Essen, who could not give vent to her ambition to become an actress while still married to her first husband, Baron Carl Gustaf Wrangel, a Captain in the Swedish Guards; her husband's position made it impossible for her to perform in public. When she married Strindberg on December 31, 1877 there were no longer any impediments to realizing her talents and Strindberg, as an artist and liberal, at first encouraged her to become an actress. Although not extraordinarily gifted, she made her debut at the Royal Theatre on January 27, 1877 and became attached to this Swedish national acting company for four years. Strindberg coached her in her parts and wrote plays with roles intended for her. For some five years their marriage was reasonably happy, but as Siri succumbed more and more to her ambitions and to her desire to shine in bohemian circles Strindberg grew increasingly irritated and became doubtful of her fidelity. Quarrels broke out, separations and reconciliations played havoc with their marriage, and their once cherished ideal of a partnership between two artists collapsed.

Comrades was first produced professionally in Vienna, in 1905, at the *Lustspieltheater*. It did not have a production in Strindberg's native Sweden until he presented the play himself at his Intimate Theatre (*Intima Teatern*) in Stockholm in 1910. It was first staged in New York in a German translation in 1917, at the Irving Place Theatre, where the part of the husband Axel was played by Rudolf Christians, the actor-father of the late Mady Christians. The comedy, which has been performed in many European countries, was filmed in Germany in 1919 with Strindberg's third wife Harriet Bosse in the leading part of the wife Bertha.

PERSONS IN THE PLAY

Axel Alberg, a painter
Bertha Alberg, née Ålund, his wife; also a painter
Abel, a friend of theirs
Willmer (Gaga), a writer
Doctor Östermark
Mrs. Hall, formerly married to Dr. Östermark
Amélie Hall } her daughters by a late marriage
Thérèse Hall
Lieutenant Carl Starck
Mrs. Starck, his wife
The Maid
A male model
Two moving-men

ACT I

(THE SETTING.—*An artist's studio in Paris, on the first floor. The room has glass doors leading to a garden; in the rear, a large studio window, also a door that leads to the vestibule. Hangings, armor, costumes, sketches and plaster of Paris figures and plaques, etc., on the walls. On the left, a door to* AXEL'S *room. On the right, a door to* BERTHA'S *room. In the center of the room, somewhat to the right, a platform used for models. To the left, an easel with accessories. A sofa. A large parlor stove with transparent isinglass doors through which the burning coal can be seen. A lamp hangs from the ceiling.*

The time is in the late eighteen-eighties.)

AXEL (*is seated, painting a canvas on an easel*). So you, too, have come to Paris?

THE DOCTOR. Everything gravitates to Paris—as to the center of the universe. And so you are married? And happy?

AXEL. Oh, so–so. . . . Yes, I am fairly happy—that is to say—

THE DOCTOR. What?

AXEL. Tell me . . . You tell me you are a widower. Consequently you have been married. How was married life?

THE DOCTOR. Excellent—for her.

AXEL. And for you?

THE DOCTOR. *Comme ci, comme ça.* But you understand, one has to compromise. And that's what we always did—as long as we could.

AXEL. Just how did you do it?

THE DOCTOR. Why—I gave in!

AXEL. You?

THE DOCTOR. Yes. You would never have believed it of a man like me, would you?

AXEL. No, I never would!—But tell me—you don't put much faith in women, do you?

THE DOCTOR. No, indeed! I put no faith in them! But I love them!

AXEL. In your own particular way, yes!

THE DOCTOR. Yes—in my own particular way! How do you love your wife?

AXEL. Well, you see, we have made an arrangement between ourselves to be as two comrades; and friendship is both finer and more enduring than love.

THE DOCTOR. H'm.—So Bertha paints also? Does she paint well?

AXEL. Passably.

THE DOCTOR. We used to be good friends once, she and I . . . of course we quarreled a little. . . . Ah, you have some visitors coming.—Well, if it isn't Carl and his wife—

AXEL (*jumps up from his seat*). And Bertha isn't at home! *Sacristi!* (LIEUTENANT CARL STARCK *and his wife enter.*) Ah! Welcome! This seems to be the meeting-place of people from all corners of the earth. How do you do, Mrs. Starck! You seem fit after your journey.

MRS. STARCK. Thank you, Axel dear, it has been a genuine pleasure trip for us! But where is Bertha?

CARL. Yes, where is your little wife?

AXEL. She is at the *Académie Julien,* but I expect her home any minute. Won't you sit down?

(THE DOCTOR *greets* LIEUTENANT *and* MRS. STARCK.)

CARL. Not now, thank you. We simply wanted to drop in for a minute and see how you had it here. But we will be here next Saturday, the first of May.

AXEL. Of course. So you received the card with our invitation, then?

MRS. STARCK. Yes, it caught up with us in Hamburg.— And—what is Bertha doing these days?

AXEL. Well, she paints—she as I. We are just waiting for her model to arrive. So I think . . . I can't ask you to stay, to be quite frank . . .

CARL. You don't think we are bashful, do you?

MRS. STARCK (*hesitantly*). It is not one of those models that—that undresses?

AXEL. Why, yes.

CARL. A man! Hell, no!—No, that's one thing I won't let my wife in for! Alone with a naked man, ha!

AXEL. You still have your prejudices, haven't you, Carl?

CARL. Well, I must say—

MRS. STARCK. For shame!

THE DOCTOR. Yes, and I say the same!

AXEL. Well, I can't say it's exactly to my taste, but as long as I must have a female model, why—

MRS. STARCK. Oh, a female—why, that's different—

AXEL. Different?

MRS. STARCK. Yes—that *is* a different thing. Even if there is a similarity between the two, there *is* a difference.

(*There is a knock at the door.*)

AXEL. There he is!

MRS STARCK. Then we are going! So—goodbye, then, and *au revoir!* Give my very best regards to Bertha!

AXEL. Goodbye, then—since you are so timid. . . . And *au revoir!*

CARL AND THE DOCTOR. Goodbye, Axel!

CARL (*to* AXEL). At least, *you* intend to stay in here, too, don't you?

AXEL. No. Why do you ask?

CARL (*leaves, shaking his head*). Ugh!

AXEL (*alone, he continues painting. Then there is another knock at the door.*) Come in! (THE MODEL *enters.*) So, you are back again? My wife hasn't come yet.

THE MODEL. But it will soon be twelve o'clock, and I have another appointment elsewhere.

AXEL. Well, well!—Yes, it's too bad, but—h'm—I can only think something must have happened at the academy to prevent her from— How much does she pay you?

THE MODEL. Five francs, as usual.

AXEL (*takes out his wallet and gives him a bill*). Here you are! But you can wait a few minutes at least, can't you?

THE MODEL. Why yes, if you want me to.

AXEL. Yes, you may as well. Sit down a moment. (THE MODEL *goes behind the screen.* AXEL *is alone on the stage. He whistles while he paints. Then* BERTHA *appears.*) Well, how do you do, my dear! You came at last!

BERTHA. At last!

AXEL. And your model is waiting for you!

BERTHA. Oh no! Has he been here again?

AXEL. You had asked him to come at eleven.

BERTHA. Had I? Why, no! Is that what he said?

AXEL. Yes, but didn't you engage him for yesterday also?

BERTHA. Perhaps I did—but, in any case, the professor

would not let us off. You know how it is when the term is about to end . . . one is a little anxious. I hope you are not angry with me, Axel?

AXEL. Angry? No—but this is the second time it has happened; and he charges five francs—in this case, for nothing!

BERTHA. Am I to blame if the professor refuses to let us off, am I? Why must you always scold me? I have never—

AXEL. Have I scolded you?

BERTHA. What do you mean? Haven't you—

AXEL. Well, well, well—I have been nagging at you, of course! Forgive me—forgive me for thinking it was your fault!

BERTHA. Well, then, that's over with! But how did you pay him—did you pay him?

AXEL. Oh yes, I forgot—Gaga returned the twenty francs he borrowed from me.

BERTHA (goes to fetch a household ledger). Oh so! He paid back the loan. Well, then I'll enter it in the ledger. Just to keep the accounts straight. The money is yours, so you can do what you please with it, of course; but as you have left it to me to look after our finances, why— (She writes.) "Received: fifteen francs; paid out to model: five francs."—Now that's done!

AXEL. Oh but you should have put: twenty francs received.

BERTHA. Yes, but there is only fifteen here.

AXEL. Yes, but I did receive twenty.

BERTHA. Yes, but there is only fifteen here on the table. Can you deny that?

AXEL. No—no, I am not saying there isn't. There is fifteen francs lying on the table. And there is—

BERTHA. Why must you always quarrel?

AXEL. Have I—? Your model is waiting—

BERTHA. Oh, is he? Will you help me to arrange things . . . please!

AXEL (arranges the platform; then he calls to the model behind the screen). Have you disrobed yet?

THE MODEL (from behind the screen). In just a second, Monsieur!

BERTHA (closes the door; then she puts some wood in the parlor stove.) There! Now you have to go out!

AXEL (lingering). Bertha!

BERTHA. Yes.

AXEL. Is it absolutely necessary—this—with a nude model?

BERTHA. Yes, it is.

AXEL. H'm! Oh!

BERTHA. I thought we thrashed that argument out long ago.

AXEL. So we did. But I can't help thinking it's abominable just the same.   (*He goes out, left.*)

BERTHA (*takes up a paintbrush and palette. Then she calls to* THE MODEL *behind the screen.*) Are you ready?

THE MODEL. I am ready.

BERTHA. Then let us start! (*There is a pause.*) Let us start! (*There is a knock at the door.*) Who is it? I have a model here.

ABEL (*from outside*). It is I—Abel! I bring you news from the Salon!

BERTHA. From the Salon! (*To* THE MODEL.) Put on your clothes! We have to postpone our séance!—Axel! Abel is here with news from the Salon!

(AXEL *comes in and* BERTHA *opens the door for* ABEL *and* WILLMER.)

WILLMER. How do you do, good friends! Tomorrow the jury goes to work! Here, Bertha,—here are your pastel colors. (*He takes out a parcel from his pocket.*)

BERTHA. Thank you, Gaga dear. How much did they cost? I imagine they cost quite a lot!

WILLMER. Oh no, nothing worth mentioning.

BERTHA. So—o? They are starting judging tomorrow. . . . Did you hear that, Axel?

AXEL. I heard, my dear!

BERTHA. Would you like to do me a really big favor, Axel? Would you?

AXEL. I always want to do whatever I can for you, my dear.

BERTHA. You really would? Well, then,—you know Roubey, don't you?

AXEL. Yes, I met him in Vienna and we became what is called good friends.

BERTHA. You know he is on the jury, don't you?

AXEL. Well—what of it?

BERTHA. I know you will be angry now. . . . I know you will . . .

AXEL. So you know that? Well, then, don't make me angry.

BERTHA (*caressing him*). You wouldn't make any sacrifice for your wife, would you?

AXEL. I wouldn't go begging—no, that I wouldn't.

BERTHA. I don't mean for yourself—you will have no trouble getting in, I don't think . . . but for your wife.

AXEL. Don't ask me, please!

BERTHA. I ought never to ask you for anything!

AXEL. Yes—things I can do for you—without sacrificing . . .

BERTHA. Your manly pride!

AXEL. You may call it that.

BERTHA. But I—I would sacrifice my pride as a woman if I could do anything to help you.

AXEL. You women *have* no pride.

BERTHA. Axel!

AXEL. I beg your pardon, I beg your pardon!

BERTHA. I have a distinct feeling you are jealous of me! I am sure you wouldn't like to see one of my paintings accepted at the Salon.

AXEL. Nothing would make me happier than to see your work accepted at the Salon.

BERTHA. But would it also make you happy if *my* work were accepted, and *yours* refused?

AXEL. That's something I would have to think about twice. (*He places his right hand over his heart.*) I am quite sure it would give me an uncomfortable feeling! I am certain it would! Not only because I am a better painter than you are, but because—

BERTHA. Speak out! Because I am a woman!

AXEL. Yes, that too. It's curious—but I have a feeling that you would be trespassing, that you would sit warming yourself at the stove and then step in and pillage after the battle was over. . . . Forgive me for telling you this, Bertha—but that is the way my thoughts run.

BERTHA. Do you see now that you are not any different from the rest of your sex, not at all different!

AXEL. Not different from the rest, eh? Let us hope so!

BERTHA. And lately you have become so superior. You never used to be like that.

AXEL. I suppose it is because I *am* superior! If you women want to do something, do something which we men have not done before!

BERTHA. What? What's that you say? Have you no shame?

WILLMER. Now, now, my dear friends!—Oh but, for

heaven's sake . . . Bertha, don't get so excited! (*He gives her a glance which she tries to interpret.*)

BERTHA (*with a change of attitude*). Axel, let us be friends! And just listen to me for a moment! Do you think my position in your house—for it *is* yours—is a pleasant one? You pay for my subsistence, for my lessons at *Académie Julien* —while you yourself can't afford to take any lessons. Do you think I can endure to see how you wear out your talent and yourself by doing these drawings, only occasionally getting an opportunity to paint? You haven't even been able to afford using a model, yet you have been paying for mine, at no less than five francs an hour. You yourself are not aware of how good, how noble, how sacrificing you are; but at the same time you have no idea how I suffer when I see you wearing yourself out for me. Oh, Axel, you can't conceive of how I feel in my position. What am I to you? In what capacity am I in this house? Oh, I blush when I think of it!

AXEL. Why, what—what. . . . Aren't you my wife?

BERTHA. Yes, but—

AXEL. Well? . . . Well?

BERTHA. But—but you are keeping me!

AXEL. Well, do you think I shouldn't?

BERTHA. Why, yes—that used to be the way—in marriages of the past. But we were not going to have it that way. We were going to be comrades.

AXEL. What nonsense is this? Shouldn't the husband take care of his wife?

BERTHA. I don't want it that way! And you, Axel, must help me. I am not your equal as long as we have it the way it is now. But I *could* be your equal if you would humble yourself for once—one single time! You wouldn't be the only one to go to a member of the jury and speak a good word for someone else. If you did it for yourself, it would be a different thing—but it is for me, for me! . . . Now I am going to ask you again—and as nicely as I can. Raise me up from my inferior position, raise me to your level and I shall be grateful to you, I shall never again annoy you by reminding you of my position, Axel,—never!

AXEL. Don't ask it of me, please! You know how weak I am!

BERTHA (*embracing him*). Yes, I *shall* ask you—I shall ask you until you grant me my wish! Oh, now, don't act so proud—be human! There, now! (*She kisses him.*)

AXEL (*to* WILLMER). What do you say, Gaga? Don't you think women are terrible tyrants?

WILLMER (*uncomfortable*). Yes, especially when they are submissive!

BERTHA. Well, now,—are the skies bright again? You *will* do it, Axel, won't you? And now—put on your black coat— and then, when you come home, we'll all go out and have dinner.

AXEL. How can you be sure that Roubey will be at home and that he will see me?

BERTHA. Don't you think I have made sure of that?

AXEL. Oh, you certainly are full of intrigue, Bertha!

BERTHA (*goes over to the closet and takes out a black cut-away*). Oh, but one *has* to be, if one wants to get any-where. See, here you have your black cutaway! There now!

AXEL. But this is horrible! What am I to tell the man?

BERTHA. H'm. You ought to be able to invent something to say to him on your way there. Tell him that your wife . . . no—tell him you are expecting—a christening—soon—

AXEL. Aren't you ashamed, Bertha?

BERTHA. Well, then—tell him you can get him a decora-tion!

AXEL. Why, you shock me, Bertha.

BERTHA. Then say whatever you like! Come here now and let me fix your hair so that you look presentable. Do you know his wife?

AXEL. I never met her.

BERTHA (*brushes his hair briskly into a bang*). Then you must get to know her. I am told she has a great deal of in-fluence; but she doesn't care for women.

AXEL. What are you doing with my hair?

BERTHA. I am fixing it the way gentlemen wear it today.

AXEL. But I don't want to look like that!

BERTHA. There now! You look perfect! Now do as I tell you!

(*She goes to the chiffonier and takes out a small box con-taining the Russian Order of St. Anne. She tries to at-tach it to his lapel, but he rebels.*)

AXEL. No, Bertha, now you are going too far! I never wear any decoration.

BERTHA. But you accepted it, didn't you?

AXEL. Yes, I couldn't very well return it. . . . But I never wear it.

BERTHA. Do you belong to any political party which is so radical that it forbids an individual from accepting a decoration?

AXEL. No, I do not, but I belong to a circle of friends who have promised one another not to show off our individual merits on our sleeves.

BERTHA. But who nevertheless have accepted medals from the Salon!

AXEL. Which are not worn on our coats!

BERTHA. What do you say about it, Gaga?

WILLMER. As long as decorations for merit exist, you would be doing yourself a disservice by going about stigmatized without one. Not many would want to do that. As far as I am concerned, they can do away with decorations; but I can't take them away from those who feel differently.

AXEL. Yes, but when my comrades—who are more deserving than I am—fail to be honored, then I belittle them by wearing my ribbon.

BERTHA. But the decoration is not seen under the overcoat; and, not being seen, no one will know—and you have stigmatized no one.

WILLMER. Bertha is right. You wear your order under the outside coat; consequently you don't display it to everyone.

AXEL. You talk like Jesuits! If one gives you a finger, you will soon take the whole arm.

(ABEL enters, dressed in a fur coat and fur cap.)

BERTHA. There is Abel now! Come, Abel, and sit as judge in this controversy!

ABEL. How do you do, Bertha. How do you do, Axel. And how are you, Gaga? What is the argument about?

BERTHA. Axel does not want to wear his decoration because he does not wish to hurt his fellow artists' feelings.

ABEL. Naturally a comrade's feelings have to be considered before one's wife's—that is a natural law among the many, of course. (She seats herself at a table, takes a pouch of tobacco from her pocket and starts to roll herself a cigarette.)

BERTHA (fastens the ribbon in the buttonhole of AXEL's cutaway and puts the decoration itself back in the box). He can do me a favor without hurting anyone—yet it looks to me as if he would rather do me harm.

AXEL. Bertha, Bertha! You all make me completely mad.

. . . Of course, I don't consider it a crime to wear that ribbon, and I have never sworn not to wear it; but it has
been one of our tenets that it is unsportsmanlike to use it
to further one's own way.

BERTHA. Not manly, I take it! But you are not going on an
errand for yourself this time; you are going on an errand for
me.

ABEL. You have a representative duty, Axel, to the woman
who has offered you her life!

AXEL. I feel instinctively that what you are saying is false,
though I haven't time to think out an answer. But there *is*
an answer! It is as if you were casting nets about me while
I am sitting engrossed in my work. I feel the net being
spread, and my foot gets tangled when I want to kick it
aside. But you just wait until I have my hands free; then
I will get my knife out and cut your net to pieces.—What
was it we were talking about? Oh yes, I was to pay someone
a visit. Well, then—let me have my gloves and my overcoat! Goodbye, Bertha! Goodbye!—Oh, I forgot—where does
Roubey live?

WILLMER, ABEL and BERTHA (*in chorus*). Sixty-five Rue
des Martyrs!

AXEL. Why, that's right close by!

BERTHA. It's just on the corner! Thank you, Axel, for going! Well, does the sacrifice seem such a heavy one?

AXEL. All I can say is that I am tired of all your talk and
that it will be a relief to get out in the fresh air. Goodbye!
(*He leaves.*)

ABEL. I feel sorry for Axel! I really do.—You didn't know
he has been refused by the Salon? . . .

BERTHA. How about me?

ABEL. Your fate hasn't been decided. They haven't come
to you yet because you were entered under your own name,
spelled in the French way with an 'O'.

BERTHA. Then there is still hope for me!

ABEL. For you, yes—but none for Axel.

WILLMER. Now there will be a scene!

BERTHA. How do you know that he has been refused?

ABEL. H'm. I met someone who should know, and he
told me. And when I came here, I was a little afraid that I
would be witnessing a scene. But evidently he has not received word yet.

BERTHA. No, not as far as I know. But, Abel, are you absolutely certain that Axel will see Mme. Roubey and not Monsieur Roubey?

ABEL. Why should he go to see Monsieur Roubey? He has nothing whatever to say, while, on the other hand, Mme. Roubey is chairman of the Women Painters' Protective Association.

BERTHA. So—I am not refused—not yet!

ABEL. No, as you just heard, and Axel's visit may do a great deal of good. He has a Russian decoration, and Russia is very popular at present in France. Just the same, I feel sorry for Axel.

BERTHA. Sorry! Why feel sorry? There isn't room for everybody's paintings on the walls at the Salon. And so many women are constantly being refused that a man should be given a taste of how it feels. But you may be sure that if I should be accepted, we shall no doubt hear that *he* has painted my canvas—that *he* has taught me—or that he has paid for my lessons. But as it isn't true, I am not going to pay the slightest attention to it.

WILLMER. Now we will be seeing something we don't see every day!

BERTHA. No, I believe—that is, if I should not be refused —that we shall be seeing something quite ordinary. Nevertheless I can't help having a certain dread if that moment should come. Something tells me that from then on things will never be the same between Axel and me.

ABEL. And I thought it was just then that things would be perfect—when you two were on equal terms.

WILLMER. It seems to me your mutual position will be better defined and your own much more pleasant when you begin to sell your pictures and are able to take care of yourself.

BERTHA. It ought to be! But we'll see! We'll see!

(THE MAID *enters. She hands* BERTHA *a green envelope, and exits.*)

BERTHA. There it is! A green letter—addressed to Axel! He has been refused! Ah, but this is terrible! Nevertheless, it is a consolation for me in case I should have the same bad luck!

ABEL. But suppose you are lucky? (BERTHA *does not answer.*) You have nothing to say to that?

BERTHA. No—I have nothing to say to that!

ABEL. Because in that case your equality would be thrown out of balance and you would be superior to him!

BERTHA. Superior? A wife having superiority over her husband! Oh!

WILLMER. It's about time that an example be set!

ABEL (*to* BERTHA). You attended the breakfast this morning, didn't you? Did you find it interesting?

BERTHA. Oh—yes.

WILLMER (*to* ABEL). But when are you going to review my book, Abel?

ABEL. I am just now in the throes of writing my criticism.

WILLMER. And it will be a favorable one, I trust?

ABEL. Very much so!—Well, Bertha, how and when do you intend to deliver the letter to Axel?

BERTHA. That's just what I am thinking about. If Axel should not have been able to see Mme. Roubey by this time and if he has not already interceded for me, he is not likely to do so now, after receiving this blow.

ABEL (*gets up*). I don't think Axel could be so unprincipled as to take revenge on you—

BERTHA. Just what does it mean to be conscionable or unconscionable? Why do you think he went where I sent him just now?—Why, because I am his wife. He would never have gone for anyone else.

ABEL. But if he had done it for someone else—would you have liked it? Would you?

BERTHA. Now you have to leave—before he returns. Goodbye!

ABEL. Exactly what I intended to do! Goodbye, Bertha!

BERTHA. Yes, now you must go! Goodbye! Both of you!

THE MAID. (*enters. She announces:*) Mrs. Hall.

BERTHA. Mrs. Hall? Who can that be? (THE MAID *leaves.*)

ABEL and WILLMER. Goodbye, Bertha!   (*They leave.*)

MRS. HALL (*enters. She is flashily but carelessly dressed and has the appearance of an adventuress.*) I don't know whether I have the honor of being known to you. . . . You are Mrs. Alberg, née Ålund, are you not?

BERTHA. Yes, that's right. Won't you sit down?

MRS. HALL. My name is Hall. Oh, my God, I am so tired. I have been running up and down so many stairs. (*Gasping for breath.*) Oh, oh, yes, yes! I think I am about to faint!

BERTHA. Is there anything I can do for you?

MRS. HALL. You know a doctor by the name of Östermark, don't you?

BERTHA. Why, yes—he is an old friend of mine.

MRS. HALL. An old friend of yours, yes! Yes! You see, dear Mrs. Alberg, I was married to him once, but we were divorced. I am a divorced wife!

BERTHA. Oh! He never told me that!

MRS. HALL. No, one doesn't talk about such things.

BERTHA. He told me he was a widower.

MRS. HALL. Oh well, you were a young girl when it happened, and I imagine he is not very anxious for it to be known.

BERTHA. Just think—and I always thought that Dr. Östermark was such an honorable man.

MRS. HALL. Well, he is the right one to be called that! He is a very, *very* fine gentleman, I can tell you!

BERTHA. Yes—but why do you come here to tell me all this?

MRS. HALL. Oh, just wait, dear Mrs. Alberg,—just wait, and you will soon understand. You are a member of our society, are you not?

BERTHA. I am—certainly.

MRS. HALL. I was sure you were!—Now you just wait!

BERTHA. Did you have a child by him?

MRS. HALL. Two—two children, both girls, Mrs. Ålund.

BERTHA. That makes quite a difference! And he left you without support, did he?

MRS. HALL. Just wait a moment! He gave me a paltry sum each year to subsist on. It wasn't even enough to pay the rent with! And now that the girls have grown up and are ready to step out into life—now he writes me that he is ruined and therefore can't send me more than half the amount. Isn't that something? Now—just now, when the girls are grown up and about to step out into life . . .

BERTHA. This we must do something about! He will be coming to see us in a few days. You know, of course, Mrs. Hall, that you have the law on your side and that the courts can compel him to pay up? And he shall be compelled to do it! Do you hear! So—o, men think they can bring children into the world and then abandon them, cast out both them and the mother! Oh! He will find out!—Let me have your address, will you?

MRS. HALL (*hands* BERTHA *her visiting card*). Dear Mrs. Alberg, you will not be offended if I should ask you to do me a small favor, would you?

BERTHA. You can depend on me in every way. I shall write to the secretary immediately.

MRS. HALL. Oh, you are so infinitely kind, but before the secretary will have time to answer, I and my poor, impoverished children may have been thrown out in the street. Dear Mrs. Alberg, would it be possible for you to lend me a small amount—let us say, twenty francs?

BERTHA. No, Mrs. Hall, I haven't any money at all. For the present I am dependent upon my husband for all my needs. And don't think I will ever hear the end of it! It is hard to have to subsist on charity when you are young . . . but perhaps better days are coming for me, too.

MRS. HALL. Oh, dear, dear Mrs. Alberg, you must not refuse me! If you do, I'll be a lost soul. For heaven's sake, help me!

BERTHA. Are you in such great and dire need?

MRS. HALL. And you ask me that?

BERTHA. I'll give you what money I have—as a loan— (*She goes over to the chiffonier.*) Twenty—forty—sixty— eighty— There is twenty missing here. . . . What can I have done with that? H'm. The breakfast meeting! (*She makes a notation in the household ledger.*) Paint: twenty; diverse: twenty.—There!

MRS. HALL. Oh, thank you, dear Mrs. Ålund! Thank you!

BERTHA. Well—now I can't give you any more of my time today. Goodbye—and you can depend on me!

MRS. HALL (*with some hesitation*). Just one more thing!

BERTHA. No, now you must go!

MRS. HALL. Just one moment! What was it I wanted to say . . . ?—Oh well, it doesn't matter!   (*She goes out.*)

(BERTHA *is alone on the stage for a few moments. Then* AXEL *enters.* BERTHA *quickly hides the green letter in her pocket as soon as she hears his steps.*)

BERTHA. Back so soon? And did you see her—or him?

AXEL. I didn't see him, but I saw her. And it was a good thing I did. I congratulate you, Bertha! Your painting has been accepted!

BERTHA. Oh, really! You don't say so? And how about your own?

AXEL. Nothing has been decided yet, but unquestionably mine will be accepted also.

BERTHA. You really think so, do you?

AXEL. Of course.

BERTHA. Oh, I am accepted! What joy! What joy!—Oh, but why don't you congratulate me?

AXEL. I already did, didn't I? I thought I said just those

words: I congratulate you!—Besides, one should never dispose of the skin until after the bear has been shot. To be accepted by the Salon is easy enough. It is merely a piece of luck. It may depend on what letter your name begins with. Your name was listed under *O* because that letter is nearest in sound to the Swedish Å and as they began with the letter *M* today, you were closer at hand.

BERTHA. And so you mean to say it was because my name begins with an *O* that I was accepted?

AXEL. Not entirely for that reason.

BERTHA. Well, then, if you are refused, I suppose it will be because your name begins with an *A*?

AXEL. Not only because of that but it might be one of the reasons.

BERTHA. You know, I don't think you are quite so noble as people say you are. You are envious.

AXEL. Why should I be envious when I don't know yet how things will go for me?

BERTHA. But when you do find out?

AXEL. What's that?

(BERTHA *hands him the green letter.* AXEL'S *hand goes to his heart. He sits down.*)

AXEL. What's this? (*He summons up his courage and reads the letter.*) This is something I hadn't expected! This is a most unpleasant blow!

BERTHA. Well, now I suppose *I* have to help *you!*

AXEL. You seem to take a malicious joy in this, Bertha. I really think I am beginning to feel a great hatred against you growing inside me.

BERTHA. Perhaps I appear happy because I have been successful. But if one is bound to a man who shows no happiness over his wife's success, then it is difficult for her to feel compassion for him when he has a misfortune.

AXEL. I don't understand just what it is, but it seems to me as if we had become enemies at this moment. The struggle for position has come between us. From now on we can never be friends again.

BERTHA. Is it so difficult for you to yield when you see the more capable one victorious.

AXEL. You are not the more capable one!

BERTHA. In any case, the jury must have thought so!

AXEL. The jury? But you must know that your paintings are not any better than mine!

BERTHA. Are you so certain of that?

AXEL. Yes, there can be no question of that. And besides, you worked under more favorable conditions than I did. You did not have to stoop to taking in drafting work, you could go to the Academy and study, you could have models, and—you are a woman!

BERTHA. Yes—now I'll be hearing all this again—that I have been living on you . . .

AXEL. Between ourselves, yes—but that is something no one will ever know, unless you yourself go around talking about it.

BERTHA. Oh, everybody knows about it already. But tell me, how is it that you don't feel hurt when one of your comrades, one of your men friends, has been accepted?

AXEL. That is something I have to give some thought to. . . . You see, we men have never considered you women with a critical eye. We have merely judged you with our feelings. For that reason I have never given any thought to our respective positions. Now that the shoe pinches, it no longer seems to me as if we were comrades—for I am now beginning to feel that you have no business being here. A comrade is a more or less loyal competitor, a friendly enemy. You have been in hiding behind the bushes while we engaged in battle; and afterward, when the table was set, you seated yourselves at it as if it were in *your* home!

BERTHA. For shame! Have you ever let us women take part in any battle? Have you?

AXEL. You have always had the chance, but you have never wanted to, or been able to. In our particular profession, which you are now encroaching upon, the technique has gone through its full length and breadth of development and been perfected by us men before you came on the scene. And now you are purchasing the work of centuries at an art academy for ten francs an hour—and with money which we men have earned by our work.

BERTHA. Now, at least, you are not being noble, Axel!

AXEL. When was I ever noble? Yes, when I allowed you to wear me down like an old shoe. . . . But now that you are above me, I can no longer endure being noble. I can no longer think of continuing my painting but must give up my life's dream and devote myself to nothing but drafting.

BERTHA. You won't have to. As soon as I begin to sell, I can take care of myself.

AXEL. Besides—what kind of union is it we have entered

into? Marriage should be built upon mutual interests; ours is built on conflicting interests.

BERTHA. I'll let you brood over that by yourself. I am going out to eat dinner now. Are you coming along?

AXEL. No, I wish to be alone with my disappointment.

BERTHA. And I need company to celebrate my good fortune.—Oh, I forgot, we are having a gathering this evening—here! I suppose that will have to be abandoned, now that you are so full of grief.

AXEL. It won't be much of a pleasure but I suppose we have to go through with it. Let them come!

BERTHA (*dressing herself to go out*). But you have to take part—otherwise they will think you are afraid to look them in the face.

AXEL. I'll be there; you don't have to worry! But you have to give me some money before you go—

BERTHA. There is no money left.

AXEL. No money?

BERTHA. No. There can be an end to money, too.

AXEL. Can you lend me ten francs, then?

BERTHA (*takes out her wallet*). Ten francs. Yes—if I have it. Here you are!—Aren't you coming along? (AXEL *does not reply.*) Say something! They will think it strange if you don't come.

AXEL. And play the part of the conquered lion hitched on to your triumphal chariot! No, indeed! I need a few hours to learn my role in time for this afternoon's performance.

BERTHA. Well, goodbye then!

AXEL. Goodbye, Bertha! And may I ask you one favor?

BERTHA. What is it?

AXEL. Don't come home drunk! Today it would be more unpleasant than usual!

BERTHA. It is none of your business how I come home.

AXEL. Yes, it is. I feel myself responsible for you as for a relative because you bear my name. And besides, it is still so repulsive to me to see a drunken woman.

BERTHA. Why is it more repulsive than to see a drunken man?

AXEL. Well—why? Perhaps because you women can't stand being seen with the veil cast aside.

BERTHA. Goodbye.—You are a great old talker! . . . You won't come? (*She goes out.*)

AXEL (*gets up, removes the cutaway and puts on another coat*). No!

ACT II

(THE SETTING.—*The same as in Act I. A large table surrounded by chairs is placed in the center of the room. On it are writing materials, paper and a chairman's gavel. AXEL is seated, painting. ABEL sits in a chair close by, smoking.*)

AXEL. So they have finished dinner and are now having their coffee? Was there much drinking?

ABEL. Oh yes! Bertha kept boasting and was unpleasant.

AXEL. Tell me one thing, Abel. Are you my friend or are you not?

ABEL. Why—well . . . I don't know.

AXEL. Can I depend on you?

ABEL. No, you cannot.

AXEL. Why not?

ABEL. Because that's the way I seem to feel.

AXEL. Tell me, Abel . . . you have the mentality of a man and one can talk reason with you. . . . Tell me how it feels to be a woman. Is it so terrible?

ABEL (*jestingly*). Why, of course. It's like being a Negro.

AXEL. That's curious! Listen, Abel, you know I have a passion for fairness and justice.

ABEL. I know you are a dreamer; and that is why you will never have any success.

AXEL. But you will have it because you have no feeling for anything?

ABEL. Yes.

AXEL. Abel, do you never feel the need of a man's love?

ABEL. How silly you are!

AXEL. Have you never found anyone?

ABEL. No. There is such a dearth of men.

AXEL. Yes—but don't you think I am a man?

ABEL. You!—No!

AXEL. I thought I was.

ABEL. Do you call yourself a man? You who are toiling for a woman and goes about dressed like a woman—

AXEL. I—dressed like a woman?

ABEL. You have a bang and go barenecked, while she wears a high collar and has her hair cut like a boy. Watch out, Axel! Soon she will take the pants from you!

AXEL. What silly nonsense!

ABEL. And what is your position in your own house? You come to her for money like a beggar, and she has placed you under her guardianship. No—you are not a man! And that's exactly why she took you when her affairs were snarled.

AXEL. You hate Bertha. What is it you have against her?

ABEL. I don't know—but perhaps I, too, have been given a touch of your passion for fair play.

AXEL. Tell me—don't you believe in that great cause of yours, or do you?

ABEL. Sometimes. Not always. What *is* there that one can believe in these days? There are times when it seems to me as if the things of old were the best. As mothers we had a position of respect and honor because as mothers we fulfilled our duties to the nation and society. As housewives we were absolute; and our task of bringing up the new generation was not one to be ashamed of. Give me a cognac, Axel! We have been doing a lot of talking.

AXEL (*goes to fetch a bottle of cognac and glasses*). Why do you drink so much?

ABEL. I couldn't tell you.—I must be out of date—

AXEL. Just what do you mean?

ABEL. I mean—if I met a man who knew how to rule a woman—

AXEL. And if you met such a man. What then?

ABEL. Then I would—what is it they call it now—love him! Just think, if all this sound and fury were nothing but humbug. . . . Suppose it were!

AXEL. Yes, I don't doubt it is an organized movement of some sort—whatever it may be!

ABEL. Yes—there are so many movements going on, both forward and backward.—And anything stupid or inane can also grow into a movement; all you need is to have a majority!

AXEL. If it were something of that sort, then you women have made a hell of a lot of noise and uproar for nothing. Soon it will get to be intolerable to live any more.

ABEL. We make so much commotion that you get dizzy! That's exactly the point!—Well, Axel, from now on your position will be a little better, now that Bertha has had a chance to sell.

AXEL. Sell? Has she made a sale?

ABEL. You mean you don't know? The small canvas with the apple tree.

AXEL. No—she hasn't said anything to me! When did this happen?

ABEL. The day before yesterday. And you don't know? Oh, I suppose she plans to surprise you with the money—

AXEL. Me? She takes charge of everything that comes in, herself.

ABEL. Does she? Then I suppose— Sh! Here she comes. (BERTHA *enters*.)

BERTHA (*to* ABEL). Oh—good evening—are you here? Why did you leave the party?

ABEL. I thought it was boring.

BERTHA. Yes—enjoying the good fortune of others isn't really much fun.

ABEL. No.

BERTHA (*to* AXEL). And you sit here painting so very diligently, Axel!

AXEL. Yes, I am sitting here dawdling.

BERTHA. Let me see! It is quite good, but the left arm is too long—

AXEL. So you think!

BERTHA. I *think*? Can't I see? Give me the brush! (*She snatches the brush from him.*)

AXEL. No—stop it! Have you no shame?

BERTHA. What's that you say?

AXEL (*angered*). I said: Have you no shame! (*He rises.*) Are you going to teach me how to paint?

BERTHA. And why not?

AXEL. Because I am the one to teach you! You can teach me nothing.

BERTHA. It seems to me you treat your wife with very little respect. You ought to have some respect for—

ABEL. Now you are old-fashioned, Bertha! Why should a man have any special respect for a woman when they are supposed to be equals?

BERTHA. So—o, you think it is right for a man to be rude to his wife, do you?

ABEL. Yes, when she is nasty to him.

AXEL. That's right! Tear each other's eyes out!

ABEL. Oh no—the matter is much too unimportant for that!

AXEL. Don't say that!—Listen, Bertha. . . . Since our economy from now on will be subject to some changes, I would like to know just where we stand. Will you let me see the household ledger?

BERTHA. You are taking a noble revenge just because you had your painting refused!

AXEL. What has the ledger to do with revenge? What connection can the ledger possibly have with my disappointment at the Salon? Let me have the key to the chiffonier!

BERTHA (*searching her pockets*). Certainly!—H'm! That's strange—I thought I had it just a moment ago!

AXEL. Look for it!

BERTHA. You speak in such a commanding tone! I don't like it!

AXEL. Find the key!

BERTHA (*goes about the room looking for the key*). Oh, but this is more than I can explain! The key is lost! I can't find it . . . I must have lost it!

AXEL. Are you certain it is lost?

BERTHA. I'm absolutely certain!

AXEL (*goes over to the speaking tube and whistles. There is a pause.* THE MAID *enters.*) I want you to get a smith!

THE MAID. A smith?

AXEL. A smith who opens locks—a locksmith!

THE MAID (*to whom* BERTHA *has given a surreptitious look*). I'll go and get one—at once!   (*She goes out.*)

AXEL (*changes coats. He removes the ribbon from the buttonhole and flings it on the table.*) Excuse me, ladies!

BERTHA (*in a soft tone of voice*). Don't mind us! Are you going out?

AXEL. I am going out.

BERTHA. Aren't you going to be here for the meeting?

AXEL. No, I am not!

BERTHA. Oh, but they will think you very rude!

AXEL. Let them think so! I have things that are more important than listening to your cackling.

BERTHA (*uneasy*). Where are you going?

AXEL. I don't see why I should tell you when I don't ask you where you are going?

BERTHA. I hope you are not forgetting that we have invited guests to drop in tomorrow evening after the carnival?

AXEL. Guests? Yes—you are right. . . . Tomorrow evening! H'm.

BERTHA. We couldn't possibly call it off. Dr. Östermark and Carl both arrived today, as you know, and I have asked them to come—

AXEL. So much the better!

BERTHA. Be sure to come home in time so that you can try on your costume!

AXEL. My costume. . . . Yes, of course. I am to play the role of a woman.

THE MAID (*enters*). The smith was busy, but he said he would be here in a couple of hours.

AXEL. So—he was busy. . . . Well, perhaps the key will show up meantime. . . . Now I have to go. Goodbye!

BERTHA (*in a submissive voice*). Goodbye then! Don't come home too late!

(ABEL *nods a goodbye to* AXEL.)

AXEL. I don't know when I'll get back. Goodbye!

(*He leaves.*)

ABEL. How cocky your lord and master was.

BERTHA. How impudent, how impertinent of him! You know, I would like to humiliate him . . . so deeply that he would come crawling after me.

ABEL. Yes, he doesn't seem to have been put in his place by his defeat at the Salon.—Tell me, Bertha, have you ever really loved that fool?

BERTHA. Loved?—I rather liked him, for he was kindhearted. But he is stupid, and when he antagonizes me I feel as if I could hate him. Can you imagine—somebody has already spread the rumor that he painted my picture.

ABEL. If it has gone that far, then you certainly must do something drastic.

BERTHA. If I only knew what?

ABEL. I am usually quick at thinking up such things. . . . Why, yes,—let me see! Listen! Suppose you went and fetched his refused painting tomorrow evening and brought it home while the guests were here!

BERTHA. No—that would look as if I were gloating. That would be a little cruel.

ABEL. Oh, but suppose I did it! Or Gaga! That would be still better. We could have the concierge send for it in Axel's name. It will have to come home anyway—and everybody knows Axel has been refused—it is no secret.

BERTHA. No, really, I—

ABEL. What? If he spreads false rumors, you have every right to defend yourself, don't you think?

BERTHA. I wouldn't mind seeing it done, but I don't want to have anything to do with it myself! I want to be able to swear that I am innocent—that my conscience is clean.

ABEL. It will be! I'll take care of the whole thing.

BERTHA. What do you suppose he wanted the household ledger for? He has never asked to see it before. Do you imagine he has some intrigue up his sleeve?

ABEL. You may be certain of that. I am sure it is something of that sort. He wants to see if you have entered the three hundred francs you received for the painting on the credit side.

BERTHA. Which painting?

ABEL. The painting you sold to Mme. Roubey.

BERTHA. How do you know that?

ABEL. Why, the whole world knows that!

BERTHA. Does Axel also know?

ABEL. Yes. I mentioned it to him by chance. I took it for granted that he knew. It was terribly stupid of you not to tell him at once.

BERTHA. What business is it of his if I make a sale?

ABEL. Why, certainly—in a way it is . . . I should imagine it is.

BERTHA. Well—in that case, I shall simply tell him that I didn't want to make him feel even more disappointed, since he had had the disappointment of seeing me hung at the Salon.

ABEL. Strictly speaking, he has nothing to do with what you make since you have a clause to that effect in your marriage contract. And you have every reason to be severe with him—if for no other reason than to make an example of him.—So, stand your ground tonight if he starts preaching a sermon to you!

BERTHA. Don't worry! I know how to take care of him. But —to speak about something else. What are we going to do about the Östermark matter?

ABEL. Östermark—yes, he is my great enemy. Let me handle him! We have an old account to settle, he and I. . . . You just don't worry! We'll manage him, no question about that, for we have the law on our side.

BERTHA. What do you intend to do?

ABEL. We shall confront the two parties, as they say.

BERTHA. Exactly what does that mean?

ABEL. Invite Mrs. Hall and her two daughters to come here! Then we'll see how he takes it.

BERTHA. No—I want no scandal in my house!

ABEL. Why not? Can you deny yourself a trump like that? If you carry on a war, you kill your enemies; you don't merely wound them. And this is war! And that's that!

BERTHA. Well, but think—a father and his wife and two daughters, whom he hasn't seen for eighteen years—

ABEL. Well—he'll see them now.

BERTHA. You are terrible, Abel!

ABEL. I am just a little stronger than you are! Marriage must have made you soft. Are you living together like man and wife, eh?

BERTHA. How silly you are!

ABEL. You have angered Axel—you have trampled on him—but he can still bite you in the heel.—What do you say?

BERTHA. Do you think he would dare to do anything?

ABEL. I think he will make a scene when he comes.

BERTHA. Oh, don't worry. I'll give it to him good—and worse.

ABEL. Do you think you can? That business about the key to the chiffonier—that was stupid. Very stupid!

BERTHA. Perhaps it was. But once he has been out for an airing, he'll be nice again. I know him.

THE MAID (*enters with a large bundle*). There is a messenger outside who brought this costume for Mr. Alberg.

BERTHA. Oh! Good! Give it to me!

THE MAID. But it must be for you, Madame; it's a woman's costume.

BERTHA. No, there is no mistake. It's for *Monsieur*.

THE MAID. Oh, heavens, is Monsieur going to be dressed in skirts, too?

BERTHA. Why not—when *we* go dressed in skirts. (*To* THE MAID.) That's all! That's all! (THE MAID *leaves*.)

(BERTHA *opens the bundle and takes out a dress for a Spanish lady*.)

ABEL. Why, that certainly was a clever idea you had! Oh, it's wonderful to get a chance to outwit one's stupidities.

(WILLMER *enters accompanied by a messenger who carries a load of packages. He is dressed in black tails with white lapels. He wears a boutonnière and kneebreeches, red tie and turned-up cuffs.*)

WILLMER. Good evening! Are you alone? Here, Bertha, are

the candles—and here are the bottles. One Chartreuse and two Vermouth—and here are two packages of tobacco, and the rest of it.

BERTHA. Oh, what a nice boy you are, Gaga!

WILLMER. And here is the bill—all paid!

BERTHA. All paid! Then you have put out the money again.

WILLMER. Oh, well, there is plenty of time to settle that. But now you must hurry, for the old lady will soon be here, I'm afraid.

BERTHA. Will you unpack the bottles, Gaga, while I put the candles in the candlesticks?

WILLMER. Why, of course, I will.

(BERTHA *opens the package of candles on the table.* WILL-MER, *nearby, removes the tissue paper from the bottles.*)

ABEL. This looks quite family-like. I shouldn't wonder if you would have turned out to be a nice little husband, Gaga.

(WILLMER *puts his arm round* BERTHA'S *neck and kisses her at the nape.*)

BERTHA (*turns round and slaps him in the face*). Have you no shame, you young whipper-snapper? How dare you?

ABEL. If you can stand that, Gaga, you can stand any-thing.

WILLMER (*in a rage*). Whipper-snapper? Don't you know who I am? Have you forgotten that I am an author of rank?

BERTHA. You—who write such drivel!

WILLMER. You didn't call it drivel when I wrote about you!

BERTHA. You wrote down our conversation—that's all you did!

WILLMER. Watch out, Bertha, you know I can ruin you.

BERTHA. So! You come with threats, you puny little black-guard! What do you say, Abel? Shall we give the little imp a sound thrashing?

ABEL. Bertha, watch what you say!

WILLMER. So . . . I have been your little lap-dog and been held in leash by you, have I? But don't forget—I can bite, too!

BERTHA. Show me your teeth!

WILLMER. No—but I will let you feel them!

BERTHA. Oh so! Come on then! Come on!

ABEL. Now, now, take it easy, before you come to regret it!

WILLMER (*to* BERTHA). Do you know what people call a married woman who accepts gifts from a young bachelor?

BERTHA. Gifts?

WILLMER. For two years you have been accepting presents from me—

BERTHA. Presents! I ought to give you a good beating, you false little creep, always hanging on to my skirts. So you think I can't get the best of you, do you?

WILLMER (*with a shrug of the shoulder*). Perhaps you could.

BERTHA. You dare to cast aspersions on my honor—

WILLMER. Honor! H'm! Is it to your honor that I have been buying a whole lot of household goods which you have charged to your husband's account?

BERTHA. Get out of my house, you scoundrel!

WILLMER. Your house! When one deals with comrades, one doesn't have to be too finicky—but when it comes to enemies, one splits hairs. And you shall have to reckon with me, you adventuress,—you can rely upon that!

(*He leaves.*)

ABEL. You are going to destroy yourself because of your stupidity, Bertha! To let a friend leave as an enemy—that is a dangerous thing!

BERTHA. Ah! Let him come! He had the audacity to kiss me! He dared to remind me that I am a woman!

ABEL. Well, you know that is something men can always be counted on to remember! You have been playing with fire, Bertha!

BERTHA. With fire! Isn't it possible for a man and a woman to live together as comrades without striking fire?

ABEL. No. You may be sure that as long as there are two sexes, just as surely will there be fire.

BERTHA. Well—then that's something that has to be done away with!

ABEL. Yes—it should be. . . . But just try!

THE MAID (*enters. She is trying hard to restrain her laughter.*) There is a lady outside who calls herself Richard—Richard Wahlström . . .

BERTHA (*goes toward the door*). Oh, Richard is here!

ABEL. Why, then we can start the meeting. Now it remains to be seen if we can disentangle the snarl you are in.

BERTHA. Disentangle it, or cut it off!

ABEL. Or be enmeshed in it!

ACT III

(THE SETTING.—*The same as in the previous acts. The hanging lamp is lighted. Through the studio window the moonbeams can be seen illuminating the garden outside. The parlor stove is also lighted.* BERTHA, *dressed in a negligee of lace, is busy sewing on the Spanish female costume.* THE MAID *is pleating a ruff.*)

BERTHA. It is no fun to have to sit up waiting for your husband.

THE MAID. Do you think it is more fun for your husband to have to sit up and wait for you, Mrs. Alberg?—This is the first time he has been out by himself—

BERTHA. Well—what does he occupy himself with when he is at home alone?

THE MAID. He keeps painting on pieces of wood!

BERTHA. On pieces of wood!

THE MAID. Yes, he has a large pile of wood that he is painting.

BERTHA. H'm. Tell me one thing, Ida. Has Mr. Alberg ever been indiscreet—forward—to you?

THE MAID. Never! No, he is a real gentleman.

BERTHA. Can I rely on that?

THE MAID (*emphatically*). Does Mrs. Alberg think I am one of those . . . ?

BERTHA. What time is it now?

THE MAID. It's around eleven-thirty.

BERTHA. Oh! Then you had better go to bed.

THE MAID. Aren't you frightened of being alone in the dark among all these skeletons?

BERTHA. I—frightened? Sh! Someone just came in through the front door. . . . Goodnight now!

THE MAID. Goodnight, Mrs. Alberg. Sleep well!

(*She goes out.*)

(BERTHA, *alone, puts away the costume, throws herself on the sofa, and arranges the lace on her negligee. Then she suddenly jumps up, turns down the lamp a little, and, feigning sleep, again resumes her position on the sofa. There is a pause; and then* AXEL *enters.*)

AXEL. Anybody here?—Are you there, Bertha? (BERTHA *is silent.* AXEL *goes over to the sofa.*) Are you asleep?

BERTHA (*gently*). Ah—is it you, Axel dear? Good evening! I was lying down and fell asleep, and I had such a bad dream . . .

AXEL. You are lying! I saw through the window when you arranged yourself on the sofa just now.

(BERTHA *jumps up.*)

AXEL (*calmly*). Let's have no seduction scenes in night-gowns! And no melodrama! Just be sensible and listen to what I have to tell you! (*He seats himself in a chair that he has placed in the center of the floor.*)

BERTHA. What is it you have to tell me?

AXEL. A whole lot of things—but I shall begin at the end. We have to dissolve this concubinage.

BERTHA. What! (*She throws herself on her back on the sofa.*) Oh, my God; and I should live to hear this!

AXEL. Stop being hysterical! If you don't, I'll empty the water carafe on your lace work!

BERTHA. This is your revenge because I got the best of you in an open competion!

AXEL. It has nothing whatsoever to do with that!

BERTHA. You have never loved me!

AXEL. Yes, I have been in love with you—and that was my only reason for marrying you. . . . But why did you marry me? Because your affairs were in a bad snarl, and you were anemic!

BERTHA. It's a good thing no one is around to hear us!

AXEL. It would not be such a bad thing if someone did hear us. I have treated you as a comrade, with unlimited confidence in you, and I have also made certain minor sacrifices as you well know. . . . Did the locksmith come?

BERTHA. No, he didn't show up.

AXEL. There is no need of him now! I have been through your accounts.

BERTHA. Oh so,—you poke your nose into my books!

AXEL. The household ledger is our common property. You

have written down false items of expenditures and have neglected to enter all income.

BERTHA. Well, you know, of course, we women are not
taught bookkeeping in the schools.

AXEL. Nor are we men for that matter! And as far as
education is concerned, you have a much better education
than I have. You went to a seminary; I only attended a
public school.

BERTHA. It isn't books that give you education.

AXEL. No—it's the mothers! And I must say it is strange
that they can't teach their daughters to be honest. . . .

BERTHA. Honest! I just wonder whether most of the criminals are not to be found among the men!

AXEL. Most of those who are punished, you ought to say,
—but back of ninety-nine per cent of the crimes committed
by males, one can, along with a certain judge, ask the question: *Où est la femme?*—However, let us return to you.—
You have lied to me—lied from beginning to end—and
finally you have defrauded and cheated me. To give but one
example: you have marked down twenty francs for paints
instead of twenty francs for breakfast at the Marguéry.

BERTHA. That wasn't true. It cost only twelve francs.

AXEL. And so, without further ado, you pocketed eight!
—And then you never entered the three hundred francs you
received for your painting.

BERTHA. "What a woman through her own work and effort
may gain, she alone shall possess." That is what the law says.

AXEL. Consequently it was no paradox? No monomania?

BERTHA. No, I imagine it was not!

AXEL. Well, let us not be petty. You look after yours, and
have looked after what is mine in an indefensible manner.
However, don't you think that—between comrades—you
ought to have told me that you had made a sale?

BERTHA. It was none of your business.

AXEL. It was none of my business, eh? Well—in that case
nothing remains for me to do but get a divorce.

BERTHA. Divorce! Do you think I would accept the shame
of being a divorced wife, do you? Do you think I will allow
you to drive me out of my own home, like a servant sent
packing with her trunk?

AXEL. If I wanted to, I could have you thrown out in the
street—but I want to be human to you and so I propose to
get a divorce on the grounds of incompatibility.

BERTHA. Speaking the way you do, you could never have been in love with me.

AXEL. Why do you think I kept begging you to marry me? Answer me that!

BERTHA. Because you wanted me to love you.

AXEL. Oh, such holy, inviolable, venerated idiocy! I could charge you with fraud, for you have been borrowing from Willmer and charged the amounts to me.

BERTHA. Ah, that little creep has been busy tattling again!

AXEL. I just left him after having paid him three hundred and fifty francs that you owed him. But let us not be petty about money. We have other things to settle—things much more important. You have allowed this scoundrel to pay for a part of my household expenses. By permitting this, you have completely ruined my good name. What have you done with the money?

BERTHA. What you tell me is a lie—every word of it!

AXEL. You have spent it having a good time, haven't you?

BERTHA. No, I have saved it—and to save is something you know nothing about, you spendthrift!

AXEL. Yes, you are certainly a saving soul! That negligee cost two hundred francs, and my dressing gown cost twenty.

BERTHA. Is there anything else you have to say?

AXEL. Nothing—except that from now on you have to be prepared to take care of yourself. I have no longer any desire to make wood paintings and let you get the benefit of what I earn.

BERTHA. Oh so, you think you will get out of the responsibilities you assumed when you enticed me into becoming your wife. You'll see! You'll see!

AXEL. Now that my eyes have been opened, I begin to see much of what happened in the past in its true light! It almost seems to me as if you schemed to marry me. Yes, it almost seems as if I were a victim of what you women like to call a seduction. . . . It now looks to me as if I had fallen into the hands of an adventuress who tried to entice my money away from me in a hotel-room; and I almost feel as if I had been living in sin after being married to you! (*He gets up.*) As you stand there with your back turned to me and I see the back of your head with your cropped hair, I feel as if —well, it's just as if—ugh!—as if you were Judith and had given your body to me so that you could have my head. There—there is the costume I was to wear in order that you might debase me! Yes, for you knew it would be debasing to wear these thick folds that were meant to hide in order to entice—this corseted bodice with its low neck that was intended to show off what I had to offer. . . . Oh no! Here is the payment for your love! I am casting off the chains! (*He throws down his wedding ring.*)

(BERTHA *gazes at him in astonishment.*)

AXEL (*brushes his hair back from his forehead*). You were afraid to look at my forehead because it was higher than yours, and that is why I allowed it to be concealed by my hair in order not to humiliate and defy you. But now, you will see, I shall humiliate you, and as you were not satisfied with being my equal after I had lowered myself to your level, I shall show you up for what you really are: my inferior!

BERTHA. All this—all this noble revenge—just because you are *my* inferior!

AXEL. I was your superior—even when I painted your picture!

BERTHA. When you painted my picture! . . . Say that again and I shall slap you in the face!

AXEL. You who always say you have contempt for raw force, you are always quick to clamor for it! Go ahead and strike me!

BERTHA. Perhaps you think I wouldn't get the best of you . . . (*She approaches him menacingly.*)

AXEL (*takes hold of her by the wrists with one hand and holds them firmly in his grip*). No, I don't think you would! Are you convinced now that physically I am your superior also? Are you? Will you give in or shall I have to tame you?

BERTHA. You wouldn't dare strike me!

AXEL. Why wouldn't I? I know of only one reason that could prevent me.

BERTHA. And what is that, pray?

AXEL. Because you are morally irresponsible.

BERTHA (*tries to free herself*). Let me loose, let me loose!

AXEL. When you have asked me for forgiveness! Therefore—down on your knees! (*He forces her to her knees with one hand.*) Now—look up to me—from where you are —below me! There is where you belong—it's the position you have chosen yourself!

BERTHA (*breaking down*). Axel, Axel! I don't recognize you any more! Are you the Axel who swore you would love me? Who asked me to let you carry me in your arms—who wanted to raise me up!

AXEL. I am the very same man, yes! I had strength then

and thought I was strong enough to be able to do it. . . .
But you took my strength from me piecemeal while I rested
my tired head in your lap; you sucked my red blood while I
was asleep—yet I had sufficient strength left to subjugate
you. Now get up and let us stop all this ranting and declaim-
ing. We have serious matters to discuss!

(BERTHA *gets up and seats herself on the sofa, crying.*)

AXEL. Why are you crying?

BERTHA. I don't know! Perhaps because I am such a weakling!

(*From now on* BERTHA's *change in behavior is acted out
in pantomime.*)

AXEL. You see now, don't you, that you had your strength
in me? The moment I took back what I had given you, you
had nothing left. You were like a rubber ball that I inflated:
when I let go of you, you collapsed like an empty sack.

BERTHA (*without lifting her eyes*). I don't know whether
you are right in what you say—but after we started quarreling, all my strength left me. . . . Axel, will you believe me
if I tell you that I have never before felt for you what I
feel now?

AXEL. Oh? What is it you feel, then?

BERTHA. I can't tell you! I am not sure whether it is—
love—but . . .

AXEL. Just what do you mean by love? Could it be a quiet
yearning to eat me alive once more? You say you are beginning to love me! Why not before—when I was good to
you? To be good is to be stupid—so let us be mean to each
other! Is that what you mean?

BERTHA. Yes—I'd rather have you a little mean than seeing you a weakling . . . (*She jumps up from the sofa.*) Axel,
please forgive me—but don't cast me aside! Oh, give me
your love—love me!

AXEL. The time for that is past! Yesterday—this morning—
I would have fallen for you as I now see you standing there
. . . but now it is too late!

BERTHA. Why is it too late?

AXEL. Because tonight I have broken all bonds—even the
final one!

BERTHA (*grasping his hands*). What—what do you mean?

AXEL. I have been unfaithful to you!

BERTHA (*shrinks*). Oh!

AXEL. It was the only way I could loose myself from you!

BERTHA (*collecting herself*). Who was she?

AXEL. A woman.

(*There is a pause.*)

BERTHA. What did she look like?

AXEL. Like a woman. Long hair—round breasts—etcetera. You may as well be spared the details!

BERTHA. You don't think I am jealous—of a—of a woman like that, do you?

AXEL. A woman like that—two women like that—a whole pile of women like that!

BERTHA (*catching her breath*). And tomorrow our friends are invited here. Do you wish to create a scandal and call off the party?

AXEL. No, I don't care to let my revenge turn me into a cad. Tomorrow we shall have the party—and the day after, our ways separate!

BERTHA. Yes—after this we must part. . . . Goodnight!

(*She goes toward the door on the right.*)

AXEL. Goodnight!

(*He goes toward the door on the left.*)

BERTHA (*stops*). Axel!

AXEL. Yes!

BERTHA. Oh, it was nothing!—Yes—wait! (*She approaches* AXEL, *pleading with clasped hands.*) Love me, Axel! Love me!

AXEL. Are you willing to share my love with someone else?

BERTHA. Yes! If you will only love me!

AXEL. No—that is something I cannot do. You hold no attraction for me any longer!

BERTHA. Love me, please—out of mercy! I believe I can say I mean it sincerely now, otherwise I would never humiliate myself before a man as I am doing now.

AXEL. Even if I felt compassion for you, I could not be moved to love you. All is ended between us—all is over!

BERTHA. I am pleading for your love—I, a woman,—and you push me aside!

AXEL. Why shouldn't I? Men, too, should have the privilege of saying no, even if we are not so particular.

BERTHA. Think of a woman offering herself to a man and being refused!

AXEL. Think how we men must feel pleading for the privilege of giving what you women so easily accept without having to give anything in return. If you can understand this—then you can talk about how it feels to be refused!

BERTHA (*gets up*). Goodnight! And so you say—it is the day after tomorrow!

AXEL. And you still wish to hold the party tomorrow, do you?

BERTHA. Yes, I do!

AXEL. Good! And so—the day after tomorrow!

(*They go out:* AXEL *to his room,* BERTHA *to hers.*)

ACT IV

(THE SETTING.—*The same as for the previous acts. The glass doors to the garden are now open, however, and the sun is shining outside, while the studio is brightly illuminated. The doors right and left are wide open. In the garden can be seen a serving table with bottles and glasses, etc. AXEL is dressed in a black cutaway and wears no decoration. He has on a high collar and a four-in-hand necktie. His hair is combed back. BERTHA is dressed in a dark, low-necked gown, cut in a square at the throat, with a ruff and a neckerchief. On the left shoulder she wears a flower. CARL is in civilian dress and wears an order. THE MISSES HALL are extravagantly and expensively dressed.*)

(BERTHA *enters from the garden. She is pale and has blue shadows round her eyes. ABEL comes from the door, rear; they embrace and kiss.*)

BERTHA. Welcome—and how are you? You are coming late.

ABEL. How do you do!

BERTHA (*with exuberance and surprise*). And Gaga has promised to come!

ABEL. Definitely. He was sorry and asks you to forgive him. (BERTHA *adjusts her ruff.*) What's wrong with you today? Something is wrong.

BERTHA. Why? What do you mean?

ABEL. You are not yourself today! Bertha, you are—you are—

BERTHA. Don't be silly!

ABEL. Your eyes are gleaming—they are so bright. Why —is it possible that you. . . . And you are so pale. . . . Bertha!

BERTHA (*abruptly*). I have to go out to my guests—

ABEL. Tell me—is Carl here, and Östermark?

BERTHA. They are in the garden—both of them.

ABEL. And The Misses Hall and their mother?

BERTHA. Mrs. Östermark will be here a little later, but the girls have already come. They are in my room.

ABEL. I am afraid your party will turn out to be a failure.

BERTHA. No, my dear,—it won't!

WILLMER (*enters carrying a bouquet of flowers. He goes over to* BERTHA *and, kissing her hand, presents her with the flowers.*) Please forgive me! For the sake of my love!

BERTHA. No—not because of your love, but. . . . Well, it doesn't matter! I don't know why—but today I don't care to have any enemies!

(AXEL *enters.* BERTHA *and* WILLMER *look embarrassed.*)

AXEL (*to* BERTHA, *without paying any attention to* WILLMER). Forgive me—if I disturb you . . .

BERTHA. Why, no . . .

AXEL. I merely wished to ask if you have ordered supper.

BERTHA. Yes, of course—just as you wished.

AXEL. Well—I just wanted to make sure.

ABEL. You look so solemn, both of you! (BERTHA *and* AXEL *exchange glances.* WILLMER *goes out into the garden.*) Tell me, Gaga . . .

(ABEL *hastens out after him.*)

AXEL. What have you ordered for supper?

BERTHA (*looks at him and smiles*). Lobster and chicken.

AXEL (*seems a little uncertain*). What are you smiling at?

BERTHA. At what you are thinking.

AXEL. What am I thinking about?

BERTHA. You are thinking of— No, I have no idea what you are thinking, of course—unless it were about the first supper we had together at Djurgården after we had been engaged—that evening in spring when you proposed to me—

AXEL. When *you* proposed . . .

BERTHA. Axel!—and this is to be our last—our very last time together! It turned out to be a brief summer!

AXEL. A little brief, yes. . . . But perhaps the sun will shine again.

BERTHA. Yes—for you, who can find a ray of sunshine to warm you in any street.

AXEL. What is there to prevent *you* from seeking some warmth in the same way?

BERTHA. You mean—that we might meet again some evening under the light of a street lamp?

AXEL. No—that wasn't what I meant . . . but *à la bonne*

heure! It would at least be a relationship on easy terms.

BERTHA. Yes—exceedingly so—especially for you.

AXEL. And for you, too. But much more pleasant for me.

BERTHA. There you have a noble thought!

AXEL. Now, now—let's not rake up the past. . . . We were discussing the supper, and we must not forget our guests!

BERTHA (*as* AXEL *leaves*). The supper—yes, of course! It was about the supper we were to speak!

> (*She goes into her room, agitated.*)

(THE MISSES HALL *enter from the garden. A little later* DOCTOR ÖSTERMARK *comes in.*)

AMÉLIE. I find it boring.

THÉRÈSE. Unbearable, I think. And I can't say our hosts are especially polite.

AMÉLIE. *She* is particularly objectionable in my opinion. One of those women with close-cropped hair!

THÉRÈSE. But they say there is a lieutenant coming . . .

AMÉLIE. Well, that would be a relief, for these artists are such terrible free loaders. Be quiet—that gentleman must be a diplomat—he looks so distinguished. (*They seat themselves on the sofa.*)

THE DOCTOR (*comes from the garden; he regards them through his pince-nez.*) If I may have the honor, ladies. . . . H'm. One meets so many compatriots of the fair sex here in Paris. You are also artists, I take it? Painting?

AMÉLIE. No—we don't paint.

THE DOCTOR. Oh—but just a little, no doubt! Here in Paris all ladies are in the habit of painting—themselves.

THÉRÈSE. We don't need to.

THE DOCTOR. But you play undoubtedly.

AMÉLIE. Play?

THE DOCTOR. Well, I don't mean playing cards! But all ladies play something or other.

AMÉLIE. I take it you are fresh from the country, sir.

THE DOCTOR. Just come from there, Mademoiselle. Can I be of some service to you?

THÉRÈSE. If you'll pardon me—we have no idea with whom we have the honor of speaking.

THE DOCTOR. You two ladies must have just come from Stockholm. Here in this country people can talk to each other without asking for bail.

AMÉLIE. We have not asked for any bail.

THE DOCTOR. What do you ask for then? To have your

curiosity satisfied, eh? Well—I am an old family doctor and my name is Andersson. Perhaps you ladies will tell your names also. . . . You don't have to give me your character.

THÉRÈSE. We are The Misses Hall, if you are interested, Dr. Andersson.

THE DOCTOR. Hall? H'm. I am sure I have heard that name before. Pardon me—will you forgive me if I ask you a question? It's a rather—countrified question . . .

AMÉLIE. Don't be bashful!

THE DOCTOR. Is your father still living?

AMÉLIE. No, he is dead.

THE DOCTOR. So—o?—Well—now I have gone so far that there is nothing left for me but to go ahead. Your father—

THÉRÈSE. Our father was the director of the fire insurance company in Gothenburg.

THE DOCTOR. Oh, was he? Oh, then I beg your pardon! Paris is fun, isn't it?

AMÉLIE. Very much so!—Thérèse, did you notice where I left my shawl? There is a cold draft here. (*She rises.*)

THÉRÈSE. You probably left it in the pavilion in the garden. (*Gets up.*)

THE DOCTOR (*rises also*). No—don't go away. Let me get it for you—I'll find it for you.—No, sit still, sit still! Just sit still now. (*He goes into the garden.*)

(*Soon after,* MRS. HALL *comes from the right. She is somewhat inebriated, with flaming red cheeks. She speaks thickly.*)

AMÉLIE. Ah, there is mamma! And she is that way again!— What did you have to come here for, mamma?

MRS. HALL. You just keep quiet! I have as much right here as you have—

THÉRÈSE. Why did you have to drink? Just imagine if anyone should come.

MRS. HALL. I haven't been drinking. . . . You are talking nonsense.

AMÉLIE. It would be terrible if the Doctor should come back and see you. Come—let us go in here—then you can get a drink of water.

MRS. HALL. That's a nice way to treat your mother—and to tell her that she has been drinking . . . to tell your own mother—

THÉRÈSE. Stop talking and come in here at once. (*They lead her into the room on the left.*)

MRS. HALL (*obstreperously*). To treat your mother in this way. . . . Have you no respect for your own mother?

AMÉLIE. Not much. Hurry up now!

(*They go out to the left.*)

(AXEL *and* CARL *enter from the garden.*)

CARL. Why, you look real fit, my dear Axel, and you seem much more masculine than you used to.

AXEL. Well—I have emancipated myself.

CARL. You should have done that from the beginning, as I did.

AXEL. As you did?

CARL. As I did, yes! I assumed my position as the head and master of the family from the very first. I felt it belonged to me for two reasons: my superior intelligence and my own nature.

AXEL. How did your wife like that?

CARL. Do you know—I forgot to ask her! But judging by what I saw, she found it quite as it should be. If a woman gets a *real* man, one can make human beings even of women!

AXEL. But don't you think that they both should have as much to say?

CARL. Power is not divisible! Either you take orders or you do the commanding. Either you or I! I preferred the *I* to the *you*—and she had to be satisfied!

AXEL. Yes, yes. . . . But she had the money, didn't she?

CARL. Not a farthing! All she brought with her was a soup spoon of silver. But she demanded that it be included in our marriage contract as her private property. She is a woman of principle, you see. But she has a good heart—she is so kind to me, you see—but then I am kind to her also. It's a joy to be married, I think—eh? And her cooking—ah, it is superb!

(THE MISSES HALL *enter from the left.*)

AXEL. May I present Lieutenant Starck—The Misses Hall.

CARL. It's a pleasure to make the acquaintance of you two lad—ladies. . . . (*He suddenly becomes aware that he has met them before.* THE MISSES HALL *seem embarrassed and make their way to the garden.*) How do these ladies happen to be here?

AXEL. Why do you ask? They are friends of my wife. It's the first time they have been here. Do you know them?

CARL. Yes—in a way.

AXEL. What are you trying to say?

CARL. H'm. I ran into them in St. Petersburg one night!

AXEL. One night?

CARL. Yes.

AXEL. Aren't you making a mistake?

CARL. No—I am not mistaken. The two were known to everybody in St. Petersburg.

AXEL. And Bertha allows them to come to my house!

BERTHA (*comes tearing in*). What is the meaning of this? Have you been insulting the girls?

AXEL. No—but . . .

BERTHA. They came out into the garden crying and said they could not remain in a company with these gentlemen. What happened?

AXEL. Do you know these ladies?

BERTHA. They are friends of mine! Isn't that enough? Or isn't it?

AXEL. Not quite. . . . Well, but if . . .

THE DOCTOR (*enters from the garden*). What do you mean by this? What did you do to the two little girls who just left? I offered to help them on with their coats, but they simply wouldn't let me, and their eyes were filled with tears.

CARL (*to* BERTHA). I must ask you, Bertha: Are these girls friends of yours?

BERTHA. Yes, they are! But if my protection is not sufficient, perhaps Dr. Östermark will take them under *his* protection—since he has a certain duty and obligation to do so . . .

CARL. Somebody has made a mistake here. You mean that I, having had a certain relationship with these ladies, should take the part of their knight-errant?

BERTHA. What kind of relationship do you mean?

CARL. A temporary one—such as one has with ladies of that sort!

BERTHA. Ladies of that sort? You are lying!

CARL. I am not in the habit of lying!

THE DOCTOR. But I don't understand all this—what have I to do with these young ladies?

BERTHA (*sarcastically*). You mean you prefer not to have anything to do with your own children whom you have abandoned?

THE DOCTOR. These young ladies are not *my* children. I don't understand this at all—

BERTHA. These two ladies are your daughters by your divorced wife.

THE DOCTOR. Since you seem to think you have the right

to be both tactless and inquisitive and to put my personal
affairs on public display, I shall answer you publicly! You
seem to have found out that I am not a widower but a
divorced husband. Very well! My marriage was dissolved
twenty years ago. I had no children in that marriage. Since
then I have entered into a new relationship, and from this
I have one child, just five years old now. So you see, these
two grown girls are not my children. Now you know!

BERTHA. But you threw your wife out into the cold world—

THE DOCTOR. That, too, is untrue. She left of her own free
will—or rather, she staggered, if you prefer the truth—and
after that I gave her half of what I earned, until I . . .
until I learned that she . . . well, *that* I shall leave unsaid.
If you had the slightest understanding of what it has cost
me in work and sacrifice to keep two households going, you
would have spared me this unpleasant moment—but that is
something somebody like you would never bother to figure
out. There is nothing more you need to know—especially
since this is a matter that is of no concern to you!

BERTHA. It would interest me to know why your first wife
left you!

THE DOCTOR. I don't think it would please you to know
that she was petty, malicious and shabby, or that I was too
good to her. But just think, Bertha,—you who are so tenderhearted and sensitive—just think if these girls had really
been my daughters—these mutual friends of yours and Carl's!
Can't you imagine how it would have gladdened my old
heart to see these children again after eighteen years, if I
had really carried them in my arms night after night when
they were ailing! And just think, if she, my first love, my
wife, through whom life became real for the first time, had
accepted your invitation and come here. What a wonderful
fifth act in the melodrama you wanted to treat us to! What
a noble revenge on an innocent man! Thank you, old friend,
thank you for having repaid me in this manner for the
friendship I have given you!

BERTHA. Repaid you? Well, yes—I know I owe you a
doctor's bill . . .

AXEL AND CARL. Oh! Oh!

BERTHA. I know that, of course. I know it very well!

AXEL AND CARL. Oh, how shameful!

THE DOCTOR. Well—I am going now. I am ashamed of
you! (*With sarcasm.*) You are certainly the right kind of
person to know!—Pardon me, Axel, but I *had* to say it!

BERTHA (*to* AXEL). And you are the right kind of person —allowing your wife to be insulted!

AXEL. I don't encroach upon *your* privileges, neither when it comes to insulting nor being insulted! (*Music is heard from the garden: guitar and singing.*) The singers have arrived! Perhaps you would like to step into the garden. A little harmony after this wouldn't hurt.   (*All go into the garden.*)

(THE DOCTOR *is alone on the stage. The music from the garden can be heard softly in the room.* THE DOCTOR *walks about looking at the drawings on the left wall, all the way to* AXEL'S *room, when suddenly* MRS. HALL *comes out. She wobbles insecurely into the room, stops and sits down in a chair.* THE DOCTOR *does not recognize her. He bows to her.*)

MRS. HALL. What is that music that's playing out there?

THE DOCTOR. It's Italian—the musicians are Italians, Madam.

MRS. HALL. Is that so? It must be the ones I heard in Monte Carlo . . .

THE DOCTOR. Oh, I imagine there are a few other Italians.

MRS. HALL. Why, I believe it is none other than Öster-mark himself! Yes, indeed, there was no one quicker in his answers than you!

THE DOCTOR (*looking at her fixedly*). Ah!—To think that there are some things that are less to be dreaded than fear itself! . . . So—it is you, Carolina! And this is the moment I have fled from, dreamed of, looked for, dreaded, and wished for—wished for, in order to feel the blow, and after that have nothing more to dread or worry about! (*He takes a vial from his vest pocket and puts a few drops of the liquid on his tongue with the cork.*) You don't have to be afraid—it isn't poison. Not in the small dose I take. It's for my heart, you know.

MRS. HALL (*acrimoniously*). Oh yes—that heart of yours. Yes! You always had *that* to contend with!

THE DOCTOR. It's strange that two old people can't meet once in eighteen years without starting to quarrel.

MRS. HALL. It was always you who did the quarreling!

THE DOCTOR. By myself, eh? Don't you think we ought to end it now?—I must try to look at you—(*He takes a chair and seats himself opposite her.*)—without trembling!

MRS. HALL. I have grown old.

THE DOCTOR. We get that way. . . . We read about it,

hear about it, see it, feel it ourselves—and yet it's horrible—it frightens us. I, too, am getting old.

MRS. HALL. But you are happy in your new—life?

THE DOCTOR. Quite frankly: it is much the same monotony. . . . Even if different, it is rather like the past.

MRS. HALL. Perhaps the olden days were better?

THE DOCTOR. No—they were not better, because they were so much like my life today! But the question is whether my life now should not have been better just because—and only because it is like the past. We flower only once—and after that we go to seed. What comes later is nothing but aftermath. . . . And how about yourself? What kind of life are you leading?

MRS. HALL (offended). What kind of life am I leading?

THE DOCTOR. Don't misunderstand me! I mean—are you satisfied with your—your life. . . . I mean— Oh, why must one always choose one's words so carefully when talking with women?

MRS. HALL. Satisfied? H'm . . .

THE DOCTOR. Yes, you were never satisfied! But when one is young, one always wants to have everything first class—and when one gets to be old one has to be content with third class. Oh well! You have told Mrs. Alberg here that your daughters are my children!

MRS. HALL. I have? That's not true!

THE DOCTOR. You still have not learned to tell the truth! In olden days, when I didn't know as much as I do now, I used to reproach you for it, but I realize now that it is part of your nature. You seem to believe the lies you tell—and that, you know, is dangerous! But it doesn't matter. . . . Are you leaving—or would you prefer that I leave?

MRS. HALL (gets up). I am going . . . (She collapses and falls back into the chair while her arms are groping about for support.)

THE DOCTOR. What? Are you drunk? Oh, this is really disgusting, terribly disgusting! Oh! Oh, the shame of it! I think I am about to cry! . . . Carolina! . . . No, this is more than I can stand!

MRS. HALL. I am sick!

THE DOCTOR. Yes, when you drink too much, you bring on sickness. But—this is harder for me to take than I thought. I have done away with unborn little children in order to save the mother's life—I have felt their trembling little bodies struggling against death—I have sawed through live tissue and seen the marrow creep out like butter from healthy bone—but never have I felt such pain, such suffering, not since the day you left me. For that day I felt as if I had lost a lung and as if I could only gasp with the other. . . . Oh, I feel as if I were about to suffocate!

MRS. HALL. Help me to get out of here! There is too much noise here! And I don't see why we came here in the first place! Let me take your hand!

THE DOCTOR (*leads her to the door, rear*). The time before it was I who asked you for your hand; and it rested on me so heavily—that delicate little hand of yours. It once struck me in the face—that little delicate hand—and still I kissed it. Alas, now it is withered, and it no longer strikes. Oh, *Dolce Napoli!* Joy of life—where did you disappear? You went the way she did—she—the bride of my youth!

MRS. HALL (*in the doorway to the vestibule*). Where is my coat?

THE DOCTOR (*closing the door*). Out in the hall, no doubt. —This is horrible! (*He lights a cigar.*) Oh, *Dolce Napoli!* I wonder whether it is really so lovely in that cholera-infested fishing harbor? Fraud—deception—brides—love—Naples— joy of life—old-fashioned—modern—liberal—conservative— ideal—real—natural—fraud, fraud from beginning to end!

(AXEL, ABEL, WILLMER *and* LIEUTENANT *and* MRS. STARCK *enter.*)

MRS. STARCK. Are you leaving, Doctor?

THE DOCTOR. Excuse me, this is merely a matter of *quid pro quo.* We were obliged to identify two strangers who had crashed the party.

MRS. STARCK. The girls, you mean?

CARL. Yes, and you have nothing to do with that! I don't know—I feel as if an enemy were hovering about in here . . .

MRS. STARCK. Oh, Carl dear, you always imagine you see enemies everywhere.

CARL. No—I don't see them—but I feel them.

MRS. STARCK. You just come to me, then, and I'll defend you.

CARL. Yes, you are always so good to me.

MRS. STARCK. Why shouldn't I be? You always are so thoughtful.

(*Just then the doors in the rear are swung open and two men, carrying a painting, enter, followed by* THE MAID.)

AXEL. What's the meaning of this?

THE MAID. The concierge said to bring it into the studio because he had no room for it.

AXEL. What sort of nonsense is this? Take away the painting!

THE MAID (*to* BERTHA). But Mrs. Alberg sent for her painting herself. Didn't you, Mrs. Alberg?

BERTHA. That isn't true—and besides it isn't my painting. It is Mr. Alberg's. Put it over there! (THE MAID *and the two men leave.* AXEL *places himself in front of the painting.*) Step aside, Axel, and let us look at it!

AXEL (*steps aside*). There is a mistake somewhere.

BERTHA (*with a shriek*). Why, what is this? There has been a mistake! What's the meaning of all this? The painting is mine—but the number is—the number is Axel's! Oh! (*She collapses.*)

(THE DOCTOR *and* CARL *carry* BERTHA *into her room on the right. The women follow.*)

ABEL. This will be the end of her.

MRS. STARCK. Heaven help us, what is this! Poor little girl! Doctor Östermark, why don't you do something! Say something! And Axel—you stand as if you had lost your wits! (*She follows* ABEL *into the room, right.*)

(AXEL *and* WILLMER *are alone on the stage.*)

AXEL. This is of your doing!

WILLMER. Mine?

AXEL (*grabs him by the ear*). You, yes—but not altogether! But I'll give you something for your part in it! (*He leads him to the door which he opens with his foot; with his other foot he gives* WILLMER *a kick so that he tumbles outside.*) Out with you!

WILLMER. You'll be repaid for this!

AXEL. I expect I will!

(DR. ÖSTERMARK *and* CARL *enter.*)

THE DOCTOR. What is all this about the painting?

AXEL. It is supposed to represent sulphuric acid!

CARL. But tell me—is it you who have been refused, or is it she?

AXEL. I was refused, for submitting her picture! I wanted to help her along, like a good comrade, and so I changed the numbers around.

THE DOCTOR. Yes, but there is still something else! She says you don't love her any more.

AXEL. In that she is quite right. That is the way it is— and tomorrow we each go our own way.

THE DOCTOR AND CARL. Go your own way?

AXEL. Yes. Where there are no bonds to be severed, they loosen by themselves. Ours has not been a marriage; we have merely been living together—or something still worse!

THE DOCTOR. The air in here is foul! Come, let us get out of here!

AXEL. Yes—I want to get out . . . get out of here!

(They walk toward the rear.)

ABEL. What? Are you gentlemen leaving?

AXEL. Are you surprised?

ABEL. May I have a word with you?

AXEL. Go ahead!

ABEL. Won't you go in to Bertha?

AXEL. No!

ABEL. What have you done to her?

AXEL. I have humbled her.

ABEL. I can see you have. Her wrists were blue. Look at me!—I never thought you had it in you! Well, victorious one, now you can triumph!

AXEL. An uncertain victory which I never wished for!

ABEL. Are you so sure of that? *(She moves close to him and says in a soft tone of voice:)* Bertha loves you—after you—after you put her in her place!

AXEL. I know. But I don't love her any more.

ABEL. Won't you go in to her?

AXEL. No—it's all over! *(He takes* THE DOCTOR *by the arm.)* Come!

ABEL. Is there nothing you want to say to Bertha?

AXEL. Nothing! Yes—tell her that I have nothing but contempt for her—that I despise her!

ABEL. Goodbye, my friend!

AXEL. Goodbye, my enemy!

ABEL. Enemy?

AXEL. Are you my friend, perhaps?

ABEL. I don't know! Perhaps I am both! Perhaps neither! I am a bastard!

AXEL. Aren't we all, don't you think?—we being a cross between man and woman. . . . Perhaps you have been in love with me in your own particular way, since you wanted to estrange Bertha and me.

ABEL *(rolling a cigarette)*. Been in love?—I just wonder how it would feel to be in love? No—I can't love. I must be a defective, a misfit of some sort. For I enjoyed watching you two, until the envy of the misfit set me afire.—But perhaps you have been in love with me?

AXEL. No—upon my soul! To me you were merely an interesting and amusing comrade who happened to be dressed as a woman. You never gave me the impression of belonging to the other sex; and love, you see, can and should exist only between individuals of opposite sexes.

ABEL. You are speaking of sexual love?

AXEL. Is there any other kind of love?

ABEL. I don't know.—But I think I ought to feel sorry for myself! And this hate—this terrible hate! Perhaps it would disappear if you were not so hesitant about loving us —if you were not so—how shall I put it—so moral, I believe that's the word!

AXEL. But why in heaven's name don't you try to act a little more agreeably, more amiably? And why do you get yourself up in a manner to make one think of the penal code when one sees you?

ABEL. You think I am so terrible to look at then?

AXEL. Yes, if you will forgive me for saying it—you are terrible to look at.

BERTHA (*enters. To* AXEL): Are you thinking of leaving?

AXEL. That was my intention, yes,—a moment ago. But now I have decided to stay.

BERTHA (*softly*). What? You . . .

AXEL. I am staying in my home.

BERTHA. In *our* home.

AXEL. No—in *my* home! In *my* studio—furnished with *my* furniture!

BERTHA. And what about me?

AXEL. You may do as you please—but you must be conscious of what you risk. You see, I have applied for a year's separation from bed and board. If you should remain—that is, if you visit me or seek me out during that time, you will have to choose between imprisonment or being looked upon as my mistress! Do you care to stay?

BERTHA. Ah!—Is that what the law says?

AXEL. That is what the law says!

BERTHA. Then you are putting me out, in other words?

AXEL. Not I—the law is!

BERTHA. And do you think I will be satisfied with that?

AXEL. No—I don't. You will not be satisfied until you have skinned me alive.

BERTHA. Axel! Don't talk like that! If you only knew how I—love you!

AXEL. I don't find that at all unreasonable—but I no longer have any love for you.

BERTHA (*rising quickly*). Because you are in love with *her* there! (*She makes a gesture in the direction of* ABEL.)

AXEL. No, I can assure you I am not! And I never have been in love with her and never will be! What an unbelievable conceit! As if there were no other women in the world —and more attractive than you two!

BERTHA. But she is in love with you!

AXEL. That may be! I believe she has even indicated something in that direction. Yes, I seem to remember she said it quite frankly.

BERTHA (*in a changed manner*). You are really the most insolent human being I have ever known!

AXEL. I am not surprised!

BERTHA (*putting on her hat and coat*). And now you intend to cast me out into the street? Is that what you really intend to do?

AXEL. Yes—or wherever you prefer!

BERTHA (*in a rage*). Do you think a woman can allow herself to be treated in this way?

AXEL. You once asked me to forget that you were a woman. Very well—I forgot it!

BERTHA. And you know that you owe something to one who has been your wife, don't you?

AXEL. You want me to pay for your good comradeship? Is that the idea? A life annuity institution, eh?

BERTHA. Yes!

AXEL. Here is a month's advance! (*He puts a few bills on the table.*)

BERTHA (*takes the money and counts it*). You still have some honor left in you!

ABEL. Goodbye, Bertha,—I am leaving!

BERTHA. Wait a second, and I'll go with you.

ABEL. No—from now on our ways part.

BERTHA. What? . . . Why so?

ABEL. I am ashamed of you!

BERTHA (*astounded*). Ashamed?

ABEL. Yes, I am ashamed! Goodbye!   (*She leaves.*)

BERTHA. I just don't understand. Goodbye, Axel! Thank you for the money!—Are we friends? (*She takes him by the hand and holds it.*)

AXEL. As far as I am concerned, we are not! Let go my hand, or I'll begin to think you are trying to seduce me again! (BERTHA *lets go his hand and walks toward the door.* AXEL, *to himself, with a sigh of relief:*) Nice comrades! Oh!

THE MAID (*comes in from the garden entrance*). Mademoiselle is waiting for Monsieur!

AXEL. Oh yes!—I'll be there in a moment!

BERTHA. Is she your new comrade?

AXEL. No, this one is no comrade. She is my mistress.

BERTHA. And wife-to-be?

AXEL. Perhaps! For I want to see my comrades at the café —but at home I want to have a wife! (*He makes a movement as if to leave her.*) Will you excuse me?

BERTHA. Goodbye, then! Shall we never see each other again?

AXEL. Why—why not!—But at the café!—Goodbye!

(BERTHA *leaves.*)

TO BETTY SHANNON

THE STRONGER
A PLAY IN ONE SCENE

The Stronger is the outstanding dramatic monologue in the modern theatre. It is a complete play despite the fact that Strindberg employed only a single speaking character. This little work is also a marvel of dramatic construction. The action constitutes a drama of discovery (Mrs. X's discovery of her husband's infidelity with Miss Y) and a drama of revelation or, one might say, self-revelation, since Mrs. X unintentionally reveals facets of her character in the course of her monologue. *The Stronger* is altogether an acting piece and requires multi-dimensional realization by the actress who performs the role of Mrs. X. The other, non-speaking character, Miss Y, also needs more than routine performance. Whether Mrs. X is "the stronger woman," as she claims to be, is a matter to be decided by the audience, and the attitude of the audience will be greatly influenced by the interpretation given to the two roles. "In the end," writes V. J. McGill in *August Strindberg: The Bedeviled Viking,* "we are in some doubt as to which of the two women is 'The Stronger', the quiet sphinx-like vampire or the talkative and, at last, triumphant wife." *The Stronger* is a *tour de force* not only when acted but on the printed page. It is highly probable that the young O'Neill was influenced by Strindberg's short masterpiece to write his early dramatic monologue *Before Breakfast,* a less subtle and complex work but nevertheless also a theatrical feat which involves one speaking and one non-speaking part—in this case a nagging common woman and her desperate husband.

Strindberg wrote *Den Starkare,* or *The Stronger* (originally billed as *Den Starkaste,* "The Strongest") in 1889, along with two other one-act plays, *Pariah* and *Simoom,* under the influence of Antoine's naturalistic little "free" theatre in Paris, the *Théâtre Libre,* for which several avant-garde play-wrights wrote short, fifteen-minute pieces known as *quarts d'heure.* In an early effort to follow Antoine's example, Strindberg in association with his already totally estranged first wife Siri von Essen (who was to play all the leading fe-male roles) tried to establish a Scandinavian *Théâtre Libre,* or experimental theatre, in Copenhagen, where he had in-fluential admirers such as Georg Brandes, the world-famous critic and his brother Edward. *The Stronger* (with the author's wife playing Mrs. X) appeared on the triple bill, along with *Pariah* and *Creditors,* with which he opened his Scandinavian Experimental Theatre on March 9, 1889. This first effort of Strindberg's to establish a theatre of his own collapsed after three performances of this bill at Copenhagen and one at Malmö.

Max Reinhardt presented *The Stronger* at his *Kleines Theater* in Berlin in the spring of 1902, and this miniature play, which provides a challenging role for a star-actress, has been extensively performed since then throughout Europe. It was first presented in London in 1909 and in the United States (in Milwaukee and Madison, Wisconsin) in 1911–1912. New York and Chicago first saw a performance in 1913. A recent professional performance was the Phoenix Theatre production in New York as adapted and staged by George Tabori in February 1956, with Ruth Ford playing Mrs. X and Viveca Lindfors the silent Miss Y. In Arvid Paulson's translation it was also successfully televised, along with *Miss Julie,* on the "Play of the Week" program in New York. It has since been shown throughout the United States.

PERSONS IN THE PLAY

MRS. X., a married actress
MISS Y., an unmarried actress
A WAITRESS

(THE SETTING.—*A corner of a café for ladies. Two wrought iron tables; a sofa upholstered with red shag; several chairs. MISS Y. is seated at one of the tables. Before her is a half empty bottle of ale. She is reading an illustrated periodical, which she later exchanges for others on the table. MRS. X. enters. She is dressed in winter apparel and wears a hat and cloak. She carries a Japanese shopping bag or basket, of exquisite design, on her arm.*)

MRS. X. How do you do, Amelie dear! You are sitting here all by yourself on Christmas Eve—like some poor bachelor . . .

(MISS Y. *looks up from the magazine, gives MRS. X. a nod, and resumes her reading.*)

MRS. X. You know it hurts me to see you sitting here— alone—alone in a café, and, of all times, on Christmas Eve. It makes me feel as bad as when I once saw a wedding party in a restaurant in Paris. The bride sat reading a comic paper, while the bridegroom was playing billiards with the wedding guests. Ugh, I thought to myself, with a beginning like that, what will the marriage be like—and how will it end? *He,* playing billiards on their wedding night! —And *she* reading a comic paper, you mean to say? . . . Ah, but there is a certain difference, don't you think?

(THE WAITRESS *enters with a cup of chocolate which she places before MRS. X. Then she leaves.*)

MRS. X. Do you know what, Amelie! I believe you would have been better off if you had married him. . . . You remember that I urged you from the very first to forgive him. You remember that? You could have been his wife now, and had a home of your own. . . . Do you recall how happy

175

you were last Christmas when you spent the holidays with
your fiancé's parents out in the country? How you sang
the praises of domestic life and literally longed to get away
from the theatre?—Yes, Amelie dear, a home is the best
after all—next to the theatre. And children, you know. . . .
Well, but you wouldn't understand that!

(MISS Y. *expresses disdain.*)

MRS. X. (*sips a few teaspoonfuls of her chocolate. Then
she opens her shopping bag and brings out some Christmas
presents.*) Here—let me show you what I have bought for
my little ones. (*She shows her a doll.*) Look at this one!
This is for Lisa. . . . Do you see how she rolls her eyes and
turns her head! Do you? Do you see?—And here is a pop-
gun for Maja. . . . (*She loads the toy gun and pops it at
MISS Y.*)

(MISS Y. *makes a gesture of fright.*)

MRS. X. Did I frighten you? You didn't think I was going
to shoot you, did you? Did you?—Upon my soul, I really
think you did! If *you* had wanted to shoot *me*, I wouldn't
have been surprised. After all, I have stood in your way—
and I realize that you can never forget that . . . even though
I was entirely blameless. You still believe that I schemed to
have you dismissed from the Grand Theatre—don't you?
But I didn't! You may think whatever you like, but I had
nothing to do with it! I realize, however, that no matter
what I say, you will still believe I was responsible for it!
(*She takes out a pair of embroidered bedroom slippers from
the bag.*) And these are for my better half. I embroidered
them myself—with tulips. You understand, I hate tulips,
but my husband has to have tulips on everything. . . .

(MISS Y. *looks up from her magazine with an expression
of irony mixed with curiosity.*)

MRS. X. (*places a hand inside each slipper*). See what tiny
feet Bob has! See? And I wish you could see how ele-
gantly he walks! You never saw him in slippers, did you?

(MISS Y. *laughs aloud.*)

MRS. X. Look, let me show you! (*She makes the slippers
walk on the table.*)

(MISS Y. *gives another loud laugh.*)

MRS. X. And when he gets angry, he stamps his foot,
like this: "Damnation! These stupid maids who never can
learn to make coffee! And look at this! The idiots don't
even know how to trim a lamp wick!" And when there is a
draft from the floor and his feet are cold: "Heavens! It's

freezing cold, and the incorrigible fools let the fire go out in the grate!" (*She rubs the sole of one slipper against the top of the other.*)

(MISS Y. *gives a shriek of laughter.*)

MRS. X. And when he comes home, he goes hunting for his slippers which Marie has put under the chiffonier. . . . Oh, but it's a shame to sit and make fun of my own husband like this. After all, he is so nice. He is a good little husband. . . . You should have had a husband like him, Amelie!—What are you laughing at, if I may ask? What is it? What's the matter?—And the best of it is that he is faithful to me—yes, that I know. He has told me so himself! . . . Why the sneering grin? He told me that Frédérique tried to seduce him while I was on a tour in Norway. . . . Can you imagine such impudence! (*There is a silence.*) I would have torn her eyes out! That's what I'd have done, if she had come near him while I was at home! (*Again there is silence.*) I was lucky enough to hear about it from Bob himself before being told by some gossip. . . . (*Silence.*) But Frédérique was not the only one, let me tell you! I can't understand it, but women seem to be absolutely crazy about my husband. They must think he has something to say about the engaging of the artists, because he is on the board of administration. . . . I would not be surprised if you, too, had used your wiles on him! I never did trust you too much. . . . But I know now that he could not be interested in you—and it seemed to me you always acted as if you bore some sort of grudge against him. . . . (*There is a silence and they regard each other with some embarrassment.* MRS. X. *continues.*) Why don't you come home to us this evening, Amelie, just to show that you have no hard feelings—at least not against *me*. . . . I can't explain just why—but I think it is so unpleasant to be bad friends—with you especially. Perhaps it is because I stood in your way that time (*In a slower tempo.*) . . . or . . . I can't imagine . . . what the reason could have been—really . . . (*There is a silence.*)

(MISS Y. *gazes fixedly and curiously at* MRS. X.)

MRS. X. (*pensively*). Our relationship was such a strange one. . . . The first time I saw you, I was frightened of you. I was so frightened that I didn't dare to let you out of my sight. No matter when or where I went—I always found myself next to you. . . . I didn't have the courage to be your enemy, and so I became your friend. But whenever you came to our home, it always led to discord. I noticed that my husband could not bear the sight of you and it made me feel ill at ease—as when a garment does not fit. I did everything I could to persuade him to show you some friendliness, but it was no use—not until you announced your engagement! Then suddenly a violent friendship blossomed between you two! At the time it appeared as if only then you dared to show your true feelings—when it was safe for you to do so! And then—what happened afterwards? . . . I didn't feel any jealousy—and that seems strange to me now! And I can remember the scene at the christening, when you were the godmother, and I had to coax him to kiss you. When he did, you were so abashed and confused—and quite frankly, I didn't notice it at the time, didn't give it a thought. I never thought of it until—until this very moment. . . . (*She rises violently, impassioned.*) Why don't you say something? You haven't uttered one single word all this time! You have let me sit here, talking on and on! You have been sitting there, drawing out of me all these thoughts that have been lying like raw silk in the cocoon—thoughts . . . yes, even suspicions. . . . Let me see! Why did you break off your engagement? Why did you never come to our home again after that? Why won't you come to our home tonight?

(MISS Y. *seems to be about to break her silence.*)

MRS. X. Don't speak! You needn't say a word! Now I understand everything! It was because of this—and that—and that! That's it exactly. Now the accounts are balanced! Now I know the answer!—For shame! I won't sit at the same table with you! (*She moves her things to the other table.*) That is why I had to embroider tulips on his slippers—because you liked tulips. . . . That's why we—(*She throws the slippers on the floor.*)—why we had to spend the summers at Lake Mälar—because you didn't like the open sea; that's why my son was named Eskil—because that was your father's name; that's the reason I had to wear your colors, read your authors, eat your favorite dishes, drink what you liked—your chocolate, for instance. . . . That is why—Oh, my God—it's frightening to think of it—horrible! Everything, everything came to me from you, even your passions! Your soul crept into mine, like a worm into an apple, worming its way, boring and boring, until nothing was left but the rind and a speck of black dust inside. I tried to get away from you, but I couldn't! You charmed me, bewitched me like a snake, with your black eyes. . . . Every time I lifted my wings to escape, I felt myself being dragged down again: I lay in the water with bound feet—and the harder I fought to keep afloat, the further down I went—down, down, until I sank to the bottom, where you lay in wait like a giant crab to seize me with your claws—and there is where I am now.

Ugh! How I detest you, hate you, hate you! But you—all you do is to sit there silent, cold and impassive! You don't care whether it's new moon or full moon, Christmas or New Year—whether people around you are happy or unhappy! You have neither the capacity to hate nor to love; you are as cold-blooded as a stork watching a rat-hole; you are incapable of scenting your prey and pursuing it—but you know how to hide in holes and corners and exhaust your prey. Here you sit—I suppose you know people call this corner the rat trap, in your honor—scanning the newspapers in the hope that you may read about someone who has had bad luck or been struck by misfortune, or about someone who has been dismissed from the theatre. . . . Here you sit, lurking for victims, figuring out your chances like a pilot in a shipwreck. Here you receive your tributes! Poor Amelie! You know, in spite of everything, I feel sorry for you, because I am aware that you are miserable—miserable like some wounded beast!—and made spiteful and vicious because of having been wounded! I find it hard to be angry with you, despite feeling that I ought to be—but, after all, you are the weaker one. . . . As for the episode with Bob—well, I shan't let that bother me. . . . It hasn't really harmed me! And if *you* got me into the habit of drinking chocolate, or if someone else did, matters little . . . (*She takes a spoonful of chocolate; then, common-sense-like.*) Besides, chocolate is a healthful beverage. And if you have taught me how to dress—*tant mieux!* My husband has become all the more fond of me as a result! That is one thing I have gained, and that you lost. As a matter of fact, judging from what I have seen, I think you have already lost him! But no doubt it was your intention that I should leave him—as you did—and which you now regret. But, you see, that's just what I don't intend to do! We must not be one-sided or selfish, you know. But why should I take only what someone else doesn't want? All said and done, perhaps I am at this moment really the stronger. . . . You never received anything from *me* —while *you* gave something to me! And now I have had the same experience as the proverbial thief had: When *you* woke up, *I* possessed what *you* had lost! And why was it that everything you touched became sterile and empty? Your tulips and your passions proved insufficient to keep a man's love—while I was able to keep it. Your authors could not teach you the art of living—as I have learned it. Nor did you bear a little Eskil—even if your father bore that name. . . . And why are you forever silent, your lips eternally sealed? I confess I used to think it a sign of strength—but perhaps it is only because you have nothing to say! Perhaps it is for lack of thoughts! (*She rises and picks up the slippers from the floor.*) Now I am going home—and I take the tulips with me. Your tulips! You found it hard to learn from others—you found it hard to bend, to humble yourself—and so you broke like a dry reed—and I survived! I thank you, Amelie, for all that you have taught me! And thank you for teaching my husband how to love! Now I am going home— to love him!   (*She leaves.*)

THE BOND
A TRAGEDY IN ONE ACT

Bandet or *The Bond* is one of the many plays Strindberg based on personal experience. Its source is his compulsive and devastating "love-hate" relationship with his first wife Siri von Essen and the termination of the marriage under painful and humiliating circumstances. Siri had much cause for complaint and accused her husband of cruel behavior and desertion; but he also had, or thought he had, reasons for petitioning for a divorce on the grounds that Siri's conduct made her unfit to bring up their children. He was especially vehement on the subject of her attachment to a young woman whom he considered to be sexually inverted. But the chief source of contention between Strindberg and Siri, who was already resolved to get a divorce from him, was the custody of their three children. An official separation for a year, prior to the granting of a divorce, was handed down by the court on March 24, 1891. It was a crushing blow to Strindberg when the children were placed in their mother's custody after the bitter wrangle in the Court of Justice.

The Bond (earlier translated into English under the title of *The Link*) was Strindberg's reaction to those proceedings. But it would be a mistake to assume that the embittered author was incapable of writing objectively about himself and Siri. The very contrary is the case; both the husband and the wife are shown in this taut play as compulsively driven to recriminations in spite of their determination to behave circumspectly in court. An irrational force (call it the force of their love-hate) overwhelms their reason until they find themselves indecently clawing at each other, with the result that they prove themselves equally unfit to receive the custody of their child. *The Bond* is another example of Strindberg's intensely concentrated and highly charged type of naturalism. There is no room for relaxation or for respite from the "sex-duel" in this overpowering divorce-drama.

The play was written in 1892 soon after the trial, and was first published in Sweden in 1897. It had its première at Max Reinhardt's *Kleines Theater* in Berlin in March 1902, with the famous actor Emmanuel Reicher in the role of the husband and Rosa Bertens as the wife. The first Swedish production was Strindberg's own presentation of the play at his experimental Intimate Theatre in Stockholm on January 31, 1908, where it was given fifty performances. The Royal Theatre in Stockholm presented the play in 1915 and in 1928.

PERSONS IN THE PLAY

The Judge, 25 years old
The Pastor, 60 years old
The Baron, 42 years old
The Baroness, 40 years old
Alexander Eklund
Emanuel Vickberg
Karl Johan Sjöberg
Erik Otto Boman
Erenfrid Söderberg
Olof Andersson of Vik
Karl Peter Andersson of Berga
Axel Vallin
Anders Erik Ruth
Sven Oskar Erlin
August Alexander Vass
Ludvig Östman
The Clerk of the Court
The Sheriff
The Constable
The Attorney
Alexandersson, a farmer
Alma Jonsson, a housemaid
The Dairy Maid
The Farmhand
Male and female spectators, young and old

(THE SETTING.—*A village hall, in which circuit court is held. In the rear is a door with windows on each side. Through the windows can be seen the churchyard and a detached bell-tower. To the left, a door. To the right, the judge's seat: a high desk on a platform. The desk is embellished with gilt ornamentations of the sword of justice and a pair of scales. On each side of the desk, tables and chairs for the twelve jurymen. In the center of the hall are benches for the spectators. The walls are lined with built-in closets, to the doors of which are tacked reports listing current official market prices for the county, announcements and communications, bulletins, etc.*

The play takes place in the eighteen-nineties in a small community in Sweden.)

THE SHERIFF. Did you ever see such a lot of people at a summer session?

THE CONSTABLE. No—not for the last fifteen years—not since the time of the famous Alder Lake murder.

THE SHERIFF. Well—this case, I dare say, is as good as any double murder—even of your own parents. That the baron and the baroness are divorcing each other, that alone is a scandal; but when their two families start wrangling about property and land holdings, too,—then you can well imagine what a blaze it will be. All that's missing now is a fight over their only child—and then King Solomon himself wouldn't be able to sit in judgment.

THE CONSTABLE. Well—what's behind it all, anyhow? Some people say one thing, others say something else—but somebody is to blame, wouldn't you think?

THE SHERIFF. It's never the fault of one when two people

quarrel, as the saying goes. And then again, it may be the fault of only *one* that they do. Take my old porcupine at home, for example. They tell me she storms hither and thither, quarreling with herself, when I am away. But in this case it's not a question of just a quarrel; this is a full-blown criminal case as large as life. And in most such cases one of the parties is the plaintiff—meaning that he has been wronged, and the other party the defendant, meaning that he is the one who has done wrong. Who is the guilty one in this case— that is not easy to say, for both parties are plaintiffs, and at the same time defendants.

THE CONSTABLE. Well, well. . . . Yes, we live in strange times, we do. One would think women had gone crazy. Every now and then my old woman comes with the idea that if there was any justice in the world I ought to bear children, too! As if the Lord didn't know just what He was doing when he created us human beings! And then she oozes out long harangues about her being human, too—as if I didn't know that before—as if I had ever said she wasn't—and that she is fed up with being a servant to me . . . when the truth is that I am the one who really slaves for *her*.

THE SHERIFF. Is that a fact? So you, too, are suffering from the same plague in your house? My old woman has the habit of reading a newspaper she brings home from the manor house; and one time she will tell me that a young Dalecarlian woman has taken up bricklaying—as if that was something so remarkable—and another time she will tell me that some old crone has attacked her sick husband and given him a beating! What in the world is the meaning of all this is more than I can fathom; but it looks to me as if she, my wife, was peeved at me because I am a man!

THE CONSTABLE. Yes, I must say it is all very strange. (*He offers* THE SHERIFF *some snuff.*) We are certainly having beautiful weather! The rye looks like a rug of fur, and we got rid of the frosty nights quickly.

THE SHERIFF. I have nothing in the field to harvest, and good years are bad years for me: no distress to levy on anyone, and no auctions. Do you know the new circuit judge who is to sit in court today?

THE CONSTABLE. No, but I have heard people say he is a young man who only recently took his bar examination and today is sitting on the bench for the first time.

THE SHERIFF. I have also heard that he is a bit of a pietist. . . . H'm.

THE CONSTABLE. H'm. H'm.—The church service for the opening of the court session is taking a long time today . . .

THE SHERIFF (*places a large Bible on* THE JUDGE'S *desk and twelve smaller ones on the jurymen's desks*). They can't be much longer now. They have been in there almost a whole hour.

THE CONSTABLE. He is a wonder at preaching, the pastor is, once he gets started. (*There is a pause.*) Will the baron and the baroness be here themselves—I mean in person?

THE SHERIFF. Both he and she! So there is sure to be an uproar. . . . (*The bell in the bell-tower starts ringing.*) There now—it's over! Go over the tables with a dust rag—then we'll be all ready to start.

THE CONSTABLE. And the inkwells are filled, aren't they?

THE BARON (*enters. In a subdued tone to* THE BARONESS). And so, before we separate for a year, we are agreed, entirely agreed on all points, aren't we? But first of all: no recriminations before the court!

THE BARONESS. Do you think I would lay bare all the intimate details of our married life before a lot of curious peasants?

THE BARON. Exactly! Furthermore, you will have the child with you during the period of the interlocutory decree, provided that he may visit me whenever I so desire, and that he is educated in accordance with the principles I stipulated, and which you approved.

THE BARONESS. That's right!

THE BARON. Further, that I—during the year of separation—provide for you and the child with three thousand crowns from the net income of the estate.

THE BARONESS. I agree.

THE BARON. Then I have nothing to add, and so I only wish to bid you goodbye. Why we are divorcing only you and I know; and for the sake of our son, no one else must know. And for his sake also, I beg of you not to enter into any contest so that we are provoked into soiling the names of his parents. Who knows—once he has come out into life, he may yet have to suffer because his parents are divorced.

THE BARONESS. I shall start no contest as long as I may keep my child.

THE BARON. That settled, let us concentrate our attention solely upon our child's welfare and forget what has come between us two. And remember one thing more: if we start fighting about the child and challenge each other's fitness as guardians, the judge might take him away from us both and place him with some pietists, and they would bring him up to hate and despise his parents.

THE BARONESS. He couldn't do that!

THE BARON. Yes, my dear—for that is the law!

THE BARONESS. It's a stupid law!

THE BARON. Perhaps it is—but it *is* the law; and the law is the same for you and me as for everybody else!

THE BARONESS. Why, that's monstrous, unheard of! And I would never submit to it!

THE BARON. But you don't need to as we have decided not to challenge each other. We have never been able to agree in the past, but on this point we are of one mind, are we not—that we are to part without any ill-feeling on either side? (*To* THE SHERIFF.) Is it permissible for the Baroness to wait inside?

THE SHERIFF. You are very welcome! Step in here! (THE BARON *escorts* THE BARONESS *to the door, left; then he goes out through the door in the rear.* THE ATTORNEY, THE HOUSEMAID, THE DAIRY MAID *and* THE FARMHAND *enter*.)

THE ATTORNEY (*to* THE HOUSEMAID). You see, my friend —that you have stolen, I don't doubt for a moment. . . . But as long as your employer, farmer Alexandersson, has no witnesses to prove it, you are innocent. But because your employer has called you a thief in the presence of two witnesses, *he* is guilty of slander. Therefore you are now the plaintiff, and he is the defendant. And just remember this one rule: the first duty an accused offender has—is *to deny!*

THE HOUSEMAID. Yes, but you just said that I am not an offender but that farmer Alexandersson is.

THE ATTORNEY. You are an offender because you have stolen; but because you have demanded a lawyer, it is my positive duty to wash you clean and try to have your employer convicted. And so I say again, and for the last time: Deny! (*To the witnesses.*) And as for the witnesses, what are they going to witness to? Listen carefully now! A good witness sticks to the matter at hand. And therefore you must constantly bear in mind that it is not a question of whether Alma Jonsson has stolen or has not stolen; the only question before the court is whether Alexandersson has said that she has stolen—for, and note this well, Alexandersson has no legal right to prove what he said—but we have. Just why it is so, only the devil knows! And anyhow—that's none of your business. Consequently: keep your tongues straight in your mouth and your hands on the Bible!

THE DAIRY MAID. Lord in Heaven, I am scared. . . . I have no idea what to say!

THE FARMHAND. You just say after me, and you won't be telling any lies.

(THE JUDGE *and* THE PASTOR *enter.*)

THE JUDGE. I want to thank you for your sermon, Pastor.

THE PASTOR. Oh, don't mention it, Judge.

THE JUDGE. Well—as you know, this is the first time I am presiding in a court. I confess I was timid about entering a legal career in the beginning. I really took it up against my will—it was foisted upon me. Because, for one thing, our laws are so imperfect, our judicial institutions so unsatisfactory, and human nature so made up of falsehood and hypocrisy that I have often wondered how any judge could even dare to express an honest, resolute opinion. And today, in your sermon, you brought to life my old misgivings.

THE PASTOR. To be conscientious is our rightful, natural duty; but to be sentimental—that will never do. And since everything else on earth is so lacking in perfection these days, we can't expect judges and their decisions to be perfect.

THE JUDGE. That may be, but that does not prevent me from feeling a tremendous responsibility when I hold the fate of a human being in my hand. Particularly, as a pronouncement of mine can affect generations to come. I am especially thinking of this divorce suit between the baron and his wife; and I feel I should ask you—since you were the one who, as the head of the Vestry Board, communicated the two required warnings to them—what you feel their mutual relationship and respective guilt may be.

THE PASTOR. In short, you would put me in the position of sitting in judgment . . . or you would let your decision be influenced by what I say. But all I can do is to refer you to the minutes of the Vestry Board.

THE JUDGE. Well, the minutes. . . . I have read them. What I want to know is what is *not* in the minutes.

THE PASTOR. The accusations the baron and the baroness made against each other at a private hearing remain my secret. Besides, how can I know which one told the truth and which one did not. I have to tell you the very same thing that I told them: "I have no reason to believe one of you more than the other."

THE JUDGE. But I should imagine you would have formed some sort of opinion as to their respective guilt during these hearings?

THE PASTOR. When I had heard one of them, I formed one opinion; but when I heard the other one I had a different opinion. Therefore, you see, I can have no definite or final opinion in this matter.

THE JUDGE. But I—who have no knowledge of what has happened—I am expected to give a final opinion.

THE PASTOR. That is the grave task a judge has. I would never undertake to bear that responsibility!

THE JUDGE. But I should think witnesses could be produced who could give evidence?

THE PASTOR. No, the baron and the baroness have never accused each other publicly. Furthermore, two false witnesses are enough to furnish valid proof of guilt—and a perjurer can do as much. Do you think that I would ever base a decision on the gossip of servants, the loose talk of envious neighbors, or on the biased and spiteful intrigues of vindictive relatives. Do you?

THE JUDGE. You are an incorrigible skeptic, Pastor!

THE PASTOR. After having lived sixty years and having cared for peoples' souls for forty, one can't help being one. The habit of prevaricating is as ingrown in us as original sin, and all of us are liars, I believe. As children we lie out of fear, as grown-ups out of self-interest, necessity, out of a feeling of self-preservation—and I have known people who have lied out of pure human kindness. In this particular case, involving the baron and the baroness, I think you will have an exceedingly hard task to find out who is speaking the truth; and I feel I must warn you not to let yourself be prejudiced by any preconceived opinion. You yourself are newly married and are likely to be under the spell of a young woman's bewitchery. As a consequence, you may easily be influenced in favor of a young and charming lady who is not only an unfortunate wife but a mother as well. On the other hand, you have recently become a father, and as such you cannot escape being moved by the impending separation of the father from his one and only child. Be on your guard against compassion for either side—for compassion for one may spell cruelty to the other.

THE JUDGE. There is one thing, at least, that will make my task somewhat easier; and that is the fact that both parties are in mutual agreement on the main issues.

THE PASTOR. Don't rely too much on that—for that is what they all say! But once they have come before the court, then the fireworks begin. All that is needed in this case is a spark—and then the conflagration is set. Here come the jurymen now. . . . Goodbye for the time being! I am staying —but I'll keep out of sight!

(*The twelve* JURYMEN *enter and take their places.* THE SHERIFF, *in the open doorway, summons the participants with a bell.* THE JUDGE *takes his seat, while spectators and witnesses crowd into the courtroom.*)

THE JUDGE. Referring to the regulations of the penal code, in chapter 11, paragraphs 5, 6 and 8, I herewith declare the proceedings of this court opened. (*He whispers to* THE CLERK OF THE COURT, *and then says.*) Will it please the members of the Jury, who have just been selected to take the oath. . . .

THE JURYMEN (*rise. They place their right hands on their respective Bibles, then speak in unison except when their individual names are called.*)

I, Alexander Eklund,
I, Emanuel Vickberg,
I, Karl Johan Sjöberg,
I, Erik Otto Boman,
I, Erenfrid Söderberg,
I, Olof Andersson of Vik,
I, Karl Peter Andersson of Berga,
I, Axel Vallin,
I, Anders Erik Ruth,
I, Sven Oskar Erlin,
I, August Alexander Vass,
I, Ludvig Östman,

(*All together, in a low pitched, measured tone of voice.*) promise and swear before God and on his holy Gospel that I will and shall, according to the best of my judgment and conscience, decide fairly in all cases, no less for the poor than for the rich, and give judgment according to the laws of God and the statute laws of the Kingdom of Sweden— (*In a higher pitch and somewhat louder.*)—never to twist or distort the law, or support what is not right, neither for the sake of close or distant kinship, friendship, envy or enmity, nor out of fear, nor for bribes nor gifts, nor for any cause whatsoever, no matter what form it may take, nor cause him to be judged guilty who is without guilt, nor him judged innocent who is guilty.

(*In increased tone of voice.*) Furthermore, I shall neither before judgment is passed nor afterward, neither to those who are parties to any action nor to any others, disclose any deliberations that may be held by this Court behind closed doors. All this I will and shall, as an honest and upright member of the Jury, faithfully keep without perfidy, subterfuge or deception. . . . (*There is a pause.*) . . . Upon my life and soul, so help me God! (*The* JURORS *seat themselves.*)

THE JUDGE (*to* THE SHERIFF). Call the case of Alma Jonsson versus the farmer Alexandersson.

(THE SHERIFF *calls the case and* ALEXANDERSSON, THE HOUSEMAID, THE ATTORNEY, THE FARMHAND *and* THE DAIRY MAID *enter.*)

THE SHERIFF (*calls out*). The housemaid Alma Jonsson versus the farmer Alexandersson.

THE ATTORNEY. I desire to present my power of attorney. I appear on behalf of the plaintiff, Alma Jonsson.

THE JUDGE (*examines the document; then says*). The housemaid Alma Jonsson has in a summons served on her former employer, Alexandersson, brought charges under the sixteenth chapter, paragraph 8, of the penal code, providing for six months of imprisonment or a fine, accusing said Alexandersson of having called her a thief, without proof or support for this accusation and without bringing legal action against her for this alleged theft. What have you to say in your defense, Alexandersson?

ALEXANDERSSON. I called her a thief because I caught her stealing.

THE JUDGE. Have you any witnesses who saw her steal?

ALEXANDERSSON. No, it so happened that I had no witnesses with me for I usually walk about by myself.

THE JUDGE. Why didn't you institute proceedings against the girl?

ALEXANDERSSON. Because I don't believe in lawsuits. And, besides, employers like me are not in the habit of doing anything about household thefts; partly because they are such common occurrences, and partly because we don't want to do anything to hurt their future.

THE JUDGE. Alma Jonsson—what have you to say to this?

ALMA JONSSON. Why, I . . . I . . .

THE ATTORNEY (*to her*). You say nothing! (*To the Court.*) Alma Jonsson, who in this case is not the defendant but the plaintiff, requests that the Court hear the witnesses in order that they may prove the fact that Alexandersson has slandered her.

THE JUDGE. As Alexandersson has already admitted that he did slander her, there is no necessity for witnesses. But on the other hand, it is of importance for me to know whether Alma Jonsson is guilty of stealing. For, if Alexandersson had good grounds for calling her a thief, this will serve as a mitigating circumstance when the judgment is handed down.

THE ATTORNEY. I ask for permission to take exception to the statement just made by the Court. According to Chapter 16, paragraph 13, of the Penal Code, anyone charged with having slandered another shall be denied the right to present evidence as to the truth of his offensive remarks.

THE JUDGE. I ask the parties in the case, the witnesses and the spectators to empty the courtroom that the Court may deliberate. (*All leave except* THE JUDGE *and the members of the Court.*)

THE JUDGE. Is Alexandersson a man whose word can be believed?

THE JURY (*as one*). Alexandersson is a reliable man.

THE JUDGE. Has Alma Jonsson the reputation of being an honest person?

BOMAN. I had to discharge Alma Jonsson last year for petty thievery.

THE JUDGE. In any case, I have to sentence Alexandersson to pay a fine. There is no other way out. Is he a poor man?

ÖSTMAN. He still owes the government for taxes; and last year he had a bad harvest. I'm afraid a fine will be more than he can stand.

THE JUDGE. Despite this I see no grounds for postponing the suit. The case is a clear one, as long as Alexandersson is not permitted to give his side of the story.—Is there anything more to add, or has anyone any objection?

EKLUND. I simply would like to make a general observation. . . . A case like this—where the one party is not only innocent but also has been injured and yet has to take the punishment while the thief has his so called honor and good character restored—a case like this can have dire consequences. People will be likely to be less forbearing toward their fellowmen and neighbors, and lawsuits may become more frequent.

THE JUDGE. That may be so, but general reflections have

no place in the official records, and sentence has to be meted out. For that reason I shall only ask you, the Jury, this one question: Is Alexandersson guilty according to Chapter 16, paragraph 13, of the Penal Code, or is he not?

THE JURYMEN (*in unison*). Guilty.

THE JUDGE (*to* THE SHERIFF). Summon the parties in the case and the witnesses!

(THE SHERIFF *summons the parties in the case. They, the* SPECTATORS *and others, not members of the Court, enter. The* SPECTATORS *seat themselves.*)

THE JUDGE. In the case of Alma Jonsson versus farmer Alexandersson, the latter is sentenced to pay a fine of one hundred crowns for slandering the plaintiff, Alma Jonsson.

ALEXANDERSSON. But I saw her do it—I caught her stealing! That's what one gets for being charitable!

THE ATTORNEY (*to* ALMA JONSSON). Now, do you see! If one only keeps denying and contesting, the case is won! Alexandersson was a fool not to contest. If I had been his attorney and had contested your case against him, I would immediately have challenged and taken exception to your witnesses—and then you would have been left high and dry! Now let us go outside and settle our account. (*He,* ALMA JONSSON *and her* WITNESSES *leave.*)

ALEXANDERSSON (*to* THE SHERIFF). And now I suppose I have to give Alma Jonsson a letter of reference and swear that she has been honest and dependable!

THE SHERIFF. That's something that doesn't concern me!

ALEXANDERSSON (*to* THE CONSTABLE). And for this I have to lose my farm and everything I own! Who would have thought that justice works like this—that the thief reaps the reward and the victim gets flogged! Hell and damnation!— Come and let's have a cup of coffee with something strong in it! Come as soon as you get through, Öman. . . .

THE CONSTABLE. I'll be with you in a little while—but don't make any noise!

ALEXANDERSSON. Yes, by all the devils, I'll make a noise —even if it should cost me three months!

THE CONSTABLE. Don't make any noise! Don't make any noise—and I'll be there!

THE JUDGE (*to* THE SHERIFF). Call the divorce suit between Baron Sprengel and his wife, née Malmberg. . . .

THE SHERIFF (*calls out*). The divorce suit between Baron Sprengel and his wife, née Malmberg!

(THE BARON *and* THE BARONESS *come in.*)

THE JUDGE. In the proceedings brought by Baron Sprengel against his wedded wife, Baron Sprengel declares that it is his intention to continue the marriage no longer, and he requests that—as the warnings of the Vestry Board have proved to be of no avail—the couple be given a year's separation from bed and board. Has the Baroness anything to say with regard to this request?

THE BARONESS. I have no objection to the separation itself, but I have one condition to make: I insist that the child remain with me.

THE JUDGE. The law recognizes no stipulations made in advance in such cases. It is for the Court to decide about the child.

THE BARONESS. This seems exceedingly strange to me.

THE JUDGE. And for that reason it is of the utmost importance to the Court to learn which one of the two parties is the cause of the dissension that has resulted in the suit before it. According to the appended minutes of the Vestry Board, it appears that the wife admits to having shown at times a quarrelsome, difficult disposition; the husband, on the contrary, has admitted to no misbehavior or misconduct. Thus the Baroness seems to have acknowledged . . .

THE BARONESS. That is a lie!

THE JUDGE. I find it difficult to believe that the minutes of the Vestry Board—which have been witnessed by the rector and eight other trusted men—can be inaccurate.

THE BARONESS. The minutes are false!

THE JUDGE. Outbursts like these cannot be made with impunity before this Court.

THE BARON. I should like to draw the Court's attention to the fact that I voluntarily offered to surrender the child to the Baroness on certain conditions.

THE JUDGE. I repeat once again what I said a few moments ago—that it is the Court and not the plaintiff and the defendant that will pass judgment in this case. Consequently, Baroness, you deny you are the cause of the differences between you and the Baron.

THE BARONESS. Yes, I do. And it is never the fault of one that two quarrel.

THE JUDGE. This is no quarrel—it is a legal action, a breach of the law! And if I may say so, it seems to me that the Baroness is plainly showing a quarrelsome temperament and a reckless behavior.

THE BARONESS. Then you don't know my husband!

THE JUDGE. Will you be good enough to explain yourself! I can't base a decision on innuendo.

THE BARON. In that case I must ask to have my suit withdrawn and I'll seek a divorce in other ways.

THE JUDGE. The case has already been taken cognizance of and must proceed to its determination. . . . You assert then, Baroness, that your husband is to blame for your estrangement. Can you prove this?

THE BARONESS. Yes, it can be proved.

THE JUDGE. Will you please do so. But give due consideration to the fact that the question of the Baron's being the father is at stake, and with it the rights to the estate and property.

THE BARONESS. *That* he has forfeited many times over, not least when he denied me both sleep and food.

THE BARON. I feel compelled to mention that I have never denied the Baroness her sleep. I have merely asked her not to sleep all through the morning, because by so doing she neglected the household, and the child failed to get proper attention. And as to the food, I have always left the concern about this to the Baroness. I have only disapproved of certain unnecessarily extravagant social affairs, as the neglected household did not permit of such expense.

THE BARONESS. He has let me lie in bed, ill, and has refused to summon a physician.

THE BARON. The Baroness had a habit of always becoming sick whenever she couldn't have her own way; but invariably such sickness would disappear before very long. After I had called in a professor from the city one time and he had diagnosed her ailment as mere sham I refrained from summoning a doctor the next time the Baroness was taken sick. That was when she found that the new pier-glass cost fifty crowns less than intended.

THE JUDGE. All these things are not of the nature that can be taken into consideration in judging a case of this seriousness. There must be deeper motives than that.

THE BARONESS. It seems to me that when a father refuses to let the mother of their child look after its education and upbringing, that this can be counted as a motive.

THE BARON. First of all, the Baroness has had a maid to look after the child; and whenever she herself tried to care for the boy, she did everything the wrong way. Secondly, she has tried to bring up the boy as one of her own sex. She had him wear feminine dresses until he was four years old, for instance; and to this very day, at the age of eight, his hair is the length of a girl's. And she makes him sew and crochet and has him play with dolls. All this I consider detrimental to the child's normal development toward manhood. On the other hand, she amuses herself with dressing up the daughters of the farmhands and servants as boys, has their hair cut short, and puts them to do such work as boys usually perform. In a word: When I noticed symptoms of psychotic aberration and deviation of the kind that lead to conflict with Chapter 18 of the Penal Code, I took the boy's upbringing in hand myself.

THE BARONESS. And despite this you are still willing to entrust the child to his mother's care?

THE BARON. Yes, because I never could think of being so cruel as to take away a child from its mother, and because the mother has promised to mend her ways. Besides, my promise to her was a conditional one. It was only given with the provision that it did not conflict with the law and that no appeal to the courts were to be made. But now that we have come to the point that accusations and recriminations have been made, I have changed my mind—especially since I, instead of being the plaintiff, have now been made the defendant.

THE BARONESS. That is the way this man always keeps his promises!

THE BARON. My promises, like those of others, have always been conditional; and as long as the conditions have been fulfilled, I have kept my part of the bargain.

THE BARONESS. Furthermore, when we were married he assured me that I would have my personal freedom in everything . . .

THE BARON. So I did, providing that the laws of common decency were not violated. But when her transgressions went too far and license took the place of freedom, I felt she had overreached herself and imposed upon my good will.

THE BARONESS. And after that he tormented me with the most outrageous jealousy! That alone is enough to make it unbearable to live together! And to make matters worse, he made himself ludicrous by being jealous even of my doctor.

THE BARON. This so called jealousy consisted in nothing more or less than my advice to her not to accept the services of a notorious and gossipy masseur for an ailment which is customarily treated by a woman. However, the Baroness may have in mind the time I showed the superintendent of our estate the door for smoking in the drawing-room and offering my wife a cigar.

THE BARONESS. As we have started backbiting and revealing our intimate secrets, we may as well let out the whole truth. The Baron is guilty of adultery. Is not this enough to make him unfit to bring up my son?

THE JUDGE. Can you prove this, Baroness? (*She hands* THE JUDGE *a packet of letters.* THE JUDGE *glances through some of them.*) When did this occur?

THE BARONESS. A year ago.

THE JUDGE. According to the statute of limitation, the time for legal prosecution has expired; but the circumstances in themselves weigh heavily against the husband and may result in his losing the child and the right to a share of the common property. Does the Baron acknowledge this breach of the marriage pledge?

THE BARON. Yes—and with both shame and remorse. But there were circumstances which should be regarded as extenuating. I had been forced into a humiliating celibacy, a cold and calculated scheme of the Baroness'. And this despite the fact that I simply asked, in a decent way, to be given—as a favor—what the law prescribes as my conjugal right. I grew tired of having to pay for her love. For she had introduced prostitution into our married life. First she sold her favors for power; and later, in return for gifts and money! At last I found myself driven to seek an irregular intimacy outside the marriage—a relationship the Baroness explicitly consented to.

THE JUDGE. Did you consent to this, Baroness?

THE BARONESS. That is not true! I demand the Baron prove this!

THE BARON. It is true that I cannot give proof, as long as my only witness, my wife, denies it.

THE JUDGE. A fact need not be untrue merely because it cannot be proved. However, a bargain of this sort is contrary to existing laws. It constitutes moral turpitude, and it has no standing before the law. Thus far, Baron, the evidence I have heard is not in your favor.

THE BARONESS. And as the Baron has ackowledged his guilt with shame and remorse, I—being now the plaintiff and no longer the defendant—request that the Court proceed to render a decision since there is no need for further evidence.

THE JUDGE. As the presiding officer of this Court I would

like to hear what the Baron may have to say in his defense, or at least in justification of his act.

THE BARON. I have already admitted my guilt as an adulterer and have mentioned as extenuating circumstances that it was partly due to desperate need—when I, after having been married ten years, suddenly found myself deprived of my conjugal rights; and partly because it was done with the whole-hearted consent of the Baroness herself. As I now, however, have every reason to believe that all this was done for the purpose of entrapping me and making me seem guilty, it is my duty, for the sake of my son, to go a little further and . . .

THE BARONESS (*with an involuntary exclamation*). Axel!

THE BARON. The real cause of my breaking my marriage vows—was the Baroness' unfaithfulness!

THE JUDGE. Have you any proof, Baron Sprengel, that the Baroness was unfaithful to you?

THE BARON. No! What proof I had at one time I destroyed in order to protect the family honor. But I dare say that the Baroness will still admit to the confession she once made to me.

THE JUDGE. Does the Baroness admit to this breach of your marriage vow? And if so, did it occur before the Baron's aberrant conduct so that it might be assumed to have been the cause of it?

THE BARONESS. No!

THE JUDGE. Are you prepared to take an oath on your innocence with regard to this charge?

THE BARONESS. Yes.

THE BARON. God in Heaven! No! She must not do it! She must not perjure herself for my sake!

THE JUDGE. I ask you once more: Are you willing to swear to it, Baroness?

THE BARONESS. Yes!

THE BARON. Allow me to point out that the Baroness is now the plaintiff in the case and as such is not required to take the oath.

THE JUDGE. As long as you have accused her of an offense, she is a defendant. What is the opinion of the Jury?

VICKBERG. As long as the Baroness is a party to the proceedings, it seems to me she can hardly be a witness in her own behalf.

ERLIN. It is my opinion that if the Baroness is allowed to witness under oath, the Baron should have the same right;

but as it is against the law to put oath against oath, the whole matter remains in the dark.

VASS. But it can't be a question of taking an oath as a witness in this case; here it is a question of an oath in defense of a party's innocence.

RUTH. Then that is the first question we have to settle, I suppose.

VALLIN. We can't do that in the presence of the two parties in the case; and we can't deliberate in public.

SJÖBERG. The Jury has the right of free speech, and it is not limited by any condition of secrecy.

THE JUDGE. With so many opinions to choose from, I have very little to guide me. But as the guilt of the Baron can be proved, and that of the Baroness has not yet been proved, I must ask that the Baroness take the oath and swear that she is innocent.

THE BARONESS. I am ready!

THE JUDGE. No—wait just a moment! Baron, could you —if you were given time to do so—could you produce witnesses, or proof of your assertions?

THE BARON. I neither can nor wish to do that. I am not anxious to have my disgrace spread abroad.

THE JUDGE. The deliberations of the Court are adjourned while I hold a discussion with the chairman of the Vestry Board.

(THE JUDGE *leaves the bench and goes out, left.* THE JURYMEN *are deliberating between themselves in a subdued voice.* THE BARON *and* THE BARONESS *remain in the background. The* SPECTATORS *are gathered in groups, discussing the testimony,* etc.)

THE BARON (*to* THE BARONESS). You do not hesitate to commit perjury?

THE BARONESS. I shrink from nothing when my child is at stake!

THE BARON. But suppose I had proof?

THE BARONESS. But you haven't!

THE BARON. The letters are burned—but the certified copies are still in existence.

THE BARONESS. You are just lying to frighten me!

THE BARON. To show you how deeply I love my child and in order to save his mother—since I seem to be doomed anyhow—here you will find the proof. . . . And don't show yourself ungrateful now. (*He hands her a packet of letters.*)

THE BARONESS. That you were a liar—that I knew before; but that you were so low as to stoop to have the letters copied, that I could not have believed!

THE BARON. That's the thanks I get! But now we shall both be done for!

THE BARONESS. Yes—let us both go down—then at least there will be an end to this struggle!

THE BARON. Do you think it is better for the child to lose both his parents and to be left alone in the world?

THE BARONESS. That would never happen!

THE BARON. Your preposterous conceit, which makes you think yourself above both the law and your fellowmen, has incited you to take up this battle in which there can be only one loser—our son! What could you have been thinking of when you commenced this attack which could not help but draw a defense? You could not have thought of the child! No—it must have been revenge you had in mind! But revenge for what? For my discovering your guilt!

THE BARONESS. The child? Did you think of the child when you stood here befouling my name just now before this rabble?

THE BARON. Hélène! We have clawed each other bloody like two wild beasts, we have shamelessly stripped ourselves naked before all these people who are now reveling in our downfall—for we haven't a friend among those who are here. From now on our child will never be able to speak of his parents as respectable people. A good word from his father and mother will be of no help to him when he starts out in life. He will see how they and their home are shunned—how they have to sit at home in their old age, lonely and despised! And one day—he also will turn his back on us. . . .

THE BARONESS. What do you propose then?

THE BARON. Let us leave here—let us sell the estate, and then live abroad—

THE BARONESS. And start wrangling all over again! I know what it will be like! You will be meek as a lamb for a week or so, and then you'll start abusing me again.

THE BARON. Think of it—now our fate is being decided by them in there. . . . You can't have much hope that the Pastor will speak a good word for you after just calling him a liar. And as I am known to be no Christian I can't expect that they will show *me* any mercy either—Oh, I should like to hide myself in the woods under the roots of a huge tree and put my head under a rock! That is how much I feel my shame—

THE BARONESS. You are quite right. The Pastor likes neither one of us. It may happen as you say. . . . You ought to have a talk with him!

THE BARON. About what? About a reconciliation?

THE BARONESS. About anything you please—if you don't think it is too late! Just think—if it were too late already! . . . What is that man Alexandersson doing here—he is sneaking around us continuously? I have a fear of that man!

THE BARON. Alexandersson is a decent fellow.

THE BARONESS. To you he is—but not to me! I have seen those eyes of his before!—Go and see the Pastor now . . . but first take hold of my hand . . . I have a fear of something . . .

THE BARON. Of what, my dear? Of what are you afraid?

THE BARONESS. I don't know—of all of them—of everything—

THE BARON. You are not afraid of me, are you?

THE BARONESS. No—no longer! It is as if we had been dragged into a mill with our clothes caught between the wheels. . . . And all these malicious persons standing about, looking at us and laughing!—What have we done? What is it we have done in our anger and bitterness? Just think how they will revel in seeing the Baron and the Baroness standing here in their nakedness, flogging each other! . . . Oh, I feel as if I were standing here absolutely denuded—(*She buttons her coat.*)

THE BARON. Calm yourself, my dear! This is not the place to tell you what I have already told you before: that you have only one friend and one home—and we *could* start all over again! God alone knows. . . . No, we can't—we can't! . . . It has gone too far—it is the end! And this last accusation—yes, I hope it will be the last! But after all the other things, *that* had to come, too! . . . No—we are enemies for life! And if I let you keep the child, then you might marry again—I see that now! And then my child would have a stepfather—and I would have to see another man in the company of my wife and my son. . . . And I myself might be seen walking arm in arm with somebody else's strumpet. No—either you or I! One of us must be punished! You or I!

THE BARONESS. You! For if I let you have the child, you might marry someone else—and I might have to see another woman as the mother of my child! Oh—the very thought of it could make me commit murder! A stepmother for *my* child!

THE BARON. You should have thought of that before! But when you saw me chafing restlessly at the bond of love that held us together, it never occurred to you that I could love anyone but yourself.

THE BARONESS. Do you think I ever loved you?

THE BARON. Yes—one time, at any rate—when I had been unfaithful to you! That time you were sublime in your love. . . . And your pretense at scorn made you irresistible. But you also came to respect me after my transgression. Whether it was the male in me or the culprit you admired most, I do not know—but I have a feeling it was both. It must have been both, because you are the most female of women I have ever known! What a pity that you became my wife! As my mistress you would have reaped an unchallenged victory, and your infidelities would only have provided the bouquet to my new wine.

THE BARONESS. Yes, your love was always of the sensual kind.

THE BARON. Sensual as everything spiritual; spiritual as everything sensual! My weakness for you which was the very source from which my feelings took their strength gave you the idea that you were the stronger one, while in reality you were merely more malicious, more brutal, and more ruthless than I.

THE BARONESS. You—the stronger one? You—who keep changing your mind every two minutes—you who never know what you want!

THE BARON. Oh, yes—I know very well what I want, but in me there is room for both love and hate—and one minute I can love you, while I can't the next! And now I can only hate you!

THE BARONESS. But have you also thought about the child?

THE BARON. Yes—now and forever! And do you realize why? Because he is the embodiment of our love. He is the memory of our beautiful moments—the bond that links our souls together, the focal point where we will always meet without intending to. . . . And that is why we shall never be able to be parted, even if our divorce should separate us. Oh, if I could only hate you as I would like to hate you!

(THE JUDGE *and* THE PASTOR *enter, engaged in conversation. They walk downstage where they stop.*)

THE JUDGE. I realize therefore how absolutely hopeless it is trying to get at the truth and to attain justice. And to me it seems as if the laws were several centuries behind our conception of justice. Was I not compelled to sentence Alexandersson, who was innocent, and fine him, and let her —who was guilty of theft—get away with a clean character? And as for this divorce suit, I am at a loss to know what the facts are, and I haven't the conscience to pass judgment.

THE PASTOR. But a decision has to be made.

THE JUDGE. Not by me!—I shall resign my office and choose another profession!

THE PASTOR. Oh! That would cause a scandal and would only make you a laughing-stock—and it would bar you from most any other career. Just keep going, and after presiding as judge for a few years, you will soon see how much easier it will be to crush a few human fates like egg shells. Moreover, if you want to stand apart from this particular case, let the jurors outvote you—and then the responsibility will be theirs.

THE JUDGE. That is one way—and I am quite sure they will be almost totally against me. For I have formed an opinion about this case, although it is based merely on intuition so that I can't be absolutely certain. . . . Thank you for the advice!

THE SHERIFF (*who has been speaking with* ALEXANDERSSON, *walks over to* THE JUDGE). In my capacity as public prosecutor, I wish to report that the farmer Alexandersson will be a witness against Baroness Sprengel.

THE JUDGE. With relation to the adultery charge?

THE SHERIFF. Yes.

THE JUDGE (*to* THE PASTOR). This is something that may bring us a little closer to a solution.

THE PASTOR. Oh, there may be many such loose ends floating about, if you only knew how to catch hold of them.

THE JUDGE. Just the same, it is sad to see two human beings who once loved each other, now tearing each other apart in this manner. It's like seeing two animals being led to slaughter.

THE PASTOR. Well, such is love, my dear Judge!

THE JUDGE. What, then, is hate?

THE PASTOR. Hate is the lining inside the garment.

(THE JUDGE *walks over to the* JURYMEN *and talks to them.*)

THE BARONESS (*comes up to* THE PASTOR). Help us, Pastor! Help us!

THE PASTOR. As a clergyman, I cannot and must not! And you will remember, I warned you not to play with things that are so grave. It was such a simple matter to get a divorce, you said! Well, get rid of each other, then! The law does not prevent you, so don't blame the law!

THE JUDGE (*who has seated himself*). The Court will now resume its deliberations.—According to the report of the public prosecutor, Sheriff Viberg, a witness against Baroness Sprengel has come forward; and this witness is affirming that the adultery charge made against her is valid. (*With slightly raised voice.*) Farmer Alexandersson.

ALEXANDERSSON (*steps forward*). Here I am.

THE JUDGE. How can you prove your allegation?

ALEXANDERSSON. I saw it happen.

THE BARONESS. He is lying! Let him prove it!

ALEXANDERSSON. Prove it! I'm a witness this time!

THE BARONESS. Your statement is no proof, even if you are called a witness for the moment.

ALEXANDERSSON. Perhaps a witness has to have a couple of other witnesses, and the other witnesses still a couple of *other* witnesses!

THE BARONESS. Yes, it might well be called for when one has no assurance that they are not lying—all of them!

THE BARON (*steps forward*). Farmer Alexandersson's testimony will not be needed. Permit me to deposit with the Court all of the correspondence which will completely prove the Baroness' marital infidelity.—Here are the original letters. The copies are in the possession of the defendant.

(THE BARONESS *gives a shriek, but soon recovers.*)

THE JUDGE (*to* THE BARONESS). The Baroness was willing to take an oath on her innocence a moment ago?

THE BARONESS. But I didn't!—And now I think it's about time that the Baron and I call it quits.

THE JUDGE. The law does not cancel crime with crime! Each one's account has to be settled separately.

THE BARONESS. Then while we are here, I want to file a claim against the Baron for my dowry which he has squandered.

THE JUDGE. If the Baron has spent the Baroness' dowry recklessly, there is every reason for settling it now.

THE BARON. When the Baroness and I were married, she

brought with her six thousand crowns in stocks. This stock could find no buyers and later became valueless. As the Baroness, when she married, was employed as a telegrapher and refused—as she said—to be supported by her husband, we entered into a marriage settlement in which it was stipulated that each one of us was to be self-supporting. But after being married, she lost her position; and since then I have been supporting her. This I have done without protest, but now that she comes with a bill and asks for payment, I shall request permission to offer a bill of my own in return. It adds up to thirty-five thousand crowns and amounts to one-third of the household expenses during the years we have been married. This means that I myself accept two-thirds of the total expenses.

THE JUDGE. Was this agreement made in writing, and if so, is it in your possession?

THE BARON. No, it was a verbal agreement.

THE JUDGE. Have you, Baroness, anything to prove that you entrusted your dowry to the Baron?

THE BARONESS. When I did, it never occurred to me that it was necessary to get a receipt! I took it for granted that I was dealing with a man of honor!

THE JUDGE. Then it will be impossible for me to take the matter under consideration. Will the members of the Jury please retire to the small courtroom and consider the evidence and then come to a decision. . . .

(THE JURY and THE JUDGE go out to the left).

AEXANDERSSON (to THE SHERIFF). This here justice is more than I can make any sense out of!

THE SHERIFF. I think it would be wise of you to go straight home now—or you might have the same experience as that farmer in Mariestad. . . . Did you hear what happened to him?

ALEXANDERSSON. No, I didn't.

THE SHERIFF. Well—he went to court as a spectator—was dragged into a case as a witness—and ended up by getting twenty lashes!

ALEXANDERSSON. Hell and damnation! But it doesn't surprise me! I wouldn't put it past them!   (He leaves.)

(THE BARON goes down stage to THE BARONESS.)

THE BARONESS. You seem to find it difficult to keep away from me—

THE BARON. Hélène! I have stabbed you, thrust a knife

into you—and I am bleeding—for your blood is mine. . . .

THE BARONESS. And you certainly know how to conjure up charges!

THE BARON. No—only countercharges! Your courage is the courage of despair, of one who is condemned to die! And once you have come away from this, you will fall into a collapse. . . . For then you will no longer have me to load your guilt and grief on—and you will be tormented by your conscience. . . . Do you know why I have not killed myself?

THE BARONESS. Because you lacked the courage!

THE BARON. No—it was not out of fear for the fires of hell— I put no credence in that—but because I kept thinking that, even if you should be awarded the child, you will be gone in five years! (THE BARONESS *gives him a startled glance.*) For that is what the doctor has said to me! And then the boy would be without both father and mother! Think of that— alone by himself in the world!

THE BARONESS (*frantically*). Five years!—That is a lie!

THE BARON. Five years! And then—whether you want it or not—the child will be with me!

THE BARONESS. Oh no—never! My family would bring suit and take the child from you! Even if I die, my will shall survive!

THE BARON. Yes—evil has a way of surviving! It's true— it never dies! But I would like you to tell me why you are so set against my having the boy—and why you begrudge him his father, when you know that he needs me? Is it out of sheer malice and revengefulness that you so punish the child? (THE BARONESS *does not answer.*) Do you know what I told the Pastor? I told him I thought you might have some doubt about the child's parentage, and that this might be the reason for your refusing to let me have the child—thinking you did not wish me to build my happiness on a false foundation. . . . He answered me: "No, I cannot think she could have any such noble motive!" —And I do not believe you yourself know why you are so fanatical on this point. But I suppose it is our struggle for survival and continued existence that impels us to keep our hold. Our son has your body but my soul—and the soul is something you cannot destroy. In him you will have me back when you least expect it; in him you will read my thoughts, you'll find my tastes and nature and passions . . . and that is why you one day will come to hate him as you now hate me! That is what I am in dread of!

THE BARONESS. You still seem to fear that he shall be mine!

THE BARON. Because you are a woman and a mother you hold an advantage over me with those who sit in judgment on us. Even though justice may cast its dice blindfolded, the dice is almost always loaded.

THE BARONESS. Even though we are about to part, you know how to pay compliments. Perhaps, after all, you don't hate me as much as you pretend?

THE BARON. To be quite frank, I think it is not so much you that I despise as it is my own dishonor and disgrace. But I could hardly say that I don't hate you. And why—why this abominable hate? Perhaps I lost sight of the fact that you are nearing your forties and that something masculine is beginning to take root in you. Perhaps it is this touch of the male that I have felt in your kisses, in your embraces, that I find so repulsive—

THE BARONESS. Perhaps it is. For I have never told you before that my greatest sorrow in life has been that I was not born a man!

THE BARON. And so your sorrow has, perhaps, in turn brought about the greatest sorrow of *my* life! And now you are avenging yourself on one of nature's tricks by bringing up your son as a woman.—Will you promise me one thing?

THE BARONESS. Will *you* promise *me* one thing?

THE BARON. What good does it do to promise? You know we never keep our promises!

THE BARONESS. No, you are right! Let us make no more promises.

THE BARON. But will you answer a question truthfully?

THE BARONESS. Even if I told the truth, you would believe it to be a lie!

THE BARON. Yes—I would.

THE BARONESS. Can you see now that all is over between us—forever?

THE BARON. Forever! And we once vowed to love each other for eternity!

THE BARONESS. What a shame to be forced to take such a vow!

THE BARON. Why do you say that? Marriage is a bond, isn't it—even such as it is?

THE BARONESS. I could never endure any bond!

THE BARON. Would it have been better, do you think, if we had not bound ourselves?

THE BARONESS. For me it would have been better, yes.

THE BARON. I wonder! And in that case, you would have had no hold on me.

THE BARONESS. Nor you on me!

THE BARON. And so it would have been much the same as—as when you reduce a fraction. Consequently, it is not the fault of the law, nor our own fault, nor can anyone else be given the blame. And still we have to assume the responsibility! (THE SHERIFF *approaches* THE BARON *and* THE BARONESS.) And now—now the judgment is being handed down. . . . Goodbye—Hélène!

THE BARONESS. Goodbye, Axel!

THE BARON. Parting is hard! Living together—is impossible! But at any rate, the fight is over!

THE BARONESS. If it only were!—But I fear it is only about to begin!

THE SHERIFF. The parties in the case will retire while the Court is deliberating!

THE BARONESS. Axel!—A word with you before it is too late! We have to be prepared for the possibility that the child is taken from us both! Won't you drive home and take the boy to your mother—then let us flee from here, far away from here!

THE BARON. I can't help feeling you are trying to trick me again!

THE BARONESS. No, I am not! I am no longer thinking of you—and I am not thinking of myself—I have forgotten about revenge! Only save the child, do you hear! Do it, please . . .

THE BARON. I'll do what you say. But if you are deceiving me . . . Never mind, I'll do it!

(*He hastens out.* THE BARONESS *goes out, rear.* THE JURY *and* THE JUDGE *enter and resume their places.*)

THE JUDGE. We have weighed all the evidence in this case and I shall now ask the members of the jury to express their respective opinions before sentence is passed. For my own part, I find it only reasonable that the child should be awarded to its mother. While both husband and wife are equally responsible for their estangement, the mother is by nature better fitted to care for the child than the father.

(*There is a silence*).

EKLUND. According to the law presently in force, the wife's position and status is determined by her husband's, and not vice versa.

VICKBERG. And the husband is the rightful guardian of the wife!

SJÖBERG. In the marriage service—which, as we know, gives valid force to the marriage—the wife is enjoined to be subservient to the husband; therefore it seems to me that the man is superior to the woman.

BOMAN. And the children must be brought up in the faith of their father.

SÖDERBERG. From this it is clear, therefore, that the children go with the father and not the mother.

ANDERSSON of VIK. But as husband and wife, in the case before us, are equally guilty and—judging by what the Court has heard—are equally unfit to rear a child, it is my opinion that the child should be taken away from both.

ANDERSSON of BERGA. Being in agreement with Olof Andersson, I like to call to your attention that the judge in such cases appoints two reputable men to look after the children and the property involved. The income from the property shall be used for the subsistence of the husband and his wife and the child, or children.

VALLIN. In that case I should like to propose as guardians Alexander Eklund and Erenfrid Söderberg, both of whom are known for their righteousness and dependability and for their Christian character and disposition.

RUTH. I concur with Olof Andersson of Vik concerning the separation of the child from both father and mother, and with Axel Vallin concerning the two guardians, whose Christian character makes them unusually fitted to look after the child and its upbringing.

ERLIN. I concur with what Juryman Ruth has just said.

VASS. I concur.

ÖSTMAN. I concur.

THE JUDGE. As the majority of the jurymen have expressed an opinion contrary to my own, I shall ask the Jury to proceed to vote on the question. Perhaps I ought first of all to put this question to you: Is Olof Andersson's proposal that the child be taken from both father and mother acceptable to you? And are you all unanimously for it?

THE JURYMEN (*in unison*). Yes.

THE JUDGE. If there is anyone of you who is not in accord with this, he will please raise his hand! (*Silence; no movement.*) The verdict of the Jury has consequently nullified my own judicial opinion; however, I shall enter my exception in the record against this decision, which to me seems unnecessarily cruel.—Husband and wife are to be sentenced to a year's separation from bed and board under the penalty of imprisonment if they, during this period, should seek each other out. (*To* THE SHERIFF.) Call in the parties!

(THE BARONESS *enters. People stream in.*)

THE JUDGE. Is Baron Sprengel not present?

THE BARONESS. The Baron will be here immediately!

THE JUDGE (*curtly*). Whoever fails to be present, has only himself to blame. The decision of the Circuit Court is as follows: The husband and the wife in the case of Sprengel versus Sprengel are sentenced to one year's separation from bed and board; and their child shall be removed from the parents and be given into the custody of two guardians for upbringing and education. As guardians the Court has selected and approved two members of the Jury, Alexander Eklund and Erenfrid Söderberg.

(THE BARONESS *gives out a scream and falls to the floor.* THE SHERIFF *and* THE CONSTABLE *lift her up and place her in a chair. Meantime, some of the* SPECTATORS *saunter out.* THE BARON *enters. He is out of breath.*)

THE BARON. Your Honor! I just heard the Court's verdict outside, and I ask permission to take an exception to it. I challenge its validity—and also the entire jury, all of whom are my personal enemies—and the selection of the two guardians, Alexander Eklund and Erenfrid Söderberg, neither of whom possesses the financial security that is demanded of guardians. Furthermore, I shall prefer charges against Your Honor for a lack of judgment and understanding in the exercise of your office because you failed to recognize that the one who first offends against the marriage laws is the one who is guilty of causing the mate to commit a similar offense; thus the degree of their guilt is not the same.

THE JUDGE. If anyone is not in agreement with the decision rendered, he has recourse to a higher Court where he may appeal the judgment within the time limit stipulated by law!—Will the Jury please come with me now and inspect the parsonage in connection with the lawsuit pending against the assessors of the communal council . . .

(THE JUDGE *and* THE JURYMEN *go out, rear. The remaining* SPECTATORS *also leave.* THE BARON *and* THE BARON-ESS *are alone on the stage.* THE BARONESS *sits up.*)

THE BARONESS. Where is Emile?

THE BARON. He was not there!

THE BARONESS. You lie!

THE BARON (*after a silence*). Yes!—I did not take him to my mother for I can't depend on her. I took him to the parsonage.

THE BARONESS. To the Pastor!

THE BARON. Your one and only dependable enemy, yes! What other person could I have dared trust? And I did it because I read in your eyes a while ago something that told me you might have in mind doing away with the child and yourself . . .

THE BARONESS. And you saw that!—Oh, how could I have let you deceive me into believing you?

THE BARON. And what have you to say now—about all this?

THE BARONESS. I don't know. . . . I am so exhausted, I wouldn't even feel another blow. . . . It almost soothes me, comforts me, to have been given the final stab.

THE BARON. You give no thought to what will come *after* this: how your son will be reared by two peasants whose ignorance and lack of breeding and crude habits little by little will bring the child to his death; how he will be oppressed by his environment and brought down into their narrow outlook; how his mind will be strangled by religious superstition; how he will be taught to have contempt for his father and mother——

THE BARONESS. Stop! Don't tell me any more or I shall lose my mind! My Emile living with peasant wives who don't know enough to wash themselves, whose beds are infested with vermin, and who never look to see whether a comb is clean or not! My Emile—no—it must never happen——

THE BARON. But it is all a fact—all of it—and you have no one but yourself to blame!

THE BARONESS. Myself? Yes—but did I create myself? Did I implant evil in myself, sow hatred and wild passions in my heart? No! Who could have robbed me of the will and the power to fight against these evils? I look at myself now, and I feel I ought to be pitied! Don't you think I should be?

THE BARON. Yes, I do. We are both to be pitied! We tried to avoid the rocks that marriage so often breaks upon, and so we decided to live together as husband and wife without being married. But even then we quarreled for we had sacrificed one of the greatest rewards that life has to offer—the respect of our fellow-beings. And so we were married.

But we still wanted to outwit society and its laws: we were not to have a regular marriage ceremony; instead we slithered into a civil marriage. We were to be completely independent of each other, were to keep separate accounts, were not to be possessive of each other—but again we fell back into the old rut! Without any marriage ceremony—and with a marriage contract! And the marriage went to pieces! I forgave you your infidelity, and we lived together—free to do what we pleased—in voluntary separation—all for the sake of the child! But I grew tired of presenting my friend's mistress as my wife, and so it came to the point when we had to part! Do you know—do you know what we have been fighting against? You call it God—I call it Nature! And Nature drove us to hate each other, just as it impels us to love each other. And now we are condemned to inflict pain on each other as long as we have a spark of life in us. . . . There will be new proceedings in the higher courts, the case will be reopened, the Vestry Board will be asked its opinion, the cathedral chapter will be requested to comment,—and then the Supreme Court will give its decision! And finally will come my complaint to the Department of Justice, my plea for guardianship, your exceptions and challenges, your countersuits—in short, from guillotine to guillotine, without any hope of finding a merciful executioner! The property neglected—financial ruin—the child's education ignored! Then, why don't we put an end to our miserable lives? Because the child holds us back! I see you are weeping—but I can't weep! Not even when I think of the night in store for us in our desolate home! And you, poor Hélène, who now shall have to go back to your mother again—your mother whom you once left with happiness in your heart, glad to have a home of your own! To be a daughter to her again. . . . Yes, you may find it worse than to be a wife!—One year—two years—many years. . . . How many more do you think we can endure this suffering?

THE BARONESS. I shall never go back to my mother—never! I shall haunt the highways and the forests and find a place to hide, where I can scream—scream myself tired against God who has allowed this fiendish love to come into the world as a torment to us human beings . . . and when darkness falls, I shall lay myself down in the Pastor's barn so that I may be near my child when I fall asleep.

THE BARON. You think you can sleep tonight—you?

CRIMES AND CRIMES
A COMEDY IN FOUR ACTS

Crimes and Crimes (*Brott och brott*) was written in 1899 during the second great creative period of Strindberg's life. It is a curious blend of realism and fantasy, gravity and mockery, near-tragedy and comedy.

Reality seems simultaneously close and distant in this quasi-naturalistic but also quasi-expressionistic work. In it the real world, which seems very real indeed, becomes gradually transposed into a dream which becomes a veritable nightmare for a while. Then the nightmare ceases suddenly and the protagonist Maurice, like a dreamer awakening from a painful dream, finds himself back in a world that makes sense, a world in which the moral demands made upon human beings are moderate rather than absolute. Before this happens and the play winds up as a comedy, Maurice suddenly finds himself in an eerie world in which our hidden wishes are granted, our unexecuted desires produce desired results, and we are therefore held responsible for our thoughts and punished for them. In *Crimes and Crimes*, as in dreams, events start and terminate abruptly, our more or less hidden wishes are allowed realization, we are tormented by a sense of guilt without being legally guilty, and we are being punished for deeds we have not actually done. *Crimes and Crimes* comes close to being a "dream play," in which the world is transformed by fantasy. The play is therefore related to Strindberg's expressionistic phase of playwriting which produced the *To Damascus* trilogy, *A Dream Play*, *The Ghost Sonata*, and *The Great Highway*.

Crimes and Crimes is a tantalizing and troubling play. It is a subtle tragi-comedy in which Strindberg is ambivalent toward the entire race of man, which is both indicted and absolved or forgiven by the author. This work is dual in tone, haunting in feeling, and diabolically penetrative. It calls for mature readers and audiences, to whom it holds up a mirror in which they may observe their own and all mankind's failings and contradictions, their accountable miseries and unaccountable escapes from condign punishment. In the opinion of the present editor there are few plays in modern literature as challenging and as finely ground as *Crimes and Crimes*.

For Strindberg, the writing of this play was an act of deliverance from a deep-seated sense of guilt, a backward glance at the power of evil to destroy through the mind or the will, a manifestation of religious and moral understanding, and at the same time a labor of sophisticated intelligence. On the surface this quasi-expressionist drama appears to be a conventional piece of playwriting, seemingly a realistic comedy of manners in a Parisian setting, combined with a melodrama of crime and detective work—which recalls the fact that Strindberg was greatly taken with the fiction of Edgar Allan Poe. But, in this play, Strindberg was also concerned with the occult. He insisted on this mystic aspect of *Crimes and Crimes* by publishing it in a volume with another play, *Advent,* under the title of *Before a Higher Judgment* or *Before a Higher Court.* Nor did Strindberg forget his warfare with the unscrupulous "emancipated" female. The heroine Henriette, who was patterned by Strindberg after the bohemian mistress of one of his friends, a somewhat decadent Polish poet, is one of these modern "harpy-women."

Judged by elementary realistic standards, the play seems implausible and contrived; the criticism that "It all seems too pat" will readily occur to the superficial reader. Only when apprehended as a work of many-leveled fancy, imagination, and theatricality does this deceptively realistic play reveal its true worth. It then proves to be a masterpiece of irony. Strindberg has in view the complexity of human nature, its conflicting desires, instinctual lawlessness, and punitive conscience—which the individual tries to placate without actually giving up anything he really desires. In observing human deviousness in *Crimes and Crimes,* Strindberg is mordant but also amused, saturnine but also playful. He plays with his characters, and he plays with his audience. The result is a somewhat mystifying work that at first verges on tragedy, veers or seems to veer toward melodrama, and culminates in quizzical comedy. *Crimes and Crimes* is Strindberg's *Measure for Measure*; we shall not strike wide of the mark in calling it Strindberg's "dark comedy."

First performed in 1900 in Stockholm at the Royal Theatre, *Crimes and Crimes* was revived there in 1906, 1916, 1924, and 1936. In the last three of these revivals Henriette was played by the author's third wife, the gifted Harriet Bosse. The play was first presented in Germany in 1900, and the world-famous director Max Reinhardt staged it in Berlin at his *Kleines Theater* in 1902. Lubitsch filmed it in Germany in 1917, and a Swedish film version appeared in 1928.

PERSONS IN THE PLAY

Maurice, a dramatist
Jeanne, his mistress
Marion, their daughter, five years old
Adolphe, an artist
Henriette, his mistress
Émile, a laborer, brother of Jeanne
Mme. Cathérine
The Abbé

ACT I

Scene 1

(*The upper pathway of the Montparnasse cemetery in Paris. It is lined with cypress trees. In the background are seen a chapel and crosses of stone, bearing the inscription* O crux! Ave spes unica!; *also the ivy-covered ruins of a windmill.*

A woman, neatly dressed in mourning, is kneeling before a grave covered with flowers. She is softly murmuring her prayers.

JEANNE *is walking back and forth, as if waiting for some one.* MARION *is playing with some withered flowers that she has picked up from a heap of rubbish in the walk.* THE ABBÉ *is reading his breviary at one end of the path.*)

A GUARD (*enters. To* JEANNE). If you please, this is no playground.

JEANNE (*resignedly*). I am only waiting for someone who ought to be here any moment.

THE GUARD. I understand, but no one is permitted to touch the flowers here.

JEANNE (*to* MARION). Put back the flowers, my child!

THE ABBÉ (*steps forward.* THE GUARD *greets him.*) Can't the child play with the flowers that have been thrown away, guard?

THE GUARD. There is an ordinance against touching the flowers, even those that have been thrown away, for fear they might carry some contagion. Whether they do, or not, I don't know.

THE ABBÉ (*to* MARION). In that case, all we can do is

223

to obey the law.—What is your name, my little friend?

MARION. My name is Marion.

THE ABBÉ. And what is your father's name?

(MARION *remains silent, while biting her fingers.*)

THE ABBÉ. Forgive me for asking, madame—I meant no offense. . . . I was only prattling away in order to soothe the child.

(THE GUARD *has disappeared during the conversation.*)

JEANNE. I understand perfectly, reverend father, and I wish you would say something to soothe my feelings also. I am very much upset, having been waiting here for two hours.

THE ABBÉ. Two hours! And for him! How people can torture each other. *O crux! Ave spes unica!*

JEANNE. Yes . . . what is the meaning of these words I see everywhere here?

THE ABBÉ. They mean: "Oh, cross! Our only hope!"

JEANNE. Is it our only hope?

THE ABBÉ. Our only safe hope. . . .

JEANNE. I almost think you are right, father. . . .

THE ABBÉ. May I ask why you think so?

JEANNE. You have already guessed the reason. When he keeps his woman and their child waiting for two hours at a graveyard—the end is not far away.

THE ABBÉ. And if he should abandon you—what then?

JEANNE. . . . Then we must seek the river.

THE ABBÉ. Oh, no! Oh, no!

JEANNE. Yes, yes.

MARION. I want to go home, mother. I am hungry.

JEANNE. My dear child, try to be patient just a little longer. We'll be going home very soon now.

THE ABBÉ. Woe, woe unto them that call evil good, and good evil!

JEANNE. What is that woman doing there by the grave?

THE ABBÉ. H'm . . . she seems to be speaking with the dead.

JEANNE. I didn't think anyone could do that.

THE ABBÉ. She seems to be doing it.

JEANNE. Then there is no end to our misery, even when life is over?

THE ABBÉ. You don't know that?

JEANNE. Where can one get the answer?

THE ABBÉ. H'm . . . whenever you feel ready for en-lightenment, look me up in Our Lady's Chapel at St. Germain.—And here, I believe, comes the one you've been waiting for.

JEANNE. It isn't he. But it is someone I know.

THE ABBÉ (*to* MARION). Goodbye, little Marion! May God protect you! (*He kisses the child and departs.*) At St. Germain-des-Près.

ÉMILE (*enters*). Why, sister. . . . What are you doing here?

JEANNE. I am waiting for Maurice.

ÉMILE. I am afraid you'll have a long wait, then. I saw him an hour ago on the boulevard, breakfasting with some friends.—Good morning, little Marion! (*He kisses the child.*)

JEANNE. Were there any women among them?

ÉMILE. Why, of course. And what else could you expect? He is a playwright, and his new play has its première tonight. I presume they were actresses in the company.

JEANNE. Did he recognize you?

ÉMILE. He doesn't know who I am. And it's just as well he doesn't. I know my place as a workingman, and I don't like being condescended to by people who are above me.

JEANNE. But if he should leave us to shift for ourselves?

ÉMILE. Well, when that moment comes, then you may be sure I shall introduce myself. But you are not expecting that to happen. He is really fond of you, and is especially attached to little Marion.

JEANNE. I can't explain it, but I have a premonition that something dreadful is going to happen to me . . .

ÉMILE. Has he offered to marry you?

JEANNE. He hasn't promised—but he has given me hope.

ÉMILE. Hope, yes. . . . You remember what I told you at the very beginning? Hope for nothing, for men in his position don't marry out of their class.

JEANNE. But it *has* happened, hasn't it?

ÉMILE. Yes, it has happened. But do you think you would be happy among his friends? I doubt it. You wouldn't even understand what they were talking about. I sometimes take my meals, in the kitchen, at the place where he goes to eat; and I don't understand a word they say.

JEANNE. Oh, you eat there!

ÉMILE. Yes, in the kitchen.

JEANNE. Do you know—he has never asked me to go there with him.

ÉMILE. You can be grateful to him for that. It shows he has some respect for the mother of his child. For there is always a queer lot of females in that place.

JEANNE. You don't say?

ÉMILE. But Maurice never bothers with them. I must say his behavior is always correct. That shows he has an honorable character.

JEANNE. I feel as you do. But if some other woman should come along, he might easily lose his head.

ÉMILE (*with a smile*). Why imagine things? But tell me —do you need any money?

JEANNE. No, I have enough.

ÉMILE. You are not too badly off, then.—Look! Look! There on the promenade—there he comes now . . . so I'll be on my way. Goodbye, child!

JEANNE. Is it he? Yes, it is he!

ÉMILE. Don't torture him now with your jealousy, Jeanne.
(*He goes.*)

JEANNE. No, of course, I won't.

(MAURICE *enters.*)

MARION (*rushes toward him, and he lifts her up in his arms*). Father! Father!

MAURICE. How are you—how are you, my dear child! (*He greets* JEANNE.) Jeanne, can you forgive me for keeping you waiting so long? Can you?

JEANNE. Why, of course, I can.

MAURICE. But say it so that I can really believe you.

JEANNE. Come here and let me whisper it to you. (MAURICE *goes to her.* JEANNE *kisses him on the cheek.*)

MAURICE. I didn't hear anything.

(JEANNE *kisses him on the lips.*)

MAURICE. This time I heard you. And now—you know, of course, that it is today my fate is to be decided. My play opens tonight and has every chance of success—or failure.

JEANNE. I shall pray for your success.

MAURICE. Thank you! Even if it does not help, it can't hurt. Look there below—down where the haze hangs over the valley. . . . There is where Paris lies. Today Maurice is unknown to Paris—but in twenty-four hours he will be known. The cloud of smoke that has kept me hidden for all these thirty years will vanish, and I shall take visible form and begin to *be* some one. The enemies—who are all those that vainly try to do what I am doing—will writhe in agony . . . and that will compensate for the torture that I have suffered.

JEANNE. Don't speak like that—please!

MAURICE. Yes—for that is how I feel.

JEANNE. But don't say it! . . . And afterwards—what then?

MAURICE. Then we will have a roof over our heads; and you and Marion will bear the name that I have made famous.

JEANNE. Then you do love me?

MAURICE. I love you both, and both equally—though perhaps Marion a little more.

JEANNE. I am glad to hear you say that; for you may tire of me, but not of her.

MAURICE. You don't trust my feelings towards you, do you?

JEANNE. I am not sure—but I have a dread of something —a dread that something terrible—

MAURICE. You are tired and annoyed by the long wait. Once again I ask you to forgive me. What is it you fear?

JEANNE. The unpredictable—that one senses without any clear reason, through some foreboding or premonition. . .

MAURICE. But I predict success, nothing but success. And that's what it will be. All who are concerned with the production are confident; and they have had years of experience. They know how to judge a play's appeal to the public. They know what will impress the critics. So stop worrying!

JEANNE. I can't, I just can't! You know, there was an abbé here a while ago. He spoke to me so beautifully. It seems you did not destroy my faith; it was merely made weak—dimmed, as when you paint over a window with chalk. But the old priest washed away the chalk with his words, the light poured in, and once again there is life within. I shall pray for you this evening in St. Germain.

MAURICE. Now you frighten me.

JEANNE. The fear of God is the beginning of wisdom.

MAURICE. God? What is God? Who is God?

JEANNE. He gave joy to your youth and strength to your manhood . . . and He will support us through the ordeal that lies ahead.

MAURICE. What is it that lies ahead? What is it that you know? Where have you heard about this—this of which I am in ignorance?

JEANNE. I can't say—I don't know. I have had no dream, have heard nothing. But during these two horrible hours I have lived through so much misery and agony that I am prepared for the very worst.

MARION. I want to go home, mother. I am hungry.

MAURICE. Indeed you are going home, my beloved child. (*He embraces her.*)

MARION (*pathetically*). Oh, you are hurting me, father.

JEANNE. We must be getting home for dinner. . . . Well, goodbye, Maurice. And—good luck!

MAURICE. Where did I hurt you? My little child knows I wouldn't want to hurt her.

MARION. Then come home with us, why don't you?

MAURICE (*to* JEANNE). Do you know that when I hear the child plead, I feel as though it was my duty to obey. But when duty conflicts with career. . . . Goodbye, my daughter! (*He kisses the child, who puts her arms around his neck.*)

JEANNE. When shall we see you again?

MAURICE. We'll meet tomorrow, my love. And then we shall never be separated again.

JEANNE (*embraces him*). Never, never away from each other again! (*She makes the sign of the cross on his forehead.*) May God protect you!

MAURICE (*who is moved against his will*). My dear, darling Jeanne!

(JEANNE *and* MARION *leave, right, while* MAURICE *departs to the left. Suddenly they turn round simultaneously, throwing kisses at each other.*)

MAURICE (*goes to her*). Jeanne! I am ashamed! I am forever forgetting you. And you are the last one to remind me or take me to task. Here is the ticket for this evening.

JEANNE. Thank you, my dear, but you should be at your post alone; and I shall remain at mine, with Marion.

MAURICE. Your good sense is as great as the goodness of your heart. Yes, I am certain no other woman would have sacrificed her own pleasure for the sake of doing her husband a service. . . . I have to be free to move about at will tonight. And women and children don't belong on the field of battle. This you understood.

JEANNE. Don't think too highly of me—I am of no importance. It saves you from illusions. But now you shall see that I am just as forgetful as you were.—Here I have a tie and a pair of gloves I bought for you. I thought you might honor me by wearing them on your day of triumph.

MAURICE (*kisses her hand*). Thank you, my dear!

JEANNE. And, Maurice, don't forget—as you sometimes do—to go to the barber. I want you to look your best, so that others will like you, too.

MAURICE. And you will not be jealous!

JEANNE. Don't mention that word. It only gives birth to evil thoughts.

MAURICE. You know that at this moment I could relinquish tonight's victory! For it *will* be a victory for me . . .

JEANNE. Hush!Hush!Hush!

MAURICE. . . . just in order to go home with you!

JEANNE. But I wouldn't let you! Please go now, your fate is waiting for you . . .

MAURICE. Goodbye, then! And may whatever is meant to be, happen . . .

JEANNE (*alone with* MARION). *O crux! Ave spes unica!*

(*The café. To the right, a buffet with a fish bowl, containing goldfish; vegetables, fruits and preserves, etc., in dishes and jars. Further up is the entrance door. In the rear, a door leading to the kitchen, where men of the laboring class can get their meals. The kitchen has a visible exit to the garden. To the left, rear, a counter on a platform. Shelves with all types of bottles. To the right, a long table with marble top is placed alongside the wall, while a similar table stands parallel to it in the center of the café. Cane chairs at the tables. The walls are crammed with paintings.*

MME. CATHÉRINE *is seated at the counter.* MAURICE *is leaning against it, hat on head, smoking a cigarette.*)

MME. CATHÉRINE. So tonight is your big night, Monsieur Maurice?

MAURICE. Yes, tonight is the night.

MME. CATHÉRINE. Are you nervous?

MAURICE. Absolutely calm.

MME. CATHÉRINE. Just the same I wish you success. And you deserve it, Monsieur Maurice, after all your struggle against odds.

MAURICE. Thank you, Mme. Cathérine. You have been very kind to me. Without your help I would have given up long ago.

MME. CATHÉRINE. Let us not speak about that now. I like to help whenever I see honest effort and good intentions. But I don't like people to take advantage of me.—Can we depend on you to come here after the play is over and let us drink a glass with you?

MAURICE. You most certainly can. I have already promised, haven't I?

(HENRIETTE *enters from the right.* MAURICE *turns round, doffs his hat, gazes at* HENRIETTE, *who in turn scrutinizes him closely.*)

HENRIETTE (*to* MME. CATHÉRINE). Monsieur has not arrived?

MME. CATHÉRINE. No, madame . . . but he will be here very soon. Won't you sit down?

HENRIETTE. Thanks. I prefer to wait for him outside.
(*She leaves.*)

MAURICE. Who—was—that?

MME. CATHÉRINE. That was Monsieur Adolphe's friend.

MAURICE. Was—that—she?

MME. CATHÉRINE. Have you never met her?

MAURICE. No—he has kept her away from me. You'd think he was afraid that I would steal her from him.

MME. CATHÉRINE. Ha, ha! How did you like her looks?

MAURICE. Her looks? Let me see. . . . Why, I can't tell . . . I didn't see her. It was as if she had flown into my embrace the moment she entered . . . as though she had come so close to me that I could not really see her. She has left an impression in the very air—I can still see her—she is standing there—(*He goes toward the door, making a motion as if encircling a woman's waist with his arms.*) . . . Ouch! (*With a gesture as if he had pricked his finger on a pin.*) She has pins in her dress. She is one of those who stick you!

MME. CATHÉRINE (*with a smile*). You are too terrible with your women.

MAURICE. Yes, it's terrible, it's terrible. But do you know what, Mme. Cathérine? I am leaving before she returns, otherwise—otherwise— What a terrible woman!

MME. CATHÉRINE. You are not afraid of her, are you?

MAURICE. Yes—I am afraid for myself; and also—for some others—

MME. CATHÉRINE. Well, then go!

MAURICE. Why, when she sucked herself out through the door, she created a minor whirlwind that pulled me along. Yes, you may laugh—but if you look at the palm there on the buffet, you can see it's still moving. What an infernal woman!

MME. CATHÉRINE. Go then, man—before you're clear out of your mind!

MAURICE. I want to go, but I can't! Do you believe in fate, Mme. Cathérine?

MME. CATHÉRINE. No. I believe in the good Lord who

gives us strength to resist evil powers, if we ask him devoutly.

MAURICE. But you admit the existence of evil powers? . . . Could it be they that I hear coming now—out in the vestibule?

MME. CATHÉRINE. It must be. Her skirts rustle as when the clerk behind the counter tears off a piece of cloth. Go! Out, out! Through the kitchen—

(MAURICE *goes toward the kitchen door, but bumps into* ÉMILE *in the doorway*.)

ÉMILE. A thousand pardons!

(*He withdraws into the kitchen.*)

ADOLPHE (*enters, followed by* HENRIETTE). Why, if it isn't Maurice! How are you? How are you?—Henriette, may I present to you my oldest and dearest friend. Henriette—this is Maurice.

HENRIETTE. We have seen each other before.

ADOLPHE. So—o. . . . When, if I may ask?

MAURICE. Just a few moments ago . . . in here.

ADOLPHE. Oh!—Well, now you can't go until we've had a chance to talk.

MAURICE (*after a gesture of warning from* MME. CATHÉRINE). Oh, I only wish I had time—

ADOLPHE. Take time! We don't intend to stay long.

HENRIETTE. I won't interfere if you two have business to discuss.

MAURICE. We have no business to discuss. Our affairs are in too bad a state.

HENRIETTE. Then let us talk about something else. (*She takes* MAURICE's *hat from him and hangs it up*.) And now, put on your best behavior and give me a chance to get to know the great author . . .

(MME. CATHÉRINE *waves a warning to* MAURICE, *who, however, does not observe it*.)

ADOLPHE. That's right, Henriette. You catch him and hold him! (*They sit down at one of the tables*.)

HENRIETTE (*to* MAURICE). You certainly have a good friend in Adolphe, Monsieur Maurice. He never speaks of anything but you. And in such terms that I often feel myself slighted.

ADOLPHE. Yes, that's right! But on the other hand, Henriette never gives me peace on your account, Maurice. She has read your writings, and she wants to know from where you got this, or that; she keeps asking me what you look like, how old you are, what you like most. In a word: I have you morning, noon and night. It's almost as if we have lived together, we three . . .

MAURICE (*to* HENRIETTE). Dear me, why didn't you come here and look at the miracle! Then your curiosity could very quickly have been satisfied!

HENRIETTE. Adolphe didn't want to. (ADOLPHE *looks embarrassed.*) Because he was jealous . . .

MAURICE. Why should he be jealous? He knows my feelings lie elsewhere.

HENRIETTE. Perhaps he had his doubts about the constancy of your affections?

MAURICE. He couldn't possibly. I am known for my absolute fidelity.

ADOLPHE. But it was not—

HENRIETTE (*interrupts him*). Perhaps because you have not yet been put to the crucial test . . .

ADOLPHE. Oh, you know then . . .

HENRIETTE (*interrupts again*). . . . for a completely faithful man is something the world has still to see.

MAURICE. Then it will see one at last!

HENRIETTE. Where?

MAURICE. Here!

(HENRIETTE *laughs.*)

ADOLPHE. It sounds nice . . .

HENRIETTE (*interrupts him; she continues to turn entirely to* MAURICE.) Do you think I would trust my Adolphe for more than three months?

MAURICE. I have no reason to challenge your lack of confidence in Adolphe. But as to his loyalty—I can unhesitatingly testify to that.

HENRIETTE. There is no need of that. I was just talking nonsense. I take it all back. Not only because I want to feel as decent as you, but because he *is* loyal. . . . It is an ugly habit I have acquired: to see only the bad side of things. Yet—despite knowing better—I persist in doing it. But if I were together with you two for any length of time, you would eventually reform me. Forgive me, Adolphe! (*She presses her hand to his cheek.*)

ADOLPHE. You have a habit of speaking with a sharp tongue, but your actions speak a different language. What you really think, I never know.

HENRIETTE. Who can fathom the mind?

MAURICE. If we had to answer for our thoughts—would

any one of us be able to survive the chaos we create?

HENRIETTE. Do you, too, suffer from such vile thoughts?

MAURICE. Why, certainly. I commit the most cruel deeds in my dreams—

HENRIETTE. In your dreams. . . . Yes, and speaking of dreams, I. . . . No, I am ashamed to tell you. . . .

MAURICE. Go on! Tell me!

HENRIETTE. I dreamt last night that I quite calmly dissected Adolphe's chest muscles. You see, I am a sculptor. And he, kind as he always is, made not the slightest resistance. He even helped me over the obstacles—for he knows more about anatomy than I do.

MAURICE. Was he dead?

HENRIETTE. No, he was alive.

MAURICE. But that is horrible! And didn't you suffer through all this?

HENRIETTE. Not in the least. That's what astonishes me, for I am rather sensitive to the suffering of others. Isn't that true, Adolphe?

ADOLPHE. Yes, that's true. I should say unusually sensitive. And not least when it comes to animals.

MAURICE. I, on the other hand, am rather insensible both to my own and to the sufferings of others.

ADOLPHE. Now he is perjuring himself! Isn't that so, Mme. Cathérine?

MME. CATHÉRINE. Monsieur Maurice is the most kind-hearted, good-natured man I know. Can you imagine?—he threatened to call the police just because I didn't change the water for the goldfish—in the bowl over there on the buffet. Look, look . . . it is just as if they had heard what I said.

MAURICE. Now, now, we are sitting here washing ourselves clean as angels; yet we are ready to commit almost any polite crudeness just for the sake of honor, or riches, or a woman.—So you are a sculptor, mademoiselle?

HENRIETTE. In a minor sense. . . . Sufficiently, however, to make a bust. And I think I am fully capable of making one of you—something that has long been my dream.

MAURICE. By all means! That dream can at least be made real without any waiting!

HENRIETTE. I should like to commence without delay—immediately after this evening's success. Then you will be what you are destined to be.

MAURICE. You seem to be very certain of my success.

HENRIETTE. Yes! You have it written in your face that you will be the victor in this battle. You must feel it yourself.

MAURICE. Why?

HENRIETTE. Because I can feel it! Do you know, I was ill this morning—and now I am well again.

(ADOLPHE *shows signs of being disturbed and out of spirits.*)

MAURICE (*embarrassed*). Oh, I have an extra theatre ticket —only one. It is for Adolphe.

ADOLPHE. Thank you, Maurice, but I prefer to give it to Henriette.

HENRIETTE. Oh, but you shouldn't do that.

ADOLPHE. And why not? . . . You know that I never go to the theatre. I can't stand the heat there.

HENRIETTE. At any rate, you will come for me after the play is over, won't you?

ADOLPHE. If you insist. But Maurice is coming here. We shall be waiting for him.

MAURICE. I think you should make every effort to come, Adolphe. I beg you to do so. I plead with you, do you hear? . . . And if you don't want to meet us at the theatre, then let us meet at the Auberge des Adrets. . . . Shall we agree on that?

ADOLPHE. Not so fast. You have a way of deciding questions without giving anyone a chance to think.

MAURICE. What is there to think about? Do you want to call for Mademoiselle Henriette, or don't you?

ADOLPHE. You never know what all this may lead to. . . . I have a curious feeling about it.

HENRIETTE. Sh—sh—sh! No superstitions while the sun is shining! (*To* MAURICE.) Whether he comes or not, we can find our way!

ADOLPHE (*who has risen*). In any case, I must go now. I have a model coming to pose. Goodbye to you both!— Good luck, Maurice! Tomorrow you'll be on the side of good fortune! Goodbye, Henriette.

HENRIETTE. Must you go?

ADOLPHE. I must.

MAURICE. Goodbye, then. . . *Au revoir!*

(ADOLPHE *goes out after exchanging a greeting with* MME. CATHÉRINE.)

HENRIETTE. Well—that we should meet at last!

MAURICE. Do you find it so strange?

HENRIETTE. It seems like fate. . . . Adolphe has done everything to prevent it!

MAURICE. Has he?

HENRIETTE. Haven't you noticed it?

MAURICE. I have noticed it. . . . But why do you mention it?

HENRIETTE. I can't help it!

MAURICE. Shall I tell you that I was about to run out through the kitchen in order to escape meeting you!—And just then I was prevented by a man who closed the door, cutting off my retreat?

HENRIETTE. Why should you speak of that now?

MAURICE. I don't know.

(MME. CATHÉRINE *knocks over some bottles and glasses.*)

MAURICE. Don't worry, Mme. Cathérine. There is no danger.

HENRIETTE. Was that intended as a signal or a warning?

MAURICE. Both, no doubt.

HENRIETTE. Am I like a locomotive that I must be guided by signals?

MAURICE. And switches. . . . The switch is the danger point!

HENRIETTE. You can be nasty.

MME. CATHÉRINE. Monsieur Maurice is not nasty at all. He is always most kind and considerate toward his own and toward all he has relations with.

MAURICE. Hush! Nonsense!

HENRIETTE (*to* MAURICE). The old woman is impudent.

MAURICE. We can go down to the boulevard, if you like.

HENRIETTE. Let's go. I don't like this place. I feel myself clawed at by hatred.   (*She leaves.*)

MAURICE (*follows her*). Goodbye, Mme. Cathérine.

MME. CATHÉRINE. Just a moment! May I say a word to you, Monsieur Maurice?

MAURICE (*stops reluctantly*). What is it?

MME. CATHÉRINE. Don't do it! Don't do it!

MAURICE. What?

MME. CATHÉRINE. Don't do it!

MAURICE. Have no fear. . . . This lady is not for me. She merely interests me. And not too much at that.

MME. CATHÉRINE. Don't trust yourself!

MAURICE. Yes, I trust myself.—Goodbye—

(*He goes out.*)

ACT II

SCENE 1

(*Auberge des Adrets. A café in ornate 17th century style. Tables and armchairs here and there. The walls are decorated with weapons and armor; on the panel shelf stand tumblers, goblets and steins, etc.*

MAURICE, *in formal evening attire, and* HENRIETTE, *in evening gown, are seated at a table, on which stand a bottle of champagne and three filled glasses. The third glass is placed at the far side of the table, facing the audience, where an armchair seems to be waiting for an absent third person.*)

MAURICE (*placing his watch on the table*). If he isn't here within five minutes, he won't be here at all. However, let us drink to his ghost. (*He clinks his glass against the unused third one.*)

HENRIETTE (*does likewise*). To your health, Adolphe!

MAURICE. He is not coming.

HENRIETTE. He will . . .

MAURICE. . . . not come.

HENRIETTE. He will come!

MAURICE. What an evening! What a wonderful day! I still can't grasp that a new life has begun for me! Think of it, the producer is convinced I'll make a hundred thousand francs. . . . I can buy a villa in the suburbs for twenty thousand, and have eighty thousand left to live on. I shan't be able to comprehend it fully until tomorrow. I am tired, tired, tired! (*Sinks down in the chair.*) Have you ever been happy?

HENRIETTE. No!—How does it feel?

237

MAURICE. Well—I don't know that I can describe it. I *can't* describe it. I simply can't! But when I think of the envy and grief of my enemies, it stirs the feeling in me. . . . This is vile, of course, but that's how I feel.

HENRIETTE. You call that happiness—to gloat over the suffering of your enemies?

MAURICE. The victor counts the number of dead and wounded, and measures his victory by them.

HENRIETTE. Have you a thirst for blood?

MAURICE. Not by nature. But when people have trampled on you for years, you are happy when you can at last throw off the enemy and get a chance to breathe again.

HENRIETTE. Doesn't it seem strange to you that you should be sitting here alone with me—a girl of no consequence, a stranger—on an occasion such as this? I should think you would feel the urge to show yourself as a conqueror before the multitudes that throng the boulevards, in the great nightspots—

MAURICE. Yes, I presume it is a little incongruous. But I am comfortable here. Your company satisfies me.

HENRIETTE. But you are not happy?

MAURICE. No, I am not. As a matter of fact, quite the opposite. I am sad. I feel almost like weeping.

HENRIETTE. But why?

MAURICE. It's an empty happiness. A happiness filled with misgivings of disaster.

HENRIETTE. As mournful as that! As mournful as that! What is the trouble?

MAURICE. I lack the one thing that makes life worth living.

HENRIETTE. You mean you don't love her any more?

MAURICE. No, not the way I understand love. Do you think she has read my play, or expressed a desire to see it? Oh, she is good, so sensitive and self-sacrificing! But to go out with me for a rollicking time, on a night like this . . . she would consider that sinful! I once asked her to have some champagne, and—what do you think?—instead of this making her happy, she took the wine list and looked to see how much it cost. . . . And when she saw the price, she wept! She wept because Marion was in need of new stockings! I suppose all this is beautiful, in a way . . . it is touching . . . but I can't say I enjoy it. I want to have some pleasure in life! In the past I have had to go without many things; but now —now life is beginning for me! (*The clock strikes twelve.*) This is the break of a new day, the start of another world!

HENRIETTE. Adolphe is not coming.

MAURICE. No, if he is not here by this time, he won't come! And now it is too late to go to Mme. Cathérine's.

HENRIETTE. But they are expecting you.

MAURICE. Let them wait! They made me give them my promise to come. Now I take it back.—Are you anxious to go?

HENRIETTE. Not in the least!

MAURICE. You will keep me company?

HENRIETTE. With pleasure. If you think you will be satisfied with mine!

MAURICE. Why, certainly—I am asking you! How worthless the wreath of victory is, if it can't be placed at a woman's feet. . . . Yes—without a woman everything in life is barren and empty—not worth having.

HENRIETTE. Need you be without a woman? You!

MAURICE. That remains to be seen.

HENRIETTE. Don't you know that a man is irresistible in his hour of fame and success?

MAURICE. This is a new experience. I have not had a chance to put it to the test.

HENRIETTE. What a strange creature you are! At this moment, when you are the most envied man in Paris, you are sitting here brooding. . . . Perhaps you are having a bit of conscience over missing that old café woman's chicory coffee!

MAURICE. Yes, my conscience bothers me. All the way out here I can feel their indignation, their outraged feelings, their righteous resentment. My comrades from leaner days had every right to expect me to be with them tonight. The estimable Mme. Cathérine had a special share in my success—which was to have acted as a ray of hope, an incentive and example to the ones who were still struggling. And I have betrayed their faith in me. I can hear them now: "Maurice will come. He is a dependable soul. He is not the kind that is carried away by success. He never breaks his word." And now I have betrayed their faith in me!

(During this dialogue the strains of Beethoven's Sonata in D Major, opus 31, no. 2—Finale Allegretto—are heard from the adjoining room; at first played softly, then gradually increasing in volume until it becomes passionately agitated, ending on a furiously wild note.)

Who is playing like that in the middle of the night?

HENRIETTE. I suppose it's some night owls like ourselves.

—But to return to what you said just now! Your presentation of the facts is incorrect. You must remember that Adolphe promised to come and meet us. And we waited. And he broke his promise. Therefore you are not to blame.

MAURICE. You mean that? . . . I believe you while you are speaking; but when you stop talking, my conscience begins to trouble me again.—What have you in the box there?

HENRIETTE. Oh, it's only a laurel wreath. I was going to send it to you, but didn't get the opportunity. Let me present it to you now. It is said to cool a burning brow. (She rises and puts the wreath on his head. She kisses his forehead.) Hail to the victor!

MAURICE. Don't! Please!

HENRIETTE (kneels before him). Hail to the King!

MAURICE (rises). Don't! You frighten me!

HENRIETTE. You are a timid soul! You are faint-hearted! You are afraid even of good fortune! Who robbed you of your faith, your belief in yourself? Who reduced you to a dwarf?

MAURICE. A dwarf! You are right . . . I don't work like the giant up in the clouds, with a great noise and hullabaloo! I forge my sword in the silent depths of the mountains! You think I am too modest to accept the victor's wreath? No, but I am contemptuous. It is too puny a reward! You think I am afraid of the ghost there—staring at me with envy and jealousy, keeping an eye on my feelings—of whose power you haven't the faintest idea!—Away with you, ghost! (He knocks down the third, empty champagne glass.) Away with you, intruder, you absent one who has forfeited your claim—if you ever had any claim! You stayed away from the battlefield, and acknowledged your defeat. . . . Just as I now crush this glass under my foot, so I shall reduce to dust the image you have created for yourself, and which shall no longer be yours!

HENRIETTE. Excellent! Now you are singing a different tune! Bravo, my hero!

MAURICE. Now I have sacrificed my best friend, my most faithful comrade, on your altar, Astarte! Are you satisfied?

HENRIETTE. Astarte! That's a pretty name, and I accept it.—I believe you love me, Maurice . . .

MAURICE. Can't you see!—From where do you come, you daughter of misfortune? You awaken the man in me, and the desire for blood! From where do you come, and where are you leading me? I loved you even before I met you . . .

when they spoke of you, I trembled.——And when I saw you in the doorway, your spirit flew straight to mine. When you left, you remained in my arms. I wanted to flee from you, but something held me back. And this evening we were driven together like quarry in the hunter's net. Who is to blame? Your lover——who kept us apart! And who now has brought us together . . .

HENRIETTE. What does it matter who is to blame? But Adolphe must be blamed for not bringing us together sooner. He committed a crime by depriving us of two weeks of bliss. He cheated us. I am jealous of him on your account. I hate him for having robbed you of your mistress. I would like to erase the memory of him forever and void him from the past. I should like to relegate him to the unborn, the never created!

MAURICE. Let us bury him on the scrap heap of our memories, dig a ditch for him in the wild forest, and pile stones on the grave so that he'll never be able to rise again! (*Lifts his glass.*) Our fate is sealed. . . . Oh, God! What will the future hold for us?

HENRIETTE. Today begins a new sequence of time.——What have you in that parcel?

MAURICE. I don't remember . . .

HENRIETTE (*opens the package and takes out a tie and a pair of gloves*). What a frightful tie! It must have cost at least fifty centimes!

MAURICE (*snatches the tie and gloves from her*). Don't touch them!

HENRIETTE. Are they from her?

MAURICE. Yes, they are.

HENRIETTE. Give them to me!

MAURICE. No! She is far better than we are . . . better than any one I know.

HENRIETTE. I don't believe it! She is only more innocent and stupid——and stingier! The kind that weeps when you drink champagne——

MAURICE. Our child had no stockings!——Yes, she is, indeed, a good woman!

HENRIETTE. You are strictly middle class! You'll never be an artist! But I am, and I shall make a bust of you, with the imprint of the storekeeper on your face——instead of the laurel wreath on your brow.——Her name is Jeanne, isn't it?

MAURICE. How did you know?

HENRIETTE. All housekeepers are called Jeanne.

MAURICE. Henriette!

(HENRIETTE *snatches the tie and gloves and throws them into the stove.*)

MAURICE (*weakly*). Astarte! Now you are demanding a woman as sacrifice! You shall have her. But if you ask for innocent children—then you shall have to go!

HENRIETTE. I wonder what it is that attracts you to me?

MAURICE. If I knew, I would tear myself free! I think it must be something evil in you—something which I lack. . . . It is this that entices me with the irresistible charm of the new—

HENRIETTE. Have you never committed a crime?

MAURICE. No, not any real crime. . . . Have you?

HENRIETTE. Yes.

MAURICE. Tell me—how did it affect you?

HENRIETTE. It was more rewarding than a good deed. A good deed reduces you, makes you the equal of others. A criminal act brings a more desirable return, because such an act places you above others and provides a reward of its own. My crime placed me outside of life, of society and my fellow-men. Ever since, I live only half a life, a dream life— and that is why reality never catches up with me.

MAURICE. And what was it you did?

HENRIETTE. I won't tell you. I would only shock you again.

MAURICE. Don't you think it will be brought to light some day?

HENRIETTE. No, never! Yet in my subconscious I see forever the five stones on Place de Roquette, where they put up the guillotine. That is why I never touch a deck of cards. I always have a fear that the five of diamonds will turn up.

MAURICE. Was it that kind of crime?

HENRIETTE. It was that kind of crime, yes . . .

MAURICE. Why, this is terrible—still it fascinates me! But doesn't your conscience ever plague you?

HENRIETTE. Never—but let's change the subject and talk about something else.

MAURICE. Shall we talk about—love?

HENRIETTE. One never speaks about love, until it is over.

MAURICE. Were you in love with Adolphe?

HENRIETTE. I don't know. . . . His natural goodness tempted me like a beautiful, long-past memory of childhood. But there was so much about him that hurt my eye. It took me a long time to change, erase, add and subtract in order to make him into a passable figure. When he spoke, I was conscious that he was imitating you—often that he had misunderstood your thoughts or rephrased your words clumsily. You can imagine how wretched the copy seemed to me when I saw the original. That was the reason he was in such fear that we would meet. And when that moment came, he knew at once his time was up!

MAURICE. Poor Adolphe!

HENRIETTE. I feel for him, too. He takes things so terribly to heart.

MAURICE. Be quiet! Someone is coming!

HENRIETTE. Just think, if it should be he!

MAURICE. That would be insufferable!

HENRIETTE. It isn't he. . . . But if it had been, how would you have treated the situation?

MAURICE. To begin with, he would be a little annoyed with you because he had made a mistake about the meeting place. He had looked for us in vain at the wrong cafés. But his vexation would promptly change into ecstacy at the thought of his unjust suspicions. And he would love us both. At the same time he would be delighted that we had become such good friends. This had always been his dream—h'm! he is making his big speech now!—his dream that we three should form a triumvirate and set an example to the world of the perfect friendship, a friendship that demanded nothing, asked for nothing in return. "Yes, I trust you, Maurice, not only because you are my friend, but because your feelings lie elsewhere!"

HENRIETTE. Bravo! Have you been caught in such a situation before? You render it so perfectly! You know . . . Adolphe is just such a man; he can never enjoy himself with his mistress unless he is chaperoned by a friend.

MAURICE. Yes, that is why I was invited, no doubt!—Quiet! There is some one outside. . . . It's he!

HENRIETTE. No . . . it's the ghost hour! And so you imagine you hear and see things. To keep vigil at night, when one should be asleep in bed, has the same fascination for me as crime has. It seems to place one above and beyond the laws of nature . . .

MAURICE. But the penalty is ghastly. I am freezing, or shuddering—I don't know which.

HENRIETTE (*brings him her shawl and puts it over his shoulders*). Let me put this around you—it will keep you warm.

MAURICE. That's perfect. It makes me feel exactly as if I were inside your skin . . . as if my body, disintegrated from lack of sleep, were melted and molded into yours. . . . I can feel how I am being re-cast. But I am also being given a new soul, new thoughts. And here, where your breast has touched, it begins to heave again—

(*In the adjoining room the pianist has been practising the D-Minor Sonata, now playing softly, now furiously, deafeningly; at intervals there has been no sound from the room, occasionally measures 96-107 of the Finale have been heard practised separately.*)

What a monstrous creature! To be practising in the middle of the night! I am getting sick of it! I'll tell you what we'll do! Let us drive out to the Bois de Boulogne and have breakfast in the pavilion, where we can see the sun rise over the lagoons and the ponds.

HENRIETTE. A splendid suggestion!

MAURICE. But first let me send a message home to have my mail and the morning newspapers delivered at the pavilion. What do you think about inviting Adolphe, Henriette?

HENRIETTE. Well, it seems a little silly, but let us ask him. We may need an ass to pull the triumphal chariot. . . . Let him come! (*They rise.*)

MAURICE (*removes the shawl*). I'll ring, then.

HENRIETTE. Wait a moment! (*She throws herself into his arms.*)

SCENE 2

(*A restaurant in the Bois de Boulogne, a spacious, handsome room with rugs, mirrors, chaise longues, sofas, etc. In the rear, glass doors and windows looking out toward the ponds and lagoons. In the center, a table arranged with flowers, fruit bowls, wine decanters, oyster plates, a variety of wine glasses, and two lighted candelabra. To the right, a small table with newspapers and telegrams.*

MAURICE *and* HENRIETTE *are seated opposite each other at the smaller table.*

The rising sun can be seen through the windows.)

MAURICE. There can be no more doubt. The newspapers have given their verdict, and the telegrams of congratulation have confirmed my success. It is the beginning of a new life. My fate is wedded to yours, because you alone shared my hopes for triumph, for the future, all through this night. It was from your hand I received the laurel; and it seems to me you have given me everything.

HENRIETTE. What an enchanting night! Has it been a dream, or have we actually lived it?

MAURICE (*rises*). And what a morning! After such a night! It seems like the dawn of the world, illuminated by the rising sun. Only now—at this very moment—was the earth created and tore itself loose from its enveloping white mists, which are now floating away. There you see the Gardens of Eden in the rosy hue of the dawn. And here are we, the first two beings of creation. . . . You know, I am so happy I could cry to think that the rest of humanity is not equally blessed. . . . Do you hear the sound in the distance, as of sea waves pounding against a rocky shore—as of the roaring wind in the woods? Do you know what it is? It is Paris—

Paris murmuring my name! Do you see the pillars of smoke rising to the sky—thousands of them, tens of thousands! They are the offerings to me, the altar fires! And if they are not, then they must be because that is what I desire! All the telegraph keys in Europe are tapping out my name at this moment. The Orient Express carries the news to the Far East, toward the dawning sun, and ocean liners carry it westward! The universe is mine, and therefore it is beautiful! Now I would like to have wings for us both, to rise aloft and fly away from here . . . far, far away, before my happiness is sullied, before envy will disturb my dream. For it can't be anything but a dream!

HENRIETTE (*gives him her hand*). Feel—feel! You are not dreaming!

MAURICE. It is no dream, but it was. . . . You know, when I was a poor young man, I would walk in the woods below and look up at this pavilion, which to me appeared like a fairy castle; and in my imagination this room with its balcony and heavy draperies seemed to be the ultimate of bliss. To be within this forbidden castle in the air with a woman I loved, and see the sun rise while the candles were still burning in the candelabra, was the most daring dream of my youth. And now that it has come true, I have nothing more to ask of life. Would you be willing to share death with me now?

HENRIETTE. No, you madman! Now I wish to live life!

MAURICE (*rises*). To live—is to suffer. And now we have to face the reality. I can hear his steps on the stairs now . . . he puffs and pants from worry and anxiety; his heart is pounding with anguish from having lost the most precious thing in life. Do you believe me when I tell you that Adolphe is here, under this very roof? In a minute you will see him standing in this room.

HENRIETTE (*uneasily*). It was a stupid idea to invite him, and I am sorry we did. Well, now we shall see if your premonition is true.

MAURICE. One can, of course, be mistaken about such things. . . . People can change their minds.

(THE MAÎTRE D'HÔTEL *enters and presents a calling card on a tray*.)

MAURICE (*picks up the card and glances at it*). Ask the gentleman to come in. (*To* HENRIETTE.) We may be sorry for this.

HENRIETTE. Too late to regret. . . . Sh!

(ADOLPHE *enters. He is hollow-eyed and extremely pale.*)

MAURICE. Well, well. Where were you last evening?

ADOLPHE. I looked for you at the Hôtel des Arrêts. I waited there an hour.

MAURICE. In other words, at the wrong place. We waited for you at the Auberge des Adrets for several hours. And, as you see, we are still waiting for you.

ADOLPHE (*his feelings eased*). Oh, my God!

HENRIETTE. Good morning, Adolphe! You are a bird of ill fate and always torture yourself needlessly. I suppose you think we wished to avoid your company. And even though you know we have sent for you, I presume you still think you are superfluous.

ADOLPHE. Forgive me—I was wrong. It was my mistake. This has been a terrible night for me. (*They sit down. Embarrassing silence.*)

HENRIETTE (*to* ADOLPHE). Well, aren't you going to congratulate Maurice on his stupendous success?

ADOLPHE. Why, of course. . . . You have had a success beyond all doubt. No question about that. Not even your detractors can take that away from you. You have swept everything before you. I myself feel dwarfed in your presence now.

MAURICE. Don't talk nonsense. . . . Henriette, pour Adolphe a glass of wine.

ADOLPHE. No, thanks, none for me. Nothing.

HENRIETTE (*to* ADOLPHE). What is the matter with you? Are you ill?

ADOLPHE. No, but not far from it.

HENRIETTE. Your eyes . . .

ADOLPHE. What about my eyes?

MAURICE. What happened at Mme. Cathérine's last night? I suppose they are angry with me?

ADOLPHE. No—no one is angry with you. But your absence caused such a gloom that it made me feel bad. Believe me, no one was angry. Your friends understand . . . they overlooked your truancy with sympathy and leniency. Mme. Cathérine herself spoke in your defense and proposed a toast to you. We were all delighted with your success—as delighted as if it had come to one of us.

HENRIETTE. Think of it, what nice people. . . . Think, what good friends you have, Maurice.

MAURICE. Much better than I deserve.

HENRIETTE. No one has friends he does not deserve. And

you are the kind of man who makes friends. . . . Don't you sense it in the air—all the thoughts and messages of good will that go out to you today from thousands of hearts?

(MAURICE *gets up in order to conceal his emotion.*)

ADOLPHE. . . . From all those you have delivered of the nightmare that has oppressed them for generations. Humanity has been slandered, and you have rehabilitated it. For this, mankind owes you a debt of gratitude. Today we can lift up our heads again and say: "Behold! We are just a bit better than our reputation!" And that thought gives us comfort.

(HENRIETTE *tries to hide her emotion.*)

ADOLPHE. Am I intruding upon you? Let me just warm myself for a few minutes in the sunshine of your success, Maurice, and then I'll be going.

MAURICE. Why should you go? You have only just arrived.

ADOLPHE. Why? Because I have seen what I might have been spared seeing. Because now I know that my time is up. (*Silence.*) That you sent for me, I take as an act of consideration. You have made known to me what has taken place with a frankness that hurts less than deception. You hear that I have a good opinion of humanity, Maurice. I owe that to you. You taught it to me, Maurice. (*Silence.*) But, my friend, I just passed through the church of St. Germain, and there I saw a woman and a child. I wouldn't like to have had you see them. For what has happened cannot be changed. But if you had given them a thought, or a word, before you turned them adrift in the big city, you could now enjoy your good fortune with a clear conscience. And now I'll say goodbye . . .

HENRIETTE. Why do you wish to leave?

ADOLPHE. And you ask that? Would you like me to tell you?

HENRIETTE. No—I wouldn't.

ADOLPHE. Then, goodbye.   (*He leaves.*)

MAURICE. The fall of Eve. . . . And behold, they saw their nakedness . . .

HENRIETTE. How different this scene turned out from what we had imagined. . . . He is better than we.

MAURICE. In this moment I think the whole world is better than we.

HENRIETTE. Do you notice that the sun is hiding behind the clouds and the trees have lost their rosy brilliance?

MAURICE. I see, yes . . . and the blue pond has turned

black. Let us fly to where the sky is always blue and the trees always green.

HENRIETTE. Yes, let us . . . without any leave-taking.

MAURICE. No, let us bid the goodbyes.

HENRIETTE. We were to have flown. You offered wings—but you have feet of clay. I am not a jealous woman, but if you should stop to say farewell and expose yourself to two pair of arms round your neck, you would not be able to tear yourself free again.

MAURICE. You may be right. But it takes only one pair of tiny arms to hold me here.

HENRIETTE. In other words, it's the child that holds you —not the woman.

MAURICE. It's the child.

HENRIETTE. The child! Another's child! And for that I have to suffer! Why must this child stand in my way? Why must she? I am not going to let her!

MAURICE. Yes, why? How much better if she had never been born—

HENRIETTE (*walks to and fro in a state of agitation*).Yes —but she was. Like an obstructing object on the road, an immovable rock, bound to upset the cart . . .

MAURICE. The triumphal chariot! The donkey has been driven to death, but the rock, the obstruction, remains. . . . Damnation! (*Silence.*)

HENRIETTE. It is hopeless.

MAURICE. We have to marry. Then *our* child will make us forget the other one.

HENRIETTE. It's our child against hers! We must do away with—

MAURICE. Do away with—? Do you know what you are saying?

HENRIETTE (*turns*). Your child would destroy our love.

MAURICE. No, my dear. . . . Anything that stands in our way will be overcome by our love. Nothing can destroy our love . . .

HENRIETTE (*picks up a deck of cards lying on the mantel-piece and starts cutting the cards*). You see! Five of dia-monds! The guillotine! Can it be that our destiny is pre-determined? That Fate decides the turn of our thoughts, channeling them where it wills, submitting to no resistance or interference? No, I refuse to give up! I will not let my-self be trapped! Do you realize that I would go to the guillotine if my crime should be discovered?

MAURICE. Tell me about your crime—this is the moment.

HENRIETTE. No, I should only live to regret it—and you would despise me. No, no, no! . . . Have you ever heard it said that hatred can kill?—Well, my father grew to be so hated by my mother and by his children that he wasted away, as wax melts before the flame.—Oh, God! Let us speak about something else. And, above all, let us get away! The air here is poisonous. . . . By tomorrow the laurel will be withered, the triumph forgotten; and before the week is up another victor, another hero, will have captured the public's adoration. Let us get away from here and plan for new conquests. . . . But first you must go and embrace your child, Maurice, and take care of her immediate needs. You don't have to see the mother.

MAURICE. I appreciate your thinking of the child. That proves you have a heart—and it makes you doubly dear to me—a kind heart, no matter what you say yourself.

HENRIETTE. That done, you must go to the café and say goodbye to the old woman and your friends. Leave no unfinished business behind. I don't want you to be depressed on the journey.

MAURICE. I shall put everything in order. We shall meet at the station tonight.

HENRIETTE. Yes—and then—away from Paris. . . . and down to the sea and the sun.

ACT III

Scene 1

(*The café. The gas lamps are lighted.* Mme. Cathérine *is seated at the buffet.* Adolphe *sits at one of the tables.*)

Mme. Cathérine. Yes, my dear Monsieur Adolphe, that's the way it is. But you young people ask too much of life. So you become disappointed. And then you start complaining.

Adolphe. No, that isn't exactly why I complain. I am not accusing any one, and I am still fond of them both. But this sort of thing disgusts me. You see, I was more attached to Maurice—yes, so much so that there wasn't anything I would not have done for him to make him happy. But now I have lost him, and that pains me more than having lost her. I have lost them both, and therefore my loneliness is doubly painful. And there is still something else I don't quite grasp.

Mme. Cathérine. You mustn't brood too much. You must work, and seek some diversion. Don't you, for instance, ever go to church?

Adolphe. What would I be doing in church?

Mme. Cathérine. Oh, there is much to look at. And there is the music. It takes your mind away from the material and the commonplace.

Adolphe. I don't think I belong in that sheepfold, for I have no devotion in me. And you know, of course, Mme. Cathérine, that faith is a gift. And it has not been given to me.

Mme. Cathérine. Then you must wait, and you will receive it.—But what about the stories I've been hearing to-

251

day? Is it true that you have sold your painting for a very large sum of money in London, and that you have been awarded the first prize?

ADOLPHE. Yes, it is.

MME. CATHÉRINE. Oh, but in heavens name— And you don't say a word about it?

ADOLPHE. I have a fear of success . . . and, besides, it does not mean anything to me now. I dread it as I would a ghost: if you mention having seen one, it brings you bad luck.

MME. CATHÉRINE. You have always been a queer one.

ADOLPHE. I have seen so much misfortune follow in the wake of success, madame. And I have learned that adversity reveals one's true friends—while success brings nothing but false friends. You asked me whether I ever went to church. I gave you an evasive answer. Do you know that I went into Saint-Germain this morning—without really knowing why. It seemed to me as though I was in search of some one whom I could thank in the silence; but I found no one. So I just put a gold coin in the poor-box. That was all that came from my church going. And I did it merely as a matter of form.

MME. CATHÉRINE. Well, that was something. It was kind of you to think of the poor in your hour of success.

ADOLPHE. It was nothing of the sort. I did it because I could not help myself. But then something else happened to me in the church. I saw Maurice's friend, Jeanne, and his child. Run over by the wheels of his triumphal chariot, and crushed under them, the two seemed to grasp the full impact of their plight.

MME. CATHÉRINE. Well, I don't know what sort of conscience you children have. . . . But how can you explain that a kindly, conscientious, sensitive man like Monsieur Maurice could suddenly abandon both his mistress and their child?

ADOLPHE. I just can't understand it. I doubt that he himself knows what he has done. I saw them this morning— Maurice and Henriette. Everything seemed so absolutely right and natural to them—as if they could not possibly have acted differently. They behaved with such complete innocence as though they had done a good deed, or fulfilled a sacred duty. There are things, Mme. Cathérine, we cannot fathom. That is why we should not judge. You know how the whole thing came about. Maurice sensed the danger; I surmised it. I wanted to avoid having them meet; Maurice earnestly tried to escape. But it was no use. It is as if a web of intrigue had been spun by some invisible power and tricked them into each others' arms. I may be prejudiced in the matter. Yet I say without hesitation: not guilty.

MME. CATHÉRINE. Well, I must say that anyone who can forgive as readily as you, is a truly religious man.

ADOLPHE. Oh, heavens, you mean I am religious without knowing it.

MME. CATHÉRINE. But to let oneself be driven or enticed to do something wicked as Monsieur Maurice did— that is a sign of weakness or badness. If a person feels that he can't cope with temptation, he should ask for help. And it will be given. But he didn't do that. He was arrogant.— Who is that coming?—I believe it is the abbé.

ADOLPHE. What brings him here?

THE ABBÉ (enters). Good evening, Madame. . . . Good evening, Monsieur.

MME. CATHÉRINE. What can I do for you, Monsieur Abbé?

THE ABBÉ. Have you seen Maurice, the playwright, here today?

MME. CATHÉRINE. No, not today. He has a play on, and is probably busy at the theatre.

THE ABBÉ. I have . . . I have sad news for him . . . and in more respects than one.

MME. CATHÉRINE. May I ask you what it is?

THE ABBÉ. Yes, it is no secret any longer. His daughter —by the unwed Jeanne—is dead.

MME. CATHÉRINE. Dead?

ADOLPHE. Marion dead?

THE ABBÉ. Yes—she died suddenly this forenoon—without any previous illness.

MME. CATHÉRINE. Oh, God, who can understand your ways?

THE ABBÉ. The mother's grief and her sad plight demand that Monsieur Maurice come to her, and we must try to locate him.—Let me ask you a question in confidence. Do you happen to know whether Monsieur Maurice loved his child, or whether he was indifferent to her?

MME. CATHÉRINE. If he loved his Marion? Monsieur Abbé, we all know how dear she was to him.

ADOLPHE. There is no doubt about that, Monsieur Abbé.

THE ABBÉ. I am glad to hear that. That makes the matter clear to me.

MME. CATHÉRINE. Could there have been any doubt about it.

THE ABBÉ. Unfortunately, yes. There is even a rumor abroad in the neighborhood that he abandoned the child and the mother in order to go away with a strange woman. In a few hours this rumor has grown into definite accusations; and at the same time the hysteria has mounted to such a point that his life is in danger, and he is being named as the murderer.

MME. CATHÉRINE (to ADOLPHE). Here you see what happens when people don't know the difference between good and evil, and when they start flirting with sin. God punishes. . . . He does, indeed.

THE ABBÉ. I wish to say, however, I feel convinced that the man is innocent of this charge; and the mother is as certain of that as I am. But circumstances are against Monsieur Maurice—and I am afraid he will have some difficulty in clearing himself when the police interrogate him.

ADOLPHE. Have the police taken over the case?

THE ABBÉ. Yes, the police were obliged to step in to protect him against the nasty rumors and the violent temper of the mob. No doubt the commissaire will soon be here.

MME. CATHÉRINE (to ADOLPHE). Here you see what happens when people don't know the difference between good and evil, and when they start flirting with sin. God punishes—He does, indeed.

ADOLPHE. Then He is more severe than we mortals.

THE ABBÉ. What do you know about it?

ADOLPHE. Not a great deal, but I can see what has already happened.

THE ABBÉ. And understand it, too?

ADOLPHE. Perhaps not just yet.

THE ABBÉ. Let us examine the matter a little more closely. . . . There is the commissaire. (*He points toward the window.*)

THE COMMISSAIRE (*enters*). Messieurs . . . Mme. Cathérine . . . I have to disturb you for a moment and ask you a few questions concerning Monsieur Maurice. As you unquestionably know he is the victim of a horrible rumor, which I, by the way, do not believe.

MME. CATHÉRINE. None of us here believe it, either.

THE COMMISSAIRE. That strengthens my conclusions; but in his own interest I must give him an opportunity to testify.

THE ABBÉ. That is right . . . and even though the circumstances may seem questionable, he will get every opportunity to clear himself.

THE COMMISSAIRE. Appearances are greatly against him. But I have seen innocent men go to the guillotine—only to be proved guiltless later. This is what can be said against him. The child Marion, left alone by the mother, is visited secretly by the father. He evidently arrived at a time when he knew the child would be alone. A quarter of an hour later, the mother returns home—and finds the child dead. This is an unhappy circumstance for the accused. The autopsy indicates no assault, and no presence of poison of any kind. But physicians report there are newly discovered poisons that leave no trace in the system. To me the whole matter seems a coincidence. I have had experience with such cases before. But then there are other factors that make his position more vulnerable. Last night Monsieur Maurice was seen with a strange lady at the Auberge des Adrets. The conversation, according to the waiter, was about crime. The words *Place de Roquette* and *the guillotine* were mentioned. An unusual subject for conversation between two lovers of good family and position. This, however, may be discounted. Experience has taught us that people seem to dig up subjects of conversation from the very dregs of their souls after libations and late hours. More incriminating is the testimony of the *maître d'hôtel* concerning the champagne breakfast in the Bois de Boulogne this morning. He testifies to having heard them voice a desire to see a child done away with. The man is supposed to have said: "Better if she had never been born!" To which the woman is said to have replied: "You are right. But the child is there!" And later in the conversation these words were overheard: "It's our child against hers! We must do away with her"—which brought the retort: "Do away with . . . ? Do you know what you are saying?" and "Anything that stands in our way will be overcome by our love." And later: "Five of diamonds —the guillotine—Place de Roquette!"—This is difficult to get away from, just as the journey abroad that had been planned for this evening. These words are definitely incriminating.

ADOLPHE. He is lost.

MME. CATHÉRINE. What a horrible mess. One doesn't know what to believe.

THE ABBÉ. This is not the work of human beings. May God be merciful to him!

ADOLPHE. He is caught in the net and will never be able to extricate himself.

MME. CATHÉRINE. How could he ever do such a thing?

ADOLPHE. Are you beginning to suspect him, Mme. Cathérine?

MME. CATHÉRINE. Yes and no. I haven't any opinion any more in this matter.—Haven't you seen angels turn into devils overnight, and later become angels again?

THE COMMISSAIRE. Yes, it is indeed a mysterious case. However, we shall have to wait and hear his side of it. He will not be judged without a hearing.

THE ABBÉ. This is not the work of human beings . . .

ADOLPHE. It seems more like the work of demons trying to destroy men.

THE ABBÉ. If this is not the punishment for wilful sins, it is a test—and a terrible one.

JEANNE (*enters. She is dressed in mourning*). Good evening!—Forgive me for asking, but has Monsieur Maurice been here?

MME. CATHÉRINE. No, madame, but he may be here at any moment. You have not seen him then, since . . .

JEANNE. Not since yesterday morning.

MME. CATHÉRINE. Permit me to express my sympathy in your deep sorrow . . .

JEANNE. Thank you, madame.—(*To the* ABBÉ.) You are here, Father!

THE ABBÉ. Yes, my child. . . . I thought I might be able to be of some help to you—and it was fortunate that I had a chance to speak to the commissaire here.

JEANNE. The commissaire! He doesn't suspect Maurice, does he?

THE ABBÉ. No, he does not—and neither does any one of us here. But appearances are against him in a frightening way.

JEANNE. You mean on account of the conversation the waiters overheard? . . . That means nothing to me as I have heard Maurice make remarks like that before, when he has had something to drink. Then he likes to indulge in ravings about crime and punishment. Besides, it seems to have been his companion that uttered the more compromising words. I would like to come face to face with that woman.

ADOLPHE. My dear Jeanne, that woman—no matter how much sorrow she has caused you unintentionally—has done so without malice. She has done it without thought of anything—good or bad. She has merely succumbed to her passions. I know her to be a good woman. She can look you in the eye without fear or shame.

JEANNE. I value your opinion about her greatly, Adolphe— and I believe you. I can therefore lay the blame for what has happened, on myself only—not upon any one else. Yes, it is my foolishness that is now being punished. (*She weeps.*)

THE ABBÉ. You must not accuse yourself. I know you, and the deep feeling of responsibility with which you accepted your motherhood. That it cannot be consecrated by the church and civil law is no fault of yours. No, here we are faced with a very different problem.

ADOLPHE. Which is—?

THE ABBÉ. Well, tell me that.

(HENRIETTE *enters, dressed for traveling.*)

ADOLPHE (*rises resolutely and goes to* HENRIETTE). You here?

HENRIETTE. Yes. Where is Maurice?

ADOLPHE. Do you know what has happened—or don't you?

HENRIETTE. I know everything. Excuse me, Mme. Cathérine, but I was ready to leave and had to come here for a moment. (*To* ADOLPHE.) Who is that lady?—Oh!

(HENRIETTE *and* JEANNE *scrutinize each other.* ÉMILE *appears in the kitchen entrance.*)

HENRIETTE (*to* JEANNE). I wanted to say something, but it is of no importance, for whatever I say will sound like crudity or mockery. But if I should beg you to believe in your heart, madame, that I sympathize with you in your great sorrow as profoundly as any one could—no matter how close to you—you must not reject me. You must not, for I deserve your pity, even if I don't deserve your forgiveness. (*She grasps* JEANNE *by her hands.*)

JEANNE (*gazes at her*). No, I believe you—yet in the next moment there is doubt in my mind. (*She takes* HENRIETTE *by the hand.*)

HENRIETTE (kisses JEANNE's *hands*). Thank you.

JEANNE (*withdraws her hand*). No, not that! I don't deserve it! I don't deserve it!

THE ABBÉ. Forgive me, but while we are here and there

is harmony, wouldn't you care to throw some light on the uncertainty and confusion that are found in the principal charge, Mme. Henriette? I ask you to tell us, as between friends, what you implied with your conversation about *doing away with,* and about *Place de Roquette*? That these words had no relation to the little child's death, we believe we know. But it would give us peace of mind to hear what the conversation really was. . . . Won't you tell us?

HENRIETTE (after a silence). I can't tell you that. . . . I can't tell you.

ADOLPHE. Henriette—you must tell us! You must speak out and set our minds at ease!

HENRIETTE. I can't! Don't ask me!

THE ABBÉ. This is not the work of human beings . . .

HENRIETTE. To think that anything like this would ever happen to me. And in such a way—under such circumstances. (*To* JEANNE.) Madame, I swear that I am without blame in the death of your child. . . . Need I say more?

JEANNE. Not for our sake—but the sake of justice!

HENRIETTE. Justice! If you only knew how right you are!

THE ABBÉ (*to* HENRIETTE). And if you knew what you just said!

HENRIETTE. Do you understand it better than I?

THE ABBÉ. Yes.

(HENRIETTE *regards the* ABBÉ *quizzically.*)

THE ABBÉ. Have no fear, for even if I divined your secret, I would not reveal it. Besides, human justice is not my concern—only God's mercy.

MAURICE (*enters. He too, is dressed for travel; does not observe those present in the foreground. He goes straight toward the counter, where* MME. CATHÉRINE *is seated.*) Mme. Cathérine, you are not angry with me for not coming last night, are you? I am here to ask you to forgive me, before I leave for the South at eight o'clock this evening.

(MME. CATHÉRINE *is silent and taken aback.*)

MAURICE. Then you are angry with me? (*Looks round.*) What is this?—Is it a dream, or what is it?—No, I see it is not. But it is as though I viewed a scene through a stereopticon lens or through a picture window. There I see Jeanne, standing like a marble figure—and dressed in black. . . . And Henriette looks like a corpse. . . . What is the meaning of all this? (*All remain silent.*) No one answers!—Has something happened? Something dreadful? (*Silence.*) Why don't you answer me?—Adolphe, my friend, what is going on?—And . . . (*Pointing to* ÉMILE.) . . . there I see a detective!

ADOLPHE (*steps forward*). You don't seem to know—

MAURICE. I know nothing. But I would like to know.

ADOLPHE. Then—I'll tell you—Marion is dead. . . .

MAURICE. Marion—dead?

ADOLPHE. Yes, she died this morning.

MAURICE (*to* JEANNE). And that is why you are in mourning. . . . Jeanne, Jeanne—who has done this to us?

JEANNE. He—who holds life and death in his hand.

MAURICE. But I saw her in the bloom of health this morning. . . . How could such a thing have happened? Who did it? Some one is to blame for this—who is it? (*He searches out* HENRIETTE *with his eyes.*)

ADOLPHE. Don't look for the guilty one here, for no one here is guilty. I am sorry to say, however, that the police have cast their suspicions in the wrong direction—upon an innocent party.

MAURICE. In which direction? On whom?

ADOLPHE. Well, you must know that your imprudent talk last night and this morning has put you in a light that is anything but favorable.

MAURICE. You mean we were overheard? Let me try to remember what we said. . . . Yes, we did say . . . Oh, then I am lost . . .

ADOLPHE. But why don't you explain your indiscreet words? And we shall believe you.

MAURICE. I can't! I won't! I'll go to jail—what does it matter? Marion is dead! Dead! And I killed her! (*There is general excitement.*)

ADOLPHE. Think of your words—be careful what you say! Do you know what you just said?

MAURICE. What did I say?

ADOLPHE. You said you killed Marion!

MAURICE. Does any one of you really believe that I am a murderer? That I could kill my own child? Mme. Cathérine, you, who know me—tell me if you believe that I. . . . Do you believe that—?

MME. CATHÉRINE. I don't know what to believe any more. What the heart is full of, the tongue speaks . . . and you have made some pretty startling admissions . . .

MAURICE. She doesn't believe me!

ADOLPHE. Why don't you explain yourself, then? Explain what you meant by the words: "Anything that stands in our way will be overcome by our love—"

MAURICE. Oh, they heard that, too. Ask Henriette to explain.

HENRIETTE. No, I can't do it!

THE ABBÉ. There is something unwholesome about all this, and you can no longer count on our sympathy, my friends. . . . A moment ago I was willing to swear you were innocent. But I could not do it now.

MAURICE (*to* JEANNE). What you think means more to me than anything else.

JEANNE (*coldly*). First answer this question: whom did you have in mind when you used those unbelievable words at the orgy in the Bois de Boulogne?

MAURICE. Did I use such words? Perhaps I did. . . . Yes . . . yes, I am guilty—but I am also innocent. Let me go away from here, for I am ashamed of myself. I can't condone my wrongdoing. It is too great.   (*He starts to leave.*)

HENRIETTE (*to* ADOLPHE). Go with him! He may do himself harm.

ADOLPHE. You wish me to?

HENRIETTE. Who else if not you!

ADOLPHE (*without bitterness*). You are closest to him. —Wait, a carriage just stopped outside.

MME. CATHÉRINE. It's the commissaire! H'm, I have seen much in this world . . . but I never thought that success and fame could disappear so quickly.

MAURICE (*to* HENRIETTE). From the triumphal chariot to the police wagon!

JEANNE (*artlessly*). With the donkey before it—whom did you mean?

ADOLPHE. That was I, no doubt . . .

THE COMMISSAIRE (*enters. He displays a document he carries in his hand.*) Summons to the Prefect of Police without delay this evening for Monsieur Maurice Gérard—and Mademoiselle Henriette Mauclerc.—Present?

MAURICE and HENRIETTE (*respond simultaneously*). Yes.

MAURICE. Is this an arrest?

THE COMMISSAIRE. No, not yet. This is merely a summons to appear before the court of preliminary inquest.

MAURICE. And then—what?

THE COMMISSAIRE. That remains to be seen.

(MAURICE *and* HENRIETTE *walk toward the door.*)

MAURICE. Goodbye . . .

(*All show emotion.* THE COMMISSAIRE, MAURICE *and* HENRIETTE *leave.*)

ÉMILE (*enters. He goes up to* JEANNE.) Now I shall see you home, sister.

JEANNE. What do you make of this, Émile?

ÉMILE. The man is innocent.

THE ABBÉ. Yes, but from my point of view it is a despicable thing to break one's word. And when it involves a woman and a child, it is unforgivable.

ÉMILE. I am inclined to agree with you, especially as it concerns my sister. But it is not for me to cast stones. . . . For I myself was guilty of the same thing once.

THE ABBÉ. Although I am free of such errors, I am not casting stones, either. Sin brings its own judgment, and the sinner reaps his punishment.

JEANNE. Pray for him. . . . Pray for them both, Father.

THE ABBÉ. No, that is something I cannot do—for to try to change God's will is defiance. And what has taken place here must be the work of the spirits of evil.

SCENE 2

(*The Auberge des Adrets.* ADOLPHE *and* HENRIETTE *are seated at the same table that* MAURICE *and* HENRIETTE *occupied in Act II.* ADOLPHE *has a cup of coffee before him;* HENRIETTE *has nothing.*)

ADOLPHE. Then you think he'll come here.

HENRIETTE. I feel certain that he will. He was released from jail at noon, for lack of evidence, but has decided to stay indoors until dark.

ADOLPHE. The poor fellow!—Do you know that after yesterday life to me seems abominable.

HENRIETTE. How about me? I am afraid even to live, to breathe, to think. . . . I know I am being watched. . . . Not only my words—my thoughts are being watched!

ADOLPHE. So this is where you were last night when I couldn't find you.

HENRIETTE. Yes, but please don't speak of it—I could die of shame when I think of it. Adolphe, you are made of different stuff than I and he—

ADOLPHE. Sh—sh—sh—

HENRIETTE. Yes, yes! And what made me remain with him? I was heedless, thoughtless, listless. The intoxication of his triumph carried me away—I just can't explain it. If you had been here, it would not have happened. But today you are the giant and he the dwarf—more insignificant than the least of us. Yesterday he possessed a hundred thousand francs; today he is a pauper. His play has been withdrawn. He can never rid himself of the taint. Public opinion has condemned him for his unfaithfulness to Jeanne as mercilessly as if he had been the murderer. And the sharp-tongued purvey the opinion that the child died of sorrow, and that he was the cause of her death.

ADOLPHE. Henriette, you know what I think—I'd like to see you both completely cleared. Won't you tell me just what you meant by those frightful, compromising words. It couldn't be by mere chance that your conversation dwelt on murder and the guillotine . . . especially on such an occasion.

HENRIETTE. No, it was not by chance. It was something that had to come out . . . something that I cannot discuss . . . probably because I cannot prove myself blameless and clean—because I am not!

ADOLPHE. What you are saying is more than I can understand.

HENRIETTE. Then let us speak about something else. Don't you think that in our very midst—among our own, intimate friends—there may be criminals . . . criminals who have never been punished?

ADOLPHE (*disturbed*). What—just what do you mean exactly?

HENRIETTE. Don't you think that every human being—at some time or another in his life—commits some sort of act, punishable under the law, if it were discovered?

ADOLPHE. Yes, I believe we all do. But on the other hand, no evil goes unpunished—by one's conscience. (*He rises; unbuttons his coat.*) And—no one who has not broken some law, can be called truly human. (*His breathing is becoming heavy.*) For—in order to be able really to forgive, one must oneself have been in need of forgiveness. I had a friend who, to all of us, was an ideal human being. He never uttered a harsh word about anyone, forgave everything and everybody, and received and accepted insults with strange satisfaction. None of us could understand him. Finally, many years later, he confided his secret to me with these words: I am a penitent! (*He sits down.*)

(HENRIETTE *is silent. She gazes at him in wonderment.*)

ADOLPHE (*as though speaking to himself*). There are crimes that are not listed in the books of law; and these crimes may be the very worst. For these are crimes we *ourselves* must punish—and no judge is as severe as we ourselves are.

HENRIETTE (*after a silence*). Your friend . . . did he ever attain peace of mind?

ADOLPHE. After years of self-torment he found a certain degree of it, but life never held any joy for him. He never felt free to accept any honors, never felt himself worthy of a compliment or even a word of praise, no matter how well deserved. In brief, he could not forgive himself.

HENRIETTE. He could not forgive himself.—What had he done?

ADOLPHE. He had wished for his father's death . . . and when the father suddenly passed away, the son became obsessed with the idea that he had murdered him. This obsession was diagnosed as morbidity, and he was sent to an institution. He was eventually released as cured. But the feeling of guilt remained, and he continued to punish himself for his murderous thoughts.

HENRIETTE. Do you believe that the will to do evil can bring death?

ADOLPHE. You mean in a mystical way?

HENRIETTE. If you wish. . . . Let us say, in a mystical way. I am certain that in my own home my mother and sisters hated my father and brought him to his death. My father was obsessed by a sinister compulsion to oppose any expressions of opinion, or desires that we had. Whenever we had a really strong urge or craving for something, he tried to uproot it. By doing this he drove us to resist him. And we countered with a concentrated fire of hate. This finally grew so fierce that he was neutralized, lost his willpower, pined away—and ended by begging for death to take him.

ADOLPHE. And you never suffered for it in your conscience?

HENRIETTE. No! I don't even know what conscience is.

ADOLPHE. Can it be possible? You will some day—soon. (Silence.) How do you think Maurice will look when he arrives here? What do you think he will say?

HENRIETTE. How strange! Yesterday morning he and I were trying to guess the same about you, when you were expected!

ADOLPHE. You did!

HENRIETTE. We guessed entirely wrong.

ADOLPHE. Will you tell me why you sent for me?

HENRIETTE. Malice, arrogance, pure cruelty!

ADOLPHE. To think that you acknowledge your shortcomings, but don't regret them.

HENRIETTE. I presume it is because I don't feel I am entirely responsible for them. They are like the filth that daily chores and contacts—whatever they be—leave on us . . . and that we wash away at the end of the day.—But will you tell me one thing: have you really the high opinion of humanity that you say you have?

ADOLPHE. Yes, we are a little better than our reputation—and a little worse.

HENRIETTE. That was not a completely honest answer.

ADOLPHE. No, it was not. But will you give me a truthful answer to my question: do you still love Maurice?

HENRIETTE. I can't know until I see him again. But at this moment I have no longing for him. I feel I could very well live without him.

ADOLPHE. I believe you are telling the truth. Nevertheless I am afraid your fate is tied to his. . . . Hush! Here he comes.

HENRIETTE. Everything returns—everything. Exactly the same situation, and the same words as yesterday, when we were expecting you!

MAURICE (*enters. He is deathly pale, hollow-eyed and unshaven.*) Here I am, good friends—that is, if I am still the same man. The past night in jail has changed me. I feel I am a different human being today. (*He gazes at* HENRIETTE *and* ADOLPHE.)

ADOLPHE. Sit down and collect yourself; then we shall see what can be done.

MAURICE (*to* HENRIETTE). Perhaps I am not wanted.

ADOLPHE. You must not be bitter.

MAURICE. I have become stirred up and irritated during these last twenty-four hours. I am suspicious. Soon, I am afraid, I will be standing alone. Who, I ask, wants to be seen in the company of a murderer?

HENRIETTE. But you have been exonerated!

MAURICE (*takes a newspaper from his pocket*). Yes, by the police—but not by public opinion. Here you see Maurice Gérard: murderer, former playwright, and his mistress, Henriette Mauclerc—

HENRIETTE. Oh, my mother, and my sisters! My mother! Oh, Christ in Heaven! Help us!

MAURICE. Can't you see that I look like a murderer? And now I am a plagiarist, too! It is now being said that I am a thief, that I didn't write the play! So you see there is nothing left of the conqueror of yesterday. Instead of *my* name, that of my enemy Octave now appears on the billboards! And he will receive my one hundred thousand francs. . . . Oh, Solon, Solon! Such is fortune, such is honor! You may well be thankful, Adolphe, that success has not caught up with you!

HENRIETTE. Haven't you heard of Adolphe's tremendous success in London? He has been awarded the gold medal of honor!

MAURICE (*with a dark expression on his face*). No—I didn't know that! Is that true, Adolphe?

ADOLPHE. It's true, yes—but the medal has been returned.

HENRIETTE (*with stress*). You returned it! . . . Are *you* averse to receiving honors, too, just as your friend was?

ADOLPHE. My friend? (*Embarrassed.*) Oh, yes, yes . . .

MAURICE. I am glad to hear of your success—but it will place a barrier between us.

ADOLPHE. I was afraid of that, and I shall have to walk as much alone in my hour of success as you in adversity. —To think that people can be wounded by others' success. Life is, indeed, horrible!

MAURICE. That is what you say. What shall I say, then? It is as though a black veil covered my eyes and changed the shape and colors of everything in life. This room is as it was yesterday—yet completely different. I can recognize you both, of course, but your faces have changed. I am fumbling for words, because I don't know what to say to you. I ought to exculpate myself, but I can't. And I almost long to go back to jail. At least, it gave me protection from the staring faces of the curious—stares that go right through you! Maurice the murderer and his mistress! You don't love me any more than I love you, Henriette. Today you are ugly, clumsy, empty and repulsive!

(*Unobserved, two men in civilian clothes have taken their places at a table in the back of the restaurant.*)

ADOLPHE. Now wait a moment, and try to collect your thoughts. . . . There must be something in the evening newspapers about your being exonerated, and cleared of all suspicions. And with that, the accusations will come to naught. Your play must be resumed; and if the worst comes to the worst, you can write a new one. Leave Paris for a year until the incident is forgotten. And you—who have rehabilitated mankind in your drama—will begin a new life yourself.

MAURICE. Ha! ha! Mankind! . . . Ha! ha!

ADOLPHE. You have lost faith in the good altogether.

MAURICE. If I ever had any! Perhaps it was merely a mood, an affectation—a sop to the fools and the savages! If I, who was considered to be somewhat superior to the rest, can be so thoroughly rotten, how wretched they must be.

ADOLPHE. I am going out to buy the evening newspapers. A fresh viewpoint may suggest a new strategy.

MAURICE (*turns round and faces the rear of the room*). Two detectives! This means that I am under surveillance. They are hoping that I'll say something careless and compromise myself.

ADOLPHE. They are not detectives. You are just imagining things! I know these men. (*He starts to leave.*)

MAURICE. Don't leave us now, Adolphe. I fear that Henriette and I may become loud in our excitement.

ADOLPHE. Be sensible, Maurice, and think of your life ahead, your future. Henriette, try to calm him! I'll be back immediately. (*He goes out.*)

HENRIETTE. Maurice . . . tell me what you think. Are we guilty, or are we not guilty?

MAURICE. I am not a murderer. My only crime is that I talked a lot of nonsense while drinking. But it is your own crime that comes back to plague you—and which you have now grafted on me.

HENRIETTE. So you are taking that tone, are you? Wasn't it you who cast a curse on your child, who wished it out of the way, and who wanted to flee without a goodbye? And didn't I beg you to visit Marion and to show yourself at Mme. Cathérine's?

MAURICE. Yes, you did. Forgive me! You are more human than I am. The blame is mine—entirely mine. Forgive me! But just the same, the blame is *not* mine! Who has tied this net from which I cannot extricate myself? Guilty—yet not guilty. Not guilty—yet guilty. I am losing my mind from all this!—Look, they are listening to us over there!—And no waiter comes to serve us! I am going in to order a cup of tea for myself. . . . Do you want anything?

HENRIETTE. Nothing.

(MAURICE *goes into the adjoining room.*)

DETECTIVE 1 (*comes over to* HENRIETTE). I'd like to take a look at your papers, woman.

HENRIETTE. Woman? Have you no manners, or decency?

DETECTIVE 1. Did you say decency? I'll teach you manners, you prostitute.

HENRIETTE. What is it you want?

DETECTIVE 1. I'll tell you what I want! I am in charge of the loose women in this district. Yesterday you were in here with one man, today with another. You are what I call a loose woman. And women without an escort are not permitted to be served here. Now you understand why you have to leave—and you are coming with me now!

HENRIETTE. My escort is returning at once!

DETECTIVE 1. Fine escort who leaves his lady to herself.

HENRIETTE. Oh, my God, my God! My mother, my sisters!—Can't you see that I am of good family!

DETECTIVE 1. Of course, you are! And, what is more, you are a notorious figure—your name is all over the newspapers tonight. Now, come along!

HENRIETTE. Where? Where are you taking me?

DETECTIVE 1. Where do you think? To the Police Station!—to present you with a little card, a permit that provides you with free inspection and free medical care.

HENRIETTE. Oh, God in Heaven! You can't mean it?

DETECTIVE 1 (*takes* HENRIETTE *by the arm*). Can't I?

HENRIETTE (*on her knees*). Have mercy! Save me!—Maurice! Help!

DETECTIVE 1. Shut your mouth, you damned whore!

(MAURICE *enters, followed by a* WAITER.)

THE WAITER. We don't serve people like you! Pay your check and get out! And take that slut along with you!

MAURICE (*crushed. He fumbles in his wallet.*) Henriette, will you pay for me, so we can leave. I haven't a sou on me—

THE WAITER. Oh, so the lady pays for her Alphonse! Alphonse! Do you know what that means?

HENRIETTE. My God! I have no money either! Isn't Adolphe coming back soon?

DETECTIVE 1. What a filthy disgusting pair! Hurry up and get out of here—but leave something as security. These harlots usually have their fingers loaded with rings.

MAURICE. Can it be possible that we have sunk so low?

HENRIETTE (*pulls off a ring and gives it to the* WAITER). The abbé was right. This is not the work of human beings!

MAURICE. No, this is the devil's work. And now, if we leave before Adolphe returns, he'll think we are deceiving him and trying to elude him.

HENRIETTE. Yes, and that would be in keeping with all the rest. . . . And now, what is left for us but to seek the river.

MAURICE (*takes* HENRIETTE *by the hand. They go out.*) Yes—the river . . .

ACT IV

Scene 1

*(In the Luxembourg Gardens, before the statuary group
of Adam and Eve. The wind is blowing through the trees
and is stirring up leaves, straws and scraps of paper on the
ground.*

MAURICE *and* HENRIETTE *are seated on a bench.)*

HENRIETTE. Now you don't want to die?

MAURICE. No, now I am afraid to! I am afraid of freezing
down there in the darkness of the grave—with only a sheet
over me and a few shavings underneath my body. Besides,
it seems to me as if I had left something undone. . . . But I
have no idea what it is.

HENRIETTE. I have.

MAURICE. What?

HENRIETTE. It's—revenge. You suspect Jeanne and
Émile of having set those detectives after us yesterday. Such
a scheme for vengeance on a rival could only have been
plotted by a woman.

MAURICE. That's exactly what was in my mind. But, you
know, my suspicions go far beyond that. It seems to me as
though the last few days had made me see things with a
keener sense. For example, can you explain why the waiter
at the Auberge des Adrets and the maître d'hôtel at the
Pavilion were not called to testify at the hearing?

HENRIETTE. That never occurred to me. Oh, yes, now I
understand the reason. They could not testify because they
had not been listening.

MAURICE. But then—how could the Commissaire know
what we had been discussing?

HENRIETTE. He didn't know. He just figured it out. He guessed—and he guessed right. He may have had a similar case in the past.

MAURICE. Or perhaps he read in our faces what we had been saying. There are people who can read thoughts, you know.—That we should have called Adolphe, who was the victim of our deceit, an ass, was quite a natural conclusion for him to make. It's a common term of derision, just like the word *idiot*. But in this case, calling him an *ass* was closer at hand. We had been talking about a conveyance—the triumphal chariot. It's as simple as finding the fourth power when you know three.

HENRIETTE. How could we have allowed ourselves to be so completely taken in?

MAURICE. That's what comes of having a high regard for our fellowmen. That is our reward. But I want to tell you something else. . . . Back of the Commissaire—who, in my opinion, is a conniving scoundrel—I have a suspicion there is some one else.

HENRIETTE. You mean the abbé, who played private detective?

MAURICE. That is exactly who I mean. He hears so many, many confessions. And note this especially, Adolphe himself told us that he had been in St. Germain that very morning. What was he doing there? He tattled, of course, and grumbled over his problems and hardships—and then the priest made out the questions for the Commissaire.

HENRIETTE. Let me ask you one thing: do you trust Adolphe?

MAURICE. I do not trust any one any more.

HENRIETTE. Not even Adolphe?

MAURICE. Him least of all! How could I trust a man after robbing him of his mistress? Can you trust an enemy?

HENRIETTE. You have just been judging Adolphe. Let me tell you something about our friend. You know, of course, that he returned his first award, the medal he received in London. Have you any idea what his reasons were?

MAURICE. No.

HENRIETTE. He considers himself unworthy. Years ago he took a penitential vow never to accept any kind of decoration or honors.

MAURICE. Can that be possible? What could he have done to take such a vow?

HENRIETTE. He committed a crime once—a crime not

punishable by law. That is what he told me in somewhat vague language.

MAURICE. He, too! He—the paragon of idealism and virtue —who never utters a word of evil about anyone, and who is always ready to forgive.

HENRIETTE. Yes—and now you can see that we are not any worse than others. And yet we are haunted by evil spirits, night and day.

MAURICE. He, too! Then humanity has not been slandered. —But if he has been capable of committing a crime, I dare say one could suspect him of anything. Perhaps it was he who sent the police after you yesterday. . . . Now that I think of it, he stole away from us the moment he saw our picture in the newspapers. . . . And he lied when he said the two men were not police. A disappointed lover might be suspected of anything.

HENRIETTE. Could he really be so low? No, I can't believe it—I can't believe it.

MAURICE. Why can't you? He is a scoundrel, isn't he?— What were you talking about yesterday before I came?

HENRIETTE. He said nothing about you that wasn't friendly.

MAURICE. You lie!

HENRIETTE (collects herself; she then speaks in a different tone). Let me tell you something! There is still another person, whom you have not suspected. And I don't know why. What about Mme. Cathérine's wavering attitude during this ordeal? She finally stated quite openly that she considered you capable of doing almost anything under the sun.

MAURICE. Why, yes, she did say that. Yes, that proves what kind of woman she is. Anyone who can hold such a low opinion of another without cause, must be wicked herself.

HENRIETTE (looks hard at him. There is a silence.) Anyone who can hold such a low opinion of another, must be wicked . . .

MAURICE. What do you mean by that?

HENRIETTE. Exactly what I said.

MAURICE. Do you imply that I—?

HENRIETTE. Yes, that is precisely what I mean. Now— tell me, did you meet anyone besides Marion during your visit this morning?

MAURICE. Why do you ask?

HENRIETTE. I'll let you guess.

MAURICE. Well, you already seem to know. . . . I saw Jeanne, too . . .

HENRIETTE. Why, then, did you lie to me?

MAURICE. I wanted to spare you.

HENRIETTE. And now you want me to believe you—after having lied to me. I can't—for now I think that you committed the murder.

MAURICE. Just a moment! Have we arrived at the point which I most of all wanted to avoid? It's strange that what lies closest to us, we see last—and what we don't want to believe, we don't believe.—I'd like to know one thing: Where did you go yesterday morning after we parted in the Bois de Boulogne?

HENRIETTE (uneasily). Why do you ask?

MAURICE. You were either with Adolphe— but you couldn't have been, for he was at the Academy—or you were with—with Marion.

HENRIETTE. Now I am convinced you are the murderer.

MAURICE. And I am as certain that you are. For it was to your special advantage to have the child put out of the way—to remove the stone from the path, as you so precisely put it.

HENRIETTE. Those were your words.

MAURICE. And the person to whose interest it was, is the one who committed the crime.

HENRIETTE. Maurice! We have been going round and round on the treadmill, scourging each other. Now let us take a respite—or we'll both go mad.

MAURICE. You are already mad.

HENRIETTE. Don't you think it is about time we leave each other? Before we do go completely mad?

MAURICE. Yes, I do.

HENRIETTE (rises). Goodbye, then.

(TWO DETECTIVES enter, rear.)

HENRIETTE (turns round; then she goes to MAURICE). There they are again.

MAURICE. The black angels that want to drive us out of the garden . . .

HENRIETTE. And force us together, welding us into one . . .

MAURICE. . . . or sentence us to be wedded for life. Are we really going to be married—live under the same roof—

be able to close the door to the outside world, and perhaps find peace at last?

HENRIETTE. Shut ourselves in, only to torture each other to death—lock ourselves in, each one with a ghost as dowry: you tormenting me with the memory of Adolphe, and I torturing you with Jeanne . . . and Marion.

MAURICE. Don't mention Marion's name again. You know she is being buried today—perhaps this very moment.

HENRIETTE. And you are not at the funeral. Why?

MAURICE. The police have cautioned me against the frenzy of the mob, and so has Jeanne.

HENRIETTE. A coward to boot?

MAURICE. With every imaginable vice! How could you possibly have fallen in love with me?

HENRIETTE. Two days ago you were an entirely different person. I felt you worthy of being loved.

MAURICE. And now I have sunk so low—

HENRIETTE. I didn't say that. You are making yourself out to be very wicked.

MAURICE. You have made me so.

HENRIETTE. Perhaps, for as you seem to be taking on wickedness, I feel more righteous.

MAURICE. It's very much like recovering from certain illnesses.

HENRIETTE. And you have become crude and vulgar, too.

MAURICE. I am conscious of that myself. I realize I am not the same since that night in the jail. They took in *one* man and set free another—through the gate that separates us from society. You know, I feel today like an enemy of mankind. I would like to set fire to the earth, dry up the sea; for only through a conflagration of the universe can my dishonor be wiped out.

HENRIETTE. I received a letter from my mother today. She is a widow. My father was a major in the army. She was brought up in the old school, with its notions of honor and that sort of thing. Would you like to read the letter? No, you would not.—Do you realize I am an outcast. My respectable acquaintances no longer wish to have anything to do with me. If I show myself in the street, alone, at night, the police will arrest me. So you see—we must be married!

MAURICE. We loathe each other—yet we have to be married. Could hell be worse? But, Henriette,—before we tie our lives together, you must confide your secret to me so that we will be on more equal terms.

HENRIETTE. Very well, I'll tell you my secret.—I had a friend who got into trouble. You understand what I mean. I wanted to help her. Her future was at stake. But I handled the matter clumsily. As a result she lost her life.

MAURICE. You were indiscreet, but at the same time you acted with a touch of nobility.

HENRIETTE. That is what you say now, but the next time you get angry, you will be accusing me.

MAURICE. No, I will not. But I won't deny that my confidence in you has been shaken, and that I am afraid of having you close to me. But what about her lover? Is he still alive? And does he know that you were the cause of her death?

HENRIETTE. He was an accomplice.

MAURICE. But suppose he became conscience-stricken? Such a thing could happen. And he might feel the necessity of reporting you. . . . Then you would be lost.

HENRIETTE. Yes, I know. It is this constant anguish that drives me to live in a continuous whirl of recklessness. I am afraid to awaken for even a brief moment.

MAURICE. And now you want to settle a share of your anguish on me as my marriage portion. Isn't that going a little too far?

HENRIETTE. But am I not sharing your dishonor as a murderer, Maurice?

MAURICE. Let's have an end to this.

HENRIETTE. No, it isn't over yet. I shan't let go my hold until I know just what kind of man you are. I will not let you get away thinking you are better than I am.

MAURICE. In short, you are set for battle. Very well, I shall give you one.

HENRIETTE. To the bitter end!

(*The sound of the rolling of drums is heard in the distance.*)

MAURICE. The gardens are being closed.—"Cursed is the ground for thy sake; thorns and thistles it shall bring forth to thee."

HENRIETTE. "And to the woman said the Lord . . ."

A GUARD (*in uniform; politely*). The gardens are being closed, Madame . . . Monsieur . . .

Scene 2

(*The café.* Mme. Cathérine *is at the bar. She is busy writing in her ledger.* Adolphe *and* Henriette *at one of the tables.*)

Adolphe (*quietly, kindly*). For the last time I give you my word: I did not run away. On the contrary, I thought you had deserted me. You must believe me.

Henriette. But why did you try to make us believe those men were not police.

Adolphe. I thought they were not. And I said it to make you feel at ease.

Henriette. Since you tell me the reason, I believe you. And now you must also believe me, when I bare to you my innermost secret, my most secret thoughts.

Adolphe. I am listening.

Henriette. But you must not accuse me of laboring under delusions and hallucinations, as you usually do.

Adolphe. You act as if you expected just that.

Henriette. I fear nothing of the sort—but I know you, and I am used to your skepticism. And now, you will reveal to no one what I tell you. . . . You must promise me.

Adolphe. I promise.

Henriette. Will you believe me, when I say that. . . . Oh, it's something so horrible. . . . I can almost prove that Maurice is guilty—or at least that there is good reason to suspect that—

Adolphe. You don't know what you are saying!

Henriette. Listen to the end, and you may judge for yourself. When Maurice left me in the Bois de Boulogne, he said he would like to see Marion alone, while her mother was out. Now it has been brought to light that he met the mother, Jeanne. Consequently he lied to me.

275

ADOLPHE. He may have lied to you—and for some good reason. But that's no proof that he has committed the crime.

HENRIETTE. Don't you understand? Can't you understand?

ADOLPHE. No, I can't.

HENRIETTE. You don't want to.—Well, in that case there is only one thing for me to do: to go to the police. Then we'll see whether he can produce an alibi.

ADOLPHE. Henriette, let me tell you the grim, unvarnished truth. Both you and he are psychopathic cases, on the verge of insanity. You are in the clutches of the demons of dread and mistrust. You each have a certain consciousness of guilt. Therefore you try to injure each other.—Let's see whether my guess is right: doesn't he, too, suspect you of having murdered his child? Doesn't he?

HENRIETTE. Yes, that's how utterly beside himself and demented he is—

ADOLPHE. You call his suspicions insanity—but not your own.

HENRIETTE. You have to prove me wrong first—or that I suspect him unjustly.

ADOLPHE. I agree with you—and it's easy to prove. A later autopsy has shown conclusively that Marion died of a well known disease, the name of which evades me at the moment.

HENRIETTE. Is that true?

ADOLPHE. The official report is printed in the newspapers today.

HENRIETTE. I put no credence in the newspapers. Reports can be falsified.

ADOLPHE. Take care, Henriette! Or is it possible that you, without knowing it, have passed the border line? Above all, be careful that you don't make accusations that may put you behind prison bars. Be careful! (*He places his hand on her head.*) You loathe Maurice, don't you?

HENRIETTE. Beyond expression!

ADOLPHE. When love turns into hatred, it can only mean that it was tainted from the very beginning.

HENRIETTE (*somewhat calmer*). What am I to do? Tell me—you who are the only—the only one who understands me.

ADOLPHE. But you don't like being preached to.

HENRIETTE. Haven't you anything else to offer?

ADOLPHE. No—but it has helped me.

HENRIETTE. Then let's have the sermon.

ADOLPHE. Try to turn your hatred against yourself. Put the knife to your own festering canker—for there is where the trouble lies.

HENRIETTE. Explain yourself.

ADOLPHE. First of all, leave Maurice so that you cannot nurse your pangs of conscience together. Break off your artist's career, which you took up for only one reason: to pursue a life of frivolity and so-called liberty. By now you have come to see how little joy there is in it. And then go back home to your mother.

HENRIETTE. Never in the world!

ADOLPHE. Then somewhere else.

HENRIETTE. Adolphe, I presume you know that I have guessed your secret. I know why you did not accept the prize medal.

ADOLPHE. You probably do—knowing part of the story.

HENRIETTE. Yes. . . . But how did you find peace of mind?

ADOLPHE. I have tried to tell you—I became conscious of my guilt, felt remorse, and decided to lead a better life. From then on I have lived the life of a penitent.

HENRIETTE. But how can one feel remorse, having no conscience—as in my case? Is remorse an act of grace, obtained in the same manner as faith?

ADOLPHE. Everything in life that is good is an act of grace. But you will learn it is only granted to him who seeks. Go and seek! (HENRIETTE *is silent*.) And don't let the time for supplication pass by, for then your heart may harden and you may perish in the bottomless pit, past all help.

HENRIETTE (*after a moment of silence*). Is conscience the fear of punishment?

ADOLPHE. No, it is the revulsion of our better self against the evil deeds of the sinner in us.

HENRIETTE. In that case, I, too, must have a conscience.

ADOLPHE. Of course you have, but—

HENRIETTE. Tell me, Adolphe, are you what they call religious?

ADOLPHE. No, not in the least.

HENRIETTE. It is all so strange. . . . What is religion?

ADOLPHE. Well, now, that is more than I can tell you. And I don't think there is anyone who can really explain what it is. There are times when I think it must be a punishment. No one gets religion unless he suffers from a bad conscience—

HENRIETTE. Yes, it is a punishment. Now I know what I have to do. Goodbye, Adolphe.

ADOLPHE. You are leaving?

HENRIETTE. Yes, I am leaving Paris. I am taking your advice. Goodbye, my friend. Goodbye, Mme. Cathérine.

MME. CATHÉRINE. Are you leaving so soon?

HENRIETTE. Yes.

ADOLPHE. Would you like me to come with you?

HENRIETTE. No. . . . I am going alone, as I came alone, one day in the spring, with the notion that I belonged here—where I do not belong—believing that there was something called freedom—which does not exist. Goodbye.

(*She leaves.*)

MME. CATHÉRINE. I never want to see that woman again! And I wish she had never come near this place!

ADOLPHE. Who knows? There may have been some meaning in her coming here. In any case, she deserves pity—no end of pity.

MME. CATHÉRINE. I don't deny that, for that is something we all need.

ADOLPHE. As a matter of fact, she has done less wrong than some of us.

MME. CATHÉRINE. Perhaps so—but I doubt it.

ADOLPHE. You are always so strait-laced, so severe, Mme. Cathérine. Tell me one thing—have you never done any wrong?

MME. CATHÉRINE (*taken aback*). Why, of course . . . I am only a sinful creature. But anyone who has been on thin ice and fallen in, has not only the right but the duty to warn others to keep away. And one may do that without having to be considered hard or uncharitable. Didn't I warn Monsieur Maurice the moment I saw that woman enter: Watch out! Keep away from her! But he didn't heed my warning, and so he suffered the consequences. He acted like some unruly, headstrong child. When a man behaves that way he deserves a spanking—just like any disobedient youngster.

ADOLPHE. Don't you think he has had his share of spanking already?

MME. CATHÉRINE. Yes, he has, but it doesn't seem to have done him any good. He still goes around acting like a spoiled child.

ADOLPHE. That is a very sensible interpretation of a complicated case.

MME. CATHÉRINE. Humph! You do nothing but philosophize about your vices and keep worrying about them. Meanwhile the police have solved the riddle. Now, let me attend to my accounts and don't disturb me any more.

ADOLPHE. There he is . . . Maurice . . .

MME. CATHÉRINE. Why, yes, may God bless him . . .

MAURICE (*enters. His face is flushed. He sits down at* ADOLPHE's *table.*) Good evening.

(MME. CATHÉRINE *nods and continues with her bookkeeping.*)

ADOLPHE. How are things coming along with you?

MAURICE. Oh, things are beginning to clear up now.

ADOLPHE (*hands him a newspaper, which* MAURICE *does not accept*). So you have already seen it?

MAURICE. No, I don't read the newspapers any more. They publish nothing but infamies.

ADOLPHE. But you must read it.—Read it.

MAURICE. No, I don't want to.—It's full of lies. But wait till I tell you about an entirely new clue I have discovered. . . . Who do you think committed the crime? Do you know?

ADOLPHE. No one. No one.

MAURICE. Do you know where Henriette was during the quarter hour the child was alone?—Well, she was there—with Marion! It was she who did it!

ADOLPHE. You are out of your mind, man!

MAURICE. I am not mad—but Henriette is. And she suspects me and has threatened to report me.

ADOLPHE. Henriette was here just a brief moment ago. And she used exactly the same words that you are using now. You are both mad, for it has been conclusively proved by a second autopsy that the child died from a known disease—the name of which I can't recall at this moment.

MAURICE. You are not telling the truth.

ADOLPHE. That is exactly what *she* said. If you'll look in the newspapers, you can read the official medical report.

MAURICE. The medical report? Well, then it must be erroneous—it's a fabrication.

ADOLPHE. That, too, is exactly what she said.—You are both suffering from the identical mental malady—the same psychosis. But with her I got so far as to make her realize the seat of her trouble.

MAURICE. Where is she now?

ADOLPHE. She went away—far away—to begin a new life.

MAURICE. H'm. H'm.—Did you go to the funeral?

ADOLPHE. Yes, I was there.

MAURICE. Well, and . . .

ADOLPHE. Jeanne seemed resigned. She didn't utter a harsh word against you.

MAURICE. She is a good woman.

ADOLPHE. She is. How could you ever desert her?

MAURICE. I was out of my mind—inflated by my own ego. And then, too, we had been drinking.

ADOLPHE. Now you can understand why Jeanne wept when you drank champagne.

MAURICE. Yes, now I can understand. And that is why I have already written to her and asked her to forgive me. Do you think she will forgive me?

ADOLPHE. I think she will. She could never hate anyone.

MAURICE. Do you think she will forgive me completely—so wholeheartedly that she would be willing to take me back?

ADOLPHE. That is something I couldn't answer. Your treatment of her is so unforgivable that she could scarcely be expected to live with you any longer.

MAURICE. Yet I can't help feeling that she is still fond of me. . . . I feel that she will come back to me.

ADOLPHE. Don't be too sure. What makes you think she will? Didn't you suspect her and her brother—an honest and upright fellow—of having connived with the police to have Henriette picked up as a prostitute—out of revenge? Didn't you?

MAURICE. I have changed my mind.—Just the same, I can't help thinking Émile is something of a trickster.

MME. CATHÉRINE. What's that you are saying about Monsieur Émile? Now you listen to me. He may be nothing but a plain workingman—but I wish everybody was as decent and straight as he is. So don't you try to find fault with him. Émile has good common sense, and is always considerate of others.

ÉMILE (enters). Monsieur Gérard?

MAURICE. Yes—I am Monsieur Gérard.

ÉMILE. Pardon me—but there is something I would like to say to you in private.

MAURICE. You can tell me here—these are all friends of mine . . .

(THE ABBÉ enters; he seats himself.)

ÉMILE (*with a glance at the* ABBÉ). Well, perhaps I had better—

MAURICE. Don't be afraid . . . the Abbé is also a friend, even if we don't see eye to eye on—

ÉMILE. You know who I am, Monsieur Gérard, don't you? My sister asked me to bring you this. It is in answer to your letter. (MAURICE *takes the package and opens it.*) I would like to add, speaking for both my sister and myself, since I am, in a way, her guardian, that you are freed of any and all obligations to her . . . now that the natural bond between you has ceased to exist.

MAURICE. You must hate me!

ÉMILE. Hate you? I don't know why I should. However, I would like to deny here and now, Monsieur Gérard, in the presence of your friends, that either my sister or I had anything to do with such a dastardly scheme as sending the police after Mlle. Henriette.

MAURICE. I take back anything I said, and I apologize. I hope you can forgive me.

ÉMILE. I forgive you. And now I . . . I wish you all a good evening.

ALL. Good evening.   (ÉMILE *goes out.*)

MAURICE. The tie and the gloves that Jeanne gave me for the première, and which I allowed Henriette to throw into the fire. Who could have picked them up? Everything is being dug up—everything comes back. And when she gave them to me at the cemetery, she said she wanted me to look fine and handsome so that everybody would like me. She herself remained at home. What I did with her gift wounded her deeply—and how could it help but hurt her? I have no longer the right to be seen in decent company. Oh, how could I have done anything so horrible? . . . To despise, to scorn a gift coming from the warmth of her heart . . . to ridicule a sacrifice made for me! This is what I threw away—for a wreath of laurel that now crowns the rubbish heap, and a bust that should have been placed in a pillory. Monsieur Abbé—now I am coming over to you.

THE ABBÉ. We welcome you.

MAURICE. Speak the word that will help me.

THE ABBÉ. Would you wish me to contradict your self-accusations and say that you have committed no wrong?

MAURICE. Speak out, Monsieur Abbé, speak frankly.

THE ABBÉ. Then, if you'll forgive me, I find your behavior just as reproachful as you yourself have found it.

MAURICE. What am I to do? What am I to do to escape this misery?

THE ABBÉ. You know the answer as well as I do.

MAURICE. No, I only know that I am forever lost, my career at an end, my life ruined. . . . I am in complete disrepute!

THE ABBÉ. And that is why you are now searching for a new existence, a better world, in which you are now beginning to believe.

MAURICE. Yes.

THE ABBÉ. You have been living in the flesh—and now you want to live in the spirit. Are you so sure that the old world holds no more attractions for you?

MAURICE. None! Honors are an illusion, riches nothing but withered leaves, women mere intoxicants. Let me take refuge behind your consecrated walls and leave behind the horrible dream of the past two days—days that seem like eternities.

THE ABBÉ. Very well—but this is not the place to discuss such matters. Let us meet at St. Germain at nine o'clock this evening. I am preaching to the penitents of St. Lazare. This will be your first step on the long road of penance.

MAURICE. Penance?

THE ABBÉ. Yes, are you ready?

MAURICE. Yes, yes . . .

THE ABBÉ. And vigils are held from midnight until two in the morning.

MAURICE. It will be a glorious feeling—to be born again—

THE ABBÉ. Give me your hand so that you will not look back.

MAURICE (rises; extends his hand). Here is my hand—and with it my spirit, and my good will!

THE MAIDSERVANT (enters from the kitchen). A telephone call for Monsieur Maurice—

MAURICE. From whom?

THE MAIDSERVANT. It's from the theatre.

(MAURICE tries to get away, but the ABBÉ holds on to his hand.)

THE ABBÉ (to the MAIDSERVANT). Ask if there is a message.

THE MAIDSERVANT. Oh, they wanted to know if Monsieur Maurice is coming to the performance tonight.

THE ABBÉ (to MAURICE who in vain is trying to free himself from the ABBÉ's grasp). No, I won't let you go . . .

MAURICE. What performance is she talking about?

ADOLPHE. You refused to read the newspapers—

MME. CATHÉRINE AND THE ABBÉ. He hasn't read the news—

MAURICE. The newspapers are full of distortions and libel. (*To* THE MAIDSERVANT.) Tell them at the theatre that I can't come tonight—that I am going to church.

(THE MAIDSERVANT *disappears into the kitchen.*)

ADOLPHE. As long as you are determined not to read what the newspapers have to say, let me tell you. Now that you have been exonerated, the theatre has resumed the run of your play. And tonight your fellow authors are planning to pay you a public tribute from the stage in recognition of your indisputable talent.

MAURICE. You are not telling me the truth.

ALL. Yes. It is true.

MAURICE (*after a silence*). I don't deserve it.

THE ABBÉ. That sounds good!

ADOLPHE. And that isn't all.

MAURICE. Not all?

MME. CATHÉRINE. One hundred thousand francs! Do you see how everything comes back to you? And the house in the surburbs! Everything comes back—except Mlle. Henriette!

THE ABBÉ (*smiles*). Mme. Cathérine, you ought to treat such matters a little more seriously—

MME. CATHÉRINE. But I can't—I simply can't keep from laughing. (*She tries to stifle her boisterous laughter by covering her mouth with her handkerchief.*)

ADOLPHE. You know, Maurice, the curtain rises at eight tonight.

THE ABBÉ. And church is at nine.

ADOLPHE. Maurice!

MME. CATHÉRINE. Monsieur Maurice—come on and make up your mind!

(MAURICE *rests his head on the table, his hands covering his head.*)

ADOLPHE. Free him of his promise, Monsieur Abbé.

THE ABBÉ. It is not for me to set free or to bind. That is a matter for him to work out, and no one else.

MAURICE (*rises*). I am going with the Abbé.

THE ABBÉ. No, my young friend. All I can do is to give you counsel—the choice has to be your own. You owe a duty to yourself and your good name. That you came through all this as quickly as you did, proves to me that you have suffered your punishment as intensely as if it had lasted an eternity. And once Providence has given you absolution, there is nothing for me to add.

MAURICE. But why should I have to be punished so severely when I was innocent?

THE ABBÉ. Severely? Two days only! And you were not innocent. We have to answer for all our thoughts, our words, and our desires. And you had murder in your thoughts, when your evil desires tempted you to do away with your child.

MAURICE. You are right. . . . I have made up my mind. I shall meet you this evening in church and settle my accounts. And tomorrow I shall go to the theatre.

MME. CATHÉRINE. You have found the key, Monsieur Maurice!

ADOLPHE. Yes, you could not have made a better choice.

THE ABBÉ. You have given your answer—the right answer.

EASTER

A PLAY IN THREE ACTS

Although hardly the strongest of Strindberg's plays, *Easter* (*Påsk*) is undoubtedly the most attractive, and it has been the most frequently performed Strindberg work in Sweden. Strindberg wrote *Easter* in 1900, during an interval of happiness and reconciliation with life after his turbulent "Inferno" period when there had been reason to fear for his mind. The play, published in 1901, had its world première at the *Schauspielhaus* of Frankfurt am Main in March 1901 under the German title of *Ostern,* and was produced in Sweden at the Royal Theatre on April 4, 1901, with Harriet Bosse in the leading role of Eleonora. The part was later filled at the Intimate Theatre, in the spring of 1908, by Anna Flygare, a young actress who was acclaimed as the ideal Eleonora. In 1912, the nineteen-year-old Fanny Falkner, who nearly became Strindberg's fourth wife when he was sixty, acted the role at Folkets Hus Teater in Stockholm. The play became the greatest success of Strindberg's Intimate Theatre, where it had 182 performances. The Royal Theatre revived *Easter* a number of times—in 1939 with Signe Hasso in the role of Eleonora. In the United States, the first production was given in Swedish at the Little Theatre in Chicago in 1913; a reading performance in English was given in New York in 1914; and a production was presented in the latter city in 1916 by Frida Uhl, who had been the author's second wife.

Only the details are realistic; mysticism and idealism were dominant in Strindberg's thinking when he conceived *Easter* in a renewed outburst of creative energy after his mental crisis. He wrote this play while in love with Harriet Bosse, who became his third wife, and he created the leading role for her. It is the role of a gentle and loving woman whom the world regards as a lunatic. (It is in part based on the character of one of his sisters, who died in 1904 in an asylum for the mentally deranged.) Eleonora is rare among Strindberg's female characters, for she brings peace, not war, into her household and gives her family a greatly needed lesson in love.

"Eleonora," he wrote, "is she who suffers in the place of others." Harriet Bosse captivated the public in Stockholm with her playing of this role. About a month later, on May 1, 1901, she married the author.

PERSONS IN THE PLAY

Mrs. Heyst
Elis, her son; Bachelor of Arts and teacher
Eleonora, her daughter; Elis' younger sister
Kristina, Elis' fiancée
Benjamin, a student
Lindkvist

ACT I

MAUNDY THURSDAY

Music played before the rise of the curtain: Haydn: "The Seven Last Words of Christ on the Cross." Introduction: Maestoso Adagio.

(THE SETTING.—*This consists of a glass veranda on the first floor of a dwelling. It has been converted into and outfitted as a living-room. In the center, rear, is a large door leading to a little garden enclosed by a fence. A gate in the fence opens onto the street. Across the street, which like the house is situated on a height, can be seen the tops of the trees of a garden, sloping down toward the city, and a low garden fence. The leaves of the trees indicate the arrival of spring. Above the treetops are seen a church spire and the gable of a monumental building.*

The windows of the veranda—which extends across the breadth of the stage—are hung with curtains of light yellow cretonne, with a flower pattern. These curtains can be drawn. To the right of the center door, a mirror hangs on the wall between the door and the window; and below it, a calendar with visible dates.

To the left of the center door stands a large writing table, on which are piled books; there is also writing material, etc., and a telephone.

To the right of the door are a dining-table and chairs, a parlor stove with isinglass windows, and a sideboard. Down stage, left, a sewing table with a kerosene lamp. Placed near this table, two reclining chairs. A lamp hangs from the ceiling.

There are doors on both sides of the veranda: to the right, one leads to the rest of the apartment; to the left, another door, leading to the kitchen. On the street outside can be seen a street lamp with incandescent Auer burners; it is lighted.

The action takes place at the turn of the 19th century.

A sunbeam falls obliquely across the room from the left, bathing one of the chairs by the sewing table in light. On the other chair, untouched by the sun, KRISTINA *is busy drawing a tape through a pair of white, freshly laundered kitchen curtains.* ELIS *enters, his overcoat unbuttoned. He carries a large bundle of papers, which he places on the writing table, left.)*

ELIS. Good afternoon, my dear.

KRISTINA. Oh, it's you, Elis!

ELIS (*looks around*). The storm windows are out—the floor scrubbed—clean curtains! Yes, spring is here again. And the ice in the street has been removed—and the willow is blooming down by the river. Yes, spring is here. And I can shed my heavy overcoat. You have no idea how heavy it is. (*He holds up the coat as if weighing it.*) It is as if it had absorbed all the labor and pain of this winter, all the sweat and anguish, and the dust of the school room. . . . Oh! (*He hangs the coat, left.*)

KRISTINA. And now you will have a brief respite.

ELIS. Easter holiday—five heavenly days when I can take it easy, breathe out, and forget! Oh, but see, the sun has come back again. It disappeared in November. I still remember the day it vanished behind the brewery across the street. Oh, what a winter! What an endless winter!

KRISTINA (*with a gesture in the direction of the kitchen*). Sh! Sh! Sh!

ELIS. I won't say a word. I shall only rejoice that it is over at last. Ah, how good to see the sun again! (*He rubs his hands as though bathing in sun.*) I am going to bathe in sun, wash myself in light, after all this gloom and filth—

KRISTINA. Sh! Sh!

ELIS. You know, I believe we are going to have a little peace at last, and that our hardships are fading away.

KRISTINA. What makes you think that?

ELIS. Why, for one thing, because—when I passed the cathedral just now—I saw a white dove come flying toward me. And it flew down onto the sidewalk, dropping a twig it carried in its bill right at my feet.

KRISTINA. Did you notice what kind of twig it was?

ELIS. It couldn't very well have been olive; nevertheless it was a symbol of peace. And at this moment I feel an un-earthly, exalting calm.—Where is mother?

KRISTINA (*gestures toward the kitchen*). In the kitchen.

ELIS (*speaks softly, his eyes closed*). I can tell that spring is come. I can hear that the storm windows are out.—Do you know how I can hear it? . . . First of all, by the axles of the wagons.—But what do I hear now? It's the bullfinch singing! And down at the wharf they are hammering, and I can smell the fresh paint from the steamboats. I can smell the red lead.

KRISTINA. You can smell it all the way here?

ELIS. All the way here? Of course, we are *here*—but I was *there,* up there in the north, where we have our home.—How did we ever come to this dreadful town where everybody hates everybody else, and where one can never be anything but lonely? Oh yes, it was our daily bread that drew us here. But alongside the bread stalked those monsters ill luck and adversity: father's unprincipled transactions and my little sister's sickness.—By the way, do you know whether mother has received permission to visit father in prison yet?

KRISTINA. I think she was there today.

ELIS. Did she say anything to you?

KRISTINA. Not a word. She talked about other things.

ELIS. One thing is gained, however: the verdict put an end to the uncertainty, and a peculiar calm set in after the newspapers stopped writing about him. Now a year has passed. In another he will be free. Then we can start all over again.

KRISTINA. I must say I admire you—after all that you have been through.

ELIS. You shouldn't. There is nothing to admire in me. I have nothing but faults. Now you know. And I wish you would believe me.

KRISTINA. If you had to suffer for your own mistakes. . . . But you are suffering for what others have done.

ELIS. What is it you are sewing?

KRISTINA. It's the curtains for the kitchen, Elis dear.

ELIS. It looks like a bridal veil.—This fall, Kristina, we are to be married, aren't we?

KRISTINA. Why, yes—but let us first think about the summer.

ELIS. You are right—summer! (*He takes out a checkbook.*) See, the money is already in the bank. And as soon as school is over, we'll hie ourselves north to our native soil—

to Lake Mälar. The cottage stands ready to receive us, just as when we were children. The linden trees are there, the punt is drawn up under the willow tree by the beach. Oh, if only summer were here, and I could go swimming in the lake! The disgrace to the family has put a strain on me, poisoned me body and soul. I can't wait to wash myself clean again.

KRISTINA. Have you heard from your sister Eleonora?

ELIS. Yes, my poor sister . . . her mind is never at rest, and her letters are enough to tear my heart out. She wants to get out of the asylum and come home, of course; but the director is afraid to let her go, for she does things that *could* put her in prison. There are times when my conscience bothers me—bothers me indescribably because of my share in having her committed.

KRISTINA. Elis dear, you reproach yourself for everything; but what you did was merely an act of charity. It is a blessing that the poor unfortunate child is being given the care she needs.

ELIS. Yes, that's true . . . and I can't help thinking it is a little more peaceful with her away. Yes, I suppose she is as well off now as she can be. And whenever I think of how she fluttered about here, casting a shadow over anything resembling happiness—how her affliction depressed us like a bad dream, tortured us to despair—I am selfish enough to feel a sense of relief akin to joy. And I can imagine no greater misfortune than to see her step inside this house. That is the kind of wretched creature I am!

KRISTINA. That is how *human* you are.

ELIS. Yet, in spite of it, I feel the pain—the pain at the thought of what she has to endure and suffer—and my father's suffering.

KRISTINA. Some seem to be born to suffer.

ELIS. My poor Kristina! To think that it should be your fate to come into this family—doomed and damned from the beginning.

KRISTINA. Elis! You don't know whether these things are sent to us as a trial or as punishment.

ELIS. What they might seem to you, I don't know. But if anyone is without guilt, you are.

KRISTINA. "Morning brings tears; night comes with joy!" Elis, let me try to help you through this.

ELIS. Do you suppose mother might have a white tie?

KRISTINA (*uneasily*). You are not going out anywhere, are you?

ELIS. I am going to a dinner tonight. Peter disputed his doctor's dissertation yesterday. Tonight he is giving a dinner.

KRISTINA. You can't be thinking of going there?

ELIS. You can't mean that I ought to stay away merely because he proved to be a rather ungrateful student.

KRISTINA. I don't deny that his disloyalty was a shock to me. He promised to give you credit for material he used in his treatise. Instead he stole from your treatise without mentioning the source!

ELIS. Oh, heavens, that is done all the time—and I am happy to know that I was of some help to him.

KRISTINA. Did he actually invite you?

ELIS. No, come to think of it, you are right—he did not! Now, that is very strange! For years he has been talking about his doctor's dinner, as if it was a foregone conclusion that I was invited. And so, in turn, I have told everybody. If I am not invited now, it's nothing short of a slight, an insult. But never mind! This is not the first time, nor will it be the last! (*There is a pause.*)

KRISTINA. Benjamin is late. Do you think he will pass his written examinations?

ELIS. I am quite certain he will; in Latin, with honors.

KRISTINA. He is a fine boy, Benjamin is.

ELIS. Exceptionally so. But something of a dreamer. —You know, of course, why he is staying with us?

KRISTINA. Is it because—?

ELIS. Because my father embezzled funds left in trust for the son, as he did with trust property of others. You see, Kristina, this is to me the worst trial of all: to have to face these poor, defrauded orphans at school who have now become objects of humiliation and charity, unable to pay their tuition. You can well imagine how they must regard me. Only by keeping their misery constantly in mind can I overlook their cruel behavior.

KRISTINA. Your father is really better off than you are.

ELIS. Yes, he is, no doubt.

KRISTINA. Let us think of the summer, and not of the past.

ELIS. Yes, let's. You know, last night I woke up hearing the students sing. They sang: "Yes, I'm coming. Bring, you winds of rapture—to the country and the birds out there—all my love, to them and birch and linden—to the lakes, I long to see once more. See them as I did in days of childhood . . ." (*He rises, moved.*) Shall I ever see them again? Shall I ever get away from this dreadful town, from Ebal, the accursed mountain, and once again behold Gerizim? (*He seats himself by the door.*)

KRISTINA. You shall! You shall! Yes, yes . . .

ELIS. But do you think that I shall see my birches and my lindens, as I saw them in those days? Won't they be covered by the black pall that has settled over our lives and over all nature down here—ever since the day that—(*He points to the easy chair which is now in shadow.*) Look, the sun is gone.

KRISTINA. It will come back—and then to stay.

ELIS. You are right. The days are lengthening, and the shadows will fade.

KRISTINA. We are coming closer to the light, Elis. Believe me.

ELIS. Sometimes I think so. And when I remember what has passed, and compare it with our lot today, I feel hopeful. This time last year, I did not have you with me—when you broke our engagement and left me. That, you know, was my darkest hour. I literally died with every breath I drew. But when you returned, life returned. Do you remember why you left me?

KRISTINA. No, I don't, and it seems to me now as if I couldn't have had a very good reason. I merely felt I had to go away at the time, and so I went—like a sleepwalker. The moment I saw you again, I woke up, and my happiness returned.

ELIS. And now we shall never again be separated. For if you were to leave me now, I would *really* die.—I hear mother coming. Say nothing to her. Spare her. She is living in a world of her own, imagining that father is a martyr and all his victims scoundrels . . .

MRS. HEYST (*enters from the kitchen, left. She wears an apron and is paring an apple. She speaks in a friendly, somewhat childish manner.*) Good afternoon, children. Would you like to have your apple soup cold or hot?

ELIS. Cold, mother dear.

MRS. HEYST. That's right, my son. You always know what you want and speak up. Kristina never does. That's something Elis learned from his father. *He* always knew what he wanted and what he was about. And people don't like that. That's why he was made to suffer for it. But *his* day will

come, and then he'll be given justice, and the others will get
theirs. Now, what was it I wanted to tell you?—Oh, yes!
Have you heard that Lindkvist has moved to town? Lindkvist
—the biggest scoundrel of them all.

ELIS (*rises in agitation*). Lindkvist—here?

MRS. HEYST. Yes, he is living across the street from us.

ELIS. And we shall have to see him pass here day in and
day out? Isn't enough enough!

MRS. HEYST. Just let me speak to him—just once—and he'll
never show his face again. He'll never return. I know his
little peculiarities. . . . Well, Elis, how did Peter do in his
disputation?

ELIS. Oh, he did very well.

MRS. HEYST. I can well imagine. When do you think *you*
will be ready with your dissertation?

ELIS. As soon as I can afford it, mother.

MRS. HEYST (*derisively*). As soon as I can afford it! That's
not a frank answer.—And Benjamin—did he pass his written
examinations?

ELIS. We don't know yet. But he ought to be here any
moment now.

MRS. HEYST. Well, I don't exactly like Benjamin. He acts
as if he were a privileged character. But we'll soon put
him in his place. Just the same, he is a nice boy. Oh, I
almost forgot—and there is a package for you, Elis, too.
(*She goes into the kitchen and returns at once with the
package.*)

ELIS. Imagine, how carefully mother looks after everything
and knows everything that goes on. I can't help thinking,
sometimes, she is not as childish as she acts.

MRS. HEYST. See! Here is the package. Lina received it.

ELIS. Can it be a present? I am wary of gifts ever since I
received that box of paving stones. (*He places the box on the
table.*)

MRS. HEYST. I'm going back into the kitchen again.
—Won't it get chilly in here with the door open?

ELIS. No, mother, it won't be too cold.

MRS. HEYST. You mustn't hang your overcoat there,
Elis. It doesn't look very tidy.—Well, Kristina, will you
have finished my curtains soon?

KRISTINA. In just a few more minutes, mother.

MRS. HEYST. Yes, I like that Peter. I like him. He is my
favorite. Aren't you going to the dinner tonight, Elis?

ELIS. Why, yes, of course, I am going.

Mrs. Heyst. Well, then—why did you say you wanted your apple soup cold, if you are going out to dinner? You never seem to know what you want, Elis. Now, Peter—he does. Well, be sure to close the doors if it gets chilly in here, so that you won't catch cold.

(*She leaves, right.*)

Elis. Good old mother! And it's forever Peter. Do you suppose she means to embarrass you about Peter?

Kristina. Me?

Elis. Don't you know that as women get older, they often do things like that? They begin to imagine things, and get queer notions.

Kristina. What is in the package there?

Elis (*tears off the wrapping*). A birch rod for Lent!

Kristina. Who could have sent it?

Elis. The sender has not put his name on it.—Well, the birch rod can't be blamed for this prank, so I'll put it in water. There it will grow green like the rod of Aaron. "Birch —as in my days of childhood." And now Lindkvist has come to town.

Kristina. Who is this Lindkvist? What has he to do with you?

Elis. He is our principal creditor.

Kristina. But *you* don't owe him anything, Elis?

Elis. Yes, it is our debt, and we have to pay it: one for all, and all for one. The family name is dishonored as long as there is a single debt to be paid.

Kristina. Why not take another name?

Elis. Kristina!

Kristina (*has finished the curtains and puts them away*). Thank you, Elis, for that! I only said it to test you.

Elis. But you must not put temptation in my way. Lindkvist is not a rich man and needs the money he has coming to him. Wherever father put his foot, he left a battle field of dead and wounded. Yet mother goes around in the belief that he has been victimized.—Wouldn't you like to go for a walk?

Kristina. And look for the sun! Gladly.

Elis. Can you fathom this: The Redeemer suffered for our sins; still we are continually paying for them. But no one pays for me.

Kristina. If someone did pay for you—would you then understand?

ELIS. Yes, then I would understand. Hush! Benjamin is coming. Can you see if he looks happy?

KRISTINA (*looking out through the door, rear*). He walks very dejectedly. He stops at the fountain. He washes his eyes—

ELIS. This, too!

KRISTINA. Wait till he comes.

ELIS. Tears, tears!

KRISTINA. Patience!

(BENJAMIN *enters. He is a gentle, respectful youth, visibly griefstricken. He carries a portfolio and some school-books.*)

ELIS. How did you do in your Latin, Benjamin?

BENJAMIN. Not very well.

ELIS. May I look at your examination paper? What mistakes did you make?

BENJAMIN. I wrote *ut* in the indicative, although I knew it should have been in the subjunctive.

ELIS. Then you have failed. But how could you?

BENJAMIN (*resignedly*). I just cannot explain it. I knew what I *should* have written—wanted to write it the right way—yet I wrote it the wrong way. (*Dejected, he sits down on the chair by the dining-table.*)

ELIS (*sinks into the chair at the writing table. He looks over* BENJAMIN's *examination papers.*) Yes, you have written it in the indicative. Oh, God!

KRISTINA (*in a strained voice*). Well, you will have better luck next time. Life is so hard, so very hard.

BENJAMIN. Yes, it is . . .

ELIS (*sadly, yet not bitterly*). And to think that everything must come at once! And you, my best pupil! What can I then expect from the others! My standing as a teacher will be ruined. I may get no more tutoring to do, and then my whole life will go to pieces. (*To* BENJAMIN.) Now, don't take it too much to heart. You are not to blame.

KRISTINA (*exerting herself to be calm*). Courage, Elis! Take courage! For God's sake!

ELIS. From where will I take it?

KRISTINA. Where you always found it.

ELIS. Things have changed. I seem to find no more grace.

KRISTINA. It is a grace to suffer when blameless. Don't let yourself be deceived into impatience. Endure the test— for it is only a test. I feel that is all it is.

ELIS. Can a year be made shorter for Benjamin—shortened to less than its 365 days?

KRISTINA. Yes—by having a cheerful mind it can be.

ELIS (*with a smile*). Blow on the hurt and it will heal, as we say to children.

KRISTINA. Then be a child and let me say it for you. Think of your mother—the burden *she* bears!

ELIS. Let me take your hand—I am sinking! (KRISTINA *gives him her hand.*) You are trembling . . .

KRISTINA. I am not aware of it.

ELIS. You have not the strength, you try to make me think you have.

KRISTINA. I feel no weakness.

ELIS. Why is it, then, you can't impart some of your strength to me?

KRISTINA. Because I have none to spare.

ELIS (*looks out through the window*). Do you know who is coming?

KRISTINA (*goes to the window and looks outside. She kneels in anguish.*) This is too much to bear!

ELIS. He—the creditor who can attach our furniture, whenever he feels like it. He, Lindkvist, who moved here so that he can sit like the spider in his web and watch the flies—

KRISTINA. Let us go away from here!

ELIS (*gets up*). No! We shall *not* leave. The moment *you* weakened, my strength came back. He is coming up the street now. His evil eye has already spotted the prey.

KRISTINA. Go away from the window, Elis!

ELIS. No, he interests me now. His face seems to brighten as if he had already trapped his quarry. Come on, Lindkvist! He is counting the steps to the gate. He has noticed the open door and knows we are at home. He meets someone and stops to talk. He is talking about us. . . . He is looking in this direction.

KRISTINA. I only hope he doesn't meet your mother! *One* carelessly uttered word might make him our enemy for life. You must see that that doesn't happen, Elis.

ELIS. Now he shakes his stick! It is as if he had said: this is one time when justice will prevail over mercy! He unbuttons his overcoat as if to show that at least we haven't taken the clothes off his back. I can tell by his lips what he is saying. What can I answer him when he comes? "My dear sir, you have the law on your side! Take every stick of furniture! It all belongs to you!"

KRISTINA. That is all you need to say.

ELIS. He is laughing now—a pleasant laugh, nothing malicious about it. Perhaps he is not so bad after all, even if he does want his money. If he would only stop his infernal chatter and come in! Now he is swinging his stick again—these ogres with outstanding claims, they always carry sticks and wear leather galoshes that squeak "witch, witch" like a whip or a switch sweeping through the air. (*He presses* KRISTINA's *hand to his heart.*) Can you feel my heart beating? I can hear it in my right ear—it sounds like the heartbeat of an oceanliner. Thank God, at last he takes leave. And there are the galoshes again: witch, witch!—like the swishing of a birch rod. I see he wears a watch charm—then he can't be so very poor. It never fails: they always carry watch charms of carnelian, like cubes of old flesh carved from their neighbors' backs! Listen to those galoshes: witch, witch! Watch out now! He sees me! He sees me! . . . (ELIS *makes a bow toward the street.*) He nodded to me—he did! He smiles. He waves to me with his hand—and—(*He collapses over the writing table, and weeps.*)—he passed by—

KRISTINA. May God be praised!

ELIS (*rises*). He passed by! But he'll come back.—Let us go out in the sun.

KRISTINA. And the dinner—Peter's dinner?

ELIS. As long as I am not invited, I won't go. And what have I to do there anyhow, while they are enjoying themselves? Go to meet a faithless friend? It would hurt me no end to see his embarrassment—so much so that I would forget what he had done to me.

KRISTINA. Thank you for staying at home with us.

ELIS. I like it better here. You know that.—Shall we go for a walk?

KRISTINA. Yes—let's go out this way.

(*She goes out, right.*)

ELIS (*pats* BENJAMIN *on the head, on his way out*). Courage, my boy!

(BENJAMIN *covers his face with his hands.*)

ELIS (*takes the birch from the dining-table and places it behind the mirror*). It was no olive branch the dove brought. It was birch.   (*He leaves.*)

(ELEONORA *enters from the door, rear. She is a girl of sixteen, with a braid down her back. She carries a potted yellow Easter lily. Without showing any sign of seeing* BENJAMIN, *she takes a decanter from the side-*

board and waters the plant; then she places it on the dining-table, directly in front of BENJAMIN, *whom she regards quizzically, while she imitates his gestures.*
BENJAMIN *regards her with a look of astonishment.*)

ELEONORA (*indicates the Easter lily with a gesture*). Do you know what *this* is?

BENJAMIN (*with simplicity and a childlike manner*). It's an Easter lily, of course. But who are you?

ELEONORA (*in a friendly manner, yet with sadness in her voice*). And who are you?

BENJAMIN (*as before*). My name is Benjamin, and I live here with Mrs. Heyst.

ELEONORA. Do you? My name is Eleonora, and I am a daughter in this house.

BENJAMIN. How strange—I have never heard them speak of you.

ELEONORA. The dead are not spoken of.

BENJAMIN. The dead?

ELEONORA. I am legally dead, for I have committed a terrible sin.

BENJAMIN. You?

ELEONORA. Yes, I have embezzled funds entrusted to me—and for that I might be forgiven; for what is gained illicitly, shall be destroyed. But you see, there is one thing that cannot be forgiven: my father was given the blame and is now in prison.

BENJAMIN. How strangely you speak—and how beautifully. But never before has it occurred to me that my inheritance might have been ill-gotten.

ELEONORA. Mankind should not be enslaved—it must be set free.

BENJAMIN. You have freed me of the grief of having been taken advantage of.

ELEONORA. You are a ward, then?

BENJAMIN. Yes—and it is now my unfortunate lot to live off these poor people until they have paid their debt.

ELEONORA. You must never use harsh words. If you do, I shall leave you. I am so very sensitive, I cannot stand hearing anything unkind.—And you say you suffer this on my account?

BENJAMIN. Because of your father.

ELEONORA. It's the same thing: he and I are one and the same person. (*There is a silence.*) I have been very sick. —Why are you so sad?

BENJAMIN. I have had a disappointment.

ELEONORA. Why should you grieve over it? "The rod and reproof give wisdom; and he that hateth reproof shall die." —What kind of disappointment was it?

BENJAMIN. I failed in my written Latin—yet I was absolutely confident.

ELEONORA. So—you were absolutely confident . . . so confident that you could have wagered that you would pass.

BENJAMIN. That's just what I did.

ELEONORA. I thought so! You see, it turned out the way it did, because you were so sure of yourself.

BENJAMIN. And you think that was the cause?

ELEONORA. Of course, it was. "Pride goeth before destruction, and a haughty spirit before a fall."

BENJAMIN. I'll remember that the next time.

ELEONORA. That's a righteous thought . . . for "the sacrifices that are pleasing unto God, are a broken spirit: a broken spirit and a contrite heart."

BENJAMIN. Are you a pietist?

ELEONORA. Yes, I am a pietist.

BENJAMIN. I mean—a believer.

ELEONORA. That's just what I mean. Therefore, if you speak ill of God, who is my benefactor, I will not sit at the same table with you.

BENJAMIN. How old are you?

ELEONORA. For me there is neither time nor space: I am everywhere, and whenever I will. I am with my father in prison, and with my brother in school . . . I am in my mother's kitchen and in my sister's shop in America. When things go well for my sister and she makes a sale, I feel her joy; when business is bad, I suffer. But I suffer most, when she does someone a wrong. Benjamin—your name is Benjamin because you are the youngest one among my friends. Yes, my friends are all mankind. Will you be one of my flock, that I may suffer for you, too?

BENJAMIN. I don't think I quite understand what you say, but I seem to sense the meaning of your thoughts. And whatever *you* wish for, *I* shall wish for, too.

ELEONORA. Will you start by ceasing to judge people— even them, who have been judged guilty of crimes?

BENJAMIN. Yes—but I must have good grounds—I have studied philosophy, you know.

ELEONORA. Oh, have you? Then you must help me to interpret these words by a great philosopher. This is what he says: "They that hate the righteous shall be guilty of crime."

BENJAMIN. According to all logic it would imply that a person may be doomed to commit a crime.

ELEONORA. And that the crime itself is a punishment.

BENJAMIN. It is profound thinking! One might suppose it were by Kant or Schopenhauer.

ELEONORA. I don't know them.

BENJAMIN. Where did you read it?

ELEONORA. In the Holy Scriptures.

BENJAMIN. You don't say so! Are there things like that in the Scriptures?

ELEONORA. What a neglected and ignorant child you are— I wish I could teach you.

BENJAMIN. You are an angel!

ELEONORA. But I don't think there is anything bad in you. On the contrary, I believe you are a good boy.—Who is your teacher in Latin?

BENJAMIN. Dr. Algren.

ELEONORA (rises). I shall remember that!—Oh, my father is suffering now. They are treating him unkindly. (She stops short, as if listening.) Can you hear the telephone wires moaning? It's the cruel words that the soft, shiny red copper can't bear to hear. When people speak ill of their neighbors over the telephone, the copper melts into tears, and moans, and cries Shame! (Her voice becomes hard.) And their every word is written in the ledger. And at doomsday comes the reckoning!

BENJAMIN. You are very severe.

ELEONORA. It isn't I! It isn't I! How would I dare to be severe—I—I? (She goes to the stove and opens the shutter. She takes out some torn scraps of white writing paper.)

(BENJAMIN gets up to look at the paper scraps, which she pieces together on the dining-table.)

ELEONORA (to herself). How can people be so thoughtless as to confide their secrets to a stove. Whenever I go anywhere, I immediately go to the stove. But I never misuse people's secrets. I would never dare to do that, for that would give me a bad conscience. (She reads.) What in the world is this?

BENJAMIN. Why, it is a letter from Dr. Peter. . . . He writes to Kristina and makes an appointment with her. I have anticipated this for a long time.

ELEONORA (covers the letter with her hand). Oh, Benjamin! What is it you have anticipated? Speak up, you sinful creature, harboring only bad thoughts! This letter has a message that can bring nothing but good. Yes, I know Kristina—she is to be my sister-in-law. Kristina and Peter are getting together in order to ward off a disaster from my brother Elis. Will you promise me, Benjamin, to keep it a secret?

BENJAMIN. I'd be afraid to mention even one word about it.

ELEONORA. What wrongs people do when they try to hide their secrets. They think they are all wise, yet act like fools. But why did I have to meddle in their affairs?

BENJAMIN. Yes, why are you so curious?

ELEONORA. Don't you see, that's my sickness: I just have to know everything—or I get restless.

BENJAMIN. You have to know everything?

ELEONORA. It's a failing I have—I can't overcome it.—And I know what the starlings talk about, too!

BENJAMIN. The starlings? Why, they can't speak.

ELEONORA. Have you never heard that starlings can be taught to speak?

BENJAMIN. Oh yes,—that were taught, yes.

ELEONORA. Well, then, starlings can learn to speak. Now, there are those that learn to speak by themselves, that imitate—like parrots. They sit and listen, without our knowing it, of course, and then they repeat. Only a moment ago, I heard two of them chattering up in the walnut tree outside.

BENJAMIN. How funny you are! Tell me what they said.

ELEONORA. One said: "Peter!" The other one said: "Judas!" "The same to you!" said the first bird. "Fee-fee-fee," said the second bird. But have you noticed that the nightingales sing only in the garden of the deafmutes next door?

BENJAMIN. Yes, I've heard that! Why is that?

ELEONORA. Because people who can hear, don't listen to the nightingales' song; but the deaf do.

BENJAMIN. Tell me some more fairy tales.

ELEONORA. Yes, if you will be good.

BENJAMIN. How good?

ELEONORA. You must never criticize what I say. Never say: "You said so-and-so and so-and-so". . . . Do you want me to speak some more about birds? There is an evil bird that is called the rat buzzard; you can hear by the name that it lives on rats. This bird is a hateful bird, and so nature has made it hard for it to catch the rats. It knows only a single word and that sounds exactly like a cat's miaow.

Therefore, when the buzzard cries *miaow*, the rats scamper away and hide. But the buzzard is completely unconscious of making this ill-fated sound, and so it often has to go hungry for its wickedness. . . . Would you like to hear another story? Or shall I talk about the flowers? . . . You know— when I was sick, they made me take a drug made from henbane. It makes the eye into a magnifying glass. Belladonna, on the other hand, has the very opposite effect. . . . And I can see farther than other people—I can see the stars in broad daylight.

BENJAMIN. But there are no stars out now?

ELEONORA. How silly you are! Don't you know that the stars are always out? I am facing north now. I am looking at Cassiopeia. It looks like a *W* and is situated directly in the center of the Milky Way. Do you see it?

BENJAMIN. No, I can't see anything.

ELEONORA. Mark my words well now: what one human being can see, others may not be able to see. That is why you must not depend too much on your eyes. . . . Now I must say something about the flower on the table there. It's an Easter lily; it has its home in Switzerland; its chalice has drunk of the sun's light. That is why it's golden and can alleviate suffering. . . . I saw it in a florist's shop just a while ago, as I passed, and wanted it for Elis, my brother, as a gift. As I was about to go inside, I found that the door was locked—I suppose because it's Confirmation Day. I just had to have the flower, so I tried one of my own keys, and—behold! one of them unlocked the door, and there I was inside the flower shop. Do you understand the silent language of the flowers? Each and every fragrance expresses a multitude of thoughts. These thoughts took possession of me; and with my extra-sensory vision I could look into their workshops, which no human eye had ever beheld. They spoke to me of the sorrows which the gardener, through his insensitiveness, had inflicted on them. I don't want to say he had been cruel—merely thoughtless. I then put the price, one crown, on the counter—together with my card—and took the flower and left.

BENJAMIN. How thoughtless of you! Suppose they miss the flower and don't see the money.

ELEONORA. I never thought of that.

BENJAMIN. A coin can disappear. And if they find only your card, you are lost.

ELEONORA. But surely no one would think that I would take anything?

BENJAMIN (*regards her fixedly*). No?

ELEONORA (*looks at him quizzically. She gets up from the chair.*) Oh, I know what is in your mind. Like father, like child. How could I have been so thoughtless! So terribly thoughtless! Well—what is to be, will be. (*She sits down again.*) Let it come.

BENJAMIN. Isn't there some way to adjust the matter?

ELEONORA. Hush! . . . And let us talk about something else. Dr. Algren!—Poor Elis! And pity on us all! But it's Easter, and therefore we must suffer. Tomorrow, at the concert, they will play Haydn's "Seven Last Words of Christ on the Cross." . . . "Mother, behold thy Son!" (*She buries her face in her hands and weeps.*)

BENJAMIN. What was your sickness?

ELEONORA. My sickness is not unto death, but for the glory of God. . . . "I looked for the good, then the evil came unto me; and when I waited for the light, there came darkness."—What was your childhood like, Benjamin?

BENJAMIN. I really can't say. Not very bright! What was yours like?

ELEONORA. I never was a child. I was born old. I seemed to know all there is to know from birth; and when I learned something, it was just like remembering. I was conscious of people's lack of understanding and of their thoughtlessness when I was only four. . . . Out of spite they treated me cruelly.

BENJAMIN. What you say, I too seem to have felt—

ELEONORA. I could tell that you had.—What made you think that the coin might be lost at the florist's?

BENJAMIN. Because the exasperating always has to happen.

ELEONORA. You have noticed that, too!—Hush! Someone is coming! (*She glances toward the rear.*) I hear—it is Elis! Oh, what joy! My one and only true friend on this earth! . . . (*Her face saddens.*) But he is not expecting me—and he will not be happy to see me. No, he will not be glad. I know he won't be. . . . Benjamin, Benjamin, show some love in your face, and a cheerful spirit, when my poor brother comes. I'll go inside and let you break the news to him that I am here. And don't use any words that can hurt. Do you hear? They pain me so. Give me your hand!

(BENJAMIN *offers her his hand.*)

ELEONORA (*kisses him on the head*). Now! Now you are my little brother! May God bless you and keep you! (*She crosses to the right and, in passing, she pats* ELIS' *coat affectionately.*) Poor Elis!

(ELIS *enters through the door, rear. He seems worried.* MRS. HEYST *comes from the kitchen.*)

ELIS. Why, here is mother—

MRS. HEYST. So it's you? I thought I heard someone else's voice.

ELIS. I have news for you. I just spoke to our attorney. I met him on the street.

MRS. HEYST. So—o?

ELIS. The case will now go to the court of appeal. And to save time, I have to read through all the records of the trial.

MRS. HEYST. Well, that won't take you long.

ELIS (*indicates the documents on the writing table*). Oh, I thought we were through with this. And now I have to suffer this whole passion story again—all the accusations, all the testimony, and all the evidence!

MRS. HEYST. Yes, and then he'll be acquitted—

ELIS. No, mother. He has already confessed. You know that.

MRS. HEYST. Yes, but there may be some irregularity of procedure. That's what the attorney said the last time I talked with him.

ELIS. He said that merely to comfort you.

MRS. HEYST. Aren't you going to the dinner?

ELIS. No.

MRS. HEYST. Now you have changed your mind again.

ELIS. Yes.

MRS. HEYST. That's a bad thing.

ELIS. I know it, but I am being tossed like driftwood between breakers.

MRS. HEYST. I thought I just heard a voice—a voice I recognize—but I guess I must have been mistaken. (*She points to the overcoat.*) I told you not to hang your coat there, didn't I? (*She goes out, left.*)

ELIS (*walks over to the right and notices the Easter lily on the dining-table. He turns to* BENJAMIN.) Where did the Easter lily come from?

BENJAMIN. A young woman brought it.

ELIS. A young woman! What in heaven's— What young woman?

BENJAMIN. It was—

ELIS. Was it—my sister?

BENJAMIN. Yes.

ELIS (*sinks down on a chair by the dining-table. There is a silence.*) Did you speak with her?

BENJAMIN. Oh, yes.

ELIS. Oh, God! When will there be an end to this?—She was not unkind to you, was she?

BENJAMIN. She—unkind! No! She was as kind as she could be! So *very* kind!

ELIS. Strange!—Did she say anything about me? Did she show any resentment toward me?

BENJAMIN. No—just the opposite! She said you were the best friend she had on this earth.

ELIS. What could have changed her so, I wonder?

BENJAMIN. And when she left, she patted your coat hanging there, on the sleeve. . . .

ELIS. Left, did you say? Where did she go?

BENJAMIN (*pointing toward the door, right*). In there.

ELIS. Is she in there now?

BENJAMIN. Yes.

ELIS. You seem so happy and radiant, Benjamin.

BENJAMIN. She talked to me so beautifully—

ELIS. What did she talk about?

BENJAMIN. She told me enchanting stories—and talked a good deal about religion.

ELIS (*rises*). And that made you happy?

BENJAMIN. Yes.

ELIS. Poor Eleonora! She is so unhappy herself—yet she brings joy to others. (*He slowly walks toward the right.*) May God give me strength! . . .

ACT II

GOOD FRIDAY

Music preceding this act: Haydn: "Seven Last Words of Christ on the Cross." Largo No. 1. "Pater dimitti illis."

(THE SETTING.—*The same setting as in Act I. The curtains are now drawn, the light from the gas-lit street lamp shining through them. The hanging lamp is lighted; a small kerosene lamp on the dining-table likewise. There is a fire burning in the parlor stove. ELIS and KRISTINA are seated at the sewing table. They are not occupying themselves with anything.*

Facing each other at the dining-table, ELEONORA and BEN-JAMIN are busy reading, the lamp between them. ELEONORA wears a shawl over her shoulders. All are dressed in black; ELIS and BENJAMIN wear white ties.

Spread out on the writing table lie the documents of the trial; on the sewing table stands the Easter lily, and on the dining-table an old pendulum clock.

Occasionally the shadow of a passerby can be seen on the curtains.)

ELIS (*to* KRISTINA, *in an undertone*). Yes, Good Friday! And how insufferably long! And the snow lies on the pavement like straw in front of a house of death. No sound from anywhere—only the deep tones of the organ can be heard, all the way here.

KRISTINA. Mother must have gone to Vespers.

ELIS. Yes, she could not bear to go to the morning service. It hurts her to be stared at by people.

KRISTINA. People are so strange. They feel we ought to stay away. They think it would be in better taste if we did . . .

ELIS. And they may be right.

KRISTINA. Because one person makes a misstep, they seem to think the whole family should be ostracized.

ELIS. Well, that's the way life is.

(ELEONORA *pushes the lamp closer to* BENJAMIN *that he may see better.*)

ELIS (*indicating* ELEONORA *and* BENJAMIN). Look at these two.

KRISTINA. Don't they make a nice picture! And how well they get on!

ELIS. Isn't it a blessing that Eleonora has grown so calm. Let us hope she remains that way.

KRISTINA. I don't see why she shouldn't.

ELIS. Well, happiness doesn't last forever.—I have a dread feeling that anything can happen this day.

(BENJAMIN *pushes the lamp gently over toward* ELEONORA *to give her more light to see by.*)

KRISTINA. Look at them—

ELIS. Have you noticed how changed Benjamin is? His repressed defiance is gone. It has given way to a calm submissiveness.

KRISTINA. Isn't she lovely! Her whole being radiates loveliness. One could call her beautiful—but even that would be inadequate.

ELIS. And she has brought with her an angel of peace that hovers over us unseen and breathes a gentle, untroubled quietude. Even mother took on a certain calm when she first saw her—a calm I had not expected of her.

KRISTINA. Do you think she has recovered entirely?

ELIS. Well, yes, if only she didn't have this extreme sensitiveness. . . . She is now reading the story of the Crucifixion and ever so often she weeps.

KRISTINA. I can recall we always read it in school on Wednesdays during Lent.

ELIS. Don't speak too loud. . . . She has sharp ears.

KRISTINA. She can't hear us. She is not close enough.

ELIS. Have you observed the change in Benjamin? Some-thing of dignity and nobility has come into his face.

KRISTINA. That comes from suffering. The pleasures of life make everything commonplace and trite.

ELIS. It couldn't be love, could it? Could it be that these children—?

KRISTINA. Hush, hush, hush! One must not touch the butterfly's wings or it will fly away.

ELIS. I think they must be looking at each other and are only pretending to be reading. I haven't heard them turn a page.

KRISTINA. Hush!

ELIS. Look! Now she can't restrain herself . . .

(ELEONORA *rises from her chair, tiptoes over to* BENJAMIN *and drapes her shawl over his shoulders.* BENJAMIN *protests mildly, but gives in.* ELEONORA *then returns to her seat, pushing the lamp closer to* BENJAMIN.)

KRISTINA. Poor Eleonora! She has no idea how good she really is.

ELIS (*gets up*). Now I have to get back to my court records.

KRISTINA. Will it do any good to go through all these documents again?

ELIS. It serves only one purpose: to keep up hope for mother. But even though *I*, too, only pretend to be reading, I come across words that pierce my eyes like thorns. The testimony of the witnesses, the columns of figures, father's own admissions, as for instance: "the defendant admitted with tears in his eyes." All these tears, these many tears! And all these papers and documents with their official stamps that call to mind counterfeit money, or prison locks . . . and the ribbons and red seals, resembling Christ's five wounds . . . and the sentences, the endless sentences . . . the eternal torment and pain. This is, indeed, a labor for Good Friday.— Yesterday we saw the sun. Yesterday we went to the country in our thoughts. What if we should have to stay here this summer, Kristina!

KRISTINA. We would at least save a lot of money. But it would be a great disappointment.

ELIS. I would never be able to live through it. I have spent three summers here and it's like a graveyard. At high noon not a soul, or a dog, or a horse can be seen on the long gray street, winding like a trench in the fields. And up from the sewers come the rats, for the cats have gone away to the country to amuse themselves. And behind their reflector mirrors the few stay-at-homes sit spying on their neighbors to see what they are wearing. "Look, that one is still going around in winter clothes!" And they don't overlook their neighbors' run-down heels, or their neighbors' faults. And from the quarters of the poor come the hunchbacks and the cripples, creeping and crawling. They have been in hiding as have the creatures without ears or noses, the mean and the malicious, and people of misfortune. And they take seats along the great boulevard—much as if they had taken over the city. Where only a brief time ago well-dressed, handsome children, encouraged by tender words from their attractive mothers, were playing, you now see hordes of ragged ones that scold and torture one another.—I shall never forget a Midsummer Day two years ago . . .

KRISTINA. Elis, Elis! Look ahead—ahead!

ELIS. Will it be brighter there?

KRISTINA. Let us believe it will be.

ELIS (*seats himself at the writing table*). If it would only stop snowing, so that we could go for a walk.

KRISTINA. Elis, my dear, last night you wished to have the old, dark days back, so that we would not be bothered by people's stares. "The darkness is so comforting, so soothing" is what you said; "it's like pulling the blanket over your head at night."

ELIS. So you see that—no matter how you look at it—our misery has not grown less. (*He reads in the documents.*) The worst about the whole proceeding, however, is the prying questions about my father's mode of living. Here it states that we gave extravagant parties. . . . Oh, this is really too much! I can't read any more of this. . . . But I have to do it—have to read every word!—Don't you feel cold?

KRISTINA. No—but it isn't exactly warm here. Lina is out, isn't she?

ELIS. She went to communion, you remember.

KRISTINA. But mother will be home soon, won't she?

ELIS. I always worry about mother whenever she goes anywhere. She keeps her ears open for everything, and she sees everything—and *always* it is something unpleasant.

KRISTINA. You are a brooding family—more so than most families.

ELIS. That's the reason only brooders have cared to befriend us. People who like gaiety have always shunned us.

KRISTINA. I just heard mother come in the kitchen way.

ELIS. Try to be patient with her, Kristina, won't you?

KRISTINA. Why, of course. She has a harder time of it than the rest of us, I'm sure. But I just don't understand her ways . . .

ELIS. She is trying to hide her shame as best she knows—that's the reason we can't understand her. Poor mother!

MRS. HEYST (*enters. She is dressed in black. In her hand she carries a hymn book and a handkerchief.*) Good evening, children.

ALL (*except* BENJAMIN, *who greets her silently*). Good evening, mother dear.

MRS. HEYST. You are all dressed in black, as if you were in mourning.

(*There is a silence.*)

ELIS. Is it still snowing?

MRS. HEYST. Yes, there's a heavy snow fall, and the snow is wet. It's cold in here. (*She goes over to* ELEONORA *and pats her.*) Well, my little angel, I see you are reading and studying. (*To* BENJAMIN.) And you—you don't exert yourself in your studies.

(ELEONORA *takes hold of her mother's hand and presses it to her lips.*)

MRS. HEYST (*with suppressed emotion*). There, my child! There, there!

ELIS. You went to Vespers, mother?

MRS. HEYST. Yes. The curate preached—and I don't like him.

ELIS. Did you see anyone you know?

MRS. HEYST (*sits down by the sewing table*). It would have pleased me more if I hadn't.

ELIS. Then I know whom you—

MRS. HEYST. Lindkvist! And he came over to me—

ELIS. How cruel of him—how cruel.

MRS. HEYST. He asked how we were—and—and you can imagine how it frightened me. He asked if he could pay us a visit this evening.

ELIS. On a day like this—on Good Friday!

MRS. HEYST. I couldn't find anything to say. He took my silence for consent. (*There is a pause.*) He may be here at any moment.

ELIS (*rises*). Here? At any moment?

MRS. HEYST. He said he wanted to deliver some kind of paper, and that the time was short.

ELIS. He wants to take the furniture—

MRS. HEYST. But he had such a curious expression on his face. I just couldn't make him out.

ELIS. Then let him come. He has the law on his side; and we have to bow to it. We have to receive him with good grace when he does come.

MRS. HEYST. I only hope I don't have to see him.

ELIS. Well, you stay in your room.

MRS. HEYST (*with determination*). But he is *not* going to take the furniture! What would we have to sit on? How would we be able to manage, if he takes away every stick of furniture, all our belongings? We can't live in empty rooms, sleep on the floor. . . . We just couldn't do it!

ELIS. The fox has his hole, and the birds have their nests. There are creatures that are homeless, who live in the woods—

MRS. HEYST. There's where the rascals and rogues should be—not people who are honest and decent.

ELIS (*at the writing table*). Mother, I have to continue my reading now.

MRS. HEYST. Have you come across anything that's wrong yet?

ELIS. No, mother. I don't expect to find anything.

MRS. HEYST. Why, I just met the clerk of the city court, and he said there might be a possibility of some irregularity of procedure, or an incompetent witness, or some statement that might be challenged, or a case of self-contradiction.— Perhaps you are not reading it the way you should.

ELIS. Yes, mother, I am; but it is all so painful to me.

MRS. HEYST. Will you please listen to me! I met the clerk of the city court only a moment ago—and—oh, I forgot, I just told you—and he mentioned something about a burglary that was committed in town yesterday, in broad daylight!

(ELEONORA *and* BENJAMIN *give a start and are all ears.*)

ELIS. A burglary? Here in town? Where?

MRS. HEYST. It's supposed to have happened at the florist's shop in Cloister Street. But the whole thing took place under the most mysterious circumstances. What happened, they say, was this: the florist closed his shop to attend church, for his son—or perhaps it was his daughter—was to be confirmed there. When he came back around three o'clock— or it may have been four, but that doesn't matter—why, then he found the door open and some of his flowers were missing—a great many, and especially a yellow tulip —that was the one he first noticed was missing . . .

ELIS. A tulip! If you had said an Easter lily, it would have given me a fright!

MRS. HEYST. No, it was a tulip—of that I am certain— Anyhow, the police are now busy investigating. . . .

(ELEONORA *has risen, as if about to speak, but* BENJAMIN *steps up to her, whispering something in her ear.*)

MRS. HEYST. The idea! Breaking into a shop on a holy day, at Easter, when the children are being confirmed. . . . The whole town is full of such rapscallions. And people who are innocent, are put in jail.

ELIS. Don't they suspect anyone?

MRS. HEYST. No! But whoever the thief is, he is a strange one. He took no money from the cash drawer.

KRISTINA. Oh, if only this day were over!

MRS. HEYST. And if Lina would only come home! Oh, and I heard people talk about Peter's dinner—the dinner he gave last night! Even the governor was there . . .

ELIS. That certainly is surprising. Peter has always been looked on as being in opposition to the governor's party.

MRS. HEYST. I suppose he has made an about face.

ELIS. His name is not Peter for nothing, it seems.

MRS. HEYST. What have you got against the governor?

ELIS. He is always blocking everything! Everything! He opposed the rural high schools, the reserve training program for youths—he tried to prevent the innocent sport of bicycling, was against summer camps for school children—and —he has stood in my way!

MRS. HEYST. Well, I don't know anything about these things, and it's just as well. Anyhow, the governor made a speech—and Peter thanked him.

ELIS. No doubt with deep emotion—and denied his teacher, saying "I know not this man." . . . And again the cock crew. . . . Could the governor's name have been Pontius, with the surname Pilate?

(ELEONORA *stirs; seems about to speak but quiets down.*)

MRS. HEYST. You must not be bitter, Elis. We are all human and have to put up with one another.

ELIS. Hush! I can hear Lindkvist—he is coming—

MRS. HEYST. You can hear him—with the snow on the ground?

ELIS. I can hear his stick pounding the pavement—and his leather galoshes!—You go inside, mother.

MRS. HEYST. No—now I want to stay. There is something I would like to say to him.

KRISTINA. Be a dear, mother, and go inside. It will only be painful to you!

MRS. HEYST (*rises. She is shaken.*) Oh, why was I ever born!

KRISTINA. You must not say such things, mother. . . .

MRS. HEYST (*with an expression of spiritual exaltation*). Is not destruction to the wicked—and a strange punishment to the workers of iniquity?

ELEONORA (*with a scream of anguish*). Mother!

MRS. HEYST. My God, why hast thou forsaken me! And my children!   (*She goes out, right.*)

ELIS (*listens to the sounds from without*). He stopped! Perhaps he changed his mind about coming, or thought that it might be cruel! But I don't think that would keep him from coming—a man who could write the kind of letters he wrote. . . . And always on blue paper. Whenever I see a letter on blue paper, I start to tremble.

KRISTINA. What do you intend to say to him? What do you plan to do?

ELIS. I haven't the faintest idea! I have lost all my senses. I can't think. . . . Shall I fall to my knees and plead for mercy and charity? . . . Can you hear if he is coming? I hear nothing but the pounding in my ears.

KRISTINA. Let us try to think of the worst that might happen! Suppose he takes everything—

ELIS. In that case, having no furniture, the landlord will demand that we put up a bond as security for the rent.

KRISTINA (*who has been looking out into the street from behind the curtains*). I don't see him any more. He is gone.

ELIS. Oh!—You know that mother's indifference and submissiveness hurt me more than seeing her lose her temper.

KRISTINA. Her submissiveness is either feigned or imagined. Her last words just now had something of the roaring lioness in them. . . . Did you notice how she grew in stature?

ELIS. You know, Kristina, as I think about Lindkvist now, I see in him a good-natured giant who likes to frighten children. From where could I get such an idea?

KRISTINA. Thoughts come and go.

ELIS. What luck I didn't go to the dinner last night. I could swear I would have made a speech against the governor —and then I would have ruined both myself and you. What luck!

KRISTINA. There you see!

ELIS. Thanks for your good advice. You knew your Peter. You certainly did.

KRISTINA. My Peter?

ELIS. I meant—*my* Peter! Look—there he is again! We are done for—(*The shadow of a man, approaching with hesitancy, is seen on the curtains. It gradually enlarges until it takes on the shape of a giant. All are gripped by extreme fear and anguish*.) The giant! Look—the giant who wants to swallow us up!

KRISTINA. Now is the time to smile—as in fairy tales.

ELIS. I am no longer able to smile! (*The shadow diminishes and then disappears*.)

KRISTINA. Just look at his stick—and you will *have* to laugh!

ELIS. He went away! Well, now I can breathe again. . . . Now I know he won't come back before tomorrow. Oh!

KRISTINA. And tomorrow the sun will be shining. It's the eve of the resurrection: the snow will be gone, and the birds will sing.

ELIS. Your words make me *see*. They cheer me.

KRISTINA. I wish you could look into my heart—that you could read my thoughts, my good intentions, my most fervent prayer, Elis. . . . Elis, if I now . . . (*She stops abruptly*.)

ELIS. What! Speak out!

KRISTINA. If I should now . . . ask you a favor . . .

ELIS. Speak.

KRISTINA. It is a test. . . . Think of it as a test, Elis.

ELIS. A test? A trial—of me? Very well!

KRISTINA. Let me . . . . No, I dare not. You might misunderstand . . . (ELEONORA *pricks up her ears*.)

ELIS. Why do you torture me?

KRISTINA. I'll regret it—I know I will. Never mind! Elis, will you let me go to the concert this evening?

ELIS. Which concert?

KRISTINA. Haydn's "Seven Last Words of Christ on the Cross"—in the cathedral.

ELIS. With whom?

KRISTINA. With Alice.

ELIS. And whom else?

KRISTINA. Peter.

ELIS. With Peter?

KRISTINA. You see, now you look grave, and disapproving! Now I feel regret; but it is too late!

ELIS. Yes, it is a little late. Explain yourself.

KRISTINA. I told you in advance that I could not explain. Therefore I asked you to have implicit confidence in me.

ELIS (*gently*). Go. I trust you. Yet I suffer nonetheless because you seek the company of one who betrayed me.

KRISTINA. I can understand that perfectly. But remember, this is a test.

ELIS. Which I find it hard to bear.

KRISTINA. You must and you will.

ELIS. I have the will, yet I cannot. . . . But go!

KRISTINA. Your hand!

ELIS (*takes her hand*). There! (*The telephone rings.* ELIS *goes to answer it.*) Hello . . . (*To* KRISTINA.) No answer . . . Hello. . . . I hear my own voice coming back. . . . Who is it? . . . How curious! I hear my own words, like an echo!

KRISTINA. Such things do happen.

ELIS. Hello. . . . This is uncanny! (*He puts down the receiver.*) You'd better go now, Kristina—without any explanations—and without delay. I'll survive the test.

KRISTINA. If you can do that, things will go well.

ELIS. I shall.

(KRISTINA *goes toward the left.*)

ELIS. Why do you go in there?

KRISTINA. I have my things in there.—Well, goodbye for a little while.   (*She leaves.*)

ELIS. Goodbye, Kristina. . . . (*There is a pause.*) For ever. . . .   (*He rushes out, right.*)

ELEONORA. God help us! What have I done! The police are searching for the culprit, and if they should discover that I did it— Poor mother and Elis!

BENJAMIN (*in a simple, childlike manner*). Eleonora, you must say that I took it.

ELEONORA. You? Can you take another's guilt on yourself, child? Can you?

BENJAMIN. That is not hard—when you know that you are innocent.

ELEONORA. But it would not be telling the truth.

BENJAMIN. Then let me telephone to the florist and tell him how it happened.

ELEONORA. No. I have committed a wrong and I must be punished by my conscience. I have put a fear in them that it might happen again, and I must be punished by fear myself.

BENJAMIN. But if the police should come . . .

ELEONORA. It would be hard—but whatever is to be, will be!—Oh, if there would only be an end to this day! (*She lifts the pendulum clock from the dining-table and turns the hands.*) Nice little clock, go a little faster. Tick-tock, ping-ping-ping—now it's eight—ping-ping-ping—now it's nine—ten—eleven—twelve! Now it is the day before Easter—now the sun will soon rise and we'll write on the Easter eggs. I'll write these words: "Behold, the adversary hath desired you that he may sift you as wheat; but I have prayed for thee."

BENJAMIN. Why do you keep torturing yourself like that, Eleonora?

ELEONORA. I—torturing myself? Think, Benjamin, of all the blossoming flowers: the blue anemones, the snow drops that have to stand in the snow all day and all night and then have to freeze in the darkness. Think how they have to suffer. The night must be hardest for them—when it is dark and they are frightened by the shadows and can't run away. They have to stand there in stillness, waiting for dawn to come. There is suffering everywhere, everywhere—but the flowers suffer most. And the birds of passage that have come back. . . . Where are they going to sleep tonight?

BENJAMIN (*naïvely*). They pass the night in hollow trees, don't you know.

ELEONORA. There can't be enough hollow trees to take care of all of them. I have only seen two such trees in the parks around here, and the owls—that kill little birds—live in *them*. . . . Poor Elis, who thinks that Kristina has left him! But I know that she is coming back.

BENJAMIN. If you knew that, why didn't you tell him?

ELEONORA. Because Elis has to suffer—all have to suffer on this day of Good Friday, that they may be reminded of Christ's suffering on the cross. (*The sound of a police whistle is heard from the street.*)

ELEONORA (*startled to her feet*). What was that?

BENJAMIN (*gets up*). Don't you know?

ELEONORA. No . . .

BENJAMIN. It's the police!

ELEONORA. Ah! Yes—it's the same sound I heard when they came to take away father—and that was how I got sick—and now they have come to take *me*—

BENJAMIN (*places himself protectingly in front of* ELEONORA, *and faces the door*). No—I am not going to let them take you! I'll protect you, Eleonora!

ELEONORA. How good you are, Benjamin—but I can't let you.

BENJAMIN (*peers through the curtains, for a view of the street*). I see two—(ELEONORA *tries to push* BENJAMIN *away, but he gently refuses to leave.*) No, Eleonora, no—you mustn't. If you do, I—I wouldn't care to live.

ELEONORA. Go back and sit down in your chair, dear child! Go and sit down! (BENJAMIN *obeys reluctantly.* ELEONORA

*looks through the curtains, without being seen from the out-
side.*) It was only two boys! Oh, we of little faith. Do you
really think God would be so cruel when I did no wrong—
only acted thoughtlessly?—I got what I deserved. Why did I
doubt?

BENJAMIN. But tomorrow he will be here—to take the
furniture.

ELEONORA. He is welcome to do so! And we have to be
without—everything. All the old furniture that father collected for us and which I have seen since I was a little
child. Yes—we should have no possessions binding us to this
earth. Let us go out on the road that leads upwards, the
pilgrimage over stony paths that make the feet bleed, and is
full of hardship and pain!

BENJAMIN. Now you are torturing yourself again, Eleonora.

ELEONORA. Let me! But do you know what I find hardest
to part from? It's the pendulum clock there! It saw me come
into this world, and it has measured my hours and my
days. . . . (*She lifts the clock from the table.*) Hear how it
ticks—just like a heart. But when grandfather died, it stopped
ticking that very moment. It has been with us that long, or
longer. . . . Goodbye, little clock, may your heart soon rest
again!—And, do you know, it used to go faster whenever
misfortune hovered over us. It was as though it wished to
leave bad times behind, for our sake, of course. But
when things were bright, it slowed down, so that we would
enjoy the happiness longer. . . . That was the good clock.
But we had a bad clock, too. It's been relegated to the
kitchen now. It had no ear for music. The moment Elis
began playing the piano, it started to strike. We all noticed
it; not only I. That is why we put it out in the kitchen—because it misbehaved! But Lina has no love for it either—it
makes a disturbance during the nights. And she says she
can't boil eggs by it—they are always hard-boiled! You
laugh!

BENJAMIN. I can't help it.

ELEONORA. You are a nice boy, Benjamin, but you should
be more serious. Remember, the birch is behind the mirror!

BENJAMIN. But you say such droll things—I just have to
laugh. I don't see why one must weep all the time.

ELEONORA. If one does not weep in this vale of tears, where
should one weep?

BENJAMIN. H'm—

ELEONORA. You want to be amused all the day long—and so you were punished! I like you only when you take things seriously. You must bear that in mind!

BENJAMIN. Do you think we shall come out of all this, Eleonora?

ELEONORA. Yes—most of it will straighten itself out when Good Friday is over, but not everything. Today the rod, tomorrow the Easter eggs. Today snow, tomorrow thaw! Today death, tomorrow the Resurrection—

BENJAMIN. How wise you are.

ELEONORA. Yes, I can feel it clearing. We shall have beautiful weather. The snow is melting. I can smell the melting snow . . . and tomorrow the violets will be coming out on the south side of the house. The clouds have lifted—I can feel it when I breathe. And I know at once that the way to Heaven is open. . . . Draw aside the curtains, Benjamin, I want God to see us!

(BENJAMIN *rises. He draws aside the curtains, and the moonlight streams into the room.*)

ELEONORA. Oh, look at the full moon! It's the Easter moon! And now you know that the sun is still with us, even when the moon is shining. . . .

ACT III

EASTER EVE

Music played before this act:
Haydn: "Seven Last Words of Christ on the Cross."
No. 5. Adagio.
(THE SETTING.—*The same as in Acts I and II, but the curtains are now drawn aside. The outside view is enveloped in a haze. The parlor stove is lighted. The outer doors are closed.*)

ELEONORA (*seated in front of the stove, holds a bunch of blue anemones in her hand*). Where have you been all this time, Benjamin?

BENJAMIN (*enters from the left*). I wasn't gone long, was I?

ELEONORA. I've missed you terribly.

BENJAMIN. And where were you, Eleonora?

ELEONORA. I went to the market square and bought some blue anemones. I am warming them now. The poor little things were frozen.

BENJAMIN. What became of the sun?

ELEONORA. It's hiding behind the mists. There are no clouds today—only the fog from the sea. I can smell the salt . . .

BENJAMIN. Did you notice that the birds are still alive in the garden.

ELEONORA. Yes—not one of them ever falls to the ground unless it be God's will. But I saw some dead birds in the square . . .

ELIS (*comes from the left*). Has the newspaper come yet?

ELEONORA. Not yet, Elis.

(ELIS *starts to cross. When he is halfway across the stage,*

321

KRISTINA *enters from the right*.)

KRISTINA (*paying no attention to* ELIS). Has the newspaper come?

ELEONORA. No, it hasn't come yet.

(KRISTINA *crosses to the left, passing* ELIS, *who goes out, right. Neither notices the other*.)

ELEONORA. Ugh! How cold it has grown! Hate has come into this house. While we had love here, we could endure anything. But now—ugh! It's unbearably cold. . . .

BENJAMIN. Why are they asking for the newspaper?

ELEONORA. Don't you understand? They want to read about the—

BENJAMIN. About what?

ELEONORA. About all that happened! The burglary, the police, and all the rest.

MRS. HEYST (*comes from the left*). Has the newspaper come?

ELEONORA. No, mother dear.

MRS. HEYST (*goes out to the left*). Let me have it when it comes—as soon as it comes.

ELEONORA. The newspaper, the newspaper. Oh, if only the printing press would break down—or the editor be taken sick.—No, I mustn't wish for anything like that. . . . You know, I was with father last night.

BENJAMIN. Last night?

ELEONORA. Yes—in my dreams. And I was in America, too—with my sister. . . . The day before yesterday her sales amounted to thirty dollars—and she had a profit of five dollars.

BENJAMIN. Is that much or little?

ELEONORA. It's quite a lot.

BENJAMIN (*knowingly*). Did you meet anyone you know at the market square?

ELEONORA. Why do you ask? You mustn't be crafty with me, Benjamin. You are trying to pry into my secrets. You mustn't do that.

BENJAMIN. But you think you can learn mine that way.

ELEONORA. Can you hear the telephone wires buzzing? That means the newspaper is out, and now everybody is busy telephoning to everybody else! "Have you read . . . ?"— "Yes, I have read . . . !"—"Isn't it shocking . . . !"

BENJAMIN. What is shocking?

ELEONORA. Everything—everything in life is horrible. . . . But we have to be satisfied nevertheless. Think of Elis and

Kristina. They are in love—yet they hate each other to such a degree that the thermometer drops when they pass through the room. She went to the concert last evening, and today they don't speak to each other. Why, why?

BENJAMIN. Your brother is jealous.

ELEONORA. Don't mention that word.—What do you know about jealousy, except that it is a sickness, and therefore a punishment. You must stay away from all evil; for once you have brushed against it, it clings to you. Look at Elis! Can't you see how he has changed since he started reading those documents?

BENJAMIN. The trial documents?

ELEONORA. Yes. It is as if all the vileness in them had permeated his whole being and was now cropping out through him. You can see it in his face and his features. Kristina senses this, and to protect herself against his hostile behavior, she has wrapped herself in an armor of ice. Oh, those fiendish documents—I would like to burn them! They stir up nothing but falsehood, malice and revengefulness! Remember, my child, you must always keep impurity and evil away from you—not only from your lips, but from your heart.

BENJAMIN. You observe everything, don't you?

ELEONORA. Do you realize what is in store for me if Elis and the others should find out that it was I who purchased the Easter lily in that unconventional manner?

BENJAMIN. What would they do to you?

ELEONORA. I would be sent back—where I came from—where the sun never shines—where the walls are white and naked, as in a bathroom—where you never hear anything but wails and weeping—where I have wasted a whole year of my life—

BENJAMIN. Where do you mean?

ELEONORA. Where people are tortured more cruelly than in prison—where the lost and the forsaken have their home—where unrest is a part of life—where anguish and agony keep vigil night and day—and from where no one returns. . . . When you go to prison, you have been convicted. But there you are condemned, condemned and doomed! When you go to prison, you have had a trial where you could speak in your own defense. There you have no defense. Poor little Easter lily, that is the cause of all this. . . . I meant only to do good, and then did just the opposite.

BENJAMIN. Why don't you go to the florist and explain

everything. Tell him: "This is the way it happened. . . ." You are like a lamb about to be slaughtered.

ELEONORA. When it knows it is to be slaughtered, it doesn't complain, and doesn't try to escape. What else can it do?

ELIS (*enters from the left, a letter in his hand*). Hasn't the newspaper come yet?

ELEONORA. No, Elis dear.

ELIS (*turns and speaks to Lina in the kitchen*). Lina, will you go out and buy me a newspaper.

(MRS. HEYST *enters from the left.* ELEONORA *and* BEN-
JAMIN *show signs of great fear.*)

ELIS (*to* ELEONORA *and* BENJAMIN). Will you children leave us alone for a moment, please?

(ELEONORA *and* BENJAMIN *go out, right.*)

MRS. HEYST. You received a letter, didn't you?

ELIS. Yes.

MRS. HEYST. From the institution?

ELIS. Yes.

MRS. HEYST. What do they want?

ELIS. They demand we return Eleonora.

MRS. HEYST. They won't get her. . . . She is my child—

ELIS. She is my sister.

MRS. HEYST. What do you mean by saying that?

ELIS. I don't know what I mean. I can't even think!

MRS. HEYST. But I can!—Eleonora—my child of sorrow—has come with joy to us—the joy of another world! Her restlessness has turned into a peacefulness which she shares with everyone. She may or may not be of sound mind—but to me she is intelligent and has wisdom, for she knows how to bear the burdens of life better than I do—better than any of us. As a matter of fact, Elis: am I an intelligent woman? Could I have had all my senses, when I believed that my husband was innocent? And this despite the fact that I knew that he had been condemned through tangible and material proof of his guilt—and which he himself had acknowledged.—And you, Elis, can you be in your right mind, do you think, when you fail to see that Kristina is in love with you,—and instead think that she hates you?

ELIS. She has a strange way of showing her love.

MRS. HEYST. No, it isn't strange. Your coldness benumbs and deadens her feelings, and it is you who hate. But you are doing something wrong, and that is why you have to suffer.

ELIS. How can you say that I am in the wrong? Didn't

she go out with Peter last evening—Peter, who has betrayed me?

MRS. HEYST. She did, yes. And you knew that she was
going. But *why* did she go out with him? Well—you should
be able to guess that.

ELIS. No, I can't . . .

MRS. HEYST. If that's the case—then you deserve what you
get.

(*The kitchen door is slightly opened, and a newspaper is
handed from inside to* MRS. HEYST. *She takes it and
gives it to* ELIS.)

ELIS. This was the hardest blow of all! With her by my
side I could survive the rest. . . . With her gone, the last
support has been torn away from me—and this time I am
done for . . . I'm falling . . .

MRS. HEYST. Fall, but fall the right way—then you can
get up again!—What's in the newspaper today?

ELIS. I don't know. I am afraid to look in it today.

MRS. HEYST. Give it to me, and let me see the news.

ELIS. No—you'd better wait.

MRS. HEYST. What are you afraid of? What do you expect
to see there?

ELIS. The very worst.

MRS. HEYST. It isn't the first time the very worst has happened—it has happened before—in the past. Oh, Elis, my
child, if you could have seen your father go down, step by
step, to his doom, as I did, without my being able to warn
the many whom he brought to misfortune! When he fell, I
felt myself as guilty as he, for I was aware of his crime. Had
not the judge been a man of discretion and understanding,
had he not realized my trying position as wife, I, too, would
have been punished.

ELIS. What was the cause of father's downfall? I have
never been able to learn the reason?

MRS. HEYST. Arrogance—presumption—by which we all
fall!

ELIS. But why should we, who are innocent, have to suffer
for his misconduct?

MRS. HEYST. Quiet! (*There is a silence.* MRS. HEYST *takes
the newspaper and starts to read.* ELIS *stands still in agitation; then he commences to pace back and forth.*) What's
this? . . . Didn't I say that—among the things that were missing from the flower shop was a yellow tulip?

ELIS. Yes—I remember it distinctly.

MRS. HEYST. But here it says—an Easter lily!

ELIS (*alarmed*). It does?

MRS. HEYST (*sinks into a chair*). It is Eleonora! Oh God, oh my God!

ELIS. Then the suffering is not over?

MRS. HEYST. The prison or the asylum!

ELIS. But I can't believe that she has done it! I can't believe it!

MRS. HEYST. And now the family name has to be booted about and be dishonored again.

ELIS. Is she under suspicion?

MRS. HEYST. It says that suspicions point in a certain direction—one can easily imagine where.

ELIS. I must speak to her.

MRS. HEYST (*rises*). Speak gently. This is more than I can bear. She is lost—redeemed and—lost. Speak to her.

(*She goes out, left.*)

ELIS. Oh. . . . (*He goes to the door on the right.*) Eleonora, my child! Come here, let me talk with you.

ELEONORA (*comes out, her hair hanging loose*). I was just trying to put up my hair—

ELIS. It can wait!—Tell me, Eleonora my dear, where did you get that flower there?

ELEONORA. I took it—

ELIS. Oh, God!

ELEONORA (*with head bent and arms folded. She is crushed.*) But I put the money beside it—

ELIS. You paid for it, then?

ELEONORA. I did and I didn't—Something awful always has to come in the way. . . . But I didn't do anything wrong— I only meant well. You do believe me, don't you?

ELIS. I believe you, Eleonora.—But the newspaper has no way of knowing that you are innocent.

ELEONORA. Then, Ellis dear, I must suffer for that, too. . . . (*She bends her head still lower until her hair covers her face.*) What will they do to me now? They may do what they will. . . .

BENJAMIN (*enters from the right; he is beside himself*). No, you mustn't touch her—she has done nothing wrong—I know she hasn't—it was I—it was I who did it . . . (*He weeps.*)

ELEONORA. You mustn't believe him.—It was I.

ELIS. What am I to believe? Whom shall I believe?

BENJAMIN. Me! Me!

ELEONORA. No—no!

BENJAMIN. Let me go to the police. . . .

ELIS. You must quiet down . . .

BENJAMIN. No—I want to go—I want to go . . .

ELIS. Quiet, children! Mother is coming . . .

MRS. HEYST (*comes in; she is in extreme agitation. She presses* ELEONORA *to her breast and kisses her.*) My child, my child—my dearest child! You are with *me*, and you shall *stay* with me!

ELEONORA. You kissed me, mother! It is a long time since you did that. . . . What makes you do it now?

MRS. HEYST. Because—because the florist has just been here; and he apologizes for all the trouble he has caused. The missing coin has been found—and the card with your name.

ELEONORA (*rushes into* ELIS' *arms and kisses him; then she puts her arms around* BENJAMIN'S *neck and presses a kiss on his head*). You good, dear child, who wished to sacrifice yourself for me? What made you do it?

BENJAMIN (*in a shy and childlike manner*). Because I am so very fond of you, Eleonora . . .

MRS. HEYST. Put on something to keep you warm now, and go out into the garden, children. The air is clearing!

ELEONORA. Oh, yes, it's clearing! Come, Benjamin. (*She takes him by the hand; they go out together, right.*)

ELIS. May we throw the birch in the fire now?

MRS. HEYST. Not yet. We still have something left to settle.

ELIS. You mean Lindkvist?

MRS. HEYST. I can see him standing outside. . . . But he is acting in a very peculiar manner and seems unusually gentle. What a pity he is so long-winded and always talks so much about himself.

ELIS. Now that I have seen a ray of sunshine, I am no longer afraid of the giant. He may come whenever he likes.

MRS. HEYST. Whatever you do, don't antagonize him. Providence has placed our fate in his hand; and the meek—well, you know what happens to those that are overbearing and haughty.

ELIS. I know. Can you hear—the galoshes: witch, witch, wolves, wolves. Does he intend to come in with them on?

Well, why shouldn't he? It's his rugs and his furniture. . . .

MRS. HEYST. Elis! You know what this means to us all—— (*She goes out, left.*)

ELIS. I know, mother!

LINDKVIST (*enters from the left. He is an elderly, serious-looking man with a face that might frighten people. His hair is gray; he wears a toupé. He has black, bushy eyebrows and black, close-cropped side-whiskers. He wears glasses, framed in black, circle-round horn rims; big charms of carnelian on his watch chain, and he carries a stick in his hand. His black suit can be seen underneath the fur coat. He holds his top hat in one hand; wears top-boots and leather overshoes that make a creaking sound. As he enters, he scrutinizes ELIS with a curious look in his eyes*). My name is Lindkvist.

ELIS (*on the defensive*). I am Elis Heyst. Please sit down.

LINDKVIST (*seats himself on the chair to the left of the sewing table, looking fixedly at ELIS. There is a moment's silence.*)

ELIS. How can I be of service to you?

LINDKVIST (*solemnly, a little pompously*). H'm. . . . I had the honor to notify you already last evening that I intended to pay you a visit; but on second thought I found it would be improper to discuss matters of business on a holiday.

ELIS. We are very grateful.

LINDKVIST (*sharply*). We are *not* grateful! No! (*There is silence.*) However—the day before yesterday, I paid a casual visit to the governor—(*He pauses to observe what impression his words make on ELIS.*) You know the governor, do you?

ELIS. I haven't had the honor!

LINDKVIST. Then you shall have the honor!—We spoke of your father—

ELIS. I can well imagine.

LINDKVIST (*takes out a paper, which he lays on the table*). And there I got this paper—

ELIS. I have long been expecting it! But before going any further, let me ask one question.

LINDKVIST (*curtly*). You may.

ELIS. Why don't you deliver this paper directly to the executors? Then, at least, we might be spared this painful and wearisome execution?

LINDKVIST. If that's the way you feel, young man—

ELIS. Young or not, I ask neither charity nor favors—only justice.

LINDKVIST. You don't say! No charity, no favors! Take a look at this paper that I just put there on the table!—Now it goes back into my pocket. And from now on, justice! Nothing but justice!—And listen to what I have to say now, my friend! Once upon a time, I was swindled—swindled in a most miserable way, and lost everything I had. . . . I asked you in a considerate letter how much time you needed to straighten things out, and you replied with an uncivil letter, as though I were a usurer, who was bent on plundering widows and the fatherless. Yet it was I, who had been defrauded, and you were in the camp of the thieves. However, as I was a little more considerate, I contented myself by answering your discourteous note with a polite but sharp one. You know my blue paper, don't you? Eh? I can decorate it with seals, too, when I feel like it; but it isn't always I feel like it. . . . (*He glances round in the room.*)

ELIS. The furniture is at your disposal, whenever you please!

LINDKVIST. I wasn't looking at the furniture. I was looking to see if your mother was here. No doubt she is as much in love with justice as you are.

ELIS. I dare say she is!

LINDKVIST. Good! Now you might like to know that if justice—which you prize so highly—were to have its course, your mother, having been conscious of your father's manipulations, would have felt the punishment of human justice, too.

ELIS. Oh, no!

LINDKVIST. Oh yes! And it is not too late yet!

ELIS (*rises*). My mother!

LINDKVIST (*takes out another paper, this one blue, and lays it on the table*). Now you see me lay this paper here on the table. And this one is blue as you see—but it has no official stamp on it—yet!

ELIS. God in Heaven! Everything comes back!

LINDKVIST. Yes, my young lover of justice—everything comes back—everything! Now, assume I was to ask myself this question: You, Anders Johan Lindkvist, born in poverty and raised in privation to hard work, have you the right, in your old age, to deprive yourself and your children— note that I say: *your children*—of the support that you, through industriousness, foresight and sacrifices—note that I say *sacrifices*—have saved little by little? What must you do, Anders Johan Lindkvist, in order to be just? You stole nothing from anyone, but if you take offence at having been plundered, you will find it impossible to live in the community any longer . . . for no one wishes to have anything to do with the heartless man who had merely asked for the return of what was his by right. So you see that there is a kind of charity that conflicts with justice—and that goes *beyond* justice—and that is—mercy!

Elis. You are right. Take everything! It's all yours!

Lindkvist. I have the right—but I dare not use it—

Elis. I shall think of your children and never grumble!

Lindkvist (*puts back the papers in his pocket*). Good! Then we'll put away the blue paper. . . . And now let us proceed a step further.

Elis. Forgive me, but are they really thinking of prosecuting my mother?

Lindkvist. First, let us go a step further. So you say you don't know the governor personally?

Elis. No, and I have no desire to know him.

Lindkvist (*takes out the blue paper again and starts to wave it before* Elis). That is not the way—not the way! The governor, you see, was a friend of your father's when they were young, and he would like to get acquainted with you. Everything comes back—everything! Will you call on him?

Elis. No!

Lindkvist. The governor—

Elis. Let us speak about something else.

Lindkvist. You must treat me with respect, for I am a defenseless man! You have public opinion behind you! All I have is justice! What have you against the governor? He doesn't like bicycles and rural high-schools—that's one of his little eccentricities—but let's overlook that, ignore it, and confine ourselves, as man to man, to the salient points. And in the great crises of life we must accept each other with our faults and weaknesses—swallow each other hide and hair.—Go to the governor!

Elis. Never!

Lindkvist. So that's the kind of man you are?

Elis (*resolutely*). Yes, just that kind!

Lindkvist (*rises and starts pacing up and down in his squeaking overshoes, the while waving the blue paper in his hand*). This is serious! This is serious! Perhaps I'd better begin at the other end, then.—There is someone in this town who intends to start proceedings against your mother, out of vindictiveness. You can prevent it.

ELIS. How?

LINDKVIST. By going to the governor!

ELIS. No.

LINDKVIST (*goes over to* ELIS *and takes hold of him by the shoulders*). Then you are the most contemptible human being I have ever met. And now I shall speak to your mother myself.

ELIS. No, don't—

LINDKVIST. Will you go to the governor?

ELIS. Yes.

LINDKVIST. Say that again, and say it louder.

ELIS. Yes.

LINDKVIST. Then we have settled this part of my errand. (*Hands* ELIS *the blue paper*.) Here is the document. (ELIS *accepts it without reading it*.) And now we come to part number two—which was previously number one. Shall we sit down? (*They resume their seats, as before*.) You see, if we could only meet each other halfway, we would get to the end so much the quicker. Number two is my claim on your furniture.—No need for illusions. I neither can nor would like to give away my family's joint property. I intend to collect every penny that is owed to me.

ELIS. I expect you to!

LINDKVIST (*sharply*). Oh, you do, do you?

ELIS. I didn't mean to offend you—

LINDKVIST. No, I can understand you didn't. (*He pushes back his spectacles and regards him fixedly*.) The wolf! The ferocious wolf! The man with the big stick and the blood-red carnelian! The giant of the Skinnarvik Mountains, who doesn't devour children, only frightens them! Yes, I intend to put fright into you until you are out of your senses, you'll see! I'll get my money out of every single stick of furniture. I have the inventory in my pocket—and if as much as a single nail or peg is missing, you'll be put behind bars where you'll see neither sun nor Cassiopeia! Oh yes, I can devour both children and widows if I am vexed. And as far as public sentiment is concerned—bah! All I have to do is to move to another town, that's all.

(ELIS *is at a loss for words*.)

LINDKVIST. You had a friend by the name of Peter—Peter

Holmblad. He was a linguist and studied languages with you. But you wanted to make him into some kind of prophet. —Well, he turned out to be disloyal. The cock crew twice, didn't it? (ELIS *is silent*.) Human nature is fallible, like earthly matter, and human reasoning. Peter was false. I don't deny that, and I don't defend him—in this case. But the human heart is unfathomable: its gold is intermixed with dross. Peter was a faithless friend, yet despite it all—a friend.

ELIS. A faithless—

LINDKVIST. Yes—faithless . . . but nevertheless a friend. This faithless friend has, unknown to you, done you a noble service.

ELIS. This, too!

LINDKVIST (*moves closer to* ELIS). Everything comes back —everything!

ELIS. Everything evil, yes! And the good is requited with evil.

LINDKVIST. Not always. The good comes back to us also. . . . Of that I am sure.

ELIS. I suppose I have to take your word for it—or you will torture the life out of me.

LINDKVIST. Not your life—but I am bent on squeezing all your false pride, your haughtiness and maliciousness out of you!

ELIS. Go on!

LINDKVIST. I mentioned that Peter has done you a service.

ELIS. I will not accept any favors from that man.

LINDKVIST. There we are again! Now I want you to listen to me! Through the intercession of your friend Peter, the governor was persuaded to intercede in behalf of your mother. For doing this, you must now write a letter to Peter and express your gratitude. Will you promise to do this?

ELIS. No! Anyone else in the world, but not to him!

LINDKVIST (*coming close to him*). I'm afraid I'll have to squeeze you once more then. Now—you have some money in the bank, haven't you?

ELIS. Well, is that any concern of yours? I am not responsible for my father's debts, am I?

LINDKVIST. Aren't you! Aren't you! Weren't you involved, too, when you helped to eat up and drink up my children's money, when it was being squandered in this house? Answer me!

ELIS. I can't deny that I was.

LINDKVIST. And since your furniture and belongings aren't enough to cover the debt, you will immediately make out a check for the balance. You know the amount.

ELIS (*completely crushed*). Even this!

LINDKVIST. Even this! Now go ahead and write!

(ELIS *rises, takes out his checkbook and goes to the writing table. He writes the check.*)

LINDKVIST. Make it payable to Cash or Bearer.

ELIS. It won't be enough to cover the amount.

LINDKVIST. Then you have to go out and borrow the rest. Every single penny must be paid! Every single penny!

ELIS (*hands the check to* LINDKVIST). There you are . . . it's everything I own. And that puts an end to my summer holiday and my marriage! I can't give you any more!

LINDKVIST. Then you have to borrow from someone, as I told you.

ELIS. I can't!

LINDKVIST. Then you have to find someone who will furnish security.

ELIS. Nobody will furnish security for a Heyst.

LINDKVIST. I'll give you two alternatives—take your choice! Either you express your gratitude to Peter, or you pay the debt in full.

ELIS. I refuse to have anything to do with Peter.

LINDKVIST. Then you are the most obnoxious, the most contemptible creature I have ever known! You can save your mother from losing the few belongings she still has left and your financée from having her life ruined, by a trifling gesture of politeness—and you refuse to do it! There must be some motive behind this which you are loath to reveal. Why do you hate Peter?

ELIS. You may take my life, but don't keep on torturing me!

LINDKVIST. You are jealous of him? (ELIS *shrugs his shoulders.*) There's where the rub is. (*He rises and starts to pace up and down on the floor. There is a silence.*) Have you read the morning newspaper?

ELIS. I regret to say I have.

LINDKVIST. From page to page?

ELIS. No—not completely.

LINDKVIST. So—o? You have not. Then you don't know that Peter is engaged, do you?

ELIS. I didn't know that!

LINDKVIST. Do you know to whom? Guess!

ELIS. How can—

LINDKVIST. He is engaged to Miss Alice. It came to light yesterday at a certain concert, and your fiancée acted as intermediary.

ELIS. And why all this secretiveness?

LINDKVIST. And why should two young people not have the right to keep their innermost secrets from you?

ELIS. Why should I have to suffer such pain for the sake of their happiness?

LINDKVIST. Well . . . think of those who have suffered to bring you happiness: your mother, your father, your fiancée, your sister.—Sit down, and I shall tell you a story. It's short.

(ELIS *seats himself reluctantly. During the preceding scene the weather outside has cleared, and it grows brighter as the scene progresses.*)

LINDKVIST. It is now about forty years ago. I was a young lad and came to Stockholm, alone and unknown, with not a single acquaintance there, to look for employment. One *riksdaler* was my only possession. The night I arrived, it was dark; and not knowing where to find a cheap night's lodging, I inquired of people I met in the street. But no one deigned to answer. When I was near despair, a passerby stopped, and asked me why I was weeping—for I was doing just that. I explained my plight to him. He went out of his way to guide me to a hotel, and comforted me with some kind words. As I was about to enter the vestibule, a glass door leading to a shop, suddenly was flung open. It struck my elbow and there was a crash of glass. The shopkeeper was in a violent rage and held on to me. He demanded payment for the broken pane and then threatened to call the police. You can imagine my despair—with a night in the street to look forward to.—The charitable stranger, who had seen what happened, came to my rescue, went to the trouble of summoning the police, and I was saved! . . . This man was your father! So, you see, everything comes back—even the good. And because of your father, I have wiped out my claim! So—accept this paper, and keep the check! (*He rises.*) Because you find it hard to say thanks, I won't linger, especially as I find it painful to be thanked! (*He approaches the door, rear.*) Now go to your mother without delay and relieve her of all her anxiety! (*He makes an averting gesture to* ELIS, *who seems to be about to go to him.*) Go to her!

(ELIS *rushes out, left.*)

(*The doors, rear, are opened.* ELEONORA *and* BENJAMIN *come in; they are quiet and serious. They stop, frightened, when they notice* LINDKVIST.)

LINDKVIST. Well, little imps, come in, and don't be afraid. Do you know who I am? (*He assumes a different voice.*) I am the giant of the Skinnarvik Mountains, who scares the children! Boo, boo! . . . But I am not so dangerous. Come here, Eleonora. (*He takes her head between his hands and looks into her eyes.*) You have your father's kindly eyes; and he is a kind man—but he is weak. (*He kisses her on the forehead.*) There!

ELEONORA. Oh, he speaks well of father! I didn't think there was anyone who would do that—

LINDKVIST. Yes—I do. Ask your brother Elis.

ELEONORA. Then you can't want to do us any harm.

LINDKVIST. No, my dear child! No!

ELEONORA. Then help us, won't you?

LINDKVIST. My child! I can't save your father from his punishment, any more than I can help Benjamin with his Latin examination. But as for the other matter, that has already been taken care of. Life does not provide us with everything—and we get nothing without effort. . . . And now *you* must help *me.* Would you like to do that?

ELEONORA. How can I help you—poor child that I am?

LINDKVIST. What is the date today? Look and see—

ELEONORA (*removes the calendar from the wall*). Today is the sixteenth.

LINDKVIST. Very well! Before the twentieth you will have seen to it that your brother Elis has paid a call on the governor and written a letter to Peter.

ELEONORA. Is that all?

LINDKVIST. Oh, you little child!—And if he doesn't do it, the giant will come and say *boo.*

ELEONORA. Why must the giant come and scare the children?

LINDKVIST. So that they will behave.

ELEONORA. Oh, of course . . . you are right, Mr. Giant! (ELEONORA *kisses the sleeve of* LINDKVIST'S *fur coat.*) Thank you, dear Giant.

BENJAMIN. You should say Mr. Lindkvist, don't you know that.

ELEONORA. No, that's such an ordinary name. . . . There are so many of that name.

LINDKVIST. And now—goodbye, children. You can throw away the birch now—throw it in the fire.

ELEONORA. No, let it stay where it is. These children have a way of forgetting. . . .

LINDKVIST. How well you know children, dear child.

ELEONORA. Now we can go to the country, Benjamin! In two months! Oh!—if they would only pass quickly! (*She tears off one leaf after another from the calendar, scattering them in the rays of the sunlight pouring into the room.*) See, how the days fly! April, May, June—and the sun is shining on them all.—Look! . . . Now you must thank God who has made it possible for us to get to the country.

BENJAMIN (*timidly*). May I not thank him silently?

ELEONORA. Yes, you may say it silently—for now there are no more clouds . . . and so it can be heard up there. . . .

(KRISTINA *has entered from the right. She stops.* ELIS *and* MRS. HEYST *come from the left.* KRISTINA *and* ELIS, *smiling, go toward each other; but before they meet, the curtain falls.*)

CHRONOLOGY OF EVENTS

IN AUGUST STRINDBERG'S LIFE *

337

* As compiled by Erik Hedén in his biography *Strindberg*, with additional events and dates by the translator.

BIBLIOGRAPHICAL NOTE

AUTOBIOGRAPHY IN ENGLISH TRANSLATION:
  The Son of a Servant. New York: Putnam's, 1913.
  The Confession of a Fool. New York: Viking, 1925.
  The Inferno. New York: Putnam's, 1913.
  Letters of Strindberg. Edited and translated by Arvid Paulson.
    New York: Thomas Nelson & Sons, 1959.

BIOGRAPHICAL AND CRITICAL STUDIES IN ENGLISH:
  Campbell, G. A., *Strindberg*. New York: Macmillan, 1933.
  Dahlström, Carl E. W. L., *Strindberg's Dramatic Expressionism*.
    Ann Arbor, 1930.
  McGill, V. J., *August Strindberg: The Bedeviled Viking*. London,
    1930.
  Mortensen, Brita M. E. and Brian W. Downs, *Strindberg: An
    Introduction to His Life and Work*. Cambridge, 1949.
  Sprigge, Elizabeth, *The Strange Life of August Strindberg*. New
    York: Macmillan, 1949.

IN SWEDISH:
  Berendsohn, Walter A., *Strindbergs sista levnadsår*. Stockholm:
    Saxon & Lindström, 1948.
  Lamm, Martin, *Strindbergs dramer I-II*.
  ———*August Strindberg I-II*. Stockholm, 1940–42.
  Ollén, Gunnar, *Strindbergs dramatik*. Stockholm, 1948.

IN FRENCH:
  Gravier, Maurice, *Strindberg et le théâtre moderne: L'Allemagne*.
    1949.
  Jolivet, Alfred, *Le Théâtre de Strindberg*. Paris, 1931.

IN GERMAN:
  Kraus, Otto, *Strindberg, Eine Kritik*. Munich, 1918.
  Liebert, Arthur, *August Strindberg, seine Weltanschauung und
    seine Kunst*. Berlin, 1920.
  Marcuse, Leopold, *Strindberg, das Leben der tragischen Seele*.
    Berlin-Leipzig, 1922.
  von Aster, Ernest, *Ibsen und Strindberg*. Munich, 1921.

von Wiese, Leopold, *Strindberg, ein Beitrag zur Soziologie der Geschlechter*. Munich, 1918.

WORKS CONTAINING CRITICAL ESSAYS ON STRINDBERG:

Bentley, Eric, *The Playwright as Thinker*. New York: Reynal, 1946.

Clark, Barrett H. and George Freedley, *A History of the Modern Drama*. New York: Appleton, 1947.

Gassner, John, *Masters of the Drama*. New York: Dover, 1954.

Paulson, Arvid, *Strindberg's Pilgrimage Dramas*. In: *The Chronicle* (American Swedish Historical Foundation). Philadelphia, 1954-1955.

JG

PRINCIPAL WORKS

OF AUGUST STRINDBERG

PLAYS: *Mäster Olof* (*Master Olof*), 1872/1880; *Gillets hemlighet* (*The Secret of the Guild*), 1879–80/1880; *Lycko-Pers resa* (*Lucky Per's Journey*), 1881–2/1882; *Herr Bengts hustru* (*The Wife of Sir Bengt*), 1882; *Kamraterna* (*Comrades*), 1886–8/1888; *Fadren* (*The Father*), 1887; *Fröken Julie* (*Miss Julie*), 1888; *Fordringsägare* (*Creditors*), 1888/1890; *Paria* (*Pariah*), 1889/1890; *Den starkare* (*The Stronger*), 1889/1890; *Samum* (*Simoon*), 1889/1890; *Himmelrikets nycklar* (*The Keys of Heaven*), 1890–2/1892; *Debet och kredit* (*Debit and Credit*), 1892/1893; *Första varningen* (*The First Warning*), 1892/1893; *Inför döden* (*In the Face of Death*), 1892/1893; *Moderskärlek* (*Motherlove*), 1892/1893; *Bandet* (*The Bond*), 1892/1897; *Leka med elden* (*Playing with Fire*), 1892/1897; *Till Damaskus, I-II* (*To Damascus, Parts I and II*), 1898; *Advent* (*Advent*), 1898/1899; *Brott och brott* (*Crimes and Crimes*), 1898–9/1899; *Folkungasagan* (*The Saga of the Folk Kings*), 1899; *Gustaf Vasa* (*Gustav Vasa*), 1899; *Erik XIV* (*Erik XIV*), 1899; *Gustaf Adolf* (*Gustav Adolf*), 1899–1900/1900; *Dödsdansen* (*The Dance of Death*), 1900/1901; *Kronbruden* (*The Crown Bride*), 1900/1902; *Påsk* (*Easter*), 1900/1901; *Till Damaskus, III* (*To Damascus, Part III*), 1901/1904; *Engelbrekt* (*Engelbrekt*), 1901; *Carl XII* (*Charles XII*), 1901; *Svanevit* (*Swanwhite*), 1901/1902; *Kristina* (*Queen Christina*), 1901/1903; *Ett drömspel* (*A Dream Play*), 1901–2/1902; *Gustaf III* (*Gustav III*), 1902/1903; *Näktergalen i Wittenberg* (*The Nightingale of Wittenberg*), 1903/1904; *Oväder* (*Stormclouds*), 1907; *Brända tomten* (*The Burned Site*), 1907; *Spöksonaten* (*The Ghost Sonata*), 1907; *Pelikanen* (*The Pelican*), 1907; *Svarta handsken* (*The Black Glove*), 1908–9/1909; *Siste riddaren* (*The Last Knight*), 1908; *Abu Casems tofflor* (*The Slippers of Abu Casem*), 1908; *Riksföreståndåren* (*The Regent*), 1908/1909; *Bjälbo-Jarlen* (*The Earl of Bjälbo*), 1908/1909; *Stora landsvägen* (*The Great Highway*), 1909.

NOVELS: *Röda rummet (The Red Room)*, 1879; *Hemsöborna (The People of Hemsö)*, 1887; *I havsbandet (By the Open Sea)*, 1890; *Götiska rummen (The Gothic Rooms)*, 1904; *Svarta fanor (Black Banners)*, 1904/1907; *Taklagsöl (The Rearing Feast)*, 1906/1907.

AUTOBIOGRAPHICAL NOVELS: *Han och hon (He and She)*, 1875–6/ 1919; *Tjänstekvinnans son (The Son of a Servant)*, 1886; *Jäsningstiden (Fermentation Time)*, 1886; *I röda rummet (In the Red Room)*, 1886/1887; *Författaren (The Author)*, 1887/ 1909; *Le Plaidoyer d'un Fou (The Confession of a Fool)*, 1887– 8/1895; *Inferno (Inferno)*, 1897; *Legender (Legends)*, 1897– 8/1898; *Fagervik och Skamsund (Faircove and Foulgut)*, 1902; *Ensam (Alone)*, 1903; *Syndabocken (The Scapegoat)*, 1906/ 1907.

SHORT STORIES: *Giftas I (Married, Part I)*, 1884; *Giftas II (Married, Part II)*, 1885/1886.

HISTORICAL WRITINGS: *Svenska folket i helg och söcken (The Swedish People in Holiday and Everyday Life)*, 1881–2/1882; *Svenska öden och äventyr (Swedish Destinies and Adventures)*, 1882–1891/1884, 1904; *Historiska miniatyrer (Historical Miniatures)*, 1905; *Nya svenska öden (New Swedish Destinies)*, 1905/1906.

POETRY: *Dikter på vers och prosa (Poems in Verse and Prose)*, 1883; *Sömngångarnätter (Sleepwalking Nights)*, 1884.

MISCELLANEOUS: *En blå bok (A Blue Book)*, 1907–1912/1907, 1908, 1912; *Memorandum till Intima Teatern (Memorandum to the Intimate Theatre)*, 1908; *Tal till svenska nationen (Address to the Swedish Nation)*, 1910.

The English translations which follow the original titles of the above works are for the convenience of the reader, and do not necessarily indicate that the works have been translated into English.

The date of writing of each work is followed, after a slash, by the date of original publication, except when the work was written and published in the same year.

AP

Bantam Modern Classics

Ask for them at your local bookseller or use this handy coupon:

THESE BANTAM CLASSICS ARE YOUR KEY TO GREAT READING!

☐	**THE ILIAD** Homer	SC4002	75¢
☐	**THE ODYSSEY** Homer	SC5303	75¢
☐	**CANDIDE** Voltaire	HC4833	60¢
☐	**THE RED AND THE BLACK** Stendhal	SC4181	75¢
☐	**MADAME BOVARY** Gustave Flaubert	FC4297	50¢
☐	**CRIME AND PUNISHMENT** Fyodor Dostoevsky	SC4274	75¢
☐	**THE IDIOT** Fyodor Dostoevsky	NC4154	95¢
☐	**FATHERS AND SONS** Ivan Turgenev	HC4143	60¢
☐	**WAR AND PEACE** Leo Tolstoy (Abr.)	NC4781	95¢
☐	**ANNA KARENINA** Leo Tolstoy	NC4609	95¢
☐	**PUDD'NHEAD WILSON** Mark Twain	FC4608	50¢

By John Steinbeck

☐	**OF MICE AND MEN**	SC4649	75¢
☐	**CANNERY ROW**	SC5337	75¢
☐	**IN DUBIOUS BATTLE**	NC4399	95¢
☐	**SWEET THURSDAY**	NC5449	95¢

☐	**QUO VADIS** Henryk Sienkiewicz	NC4682	95¢
☐	**LORD JIM** Joseph Conrad	HC4149	60¢
☐	**CITIZEN TOM PAINE** Howard Fast	NC5537	95¢
☐	**SISTER CARRIE** Theodore Dreiser	SC4220	75¢

Ask for them at your local bookseller or use this handy coupon:

Bantam Books, Inc., Dept. BC1, Room 2450, 666 Fifth Ave.,
New York, N. Y. 10019

Please send me the Bantam Classics which I have checked. I am
enclosing $_____(check or money order—no currency
please). Sorry, no C.O.D.'s. Note: Please include 10¢ per book for
postage and handling on orders of less than five books.

Name_____

Address_____

City_____State_____Zip Code_____
Please allow about four weeks for delivery.   BC1—4/70

Wait 'til you see what *else* we've got in store for you!

Send for your FREE catalog of Bantam Bestsellers today!

This money-saving catalog lists hundreds of best-sellers originally priced from $3.75 to $15.00—yours now in Bantam paperback editions for just 50¢ to $1.95! Here is a great opportunity to read the good books you've missed and add to your private library at huge savings! The catalog is FREE! So don't delay—send for yours today!